PUSHKIN

A COMPARATIVE COMMENTARY

COMPANION STUDIES

Racine, or, The Triumph of Relevance, by ODETTE DE MOURGUES
Goethe, a Critical Introduction, by RONALD GRAY
A Generation of Spanish Poets, 1920–36, by C. B. MORRIS
Tolstoy, a Critical Introduction, by R. F. CHRISTIAN
Dostoevsky, by RICHARD PEACE

Other volumes in preparation

PUSHKIN

A COMPARATIVE COMMENTARY

BY

JOHN BAYLEY, 1925 -

Fellow of New College, Oxford

CAMBRIDGE

AT THE UNIVERSITY PRESS

1971

PG
3356
.B3

Published by the Syndics of the Cambridge University Press
Bentley House, 200 Euston Road, London NW1 2DB
American Branch: 32 East 57th Street, New York, N.Y.10022

© Cambridge University Press 1971

Library of Congress Catalogue Card Number: 75-139711

ISBN: 0 521 07954 3

Printed in Great Britain
at the University Printing House, Cambridge
(Brooke Crutchley, University Printer)

CONTENTS

CONTENTS.

FOREWORD

All first quotations from Pushkin's works discussed and translated in the text are referred to volume and page in the most recent Soviet 'Academy' edition *Polnoe Sobranie Sochineny*, Akademiya Nauk SSSR, 10 vols., ed. B. V. Tomashevsky (Moscow 1962–6), with the exception of quotations from *Evgeny Onegin*, which are identified for convenience by chapter and stanza, and of those from the letters, where date and recipient are given.

Quotations from poems are printed in cyrillic, and transliteration is used only for reference, or illustration for the benefit of readers knowing no Russian. The simplest system has therefore been adopted, without accents, and with ы, й, ый and ий all rendered by *y*. Characters in Pushkin's works are transliterated letter for letter (*Mariya, Grinev,*) but other proper names and titles are given in the anglicised form most usually met with (*Küchelbecker, Tsarevitch*).

I wish to thank Mr Neil Malcolm and Mr Michael Katz for their valuable help, and Professor Fennell for his great kindness in reading the manuscript and for numerous corrections and suggestions.

1

INTRODUCTORY AND BIOGRAPHICAL

A study in English of Pushkin's works is a more dubious undertaking than one on most other great foreign authors. As a name he lacks definition. He is present to most English-speaking readers neither as a personality in his own right nor as the creator of scenes and figures which have passed into the common culture: not even as the poet of a few memorable and translatable quotations. His place among the very greatest poets has never been taken for granted outside Russia. Significantly it is only in Germany, where the golden age of poetry had preceded Russia's by a generation or so, and where the aged Goethe was completing *Faust* only five years before Pushkin's death, that the whole of his work has been translated and widely read. Not because he in any way resembled German writers, about whom he knew little and cared less, but because Russia and Germany had in common their late entrance on the European literary scene.

'*Il est plat, votre poète*', exclaimed Flaubert to Turgenev in genuine perplexity, and indeed the chief difficulty in the way of our understanding is that Pushkin's words come before us on two levels, disconcertingly obvious and familiar in the medium of translation: inexplicably different, exciting, and unique, when we have learnt some of his own language. The foreign critic cannot ignore this gap, and must work from both sides as he attempts to bridge it. As the would-be critic of ancient literatures today must defer to the vast corpus of classical scholarship while contriving at the same time to remain independent, so the critic of Pushkin must make what virtue he can from his position outside the linguistic and textual tradition of professional Pushkin scholarship, since he is in no case to compete with it.

He can only be grateful for the results of its labours, the painstaking detail of commentaries and the precise establishment of texts. The bulk and scope of Pushkin studies befits the author whom Russians will always put in a class by himself. For the great novels which to the world at large are the real Russian contribution to

world literature, and one unequalled elsewhere, are for Pushkin's countrymen a secondary development of his primary genius. Without Pushkin, they say, no Turgenev, no Dostoevsky or Tolstoy; and the European reader can only test the truth of the assumption by as close a study as he can manage of Pushkin's work. Even so, he cannot apprehend the relation as a Russian does, who absorbs Pushkin in adolescence before reading the novelists, and for whom even today his rhyming verse remains the most authoritative and the most natural expression of the language in art,[1] but he will certainly never again see in Tolstoy and Dostoevsky self-contained and self-created provinces of the imagination. He will instead, it may be, find them to be wide seas in which the element of salt has been crystallised and tasted in concentration by reading Pushkin.

Edmund Wilson has made the point, and found an analogy in French literature:

Reading Pushkin for the first time, for a foreigner who has already read later Russian writers, is like coming for the first time to Voltaire after an acquaintance with later French literature: he feels that he is tasting the pure essence of something which he has found before only in combination with other elements. It is a spirit whose presence he has felt and with whom he is in a sense already familiar, but whom he now first confronts in person.[2]

To a lesser extent, the spirit of Dante in Italian, and of Goethe in German literature, is equally strong; while Shakespeare's prose, as well as his poetry, is in the marrow of English style. But Pushkin's relation to his country's literature remains unique, which is why the Russians claim so much for him. Too much, it is sometimes said. Does his reputation depend simply on his place in the Russian consciousness? Blok spoke of its gloomy roll-call of despots and executioners, and of the one bright name on the other side – Pushkin. His name frees his fellow-countrymen from the weight of their history, even from the burden of themselves – Pushkin is as 'unrussian' in obvious senses as Dickens is 'unenglish' – and for them this freedom constitutes a unique enchantment. But does it for us? No foreigner is in danger of supposing that because Shake-

---

[1] In his essay on *Anna Karenina* in 1887 Matthew Arnold observed that 'the crown of literature is poetry' and that the Russians had not yet produced a great poet.

[2] E. Wilson, 'In Honor of Pushkin', an essay from *The Triple Thinkers*. The best short introduction to Pushkin in English.

speare is so important in English literature, or Goethe in German, these countries set for that reason an excessive valuation on them. They have their place in world literature because of what they are, not because of a special relation with their cultures.

And yet any criterion of universality is ambiguous. Byron had, and has, an international reputation denied to Wordsworth, but most English readers would maintain that Wordsworth was the greater poet, and they would be right. No judgement can be founded on the significance of a wide appeal to a writer's entire age, and the accessibility of his personality and appeal through the medium of translations. Nor can we necessarily judge greatness by the way it may perfect and use up a form, although no masterpiece in the same genre is possible after the *Divine Comedy, Faust, King Lear* or the tragedies of Racine; and Tolstoy and Dostoevsky may have created the great novels not only of Russia but of all time, even though the novel is by its nature far less exclusive and national a form than the tragedy or the long *poema*.

We can oppose to the concept of the masterpiece, in a finalising and self-defining form, that of the work which initiates or prolongs a whole tradition. Following Edmund Wilson, we might take Voltaire as the writer most representative of the unity of French culture, though he neither created it nor inhibited later writers from achieving the fullest individual expression within it. In such a culture, as T. S. Eliot put it, 'the existing order is complete before the new work arrives' and continues after it because any novelty modifies the whole existing order. 'The past is modified by the present as much as the present is directed by the past.' In such a culture it is hard to find out who began what and when, and it may be irrelevant or misleading to inquire. Was the direction of French literature determined by Malherbe and Montaigne? Did Chaucer or Surrey lay down the course of English poetry? These are fundamentally unreal questions, though it may be proper to pose them in surveys of literature and even to suggest answers. But a culture of long standing (and Eliot has French culture most obviously in mind) is indeed a seamless garment, because 'the conscious present is an awareness of the past in a way that the past's awareness of itself cannot show'.[1] In France literature as an institution has always been greater than any individual who represents it (it is hard to imagine a French author who would consider it irrelevant to his achievement if he became, or did not become, an academi-

[1] From T. S. Eliot, 'Tradition and the Individual Talent', in *Collected Essays*.

cian) and this is indeed the touchstone of metropolitan culture which Matthew Arnold so highly valued.

An isolated culture, or a recently arrived one, is apt to be represented, if not dominated, by a single figure. Goethe and Cervantes represent to outsiders, and with justification, the spirits of their national literatures. Pushkin's contemporary Mickiewicz gave the Poles their national poem and became the focus of their cultural identity – a god-like figure to his fellow-countrymen. Pushkin is not like this. He is in the peculiar position of being regarded as the founding father, while his own *œuvre* resembles that of a genius born into a high culture and taking his place in it, not embodying it. He seems both the original Russian writer and the representative of Eliot's concept of a cultural tradition. For his genius enabled him to marry Russia and the Russian language to the whole tradition of European and classical culture. And in this he sets a precedent: no great Russian writer who follows him is definitively national.

In a letter to his friend the writer Bestuzhev, written in June 1825, Pushkin discusses the question of who comes first in the development of a new literary culture, the mediocrity or the genius. In an article in *The Polar Star* in the same year, 'A glance at Russian literature in 1824 and the beginning of 1825', Bestuzhev had maintained that genius is the first to arrive. Pushkin disputes this, pointing out that with the exception of Ovid and Lucretius the great Latin poets – Virgil and Horace – 'went along the well-marked road of imitation'. 'In Italy Dante and Petrarch preceded Tasso and Ariosto, and the latter came before Alfieri and Foscolo. With the English, Milton and Shakespeare wrote before Addison and Pope, after whom came Southey, Walter Scott, Moore and Byron. It is hard to draw any conclusion or rule from this. Your words apply fully to French literature alone.' Of the Germans, he says only that theirs is the one culture in which 'criticism preceded literature', and he deplores the lack of good criticism in Russia. The comment on German culture is shrewd, but the oddity of some of his examples shows how superficial was Pushkin's knowledge of foreign literatures at this time – the only one he knew at all well was the French. The interest of the argument is the light it throws on the Russian writers' consciousness of their culture at this period, and on Pushkin's own probable sense of himself as the inheritor of an already established national literary tradition.

Had Pushkin's genius been other than it was, Russian literature might have become what it most certainly is not – provincial.

INTRODUCTORY AND BIOGRAPHICAL

A giant on the threshold could have dwarfed the dimensions of the new temple of literature. Pushkin was not a giant but a Proteus – the term was applied to him in his own lifetime – and he modelled for his successors a wide range of literary forms. A great part of his achievement can now be seen to point towards the nineteenth-century Russian novel, but that novel itself – as Tolstoy pointed out[1] – cannot be defined in terms of its European counterpart. In Tolstoy's words: 'its whole aspect can be expressed only by itself' and this it owes to Pushkin's liberating as well as Europeanising genius. It is as if Shakespeare had shown his successors how a new kind of drama might be written, and had left them to exploit a genre on which he had set an unmistakable but not a personal imprint. Shakespeare, like Pushkin, was Protean; and his genius was as generous and as unportentous; he too was a fertilising influence in his own lifetime and in the years just after his death. When Coleridge, in the *Biographia Literaria*, called him 'a very Proteus of the fire and flood', he contrasts this kind of greatness with that of Milton, which drew all nature egocentrically into its own compass. Nevertheless, Shakespeare's genius proved in the long run as conclusive as Milton's, in that the forms it created could have no direct literary issue.

Pushkin is unique among great writers, and particularly writers of his own age, in his attitude to literary forms. All his works are an examination – often amounting to an inspired parody – of one or another of them; and it is this more than anything else which makes a complete aesthetic comprehension of his work so difficult in translation. (It is also, as we shall see, the starting-point of Russian formalist criticism, with its thesis that 'the perception of its form reveals the content of the work'.) Moreover he wrote in many forms – the narrative poem combining romance with history, the history play and novel, the folk tale in verse – forms which we do not associate, in the nineteenth century, with any very great kinds of literary achievement. The dramatic sketch, which he picked up from the now-forgotten English poet Bryan Proctor, who wrote under the name of Barry Cornwall, is, in almost every example outside Pushkin's work, downright feeble. There is something bewildering to the foreigner about a poet who makes alleged

---

[1] In an article that appeared in *Russian Archive* after the publication of the first part of *War and Peace*. Tolstoy wrote that 'the history of Russian literature since the time of Pushkin' had seen no prose work of the highest class that would qualify as a novel in the sense in which the term was understood in the west.

masterpieces out of these kinds of composition; and indeed it is not unironic that, in following the most commonplace forms of European romanticism, Pushkin (and sometimes his older friend and fellow-poet Zhukovsky as well) produced versions that are superior to their originals in the west. But it is the forms themselves that never really became self-justifying in nineteenth-century literature as the novel was to do. Though many were written, the novel in verse never achieved real status in the west – Pushkin's is the only masterpiece in the genre – and *Evgeny Onegin* is further compromised in western eyes by the impression that it is in some sense a variant of Byron's *Don Juan*, though a closer parallel would be one of Jane Austen's masterpieces, or even Stendhal's *Le Rouge et le Noir*: the fact that two such different authors can be cited in comparison is in itself bewildering to the reader outside.

Neither of Pushkin's greatest achievements in narrative poetry, *Evgeny Onegin* and *The Bronze Horseman*, appear to carry the weight of 'things unattempted yet in prose or rhyme'; their pretensions are far from being self-proclaimed, and both seem at the same time finished and unfinished. They have a formal perfection and inevitability combined with a being provisional and open-ended, a paradox of Pushkin's art that has a parallel in the structure of the greatest Russian novels. Although one of his last poems paraphrases the Horatian ode *Exegi monumentum*, and claims, with a kind of proud equanimity, that his monument has raised its unhumble head higher than the Tsar Alexander's column, he remains no more imprisoned than Horace does in a monumental *Weltliteratur* of his own making. Horace has inspired poets of every age and culture, and continues to exist in their work as much as in his own. Tyutchev said that Pushkin was Russia's *pervaya lyubov* (first love), as if a great country and a great language had been waiting, like the sleeping princess, to feel this emotion. No previous Russian writer, not even Krylov the fabulist, had affected his fellow-countrymen in the same way, though many had been more decisive innovators and pioneers than Pushkin. Derzhavin, who as an old man heard Pushkin reading his poetry at his school in Tsarskoe Selo, had himself composed an *Exegi monumentum* on the Horatian pattern. We must postpone a detailed examination of the two poems till a later chapter, but it is worth noticing that both poets repeat in their separate ways Horace's claim to remembrance in the town of his birth as the first to set the modes of Lesbian song to the Latin language.

It is obviously exasperating for a foreign reader to be told that though Pushkin is the most eclectic of poets, little of his quality can appear in translation, and it produces a natural scepticism. But the reader without any Latin cannot really do more than take on trust the quality of Horace, and must look for his monument in later European poetry, in Shakespeare and Ronsard, Ben Jonson, Campion or Dryden. It is in any case arguable that the language barrier has become less important, not through the spread of education, but because the Hegelian and Goethean idea of world literature has become accepted as a standard by readers and writers alike, the novel being the form that both embodies the attitude and lends itself to the process. Moreover as languages develop they lose their power of primary meaning and become more instrumental and also more personal, less opaque and more transparent, a medium to feel and to see by (even if the object of view is only the author) rather than the materials of linguistic art. In *What is Literature?* Sartre distinguished prose, which brings us inside language, from poetry, which leaves us outside it. And what is written 'inside' a foreign language can be without too much difficulty transposed and apprehended on the 'inside' of our own.

The apotheosis of Shakespeare's plays in the nineteenth century took place not so much because of any increased understanding and appreciation of their dramatic poetry but because of the immense scope they afforded, as *Weltliteratur*, for universal recognition and identification. The reader of 'world literature' is scarcely concerned with the words on the page. Most of us take the greatness of the ancient classics for granted by reading into them meanings based on a translation; as they recede from the patterns of our own thought and speech and language we bridge the gap, justifiably, by taking less account of the actual words in them and more of what meanings they can continue to have for us. Recreating, as he did, a new poetic language, and creating a new world of poetry, Pushkin may none the less seem at first, to the foreigner, closer to such classics than he is to modern literature.

I

The bafflement which assails an experienced reader confronted with a translation of what he is assured is one of Pushkin's masterpieces, and hence one of the great poems of the world, is in reality a very pure sensation. He is confronted by commonplace words which he can make nothing of. He cannot read virtues into them, as long conditioning has accustomed him to do with the classics, and he cannot find a personality in them of obvious originality and power, as he does in translations of great novels. In such novels the style is the man, and although some of him is lost in translation – as we lose the repetitive, preoccupied, probing sentence-structure of Tolstoy, and the sly malign play of humour in Dostoevsky – enough remains for us to meet and appraise the author man to man. By contrast, Pushkin seems both flat and anonymous.

It is this bafflement which Flaubert expressed when Turgenev attempted to show him how great Pushkin was by translating some passages. The flatness is an aspect of words that imply nothing, have no power or resonance, and a merely mechanical correspondence with the words of the original. Any attempt to make the paraphrase more lively in its own right, as in most verse translations of *Evgeny Onegin*, merely muddies the waters. But Horace too can sound flat:

> usque ego postera
> crescam laude recens, dum Capitolium
> scandet cum tacita virgine pontifex.

> I shall live on to reap
> Fresh praise in ages new, while silent maid
> And solemn priest shall climb the Capitol.[1]

In *Exegi monumentum*, the ode paraphrased by both Derzhavin and Pushkin, the language is truly monumental,[2] and its impression like a carved proclamation which in the word *tacita* can almost be touched. The words convey the whole weight of time through an image and appearance of space. But in an English equivalent the idea is no more than nobly picturesque.

Pushkin's powers of concentration can be as great as Horace's and of a very similar kind. No more than Horace does Pushkin keep himself out of his work with any air of deliberation, but his presence is as subordinate to his art as that of Horace to the *leges*. Consequently his style is never the man in the romantic and nineteenth-century sense, and we never identify with him. It is this which

---

[1] H. Macnaghten's translation.

[2] 'Impossible, en effet, de trouver une expression plus monumentale pour cette religion, monumentale entre toutes, du peuple maître du monde.' Zielinski, *Horace et la société romaine du temps d'Auguste.* (Horace's boast has turned out to be an enormous understatement, as Professor Fraenkel remarks, and yet the word *tacita* perhaps suggests to the modern ear a rite continuing eternally in the imagination. 'And, little town, thy streets for evermore / Will silent be...')

distinguishes his poetry from that of almost all other poets of his time. In *Tithonus* and *Ulysses* Tennyson sets out to achieve impersonality through a mythological convention, and his language seeks very consciously to impress with the powerful decorum of the classics. But lines like 'And see the great Achilles, whom we knew', or 'And after many a summer dies the swan', imply very little by suggesting too much. Because it is supplied from the hidden world of the poet's personality, their appearance of summation gives an effect which is the very opposite of the graven finality in Horace's lines, or in Pushkin's paraphrase of them.

Although the language of Pushkin's finest poetry does not remind us of other poets, the foreign reader assumes he belongs to the same world as that of André Chénier, Scott, Byron and De Musset, and finds nothing in a translation to disprove his assumption. The subject and treatment of *The Captive of the Caucasus* and *The Fountain of Bakhchisarai*, and also that of *The Gipsies* and *Evgeny Onegin*, seem in translation to be characteristic of their period; a rendering of the best-known lyrics sounds reminiscent of Byron and Heine, while many of the slighter ones remind us of Moore, Southey or Hood. On the surface Pushkin can be seen to have a variety of styles, suited to the kind of poem he is writing. *The Little House in Kolomna*, for instance, is so close to Byron's *Beppo* manner that the englishing of it should present few difficulties to an enterprising translator, but it is perhaps for this reason that so few have been made. The translator naturally wishes to try his skill on what is least accessible, and these are not the sparkling stylistic *tours de force* but the lyrics and shorter poems. The difficulty of rendering even *Evgeny Onegin* is not absolute – as is the case with such short and apparently simple poems as *Arion*, *Anchar*, and *I loved you* – but more obviously technical. The meagre rhyme resources of English are impossibly overstrained, and soon lapse into grotesque, and our syntax cannot begin to stand the pace which Pushkin sets by exploiting every advantage that can be won from Russian inflection, absence of particles, and flexibility of word order.

When we read in their own language the work of other Russian poets – Pushkin's predecessors Derzhavin and Krylov, his elder contemporary Zhukovsky, Yazykov and Baratynsky, even Lermontov or Tyutchev – we can distinguish between familiar differences and feel on familiar ground, and this is still more true of those nearer to us in time, the poets of Russia's *fin de siècle* 'Silver

Age', and the poets of today. We recognise their tone by its immediate resemblance to some analogue in our experience of European poetry: it is like reading known poetry in a new tongue, and it seems as if this new poetry could be variously interchangeable with its counterparts in Europe, in the same way that the poems of Byron, Schiller, or Lamartine have their Russian counterparts in Pushkin's period. The 'suggestibility' of Tennyson's lines, previously quoted, would not disappear in translation but would find everywhere some corresponding contemporary echo. The opening lines of the Prologue to *Ruslan and Lyudmila*, on the other hand, bring us a sensation for which there is no analogue. The international movements which had brought national literatures closer together, and which suggested to Goethe the growing importance of *Weltliteratur*, lose their relevance when we are confronted with the seeming isolation of Pushkin's poetic self.

Though our first acquaintance with Pushkin's poetry is a revelation, while that of his contemporaries is more like a recognition of kinds of poetry we have already experienced in another language, he can at times sound like any other poet of his period because he uses its conventionally poetic styles and tones. But after his most youthful period he can be seen to use them: they do not use him. The poetry of Zhukovsky, for example, seems of its time because its author was not able to make it anything else: Pushkin's, because he has chosen – for one reason or another – to make it sound that way.

We shall return again and again to this unique combination in his greatest poetry of a complete identity with words and style and at the same moment an equally complete detachment from them. It can seem simple and inevitable, the words 'frappent moins d'abord pour frapper plus en suite', as Montesquieu said of Raphael. But Pushkin also has Shakespeare's or Chaucer's joy in language as spontaneous artifice, and this pleasure in manipulating styles and diction has no parallel in any European poetry of his time – nineteenth-century poets may change styles or mix a variety of them, yet the process lacks the immediacy and assurance of language used by genius at its most malleable and least misgiving point of development. Parny, Chénier, and Byron are all imitated by Pushkin, but the language of all three seems limited and circumscribed beside his own.

The diction of Pushkin's poetry is a complex and specialised field of study, but even the foreign amateur can get the feel of the aesthetic processes involved, and can become aware of when and in what spirit Pushkin uses a Church Slavonic word, a Gallicism, a direct and down-to-earth colloquial construction, or the syntax and vocabulary of received poetic diction. It is this sureness of aim, this sportsman's confidence – as his style matures – which presents both the ultimate difficulty for a translator and the enduring fascination for a reader. Behind Pushkin's words we feel the confidence of a new language, as well as its already settled and characteristic poetic conventions. And we often find – as we do with Chaucer – that what seems an absolutely individual felicity is in fact a commonplace poeticism, taken over and endued with the indefinable twist of personality, the search of perspective, which confer on it the transparent authority of new utterance.

In some poems too, particularly in lyrics of description and the picturesque, we feel that a commonplace tone is not transformed in this way, that it has been merely acceded to, as other very great poets are sometimes indistinguishable among the modes of their time. But this very ordinariness has nothing vulnerable about it. A bad poem by Blok or Khodasevich, as by Yeats or Rilke, is bad in a way of which only those poets would be capable: it displays the limitations, the sillinesses, anxieties and ambitions which make such a poet vulnerable in his own personal vision, in his own proffered image of himself: it displays, above all, that concentration on the self which the modern poet carries like a brimming basin from which he is fearful of spilling a drop. An ineffective poem of Pushkin gives nothing away, for there is nothing – in this sense – to give. His triviality is as anonymous as his depth, universal qualities which cannot be marked down to a single poet's personality and world. Here again Pushkin seems to stand in the dawn of literature: though only sixty years separate them, there could be no wider gulf than that between him and the Symbolist and Acmeist poets at the beginning of the next century in Russia, however much they all admired and even identified themselves with him.

We shall go into details later, but one example of Pushkin's use of period styles might be briefly noticed here: his handling of the romantic fragment. By tradition, such a poem breaks off when the vision fades and the wind of inspiration has ceased to play in the strings of the æolian harp. It was favoured for its structural picturesqueness, on the analogy of a ruin, but still more because it allowed the poet's ego to wander free, as in so many of Coleridge's poems, abandoning itself to the stimulus of association. In the poem *Nenastny den potukh* (*The dismal day is over*) which refers to his life in Odessa in 1823–4, and very probably to his feeling for the Countess Vorontsova, Pushkin uses the fragment to convey not an individual train of association, but the operation in the mind, any mind, of a single emotion – jealousy. All the romantic paraphernalia, the landscape of moonlight and waves, the breaking off, the rows of dots,[1] have an impersonal and dramatic function, comparable almost to the broken sentences of Othello's monologue. They display with clinical precision the torments of a mind as it darts back and forth in the throes of memory; they are a study on the universal platitude: I wonder who's kissing her now? Here is the ending (the poem itself is twenty lines long):

> Теперь она сидит печальна и одна...
> Одна...никто пред ней не плачет, не тоскует;
> Никто ее колен в забвенье не целует;
> Одна...ничьим устам она не предает
> Ни плеч, ни влажных уст, ни персей белоснежных.
> Никто ее любви небесной не достоин.
> Не правда ль: ты одна...ты плачешь...я спокоен;
> Но если...

Now she sits sad and alone...alone...no one weeps and anguishes before her; no one, oblivious, is kissing her knees; alone...to no mouth does she surrender her shoulders, her moist lips, her snow-white breasts... No one is worthy of her heavenly love. Is it not so: you are alone...you weep...I am calm;...
But if... (II, 206.)

Though Pushkin is himself the sufferer, he stands beside the emotion and watches its objectification by technical means; the pointed but unobtrusive change from 'she' to 'thou', in the last two complete lines, emphasises this objectivity by showing where it breaks down. There is in this none of the self-conscious 'romantic irony' of Byron and De Musset: Pushkin on the contrary devotes himself wholeheartedly to the form's romantic possibilities. It is his craftsman's skill rather than his personal attitude which gives the effect of detachment, almost indeed of parody, for that luxuriance of dots suggests a mute commentary on the 'I die, I faint, I fail'

---

[1] The poem was printed in 1826 but no autograph exists. T. Tsyalovsky comments that Pushkin probably did intend the poem to appear in this form, the first use in Russian poetry of the typographical 'suggestion' of a fragment. *Pushkin, Collected Works*, ed. Blagoy *et al.* (Moscow 1959), vol. II, p. 671 n.

type of romantic utterance. Yet the spirit of parody which we shall frequently be noticing in Pushkin may often, as here, be summoned up not by intent, but by a singular precision and concentration directed on a form to which such qualities are usually strangers. The parodic suggestion comes from something not 'taken off' but done better, more intensively; so that a notion of the incongruous is necessarily in the air (the suggestion, for instance, that makes the ghost of Hamlet's father a kind of comment on the ghosts of other revenge tragedies). But the emotion of the poem is not the less painful and contingent for being so exactly recorded, and the sudden shift from the recollected third person to the direct intimacy of appeal makes that appeal all the more pathetic.

Nenastny den potukh is far from being one of Pushkin's great poems, indeed it is not even by his standards a particularly good one, but it does reveal something about how he handled personal experience in his poetry, and the use he made for that purpose of contemporary poetic devices. We might compare it with the stanza that Byron jotted down on the back of the MS of the first canto of *Don Juan*:

> I would to heaven that I were so much clay,
> As I am blood, bone, marrow, passion, feeling –
> Because at least the past were pass'd away –
> And for the future – (but I write this reeling,
> Having got drunk exceedingly today,
> So that I seem to stand upon the ceiling)
> I say – the future is a serious matter –
> And so – for God's sake – hock and soda-water!

Byron's dashes are as much a device of the medium as Pushkin's dots, but they indicate not the poet's control over the sensations he is experiencing but his abandonment to them. The difference in our sense of intimacy with both poets is the difference between hearing a drunk man (or a man with the pose of being drunk) extemporising with genius on his sensations and a sober one imaging them with all the concentration of art. The art of the first lies in its complete individuality, of the second in its universalising power. We feel a kind of intimacy with Pushkin when he is describing his jealousy, or a winter's day in the country, or his working life in the autumn at his country retreat, but it is a relation on the plane of an exact and sober art, and outside the particularity of place and time. Byron's display of himself was local, social, and immediate, and in its way still is: we know, or would like to know, the actual moment when he dashed down that verse – the canal outside and the decanter within seem a part of our total experience of the man and the poem. With Pushkin the experience is all in the poem. Though his life and his love affairs are as accessible as Byron's and as well or even better documented, they are not continuous with his poetry; they may be relevant but they are never essential to the awareness of him that it gives us.

The story of Pushkin's life and death is much better known in the west than his work, and in Russia it is very much a hagiography. Yet Pushkinism is not, like the worship of Goethe in Germany, romantic and reverential; it is loving and precise. When Moscow was freezing and starving after the revolution, a little circle of Pushkinists managed to come together in order to determine exactly *whose* feet – out of the many contestants for that honour – were described by him in the first chapter of *Evgeny Onegin*. There is something heroic about this wish to establish the truth in every detail, for the smallest fact in the life of a very great writer has its own incontrovertible importance, and Pushkinists expend the same meticulous care on the minutiae of his life as on the punctuation of his manuscripts. But as the world of his creation does not fit easily into the nineteenth-century concept of great literature, so it does not coincide with the story of his own life. He thought of his writing as something outside the open current of his life, a necessary activity almost like physical elimination (with which he sometimes compared it) and a useful way of earning money, not as the justification and expression of his whole being. It is never necessary for the full appreciation of his lyrics to connect them with definite episodes and people, even where such a connection certainly exists. In W. H. Auden's phrase about such poems, they are 'halcyon structures' whose logic and laws do not depend on their relation to personality and event. The fine lyrics Pushkin addressed to Amalia Riznich might have been addressed to a Greek *kore*.[1] They throb with life; they are not, as with Landor, coolly remote and classical, but they reveal a moment and an expression rather than a per-

---

[1] Compare the image at the end of Pushkin's poem to his friends exiled in Siberia after the Decembrist conspiracy, in which he looks forward to the time when their prison shall be destroyed:

i svoboda
Vas primet radostno u vkhoda.

'And freedom shall receive you joyfully at the entrance' is an image which is not only of the 'high style' but combines like archaic sculpture high formalism with intense animation and expressiveness.

sonality. By contrast some of Byron's best poems, like his lines about his wife, require that we add our external knowledge to the viewpoint of the poem, for only thus can its full human meaning become manifest.

Not that Pushkin's poems exist in an aesthetic enclave, deliberately cut off from life and from their author. In the lyrics, as in *Evgeny Onegin* and *The Bronze Horseman*, he refers constantly to himself, to his amusements and friends, likes and dislikes. But neither in his poems nor in his letters does he seem to cultivate, or even be aware of, any image of his own personality, any self-distinguishing privacy of emotion or feeling. The self-knowledge that is revealed in the *Little Tragedies* and in *Evgeny Onegin* has already become general knowledge. Pushkin seems to have had no interest in the 'game' or drama of his own life, no *besoin de la fatalité* like Byron's. His sense of 'blind fate' was that of a superstitious man, with no conviction of what it should bring to him, but equally with no gift of evading it, no capacity for prudence or surefootedness. The role of the artist's life and death, romanticised like so much else in the nineteenth century, still attracts its devotees. But the story of Pushkin's marriage, duel, and death – so frequently told, and in so much detail – has the more tragic power of exciting fear and pity without any wish for participation, or sense of ownership. He can be taken over and used for their own ends by his admirers, but they must remain outside him, as he himself – as artist – remains outside his own story.

Nor can Pushkin be said to exemplify the fate of the artist in the nineteenth century, as Edmund Wilson implies. 'It was as if in those generations where Byron, Shelley, Keats, Leopardi and Poe were dead in their twenties and thirties...where Lermontov, like Pushkin, was killed in a duel before he was twenty-seven – it was as if in that great age of the bourgeois ascendancy – and even in still feudal Russia – it were impossible for a poet to survive. There was for the man of imagination and moral passion a basic maladjustment to society in which only the student of society – the social philosopher, the historian, the novelist – could find himself and learn to function.' Pushkin's case is not only quite different from that of the other poets: he was himself also, in fact, a social philosopher, historian and novelist. And he seems to have fitted very naturally and harmoniously into his age and society, although Soviet critics – in addition to underlining Edmund Wilson's general social point – claim him as a martyr of the Imperial system, who but for its persecution would have gone on to produce even greater works than those he had already accomplished.

Dostoevsky claimed that Pushkin died with his secret yet unuttered, and that it was the destiny of the writers who followed him in Russia to decipher and reveal it. 'Pushkin died in the full bloom of his creative power, and no doubt he carried with him into his grave some great secret. And now we, with him no longer among us, are endeavouring to solve it.'[1] It may indeed have been fortunate for them that he died when he did, though it is useless to speculate if his powers were still developing and diversifying or whether – as some of the younger writers were already hinting before his death – his great work was behind him. The notion of Pushkin's secret, so dear to Dostoevsky, was elaborated by many subsequent critics, notably by Gershenzon in his book *Mudrost Pushkina* (*Pushkin's Wisdom*). For this school of criticism each of Pushkin's works contains an inner revelation, a buried meaning, which the critic has been privileged to stumble on. Such Pushkinists are obviously in danger, to quote W. H. Auden again, of 'treating a work of art by someone else as if it was their own discovered document'. Yet this need not be as bad as it sounds. It is done to Shakespeare all the time, by critics and stage directors alike, for the great structures of verbal art can be loaded with uncommitted meaning which audience or readers will scarcely fail to make explicit in their various ways. Pushkin's 'secret' – and the notion does indeed powerfully suggest itself at some stage to all his readers – lies in the very openness of his art, in what Blok called its 'secret freedom': the freedom both to be transformed by the vision of later writers and at the same time totally separated from them. (It was something like this that T. S. Eliot valued so highly, finding in Dante and in Donne an inspiration which in the medium of his own prose and poetry makes them seem poets like Laforgue, or indeed like Eliot himself.)

In fact the suggestion of a secret, in Gershenzon's if not so much in Dostoevsky's sense, is as much the result of the censorship as of Pushkin's own remarkable powers of economy and implication. In spite of all its constriction and crassness, the censorship and Pushkin's genius could, and did, work together very well. It is a puzzle to inquire whether Pushkin's peculiar gifts would have developed as they did without the bonds of external authority, the

---

[1] F. Dostoevsky, 'Pushkin Address' to *The Society of Lovers of Russian Literature* (1880).

censorship that might have deadened and nullified the open forms taken by the later nineteenth-century novel. Nicholas I and his *éminence grise* Count Benkendorf played an odious part in Pushkin's life and death, but their influence on his art was, strangely, not wholly unbenign; all-unknowingly their supervision, with its niggling condescension and conceited ignorance, helped to concentrate its power. Pushkin's poetic masterpiece, *The Bronze Horseman*, failed to pass the censorship, but was written with the hope that it might do. 'Let us have a strict censorship by all means but not a senseless one', Pushkin wrote to his friend Vyazemsky. Like all great artists he is the product of his age, and a more liberal social and political environment would not have made him a better one. The very negativism of Tsarist tyranny was a liberating factor. The censorship that really deadens and kills is the positive one of a secularised state culture, with its apparatus of arts councils and writers' unions, a culture that decrees the proper style and function of literature.

In his lifetime Pushkin did not assume the mantle of greatness, nor have it thrust upon him; and even if he had lived we can hardly imagine him assuming the national status of a Goethe or a Hugo. Not until Belinsky's articles, written when Pushkin's work was being published posthumously between 1838 and 1841, was the characteristic tone of nineteenth-century author-worship first heard, and it is this rather than their detailed appreciations which make Belinsky's essays a landmark in the history of Pushkin criticism – more perceptive and less longwinded studies had already been made by Pushkin's younger contemporaries, Shevyrev and Kireevsky.[1] Belinsky was the first great ideological journalist of the Russian intelligentsia, the first to take over Pushkin, making him the cultural figurehead for the new consciousness and ideals; it is in his writings that we first become aware of the claustrophobic phenomenon of *Pushkinism*: the sense of a body of literature ingested and absorbed by its admirers to the point where the original seems merely the starting-point of their ideas. Even the Shakespeare industry cannot empty that great reservoir: we can open the plays and be startled by something we have never seen before, and that seems never to have been used or remarked on. But

---

[1] Shevyrev's critique of Pushkin appeared in the *Moskvityanin* in 1841, and Kireevsky's article in the *Moscow Messenger* 1828. References to other critics and commentators in these paragraphs will be referred to their contexts in later discussions, and in the bibliography.

compared with the sheer bulk both of Shakespeare and of most great nineteenth-century authors Pushkin's output is small and his masterpieces so brief and economical that they seem incongruous with such an aftermath of commentary and appreciation. Some educated Russians know most of his poetry by heart, and even in detailed critical studies it is common for a passage to be cited but not quoted, as the member of a scriptural sect need give only a reference to the text on which he is about to preach.

In the history of Russian culture Pushkin is the head text for debate on every aspect of the national self-awareness, just as his works hint at every topic and glance in every direction which the national literature was to take. Dostoevsky implied that European literature too had much to learn from him, and later Soviet critics – notably Gukovsky – have claimed that in borrowing from European literature Pushkin developed forms and kinds which were in their turn to exercise a profound influence on the literature of the west. For Dostoevsky he is the most universal of authors. 'In European letters there were [the past tense is significant] geniuses of immense creative magnitude – Shakespeare, Cervantes, Schiller. But please point to even one of these geniuses who possessed such a universal susceptibility as Pushkin.' He 'reflects universal ideas, poetic images of other nations in which their genius is incarnated'. Whereas Shakespeare's Italians are really Englishmen, Dostoevsky goes on, Pushkin's *Stone Guest* suggests Spain almost as if a Spaniard had written it; his versions in poetry from the Koran embody the very spirit of militant Islam.

However sketchy and ebullient Dostoevsky's claim for Pushkin's 'universality' and power of interpretative localisation, it does none the less indicate something of real significance – Pushkin's kinship with the nineteenth-century novel, with its conscious attempts to locate characters in their environment and comprehend them as a part of it, to portray what Lukacs calls 'individuals as a whole in the whole of society'. This is Realism, the imaginative embodiment in art of the historical process, and of the part played in it by classes and individuals in the author's time; it is by invoking this term that Gukovsky claims for Pushkin the title of the first of European realists. Later in the book we shall have to consider what this claim might mean and how much importance to attach to it.

II

Though the Pushkins had never played a particularly distinguished part in Russian history they were among the oldest boyar families; but during the period of the empire they had been eclipsed by the newly ennobled aristocracy of the court. Pushkin's mother's family, the Gannibals, were descended from a princely hostage, probably Ethiopian, acquired in Constantinople by a Russian envoy and presented as a kind of curiosity to Peter the Great. He had risen to the rank of general and land-owner and founded a family – one of his sons became an admiral. Pushkin was proud both of his paternal ancestry and his African forebear, to whom he attributed his 'Negro' face, volatile temperament and strong sexual passions.

Aleksandr Sergeevich Pushkin was born in Moscow in May 1799. Neither of his parents was much interested in him – indeed his mother seems to have disliked him – and his early affections were for his maternal grandmother and the nurses and servants. But his father and his uncle Vasily were literary dilettantes, and Pushkin had the run of a large library, mostly of French books, and met in childhood many of the Russian authors of the time. At the age of twelve he was sent to the newly founded *Lycée* at Tsarskoe Selo, where Alexander I planned to produce an élite generation of soldiers and public servants. He was a clever but idle school-boy. He wrote verses in French and Russian, read desultorily in French and the classics, and formed friendships which he was to cherish for the rest of his life. His chief friend was Baron Delvig, also a precocious poet, who died young in 1831.

While still at school Pushkin was elected to the Arzamas club, an unserious little coterie of young progressives united by their opposition to the conservative clique of Admiral Shishkov, 'The Society of Lovers of the Russian Word'. The Arzamas were fashionably liberal, devotees of the European, and good-humouredly contemptuous of the reactionary world of their elders. In 1817, while nominally employed by the Foreign Office and leading the life of a young man about town in St Petersburg, Pushkin joined a more revolutionary society, The Green Lamp, where the meetings were devoted equally to dissipation and high-minded debate, with readings of poems against the government. Though The Green Lamp had affiliations with the secret Unions whose activity led to the Decembrist plot of 1825, Pushkin knew little of them and was never taken into the confidence of the more dedicated members;

they admired his poetry and appreciated what his verses and epigrams did for the cause, but considered him too frivolous and indiscreet for the responsibilities of a conspirator.

During these years Pushkin was hard-up, but he frequented the theatre and the ladies of the Petersburg *demi-monde* and was in the set of the rich and rakish young men; he may also have taken part in a duel. After his death friends and acquaintances recollected numerous events and anecdotes of this period, most of which – like all the apocryphal stories about Pushkin – could equally well be told of someone else. He certainly contracted a mild venereal disease, and during the period of treatment and convalescence wrote his first long poem, *Ruslan and Lyudmila*, which was published after his exile to the south.

In 1820 Alexander had his attention drawn to Pushkin's poems, one or two of which were directed against himself and his favourite Arakcheev, while others (*The Village* and *The Dagger*) attacked serfdom and praised tyrannicide. Exile was thought suitable. Alexander's first idea was a monastery on the White Sea, Solovki, but Pushkin's more respectable literary friends – notably Zhukovsky and Karamzin – intervened on his behalf, and he was sent instead to Ekaterinoslav in South Russia, to serve on the 'Board of Protection of Foreign Colonists'. On his arrival he was lucky enough to fall in with his friends the Raevskys, who were on their way to the Caucasus. By permission of his kindly superior, General Inzov, Pushkin went with them, took the waters, saw the scenery and fell in love with the whole Raevsky family. General Raevsky, a hero of the war of 1812, was an ideal father-figure; and his eldest son, a cynical and strong-willed young man who modelled himself on his idea of Byron, introduced Pushkin to the works of his favourite poet, and exercised a considerable influence over him.

Though she was only fourteen at the time the third Raevsky daughter, Marie, has been identified in many biographies as one of Pushkin's loves, the 'N.N.' of the 'Don Juan list' – a note of his various conquests which was found among Pushkin's papers – and the likeliest candidate for the rhapsody on a small foot in the first chapter of *Evgeny Onegin* (though even the feet of the sisters' *femme de chambre* have had their supporters among Pushkinists seeking to identify a snapshot from life for a stanza in *Evgeny Onegin*). Marie afterwards married a Decembrist and followed him to Siberia, and her devotion to a martyr in the cause of liberty is the reason, as Mirsky dryly observes, for her role in Pushkin's life being stressed by liberal-minded critics and biographers and deprecated by reactionaries such as Gershenzon – for even the legend of Pushkin's loves becomes an occasion for critical alignment. Pen-portraits of her do indeed occur at this time in the margins of Pushkin's manuscripts, but he seems in fact to have been more attracted on the Caucasian tour by her elder sister Ekaterina, an Amazon of nineteen. All that is certain is that Pushkin led a happy family life with the Raevskys, the kind of life to which his affectionate and unself-centred nature was suited when it had the chance.

General Inzov's organisation had moved in the meantime to Kishinev, a formerly Turkish town near the Russian frontier, and there Pushkin remained with a few interruptions until July 1823, finishing *The Captive of the Caucasus* and writing *The Fountain of Bakhchisarai* and *The Gipsies*. The steppe and the primitive life of its nomads appealed to him, but the town did not: he consoled himself by recalling that Ovid had also been exiled not far off. The headquarters of the southern army was near Kishinev, and there Pushkin met the formidable Colonel Pestel, a staff officer and the leading spirit of the Decembrist union, who was hanged after the abortive uprising in Petersburg in 1825. Pushkin was glad to secure an appointment to the Staff of Governor General Vorontsov in Odessa, the most lively and cosmopolitan town in south Russia. He remained there for more than a year, writing a certain amount (he began *Evgeny Onegin*), gambling a good deal, and falling deeply in love with two women, one of them the Countess Vorontsova herself.

The other was Amalia Riznich, the young wife of a Dalmatian merchant. Pushkin became her lover, but so did many others, and he experienced the extremes of jealousy. She ran away to Italy with a Polish nobleman and died of consumption two years later. Of his many poems about her the most remarkable commemorates Pushkin's memory of their parting. The suffering she caused him seems to have made his apprehension of her singularly intense, and all the more objective from its intensity: in one lyric ('Beneath the blue skies of your native land') he records not his feelings when he heard of her death but the absence of any feeling. Yet if we except the hypothetical countess of *The Little House in Kolomna*, whom Pushkin may have seen in church and loved from afar when he lodged in the district of Kolomna in his Petersburg days, Amalia Riznich is the only instance in his life and poetry of that stock romantic figure, *La Princesse Lointaine* – attained indeed but remaining for ever unpossessable, in faithlessness and in death.

Countess Vorontsova, by contrast, was a woman of character; she was kind, comprehending, and where Pushkin was concerned most likely chaste. She was certainly very fond of him, but she had a responsible role in local society, and she also probably regarded his friend Aleksandr Rayevsky as a more serious suitor. Indeed Rayevsky seems to have used Pushkin as a stalking-horse, to deflect the possible suspicions of Vorontsov, a manœuvre bitterly resented by the poet when he became aware of it. This involuntary comedy role in the affair is significant: Pushkin as a lover was never taken especially seriously even by those who were in love with him. His vulnerability was too extreme. He never achieved or wanted to achieve a tragic role; he never set himself to *become* Pushkin as Byron did to be Byron, and he lacked the regal impassivity in the role of poet and romantic nobleman that made Byron available to Claire Clairmont. As a lover he cared nothing for his dignity; as a Don Juan he lacked the attraction and confidence of reserve. It is clear that he could and did exhibit all the silliest and most universal emotions of the lover – jealousy, shyness, vanity, childish spite and wounded pride. He could also be fascinating, impetuous, and warm-hearted. The women he besieged and who indulged him often became fonder of him, and sometimes he of them, when the affair was over. The fiery Countess Zagrevskaya, who was briefly his mistress, then made him the confidant of her relations with other men. He knew, on the other hand, that Anna Kern had little feeling for him, and though the poem he addressed to her ('I remember a wonderful moment') has become an anthology piece, it has a kind of mischievously meaningful solipsism which is quite absent in the other love poems. Pushkin exploits for his own ends the artifice of the elegant French sentimental tradition, and the perfection with which he endows its banality seems exactly to reflect his awareness of the nature of his relation with the girl to whom it is addressed. He first met Anna Kern at a party in Petersburg in 1819, and again at the Vulfs's house near Mikhailovskoye in July 1825, when he wrote the poem and presented it to her inside the published copy of the first chapter of *Evgeny Onegin*. Anna Kern's memoirs, in which the event is recorded, are far from reliable, but reading between the lines it seems likely that Pushkin was already disenchanted with her when he wrote the poem, which overtly records the impression 'a spirit of pure beauty' (*geny chistoy krasoty*) had made on him when he first saw her, and the moment of ecstatic rebirth – 'to life, tears, and love' – when he met her again.[1]

Biographers have been surprised and even shocked by this contrast between the stanzas addressed to Anna Kern and the jocular crudeness with which he referred to her in his correspondence, but the two modes in fact tacitly complement each other. It is a classic instance of how Pushkinists disagree, and in great detail, on the exact relation of a lyric to the poet's life. In his study *V dvukh planakh* (*On Two Planes*) V. Veresaev maintained that the poem should not be read in a biographical context, and in *Lirika Pushkina* N. A. Stepanov took a whole chapter to argue that the *geny chistoy krasoty* of the poem should be seen as Pushkin's own muse or inspiration, momentarily and fortuitously incarnated in this vision of the girl, and hailed with a down-to-earth (*zemnoy*) relish typical of him but quite unlike the 'mystical-religious' rapture of Zhukovsky's poem. However that may be, the renewal of vitality commemorated in the poem is solipsistic and curiously bland, as if the 'fleeting vision' (*mimoletnoe videne*), officially complimented for bringing it about, would in fact be paid no further attention. For all the smooth banality of its diction, the weight and depth of the poem which make it so memorable proceed not from the flattering celebration of the 'vision' but from the significance of a poet's time, lost, wasted and regained: from the contrast between the simple statement *Shli gody* (years passed) and the poeticisms that record how they passed 'in the darkness of exile', when 'the storm's turbulent gusts scattered former dreams'.

---

[1] The phrase 'spirit of pure beauty' (*geny chistoy krasoty*) had been used by Zhukovsky in a poem addressed to the Empress Alexandra, the young German wife of Nicholas I, when she appeared as Lalla Rookh in 1821 in a pageant based on Moore's oriental poem. (Zhukovsky, who was her Russian tutor, admired her deeply, as did Pushkin himself when he saw her later on at the St Petersburg balls, and celebrated her as 'Lalla Rookh' in a fine stanza of *Evgeny Onegin*, one of the many which were taken out in revision.) Zhukovsky had written

> Akh! ne s nami obitaet
> Geny chistoy krasoty,
> Lish poroy on naveshchaet
> Nas s nebesnoy vysoty.

'Ah! the spirit of pure beauty does not live with us, only visits us sometimes from the heavenly height.'

Pushkin's poem could almost be taken as a variation on this theme, with a marked change of tempo and emphasis – Zhukovsky's poem is in graceful trochaics, and the line which Pushkin copied is significantly slowed by its iambic addition.

Pushkin hints in a few lines at the process of poetic withdrawal and rebirth which Coleridge and Wordsworth were preoccupied with in longer and more intimately personal poems, and the hint is contained not in statement but in the poise of the diction between banality and the excitement of joy.

Count Vorontsov, a cultivated anglophile with a cold heart and a passion for propriety and power (he makes a brief but telling appearance in Tolstoy's story *Hadji Murad*) looked with distaste on Pushkin and tried to keep him in his place. His adverse reports to Petersburg were strengthened by an imprudent letter, opened by the postal authorities, in which Pushkin remarked that he had been taking lessons in atheism. In July 1824 he was formally expelled from the service and ordered to live on his mother's estate at Mikhailovskoye, under the supervision of the local authorities. Pushkin had never got on with his parents, and their consternation at the mess their eldest son had got himself into did not help matters. After some painful scenes they left for the capital, taking Pushkin's younger brother and sister, Lev and Olga, along with them. Pushkin settled down to work and read, relying for company on the old nurse Arina Rodionovna and his friends the Vulfs who lived on a neighbouring estate – it was there he had his second meeting with Anna Kern and wrote the poem. He continued *Evgeny Onegin* and began *Boris Godunov*.

In November 1825 Alexander I died suddenly at Taganrog. His brother Constantine had secretly abdicated his rights in favour of the younger Nicholas, but allegiance to him was proclaimed in many towns and the Decembrists staged their attempted *coup d'état* on the Senate Square in Petersburg, nominally in favour of Constantine but hoping in fact to seize power and form a government of their own. After a fit of panic Nicholas and his supporters acted with decision and effect. The five leading Decembrists including the poet Ryleev, a friend of Pushkin, were hanged, the rest exiled to Siberia. At Mikhailovskoye Pushkin himself feared arrest. In the margins of his MSS of the time there are sketches of the hanging men, one with the phrase: 'And I myself might have dangled like a clown...' Now that the blow had fallen, Pushkin was anxious to make his peace with the new powers and he wrote to ask Zhukovsky for his intercession. In the autumn he was summoned to Moscow and there took place the celebrated confrontation with the Tsar around which grew up a whole tradition of gossip and apocryphal anecdote.

Its main tendency is to gloss over the fact that Pushkin was flattered by the new Tsar, took to him, and became for some years a loyal supporter of the new régime. He is said to have told Nicholas that had he been in Petersburg he would have been on the square with the rebels. That is certainly true, given his fearless and impetuous nature, which would have impelled him had he been given the chance, less from idealistic conviction than in the solidarity of friendship. But whatever Pushkin said or did not say he was certainly seduced by the compelling charm which the young Nicholas was capable of exercising, and by the offer of benevolent patronage. He was always more susceptible to atmosphere and personality than to abstract ideas. His schoolfriends had regarded themselves as liberals and progressives, so he had been one too. Now that authority seemed to wear a human face, and to regard him as one of the family, he saw it in a new light. His deep feeling for Russia could identify itself with a new Emperor who had dismissed the clique of reactionaries whose influence had darkened the last years of Alexander's reign. Pushkin's growing interest in the figure of Peter the Great projected itself briefly on Peter's successor, and he compared the opening of Nicholas's reign with Peter's in a poem ('In hope of all the good and glory') which his friends in Moscow did not approve of. Pushkin's interest in the perspective of Russian history had now a much stronger hold on his imagination than the liberal *idées reçues* of his youth, and here seemed the opportunity of entering that history in its actual workings and from the inside – part of the bait negligently offered by Nicholas was the project of a report by Pushkin on the possibilities of educational reform, as well as the opportunity to work later on in the historical archives.

Pushkin was involved at the centre of a great power, and one can hardly overstress the singularity and importance of this for such a poet in such an age. The politics of *Faust* are those of a model German duchy: the politics of *The Bronze Horseman* those of a rapidly expanding and ruthless empire. Pushkin was never left isolated – like Dante in exile or Wordsworth after the French Revolution – to work out a personal and compensatory vision of his own. The poem in celebration of Nicholas, the mysterious poem of farewell to the Decembrists (*Arion*), and the indignant rhetoric of the ode against the European supporters of the Polish rebellion (*To the Slanderers of Russia*) – all possess, in contrast to the youthful liberal *bien pensant* poems, the kind of authority which comes not from 'ideas' but from the pressure of involuntary experience. And this span of experience covers the time from Pushkin's reconciliation with imperial power to the measured judgement of *The Bronze Horseman*. If he had not come to terms with the system, if he had succeeded in his application – made several times during the Mikhailovskoye exile – to go abroad, he would not have achieved that bitter understanding of authority which his last works reveal.

'The Tsar has freed me from the censorship', he wrote to Yazykov in November 1826. 'He himself will be my censor. The advantage is of course enormous. Thus we shall print Godunov.' He was speedily undeceived. The middleman in the arrangement was the head of Nicholas's new special gendarmerie, Count Benkendorf. Like Vorontsov he expected Pushkin to behave like an obsequious subordinate, and the pair soon came to dislike each other thoroughly. Almost at once Benkendorf accused Pushkin of giving a reading of *Boris Godunov* to his friends in Moscow without permission. Nicholas himself raised objections to the play, and it was only released for publication, with alterations, some time later, and never performed in public. This was the pattern of future relations with the censorship, exasperating in itself and the cause of considerable financial loss to Pushkin, for his work commanded a high price and he could not be paid for what he was forbidden to publish.

He had in fact lost at a game of cards some years earlier the copyright of his shorter poems. This he had managed to buy back while at Mikhailovskoye, and a selection was printed in Petersburg in 1826 under the supervision of his friend and admirer Professor Pletnev. But though he continued *Evgeny Onegin* he now wrote comparatively little, and *Poltava*, published in 1828, was a failure. Grub Street resented his aristocratic stance, and the journalists who had earlier sung his praises now declared war on him: he was attacked by the new radicals and the government literary establishment alike.

And he was anxious to get married and settle down. He proposed in Moscow to Sophia Pushkina, a distant relation, and was refused. In 1827 he got leave to go to Petersburg and lived there for most of a year, gambling a good deal and drinking with his old companions. At the age of twenty-nine he felt aimless and worn out. The sickness of the age, which he resisted so instinctively in his writing, had got into his life. He even applied to join the army, and then – somewhat in the spirit of Byron's departure for Greece – he bolted for the Caucasus, where his brother and a friend were serving in a campaign against the Turks. The immediate cause may have been his meeting in Moscow with Natalia Goncharova, his future wife. Deeply impressed by her beauty (she was only seventeen) he asked her to marry him, but like his distant cousin she turned him down.

The Caucasus revived him. He saw some action and was foolhardy enough to have got himself killed if he had not been looked after. Although he was in trouble with Benkendorf on his return, he resumed his activities in the capital with a fresh access of vitality, helping his friend Delvig to run a periodical, the *Literary Gazette*, for which permission had just been granted. But further applications to be sent abroad on some mission were again refused.

The thing that gave him most hope was his renewed courtship of Natalia Goncharova. In the eighteenth century a fortune had been made by the Goncharovs out of a linen factory, but their descendants had squandered the proceeds and the present family was rather worse off than the Pushkins. Had they not been so Pushkin would hardly have been regarded as an eligible suitor. As it was, his connection with the Tsar and the court was a powerful inducement to Natalia, who now had time to reflect on the use that might be made of them. She was a socially ambitious girl, extremely conscious of her remarkable beauty – well suggested in the engraving of her by V. Gay – uneducated, and quite uninterested in Pushkin's literary life, which would not have mattered if she had loved him. Clearly she was not unamiable; she wanted to appear and to be a good wife, but she wanted everything else that high society had to offer. Her will was not destructive or self-insulating: she became emotionally very dependent on Pushkin and apparently confided her social triumphs and embarrassments to him up to the end. All in all, a highly commonplace figure, matching the heroic commonplace of Pushkin's own nature. To him the idea of a wife whose looks were universally admired appealed as much as the prospect of a family and home. And he seems to have been enchanted by her statuesque unresponsiveness. He had no illusions about her character and the probable nature of their life together. *Il n'est de bonheur que dans les voies communes* he wrote to a friend, quoting the last sentence of Chateaubriand's *René*. 'Trials and tribulations will not astonish me. They are included in my family budget. Any joy will be something I did not expect.'

They were married in Moscow in February 1831. In the previous autumn Pushkin had visited the little estate that his parents had agreed to settle on him near Boldino, in the Nizhni Novgorod district. A cholera outbreak prevented him from returning when he had planned, and during this remarkable 'Boldino autumn' he produced a quantity of his finest work, including the *Little Tragedies* and the *Tales of Belkin*. All he wrote during those three months bears the marks of his determination to show his critics that he was not a back-number, and that he was capable of exploring new forms and creating new masterpieces, especially in prose. From now until his death he scarcely wrote except during the autumn and at Boldino. Two years later he completed there his history of the Pugachev rebellion, and in addition to two verse tales wrote the first draft of *The Bronze Horseman*. In 1834, the last of these productive periods, he finished *The Queen of Spades* and his historical novel, *The Captain's Daughter*.

In the intervals in St Petersburg he began and put aside a number of projected novels and stories. He was desperately hard-up and needed all the money he could earn, for Natalia was extravagant and was enjoying the success in court circles which she had hoped for. So much so that the emperor humiliated Pushkin by making him a Kammerjunker, or court page, an appointment absurdly incongruous with his age and position, in order that his wife could be invited to every ball at the palace. He had to escort her and was profoundly bored. He longed for the country and the society of his children, to whom he was much attached. And he did his best to escape. Writing to Benkendorf in June 1834 he asked to be relieved of his duties so that he could spend a few years away from the capital, adding that he hoped to retain the position to work on the state archives, where he was beginning to compile materials for a study of Peter the Great. The emperor replied that no effort would be made to detain him against his will, but that if he went he must not expect any further privileges or access to the archives, 'considering that such permission may be given only to persons enjoying the particular confidence of the authorities'. The chill blackmail was entirely effective. Pushkin once more implored his old ally Zhukovsky, now tutor to the heir to the throne, to make his peace with the emperor.

Only the permission to found and edit a new critical quarterly cheered him during this time. The *Contemporary* (*Sovremennik*) was to be on the model of English reviews like the *Edinburgh*, and Pushkin had hopes of its being a successful rival both to the journals of Petersburg, dominated by the *Northern Bee* of his old enemy, the government spy Bulgarin, and the Moscow magazines, for whom the young Belinsky was already writing under the patronage of Nadezhdin, another journalist with whom Pushkin was on bad terms. The young lions of Moscow were now all for German metaphysics and transcendental philosophy, matters of no interest whatever to Pushkin. He had come to regard himself as a reactionary of letters, the leading spirit of the 'aristocrats', and he was grateful to be elected to the Russian Academy, an aged body presided over by that same Admiral Shishkov whom the Arzamas had once delighted to tease. Since then literature had become far more combative, and the period of social engagement and ideological utilitarianism was just beginning.

As well as reviews the *Contemporary* published original work, and the four numbers of 1836, the only ones edited by Pushkin, included verse and prose by himself (*The Captain's Daughter* and one of the *Little Tragedies*), poems by Zhukovsky and stories by Gogol. Under the anonymity of initials also appeared the first poems of Tyutchev, the most remarkable collection of lyric verse to be published by another Russian poet in Pushkin's lifetime. But in spite of, or perhaps because of, its remarkable quality the *Contemporary* was stillborn. It had no publicity, and other journals maintained a conspiracy of silence against it. Pushkin did not give up hope however, and on the day of his duel he wrote to a contributor asking her to translate some of the dramatic scenes of Barry Cornwall: the translation came out in the periodical after his death. The most inconsiderable of English and the greatest of Russian poets made at this moment an odd and touching yet characteristic *entente*.

The *Contemporary* did nothing to relieve Pushkin's debts, but they had become the least of his troubles. In 1834 a young French royalist *émigré*, Baron d'Anthès, had been admitted to the Chevalier guard through the influence of Baron Heeckeren, the Dutch ambassador, who had adopted him as his son. Natalia Pushkin was recognised as the most beautiful woman in the circles he now moved in, and he at once began to pay court to her. He was highly attractive; tall, good-looking, and an excellent dancer. Natalia was flattered by his attentions and enjoyed his company, but there is no likelihood that she fell in love with him: she was too much in love already with the whole social world of the capital.

Pushkin had already challenged the young Count Sollogub for showing too open an admiration for his wife, but Sollogub was both a sensible man and a devotee of the poet's work and the affair passed off without a duel. D'Anthès was a different matter. A grotesque complication was the presence in Pushkin's house of Natalia's two elder sisters, who had come to St Petersburg to find husbands. Ekaterina Goncharova fell for d'Anthès, who made use of this as a pretext for frequent visits to Natalia. Pushkin had meanwhile received anonymous notes facetiously informing him of his election to 'the Serene Order of Cuckolds', as 'historiographer' to its 'Grand Master', D. L. Naryshkin, whose wife had been the mistress of Alexander I – a clear hint that the same relation existed between Natalia and Nicholas. (In fact it almost certainly did not, though after Pushkin's death she may have been for a short while *maîtresse en titre* to the emperor.) Pushkin chose to believe that Baron Heeckeren was behind this gossip, and contemptuously refusing to call out the old man, he challenged his adopted son as a doubly convenient proxy. But Heeckeren denied any knowledge of the letters, and the affair was patched up, as so often before, through the good offices of Zhukovsky. D'Anthès actually became engaged to Ekaterina, the nominal object of his pursuit, and they were married in January 1837.

Natalia was pitiably confused by this outcome. In the many letters he had written to her since their marriage Pushkin had done his best to interest himself in her social preoccupations, had advised her with tenderness and good sense, and besought her to behave with decorum. Now (if the Countess Ficquelmont's diary is to be believed) she came to him for reassurance that she herself had been the object of d'Anthès' admiration and that he had only married her sister as a second-best. As if to confirm this, the new brother-in-law was soon as attentive to her as ever. Pushkin determined to end the matter. There is little doubt that Natalia had done her limited best to avoid scandal and had not been technically unfaithful, nor did Pushkin suppose she had, but he was tormented beyond measure by the amusement of society and its patronage of an increasingly farcical situation. A duel, if he survived it, would certainly mean exile to his estate and the end of the Petersburg nightmare.

To avoid any further intervention by friends, Pushkin sent Heeckeren a letter so grossly offensive that it could only have one outcome. D'Anthès challenged him, and a meeting was fixed for the following day. The duel took place on the outskirts of the capital in deep snow. D'Anthès fired first and Pushkin was hit. Prostrate, he managed to fire his own shot and slightly wound his opponent. His own abdominal injury was severe and there was little hope of his recovery; he died two days later and was buried secretly at the monastery near Mikhailovskoye. The authorities tried to hush matters up, and there was even a rumour, probably groundless, that Benkendorf knew of the duel but had done nothing to prevent it. Nicholas wrote to Pushkin on his deathbed, urging him to die as a Christian and promising that his family would be looked after. And so they were: Pushkin's debts were paid, arrangements were made for the education of his children, and his widow received a pension. She married an officer called Lanskoy, who had played a minor part in the events leading up to Pushkin's death. D'Anthès was expelled from Russia. Returning to France he took up politics and became a senator under Napoleon III. He died in 1895.

2

EARLY POEMS

1812 was the high point of Russia's heroic age and of its celebration in literature. Three years later the fifteen-year-old Pushkin recited an ode, *Memories of Tsarskoe Selo*, on the occasion of the passing-out exam at the *Lycée*. It was probably his first sustained effort in the heroic style, and he handles with ease and confidence the *clichés* of the new Russian and the old European heroics – the poem might be transposed into the same contemporary idiom in any European language and would be immediately recognisable. It is full of fiery steeds and Russian valour, all the properties of poetic *gloire*, inherited from the odes of Lebrun; and there is a true Gallic concentration on the declamatory possibilities of the form. It is this unselfconscious intentness on what such a poem must be and say, which is Pushkin's most durable legacy from the French, and which remains in his poetry when it no longer uses French models. Even more than the French ode – and a great deal more than the English – the Russian ode lends itself to impassioned recitation, and we can still hear in Pushkin's stanzas the ringing tones in which he himself recalled that he read them, and which moved the elderly Derzhavin who was present at the occasion. He had celebrated the achievements of Catherine and her generals in the same form, but in a language far less fluent and in rhythms not so naturally fitted to the acoustic tone. Of all Pushkin's '*Lycée* poems', the *Memories* gives the greatest promise of that mastery of a form which he was to show two years or so later in his ode *Freedom* (*Volnost*), the most accomplished of his early performances in the high style.

Not that he always took it seriously: already for the young Pushkin it was one style out of many. In *Fonvizin's Shade*, a satirical poem only rediscovered by Pushkin scholars in the nineteen-thirties, Pushkin imagines the ghost of the eighteenth-century dramatist Fonvizin conducted back by Hermes to see how literature is progressing. A passage parodies one of Derzhavin's epic flights and shows that Pushkin and his friends did not, among themselves, feel any excess of reverence for the aged poet. Nearly twenty years later Pushkin took as an epigraph for his *Egyptian Nights* a line from Derzhavin *Ya tsar, ya rab, ya cherv, ya bog* (I am tsar, I am slave, I am worm, I am God) which had been mocked by Fonvizin's ghost in the parody line *Ty bog – ty cherv, ty svet – ty noch* (You are God – you are worm – you are day – you are night) and in *The Bronze Horseman* there occurs a deadpan reference to the 'deathless verses' of Count Khvostov, another of Fonvizin's victims. The mood of *Autumn (Osen)* is, in a formal sense, determined by a generous admission – not in fact borne out by that most Pushkinian poem – that it begins from the inspiration of Derzhavin's line *Chego v moy dremlyushchy togda ne vkhodit um?* (What does not enter then my drowsy mind?).

These are indications of the strong family relation within the society of Russian poets, in which the family element made it possible to tease the older generation while retaining for them an instinctual affection and respect – we might compare it with the 'coffee-house' relation of the English Augustan poets – and this at a time when the poetic personalities of English and German literature – Goethe and Hölderlin, Wordsworth, Shelley, Byron and Keats – were to a striking extent mutually exclusive of one another. Pushkin's earliest poems are impersonal and subdued to the characteristics of their models. Among the poets of the 'Pushkin Pléiade', a rather misleading term applied to the poets who were friends and approximate contemporaries of Pushkin – Delvig, Vyazemsky, Baratynsky, Pletnev and Yazykov – all could be said to have found their voices earlier than he. Baratynsky, it is true, later developed in reaction to Pushkin a deliberately different, almost metaphysical style; but Delvig had reached the limit of his considerable talent before Pushkin had written his first really distinguished poem.

There may even be some connection between this early maturity and the fact that Delvig, like Batyushkov before him, had very little to write about. They have no access to the spacious and mutually exclusive worlds of the European romantic poets. Greek, French and Italian classic models offered them the means of attaining a limited perfection of expression in Russian verses, but they did not, like Pushkin, pursue to the limit the formal possibilities of each model they tried, subduing themselves in order to render its complete structure and perspective. Pushkin's early imitativeness is that of a long distance poet, who is learning every-

thing he can, not only in terms of style but of staying power. He
has none of the impatience of the innovator. Indeed the formalist
critic Eykhenbaum sees him as an end-product, heir and beneficiary, of Russian poetic development.

At this early stage Pushkin's chief foreign model for the long
poem is Voltaire, and for the short one, Parny. Both have great *élan*
without individuality, and feeling without personal sensibility –
just what Pushkin at this stage could best make use of. He makes
no attempt to naturalise in Russian the topographical charm of
Parny's world, with its sensual *douceur* of pre-revolutionary France,
but he clearly found it highly congenial. For us it is part of the
landscape of taste, for Pushkin it was something more exciting; he
must have identified with Parny's creole background, his naive
excitability and easily deflected ambitions (he attempted first to
become a monk, then an army officer), his anacreontic life with
kindred spirits in Paris and Feuillancourt. All the more remarkable
that Pushkin avoids committing himself to any overt identification
with Parny, even when he is virtually translating one of his poems.

À mes amis

Rions, chantons, o mes amis,
Occupons-nous à ne rien faire,
Laissons murmurer le vulgaire.
Le plaisir est toujours permis.
Que notre existence légère
S'évanouisse dans les jeux.
Vivons pour nous, soyons heureux,
N'importe de quelle manière.
Un jour il faudra nous courber
Sous la main du temps qui nous presse;
Mais jouissons dans la jeunesse,
Et dérobons à la vieillesse
Tout ce qu'on peut lui dérober.

This becomes, in Pushkin:

Добрый совет

Давайте пить и веселиться,
Давайте жизнию играть,
Пусть чернь слепая суетится,
Не нам безумной подражать.
Пусть наша ветреная младость
Потонет в неге и вине,
Пусть изменяющая радость
Нам улыбнется хоть во сне.

34

Когда же юность легким дымом
Умчит веселья юных дней,
Тогда у старости отымем
Всё, что отымется у ней.

Let us drink and be merry; let us play with life; let the blind mob bustle as they please, no need for us to imitate the foolish. Let our thoughtless youth drown itself in wine and pleasure; let fleeting joy smile at us, though in a dream. When youth with its airy vapour carries off the merriment of youthful days, then we will withhold from old age everything that can be withheld from it. (I, 409.)

Parny's poem breathes an agreeable, enervated languor. Exhausted by the long poetic tradition of pleasure his young persons indulge its rites as if in a picture by Lancret or Fragonard. Pushkin's, by contrast, seethes like champagne with an abandonment restrained only by the control of the four-stress iambic line, a much brisker measure than Parny's. The restricted poetic vocabulary that is wholly adequate for Parny's *louche* or touching elegance of feeling turns out to be equally suited, when transposed into Russian, to Pushkin's more ebullient hedonism. In a sense Pushkin never grew out of Parny: he had no need to; for Parny, more than André Chénier, was always a genuinely kindred spirit, whose distinction the Russian poet emphasised by his imitation at a time when Europe had almost forgotten him. In spite of all difference of tempo the finest lyrics of Pushkin's maturity still recall the clarity of such lines as

Que le bonheur arrive lentement!
Que le bonheur s'éloigne avec vitesse...

The first two lines of an early *Lycée* poem, *Anacreon's Tomb*, suggest a very different kind of influence:

Всё в таинственном молчанье;
Холм оделся темнотой;

All things rest in a mysterious silence; the mound has clothed itself in darkness. (I, 174.)

In 1802 Zhukovsky had published in *The European Messenger* his first translation of Gray's *Elegy*. Pushkin must certainly have read it at some time with care; we know from a letter that he was irritated by the journalist Polevoy's parody of it in the 1825 *Neva Almanac*; and it would be interesting to discover whether his power of implanting inference and the ambiguously detached authorial 'I' in his poetry owed anything to Gray's unobtrusive skill in the

Elegy in manipulating the desires and fate of the author figure in relation to its structure and its generalising convention. Certain stanzas in *Evgeny Onegin* after Lensky's death suggest that it might be so, though this is only speculation, and the appearance in that poem of Gray's beetle need not indicate a borrowing. Originating in Shakespeare, the literary beetle had become almost an eighteenth-century convention, and like other crepuscular properties is common to the poetic traditions that Pushkin knew at the time. But though he may have picked up something from the *Elegy* and from Zhukovsky's other translations, their mellifluous melancholy was not really congenial to him.

It was otherwise with Delvig. Pushkin's chief companion in verse at the *Lycée* shared his enthusiasm for anacreontics, and saluted him in an ode published in a leading magazine as a poet destined for immortality. Pushkin returned the compliment ten years later, in the finest of his *Lycée* anniversary poems, by describing Delvig as a poet who had quietly brought his gift to perfection, while he himself had squandered his talent in trifles. The praise has a courtly renaissance ring about it, but also honest self-knowledge; in spite of his virtuosity the young Pushkin is not really at his best in the Arzamasian *bezdelka*, the poem about nothing, the trifle. One of the best known of his early pieces in this vein is the epistle *To Yuriev*, congratulating him on his success in love. Pushkin ends the poem by contrasting his own experience:

> А я, повеса вечно праздный,
> Потомок негров безобразный,
> Взращенный в дикой простоте,
> Любви не ведая страданий.
> Я нравлюсь юной красоте
> Бесстыдным бешенством желаний;
> С невольным пламенем ланит
> Украдкой нимфа молодая,
> Сама себя не понимая,
> На фавна иногда глядит.

But I, an ever indolent rake, a hideous descendant of negroes, reared in farouche simplicity, knowing nothing of the torments of love – I please youthful beauty by the shameless fury of my desires. With cheek involuntarily aflame, stealthily, a young nymph, not understanding her own self, will sometimes look at a faun. (II, 44.)

This has the manner of a trifle but not the tone. It gives too much away; its boastfulness jars and recovers itself by an expert flourish for which the whole poem then seems too obviously a preparation. On reading it, Batyushkov is said to have exclaimed in envy 'How this rascal has learnt to write!' and yet the poem's virtuosity is the complete opposite of Pushkin's true excellence. It is the faithful equivalent, in art, of those aspects of the young Pushkin which, as we know, sometimes exasperated his friends in life and made him seem frivolous, flamboyant and unreliable. Such a judgement on a slight and superb piece may seem ponderous, but there is no doubt that it offends against all the canons of Pushkin's later achievement. It scrapes against the delicate skin of the form, emphasising too strongly the conceited ending that Hénault or Parny knew how to manage with such lightness in *Stances pour deux sœurs qui se ressemblaient,*

> ...On croit voir sur de verts rivages
> Vénus se mirer dans les eaux,

or in *Vers sur la mort d'une jeune fille,*

> Ainsi le sourire s'efface;
> Ainsi meurt, sans laisser de trace,
> Le chant d'un oiseau dans les bois.

Of course Pushkin's facetiously boastful intrusion into the epistle to Yuriev is not typical of his *bezdelki*, or his other erotic poems written in the context of The Green Lamp, of which some, such as *To Olga Masson* (a well-known Petersburg *cocotte*), have a splendid collective effervescence, with the poet acting as anacreontic spokesman for his friends and fellow revellers. This identification with the group suits the poet of classic temper who has not yet learnt to talk about himself with the objective calm of *Nenastny den potukh*, the poem about jealousy mentioned in the previous chapter, and of the later love lyrics.

'Leave the *bezdelki* to us' wrote Batyushkov to Zhukovsky in 1814.[1] Like Pope and his contemporaries a century before – indeed like all poets who see themselves as trustees of a national literary movement – the Russian writers disclaimed any lasting status for the fugitive poem. Their expectation was for the *poema*, the lengthy

---

[1] The letter shows how much his contemporaries expected of Zhukovsky and – even more significant – the kind of writer they expected him to be and the models they thought he should follow. 'Turgenev tells me you are writing a ballad. Why not a *poema*? Why don't you translate Pope's *Epistle to Abelard*? Perverse fellow!...You have the imagination of Milton, the tenderness of Petrarch and you write ballads.' K. N. Batyushkov, *Collected Works* (St Petersburg 1886), vol. III, p. 306.

and ambitious work which Zhukovsky was to write, and which would no doubt fuse in a new Russian style classic grandeur with the romantic and Germanic *Heldengedicht* and national legend poem. Apart from his numerous and admirable translations, which included the *Odyssey*, rendered from a German version, Zhukovsky did indeed write many such poems. Yet none, in the awaited sense, was Russian. In spite of his skill and fluency in Russian metrics, in spite of the mastery of pace and rhythm which instructed Pushkin and which make many of his translations better poems than their originals, Zhukovsky is really one of that small class of paradoxical beings, the polynational poets. His preferred metre, significantly, came to be a version of the hexameter, which Goethe and Hölderlin had made almost a national metre in Germany, and which appealed to him as a symbol of Russia's unity with the European culture of past and present. Zhukovsky was not of course a syncretic poet in the fashion of Ezra Pound, but his later long poems do appear detached from any instinctual roots, and his sympathy with German culture – he was a great favourite with the German wife of Nicholas I and he went to live in Germany after retiring from court – is in marked contrast with Pushkin's indifference to it.

Where Zhukovsky is polynational, Pushkin is Protean. He had learnt how to write heroic poetry, anacreontics, witty sensual verses, epigrams, poems of friendship. None is entirely satisfactory because each is compartmented within the limits of a separate acquired style: a long poem would bring out his latent genius for combination and would concentrate these accomplishments into something completely distinctive and *sui generis*. He needed to write a long poem in order to realise himself fully as a poet, not in order to have composed a Russian epic, like Volkov's *Osvobozhdennaya Moskva* (*Moscow Liberated*), which came out at the same time as *Ruslan and Lyudmila*. And perhaps that is why, while Volkov's poem was received with approval and respect, *Ruslan and Lyudmila* was so successful and so instantly popular. Certainly Zhukovsky had no doubts about it. After it appeared he sent Pushkin his portrait with the inscription: 'To a victorious pupil from a defeated master.'

Volkov wrote in alexandrines; and like dactylic hexameters or the free blank verse iambics which Zhukovsky also developed, these never really settle into the fibre of Russian poetry. (Pushkin, but only Pushkin, disproves this generalisation later as regards blank verse.) It might be argued that every national poetry develops a distinctive metre suited to its linguistic character, and, whatever its success with other imports, measures them ultimately against the line and stanza it comes to know best – the classical measures sanguinely brought in by academic Elizabethan poets died before the living competition of dramatic blank verse in England. Pushkin produced some good hexameters, usually for two-line Catullan miniatures; tried *terza rima*; and wrote much in alexandrines, even the long poem *Andzhelo*. Yet though never expressing himself on the subject, it seems likely that he was aware in them all of too great a resistance. The *Iliad* of Gnedich and Zhukovsky's *Odyssey* are magnificently kept going by the metre of their originals, but Russian syntax and inflection seem to favour it without naturalising it: there is nothing comparable in Russian, as there is not in English, to the golden certainty of Goethe's *Römische Elegien* or Hölderlin's measures. On the other hand Russian accommodates a wide range of imported metre with impressive ease; and seldom or never has that air of complacent patronage which accompanies French blank verse, and the quirkiness or happy bravado of English alexandrine and hexameter, which leave the reader to wonder not why they were not done well but why they were done at all.

The Russian equivalent of Shakespeare's blank verse is the Pushkinian octosyllable. Few languages lend themselves to the natural rapidity of octosyllabics, and their exigence in the matter of rhyme. Milton, Marvell and Keats – three English poets who excel in this form - all do so by exploiting the very weaknesses that it imposes on poetic exposition in English syntax: turned to account in the rapid and excited movement of *L'Allegro* and *Il Penseroso*, with their kaleidoscopic alternation of scene; in the metaphysics of haste that animates *To his Coy Mistress*; in the instant scene-setting of that brilliant fragment, *The Eve of St Mark*. But Keats did not continue his narrative poem, perhaps because the pace could not be slackened. The strain it imposes on an expanding narrative is too much for the resources of his world of sensuous and tangible conveyance. In English and French – even, despite *Faust*, in German – the iambic tetrameter is a measure that tends to impose its own character and its own uniformity on the poet: instead of using it as he wishes he must allow himself to be used by it. The romantics' way out is to break the metre, as Scott and Coleridge do in *The Lady of the Lake* and in *Christabel*, by launching into ballad variations and lines of nine or ten syllables, even sometimes an anapaestic canter – a favourite expedient of Byron's. Wordsworth in *The Waggoner* is directed by the measure to prolong the show of ponderous gaiety with which he begins: the ghost of *Hudibras* seems to be looking over his shoulder; and it was the example of *Hudibras*, and his own rejection of octosyllables for the heroic couplet, that led Dryden to remark on the metre giving no room for the thought to turn round.

Pushkin's chief foreign model was Voltaire, who with Desmahis and Chamfort used the metre in its sprightliest vein for verse letters, where it suggests the *badinage* and rapid exchange of talk. And Pushkin adapted this tone in Russian to the requirements of the long and varied poetic narrative. Voltaire would have delighted in the observation, at once expansive and straight-faced, with which Pushkin opens the fourth canto of *Ruslan*:

> Я каждый день, восстав от сна,
> Благодарю сердечно бога
> За то, что в наши времена
> Волшебников не так уж много.
> К тому же – честь и слава им! –
> Женитьбы наши безопасны...

Awaking each day from sleep, I thank God from my heart that in our times magicians are not so numerous. Furthermore – honour and glory to them – our marriages are not in danger. (IV, 60.)

so also would Chaucer:

> This maketh that ther been no fayeryes.
> For ther as wont to walken was an elf,
> Ther walketh now the limitour himself...
> Wommen may go saufly up and doun,
> In every bush, or under every tree,
> Ther is noon other incubus but he,
> And he ne wol doon hem but dishonour...
>
> (*The Tale of The Wyf of Bathe*)

Already in *Ruslan* Pushkin expands his narrative tone and scope into a universal dimension. His introductions are leisurely; his action and description command the same variety of effect that Chaucer, Ariosto, or Spenser secure over the spacious field of their verse worlds. The reader is conscious of no stricture in the verse medium but only of its powers of liberation. *Ruslan* contains in embryo all the genius of Pushkin's later iambic tetrameter poems, and, by his choice of it, the metre becomes the regular Russian metre for all subsequent poetic narrative.

Like the opening chords of a ballet suite, the first two lines of the opening canto set the tone of what is to come. A bar of silence – in more pedestrian terms a two-line gap – divides them from the curtain going up on the wedding feast at Kiev of Vladimir's daughter Lyudmila with Prince Ruslan.

> Дела давно минувших дней,
> Преданья старины глубокой.

> Deeds of days long since passed away,
> Legends of deep antiquity. (IV, 13.)

By alliteration and onomatopoeia the inference he is to draw is signalled to the reader. The phrases themselves are traditional, even formulaic: effect comes from the harmony of their juxta-position in the two lines. The first is light, caressing, faintly mocking; the second, without breaking the thread of the not wholly serious, seems to plunge deep into the true past conjured up by the first line's stylised romantic appeal. For what we are to read or hear is both real and unreal; both a sophisticated sport with the fan-tastic, and a deeper display of what the past and its magic can mean to the imagination.

By way of contrast here is the opening of *The Eve of St Mark*:

> Upon a Sabbath-day it fell;
> Twice holy was the Sabbath-bell
> That call'd the folk to evening prayer;
> The city streets were clean and fair
> From wholesome drench of April rains;
> And, on the western window panes,
> The chilly sunset faintly told
> Of unmatured green valleys cold...

Keats's first two lines leave the reader in no doubt that the magic is to be taken seriously. 'Twice holy' – Sunday and the eve of a saint's day – but the evening is also evoked quite differently, in its magical but commonplace physical feel. Keats's contrast is more leisurely and more prosaic than Pushkin's, but in both we are aware of that instant occupation of the whole field of our poetic recep-tivity that only a very great poet can achieve. Pushkin's contrast is more stylised and yet as unobtrusive – it is between the scepti-cism of Voltaire and the reverence of folk-tale – and translation reveals only the romance of long ago, as exploited by every poet of the period; for the tones of lightness and depth, detached irony and ardent identification, which are compressed into the two lines, vanish with the words that contain them.

Pushkin's extraordinary ability to keep the balance between the attitudes implicit in these two opening lines is the key to the success of the poem. This in itself is so far from being a unique achievement that it might almost be called the revival of a tradition. As the critic Kireevsky pointed out not long after *Ruslan* appeared, it owes much to Ariosto and to the 'Italian–French school'.[1] Ariosto mixes the heroic and the profane, high spirits and learned doctrine; yet like all the great poets of the Renaissance, like Spenser and Chapman after him, he subordinates uninhibited mythologising to an overall moral structure. Even where such a structure is not much in evidence, as in Shakespeare's *Venus and Adonis*, there is no question of dismantling the massive rhetorical apparatus on which it depends. The long poems of the Renaissance are never light in tone; their plans preclude the delicacy of miniature. And their romantic equivalents in Pushkin's time – Goethe's *Faust*, Wieland's *Oberon* – have the same cumbrousness of structure without the unselfconscious compounding of 'mirth and doctryne'. Facetiousness and comic relief in these long works is switched on to order and becomes elephantine in consequence. The German Muse is well aware that humour is needed after the rhapsodic message, but this calculation does not produce spontaneous variety.

Although Pushkin draws on the Ariostan tradition his power to amuse and to move, within the context of fairy-tale and legend, is really much nearer something specifically Russian, or at least with an originality developed in a Russian context – the ballet. Pushkin adored Didelot's ballads on the Petersburg stage; *Evgeny Onegin* lyrically describes one, and some scenes – like the dream of Tatyana – suggest a transposition of their atmosphere; in Pushkin's last play, *Rusalka*, he returns to a theme from operatic ballet. I have already suggested that the opening lines of *Ruslan* have a kind of musical counterpart, and its rhyme-scheme carries the analogy further: the deep chord of the opening lines, heard again when they are repeated at the poem's end, has not the finished air of a couplet – it picks up its rhymes, like notes in a phrase, after the moment of silence when the actors are revealed upon the stage. The rhyme pattern of *abab*, alternating – but not regularly – to *abba*, and interspersed with occasional couplets, gives a much

[1] 'Nechto o kharaktere poezii Pushkina,' *The Moscow Messenger* (1828).

greater flexibility and freedom to the four-stress lines than Keats's octosyllabic couplets can command.[1]

Though the point is evident enough, we might take one example of *Ruslan's* lack of any of the patterning of meanings found in the legend poems of both the Renaissance and the Romantic period. Lyudmila on her wedding night is ravished away by the invisible enchanter Chernomor, and after Prince Ruslan has rescued her he encounters his old rival Khan Ratmir, one of the three disappointed suitors who – with the distracted bridegroom – had originally ridden off to seek her. Ratmir has found a castle full of fountains and delicious damsels (Pushkin takes occasion in a brief aside to let us know that he is not Homer, to celebrate the feasting in heroic halls, but will rather follow Parny in singing the charms of a naked limb in the darkness). Ratmir succumbs, and is found by Ruslan leading an idyllic life among fisher-folk, his charmer of the castle now metamorphosed into a domestic shepherdess. The pair chat awhile, like two young men about town – '*Lyubezny Khan, Ya ochen rad...*' ('My dear Khan, I'm delighted!...') – and Ratmir accompanies Ruslan on his way, wishing him further conquests and glory, and with a twinge of sadness at their parting as he thinks of his own proud days past.

The last touch shows Pushkin superimposing a hint of his own social world – the world of friends and friendship poems – upon the *skaz*, and withdrawing it before the point becomes obvious and facetious. Marriage is the end of adventure, even with an enchanted shepherdess, and in such connubial felicity the young now and then regret their old freedom. In an early draft Pushkin made the point too explicit: in an interpolation he tells us how much he loves his heroine (a confidence he can allow himself freely later in the context of *Evgeny Onegin*) but not as a wife, for the idea of marriage does not appeal to him. This he wisely removed, and left it implicit in the encounter of Ruslan with Ratmir. In the romances of Ariosto or Spenser the role, and hence the meaning, of Ratmir would be that of the sensually deluded man, in thrall to the enchanted garden or the Bower of Bliss. In Pushkin he is a quest hero who finds himself in an agreeable situation, and so decides – rightly, as it seems to both young men – to stay with it and abandon the poem.

---

[1] Meredith's five-stress lines in *Modern Love*, rhyming *abba*, can sometimes suggest, in their speed and brilliancy, an English equivalent of one effect of Pushkin's rhyme schemes.

The tragedy in old unhappy far-off things can be implied as well as modern comedy. When he meets Ratmir, Ruslan has just left the vast severed head of a Bogatyr, elder brother of the dwarf Chernomor, with whom Ruslan had earlier conducted a kind of Ariostan skirmish until it revealed by what trick the villainous dwarf had cut it off and set it on guard over a magic sword. This head is not only a pantomime grotesque but a sombre and curiously moving portent, a survival of epic darkness in the sophisticated frivolity of the poem. It alone can die as a hero dies. Separated from its vast trunk, which rots in a far-off desert, it has longed for death; but the dwarf's magic has kept it alive. When Ruslan approaches with the captive dwarf its moment has come at last.

> Узнала витязя она
> И брата с ужасом узнала.
> Надулись ноздри; на щеках
> Багровый огнь еще родился,
> И в умирающих глазах
> Последний гнев изобразился.
> В смятенье, в бешенстве немом
> Она зубами скрежетала
> И брату хладным языком
> Укор невнятный лепетала...
> Уже ее в тот самый час
> Кончалось долгое страданье:
> Чела мгновенный пламень гас,
> Слабело тяжкое дыханье,
> Огромный закатился взор,
> И вскоре князь и Черномор
> Узрели смерти содроганье...
> Она почила вечным сном.

It recognised the Knight; and it recognised, with horror, its brother. Its nostrils extended; a reddish glow grew on its cheeks; and a last indignation showed itself in the dying eyes. In rage, in a dumb fury it ground its teeth, and with its cold tongue whispered to its brother an inarticulate reproach. But already its long suffering was ending: the brief glow died on its brow, its laboured breathing grew weaker, its huge gaze sank, and soon the Prince and Chernomor witnessesd the convulsion of death...It was sleeping an eternal sleep. (IV, 79.)

In the Russian *skazka* all turns out well in the end, and the combats are spectacular rather than grimly realistic, but in the death of the giant head Pushkin evokes something closer to the atmosphere of Germanic and heroic legend. This is all the more remarkable because the antecedents of *Ruslan* are neither ancient nor dignified. Russian folk-tale is far less important than Italianate extravaganza and contemporary Gothic and Ossianic romance – the giant head could have come from a number of chapbook sources, or even from a recollection of the huge helmet in the courtyard of Walpole's *The Castle of Otranto*. But this motley does not diminish the authenticity of the singular effects, heroic, elegiac or lyrical. If the head's last moments move us, then the quasi-comic decease of the warrior Rogdai, hurled by Ruslan from the Dnieper's bank, is a thing of gay elegiac pleasure.[1]

> И слышно было, что Рогдая
> Тех вод русалка молодая
> На хладны перси приняла
> И, жадно витязя лобзая,
> На дно со смехом увлекла,
> И долго после, ночью темной
> Бродя близ тихих берегов,
> Богатыря призрак огромный
> Пугал пустынных рыбаков.

It was rumoured that a young rusalka of that stream clutched Rogdai to her cold bosom, and embracing him hungrily, carried him off with glee to the depths. And long afterwards, in the darkness of night the warrior's prodigious shade, straying along the quiet shores, struck fear into solitary fishermen. (IV, 44.)

The mixture may have delighted the public but it did not appeal to the more serious-minded critics, or to some other poets. Those who wanted a new variation on the theme of Kheraskov's *Rossiada* or *Vladimir* were not pleased with Pushkin's perfunctory attitude towards the Kievan setting of heroic myth, and his treatment of the theme with the same lightness with which Bogdanovich had composed his very popular *Dushenka*, thirty years before. The journal *Son of the Fatherland* lamented the tale's lack of ordinary narrative plausibility, and in his preface to the second edition Pushkin answered some of the objections with a series of deadpan queries: 'Why did Chernomor leave the magic sword in the wilderness, under his brother's head? Wouldn't it have been better to have taken it home with him?'

His sarcasm might have been misplaced, for any good fantasy or fairy-tale must have its own kind of commonsense and interior

---

[1] It was no doubt this kind of elegiac beauty that made Zhukovsky good-naturedly suspect, and with reason, a parody in *Ruslan* of his own sentimental narratives.

logic, which the artist's irresponsibility can weaken. The critics' objections would indeed apply to the kind of work – it might be *Gulliver's Travels* or *The Ancient Mariner* – which requires us to 'suspend our disbelief' at the outset and expect the narrative coherence of the impossible. But Pushkin's poem does not function like this. Instead of a story told by the poet it is more like a series of *tableaux vivants* surveyed and commented on by a sophisticated spectator. There is a space between the detached scenes and the detached attitude which commands them, a relation of similarity between presentation and appraisal which we shall also find in the far more complex world of *Evgeny Onegin*.

Slonimsky observes that the genial lyricism with which the heroine's predicament in the enchanter's castle is described makes her 'lovable': for the first time a heroine of the fantastic romance is also 'human'.[1] There is something in this, but at the time the heroine struck some critics, attuned to romantic sensibility, as being more ludicrous than lovable. Writing in *The Critic* in 1821 the poet Olin testified that though the sufferings of Aminta, the heroine of Wieland's *Oberon*, made him weep, those of Lyudmila only made him laugh. The common reader was not only more sympathetic but more adaptable, appreciating Pushkin's heroine as the theatre-goer would have adored a ballerina who combined a perfect mastery of technique with an engaging disposition, incongruously sensed through the exquisite precision of her movements. When a marvellous feast appears before the captive Lyudmila she at first tearfully rejects it, but then realises she is hungry and sits down to eat. When Chernomor vainly woos her she knocks his hat off, and then alone in her room she tries it on before the glass, for what girl can resist a new hat? Promptly she becomes invisible: she removes it, and there she is again.

> Людмила шапкой завертела;
> На брови, прямо, набекрень,
> И задом наперед надела.
> И что ж? о чудо старых дней!
> Людмила в зеркале пропала;
> Перевернула – перед ней
> Людмила прежняя предстала;
> Назад надела – снова нет;
> Сняла – и в зеркале! «Прекрасно!
> Добро, колдун, добро, мой свет!
> Теперь мне здесь уж безопасно»;

[1] A. L. Slonimsky, *Masterstvo Pushkina* (Moscow 1959).

Lyudmila adjusted the hat on her brow, trying it straight, askew, and then back to front. And what's this? Oh marvel of bygone days! Lyudmila has vanished in the mirror. She turned it round; and before her stood her former self. Back again, again she's not there. She takes it off, and there she is in the glass. 'Splendid! That's fixed you, sorcerer – so much for you my dear! Now I'm in no danger.' (iv, 49.)

Pushkin records the gestures of a beautifully synchronised performance as he does those of the ballerina in *Evgeny Onegin*.

> Бдистательна, полувоздушна,
> Смычку волшебному послушна,
> Толпою нимф окружена,
> Стоит Истомина; она,
> Одной ногой касаясь пола,
> Другою медленно кружит,
> И вдруг прыжок, и вдруг летит,
> Летит, как пух от уст Эола;
> То стан совьет, то разовьет,
> И быстрой ножкой ножку бьет.

Shining, half ethereal, obedient to the conductor's enchanted wand, surrounded by a corps of nymphs, stands Istomina: while touching the floor with one foot she slowly gyrates the other; suddenly leaps, suddenly flies – flies like fluff from the lips of Aeolus – spins herself and unspins, and taps one quick small foot against the other. (i, 20.)

The split-second timing is essential. No more than the performer can the poet afford to linger into self-indulgence in his own skill and in the pleasure of what he is creating.

This is particularly true of the sex comedy. There is a striking difference between the almost touchingly inflammable womaniser that Pushkin was in real life and his self-control on the subject in his art. Without self-indulgence there can be no pornography. Parny's shade has hardly been invoked to describe the bridegroom's raptures on his wedding-night before it is brusquely dismissed by the sudden onset of the enchantment, the clap of thunder and the strange cry twice heard. The moment is genuinely uncanny, yet we may suspect that Pushkin throws off, as he will often do again, the hint of a parody; here it is at the expense of the love languors in the kinds of French literature he enjoyed. So far from receiving any sympathy, the unfortunate Ruslan is made to feel by his father-in-law and the court that the disappearance of the bride is somehow all his fault.

That artistic restraint in such matters did not come easily to Pushkin is shown by his early drafts of the scene in which Ruslan

accidentally knocks the cap of invisibility from Lyudmila's head
and beholds her lying insensible, trapped in a net by Chernomor.
The MS stammers with ecstatic phrases – 'her naked limbs...her
shoulders in the meshes...her thigh half glimpsed' – in a manner
very similar to *The Eve of St Agnes*, in the first jottings of which
Keats runs through images of Madeline undressing. Both poets
recovered their equilibrium in the course of composition, but while
Keats did so by reconciling his day-dreams with the opulent art of
his poem, Pushkin suppressed his completely. Already in *Ruslan*
he shows his preference for allowing the reader to infer, rather than
making any display of his own sensations.

It is significant that the *tableau vivant* approach, with the poet as
choreographer, breaks down at the conclusion of the poem when
Ruslan, arriving back in Kiev, finds a full-scale epic battle in
progress between Vladimir and the invading Pechenegs. Though
Pushkin gives a spirited account of the battle, decided by Ruslan's
heroic intervention, it is barely in keeping with the preceding
cantos, whose eclectic variety has depended on a much more
intimate scale. But Pushkin's contemporaries were enthusiastic;
this was the formula of the kind of poem they expected, the kind of
poem which Zhukovsky had projected ten years earlier on the
theme of Vladimir. Pushkin's schoolfriend Küchelbecker, himself
a poet and later a Decembrist, thought the finale easily the best
part of the poem, and not inferior to the battle scenes in *Poltava*.
Soviet critics are apt to agree, because here at last is something like
narodnost, the struggle of a people under their hero leader in a
'concrete' historical setting. In borrowing from Karamzin's
account of the wars of the Kievan Princes and the Pechenegs,
Pushkin altered his first draft to include more realistic details of the
fighting. But this hardly makes them less perfunctory. Though the
martial sequence is as spirited as in Chaucer's *Knight's Tale*, it is
not, poetically, as suggestive of the heroic age as is the final
passing of the betrayed and severed head. In Chaucer's tale, too,
heroic atmosphere is more impressive in descriptive suggestion than
in the actual account of battle.

Ruslan is worth looking at in some detail because it gives us an
insight into Pushkin's precocious talent in synthesising and
proportioning heterogeneous material. It is an admirable work of
art but it is also a workshop poem. If we compare it with the
Skazki, written ten years later, the contrast is not so much between

two ways of treating the marvellous, as between poetry whose internal workings are almost insolently open for our inspection, and poetry which is sealed off from it, sheathed in the simplicity of total sophistication. We noticed the neglect in *Ruslan* of the tight interior logic of fairy-tale, a neglect sardonically justified by Pushkin in his preface to the second edition. But in the *Skazki* he makes this logic the principle which both creates and conceals their art.

Neither Ruslan nor the *Skazki* are in a self-conscious sense Russian poems. Pushkin knew instinctively that – as Pevsner has put it – while great art is national, national art is bad art. And yet *Ruslan* does give us the feeling, I think, which we also may get from such apparently and incongruously different works as Pope's *Rape of the Lock* and Goethe's *Hermann und Dorothea*, of a society apprehending itself, through the medium of a great poet's craft, in a sort of microcosmic idyll. The idyll is insulated: it does not raise questions or suggest issues about such a society in the way that *Evgeny Onegin* does, or *Peer Gynt*; and its kind of appeal and popularity reflects only this happy and immediate sense of self-discovery. Before Pope's poem, polite Augustan society had not yet seen itself in this spirited and elegant, this enchantingly characteristic way. The German bourgeois found his satisfaction in his own identity majestically stylised in Goethe's idyll. And it may be that such exotically artificial and hybrid works can create and contain the image of an emergent society more potently than any conscious attempt at national or folk poetry.

When, in 1828, Pushkin added the famous Prologue to *Ruslan and Lyudmila*, did he perhaps enjoy the incongruity between the actual provenance of the poem and the Prologue's assertion that it would contain homely marvels 'smelling of Russia', tales like the traditional one of Tsar Kashchey or Baba Yaga and the hut on fowl's legs? The *Skazki*, too, though written at the height of Pushkin's poetic maturity, were in their way as unexpected and disconcerting to theoretically-minded contemporaries as *Ruslan* had been. Polevoy, by then an outspoken enemy of Pushkin's, chided him in the *Moscow Telegraph* for writing in a form 'lower than the model', a significant objection from a serious folklorist who wanted simultaneously to worship *narodnost* and to elevate it. Though most literary versions of folk poetry had been done in the same trochaic form, he also objected to the metre of the *Skazki* – the clipped tetrameter whose air of simplicity conceals the most assured craftsmanship – and advised Pushkin to go to school with the antiquarian versifier Danilov. The unfavourable reaction was general, except among Pushkin's closest friends. Even to Belinsky they seemed mere adaptations of popular material, too straight-forward to qualify as poetry. Turgenev thought them the slightest of all Pushkin's work, and it was not until Rimsky-Korsakov made an opera of *Tsar Saltan* that they became widely known. In the Soviet era they are of course praised highly as examples of how Pushkin drew his art from the traditions of the people.

The representative of the people, canonised in Pushkinian hagiography, is the Pushkin family nurse, Arina Rodionovna, whom the poet came to know well during his exile at Mikhailov-skoye after his years in the south. She had plenty of old stories, which she probably embroidered and improved on herself when she told them to Pushkin, as an intelligent and shrewd transmitter of a verbal tradition would tend to do.[1] Pushkin was very fond of her. He made her the model for Tatyana's nurse in *Evgeny Onegin*, and he addressed two poems to her, one a fragment. *Winter Evening*, the other, has become as much a part of the consciousness of the Russian reader – from childhood onwards – as nursery rhymes are to his English equivalent; but instead of the simplicity of such rhymes the poem has the sophistication of a perfectly balanced compound, as elaborate on its miniature scale as *Ruslan and Lyudmila*. It reproduces in literary terms a homely occasion, poet and nurse sitting together with a snowstorm howling outside the 'decrepit hovel' (*vetkhaya lachuzhka*), which is appropriate to the convention of story-telling on a winter's night, and leads into the other *topoi* of drinking-song and ballad of sentiment.

> Выпьем, добрая подружка
> Бедной юности моей,
> Выпьем с горя; где же кружка?
> Сердцу будет веселей.
> Спой мне песню, как синица
> Тихо за морем жила;
> Спой мне песню, как девица
> За водой поутру шла.

Let's drink, good friend of my poor boyhood, let's drown our sorrow. Where's the jug? It will cheer our hearts. Sing me a song: how the blue tit lived quietly beyond the sea. Sing me a song: how the maiden went to fetch water in the morning. (II, 288.)

---

[1] A detailed discussion of these, *Skazki Arini Rodionovni*, by M. K. Azadovsky, appeared in *Literatura i Folklor*, 1938. See the same author's *Pushkin i folklor* (*Vremennik Pushkinskoy Komissii*, III (1937)).

A single word – *tikho* (quietly) – acts as catalyst for the poetic compound. It is one of Pushkin's favourite words, usually in the simplest descriptive context and in association with night, moonlight, water, the breeze, and so on. Here it jumps what F. W. Bateson would call 'the semantic gap' between the literary commonplace of the poet and the naive life of the old nurse's vocabulary as narrator. We hear the story, as she tells it, through the medium of the poet's reaction: his nostalgia, part stylised, part actual – Pushkin's recurrent longing for *pokoy i volya* (peace and freedom) – to escape to the magic other land of art and tale where the blue-tit lived quietly. It is of importance that the nurse does not speak in the poem: we are aware of her matter-of-fact presence through the comfort it brings to the poet. The perspective of narrative and dialogue is accomplished in the four verses of a short lyric; not long after Pushkin had been working on the full-scale dialogue between Tatyana and her nurse in the third chapter of *Evgeny Onegin*.

From Arina Rodionovna Pushkin heard stories on which he made notes, still extant, recording not only the material itself but the way in which it had been told to him. One of these gives the narrative formula used in the opening lines of the Prologue to *Ruslan and Lyudmila*.

«У моря лукоморья стоит дуб, а на том дубу золотые цепи, и по тем цепям ходит кот: вверх идет – сказки сказывает, вниз идет – песни поет».

At a curving shore of the sea stands an oak; on that oak a golden chain; and on that chain walks a cat. As it walks up it tells stories – as it walks down it sings songs.

> У лукоморья дуб зеленый;
> Златая цепь на дубе том:
> И днем и ночью кот ученый
> Всё ходит по цепи кругом;
> Идет направо – песнь заводит,
> Налево – сказку говорит.

By a curving shore a green oak; a golden chain on that oak; and night and day a learned cat walks round and round on that chain: when it goes to the right it strikes up a song: to the left – it tells a tale. (IV, 7.)

The oak-tree has become green: the cat has become learned. The epithets need each other for the rhyme, but they show also *curiosa felicitas*; the plain vision of the one and the genial implication of the other (the wonder in itself, and as it is considered by the intelligence) combine to make the scene burst upon the reader with an impact far more terse and sensational than in the story formula.[1] That, for all its effectiveness in setting the scene, suggests the leisurely tempo of a simple evening's tale. By stylising and exaggerating the syntactic economy of the scene-setting phrases (the otiose verb *stoit* (stands) is cut out), Pushkin's iambics beat the directness of folktale at its own game. We might notice, too, that the learned cat is not stylised but naturalised, so that we seem to see the beast stalking left or right at the circumference of its golden chain.

Though written much later, the *Skazki* share the same secret of exaggerating, so to speak, the folktaleness of folktale – to refine an essence which has nothing primitive or old-world about it. Inference can be as sharp, meaning as contemporary, as in the narrative poem of mixed origin. Indeed in *The Tale of the Golden Cockerel* a modern fantasy has almost certainly been grafted on the form of the *Skazka*. The tales of Washington Irving in a French translation were very popular in Russia around 1833, and Polevoy noted, perhaps not unmaliciously, a resemblance between his *Knickerbocker* and Pushkin's *Tales of Belkin*. More important, the poet Anna Akhmatova has noticed that Pushkin owned a French translation of *The Alhambra*, and that a fragment of 1833, the year before *The Golden Cockerel* was written, reproduced fairly exactly the details of one of these 'Haroun al Rashid' tales, mild spoofs on the manner of the *Arabian Nights*.[2] In the Alhambra story a bronze

---

[1] Even the non-existence of articles in Russian could be said to be stylised in the opening lines of the Prologue. Compare the lines in *The Rime of the Ancient Mariner*:

> The sun's rim dips; the stars rush out:
> At one stride comes the dark;

where the definite article, thrice repeated, actually emphasises the staccato economy of the description rather than detracting from it. Avoidance of it would have slowed down the action described, while the concentration of Pushkin's two lines seems to draw attention to the linguistic conditions which make possible the swiftness of his scene-setting, the 'foregrounding' – as Dr Ullmann has called it – which Russian syntax can lend to poetic descriptions. Compare the descriptions from *Poltava*, below Ch. 4.

[2] A. Akhmatova, 'Poslednaya skazka Pushkina', *Zvezda* (1933). Akhmatova thought the plot of Pushkin's tale inferior to Irving's because its persons and their motives are insufficiently developed. Censorship and politics may have been the cause, but she seems to discount the usual working of Pushkinian economy and implication. She points out that if a political significance was intended, as it almost certainly was, the likeliest real life candidate for Pushkin's Tsar Dadon is not Nicholas but Alexander I, who had been 'warlike' in his youth, and who surrounded himself in the last years of his reign with scheming devotees of both sexes. Her firm connection of the tale

horseman is placed on a tower to warn the ruler of approaching enemies. Inside the tower are model armies which the ruler has only to knock down in order to destroy the real armies which are advancing against him. It was this detail that Pushkin reproduced in the fragment, but it is clear that its whimsical ingenuity would not have suited the *skazka*: Pushkin used instead the much older *motif*, found everywhere in legend, of the ruler sending out a succession of armies and finally going out to battle in person. The coincidence of the bronze horseman *motif* with Pushkin's poetic masterpiece of 1833 is striking but probably not significant; though it may have prompted the substitution of the golden cockerel. Though the similarities of the fragment are not reproduced in *The Tale of the Golden Cockerel* there can be little doubt that the tale was modelled on Irving's oriental fantasia rather than on any folklore source, but Pushkin cared as little as Shakespeare where his stories came from: he enjoyed them without reverence and adapted them without pedantry. Source hunting is a proper Pushkinist activity and the title of Azadovsky's article, 'Arina Rodionovna or "The Brothers Grimm"', shows how widely and inconclusively the net must be cast, for Pushkin's nurse herself had picked up many of her tales not from old traditions but from new tales and translations that had filtered through by word of mouth to a largely unlettered peasantry – but in the case of *Tsar Saltan*, *The Tale of the Parson and his Man Balda*, and the others, it cannot do much to enhance our enjoyment or our critical appreciation. *Balda* is an excellent comic tale in the straight tradition of folk *fabliau*, which suffered somewhat from the emendations Zhukovsky made to get it past the censorship: *Tsar Saltan* is a perfect lyrical masterpiece, the most formally beautiful of them all, and the one that most sustains throughout the length of a tale the atmosphere and taste of magic in the *Ruslan* prologue. *The Dead Princess and the Seven Heroes* is not on the same level, and *The Fisherman and the Fish* is pure folklore on a slighter scale.

The origins of *The Golden Cockerel* and its hint of political meaning give it a special place. More remarkable than any specific reference – for popular rhymes are after all traditionally full of cryptic or sub-

with Irving's work earned her the hostility of good Soviet Pushkinists, who resented emphasis on European models and influence, especially where the *Skazki* were concerned; and may have contributed to her inclusion among those denounced in Zhdanov's notorious 'anti-cosmopolitan' speech of 1946. See J. C. Fiske, 'The Soviet Controversy over Pushkin and Washington Irving', *Comparative Literature*, VII, 1954.

versive comment – is Pushkin's use of the *skazka* to create a gruesome little tableau of the nature, in any age, of power: its irresponsibility and its blindness. As such a 'peepshow' (to use Tolstoy's term) it would not be absurd to class it with Tolstoy's own story *Hadji Murad*, and *The Bronze Horseman*.

Tsar Dadon is a king who takes his absolute power completely for granted, and he is genuinely amazed at being held to a promise. Insensately aggressive in his prime, he now wishes for a quiet old age, but his realm is threatened from all sides and his generals are in despair.

> Ждут бывало с юга, гдядь, –
> Ан с востока лезет рать.

They would be on the watch, looking to the south, but no, from the east an army approaches. (IV, 484.)

Like Chaucer in similar contexts, Pushkin imposes a hooded irony of his own on the droll vitality of the hypothetical narrator. Dadon consults a wise man, an astrologer and eunuch, and is given a golden cockerel who stands on a spire and crows at the approach of any danger. The Tsar can sleep at last, and when he is aroused by the next alarm we hear his voice:

> «Царь ты наш! отец народа! –
> Возглашает воевода, –
> Государь! проснись! беда!»
> – «Что такое, господа? –
> Говорит Дадон, зевая, –
> А?...Кто там?...беда какая?»

'Our Tsar! Father of the people!' the general cries – 'Sovereign awake! Disaster!' 'What is it, gentlemen?' says Dadon, yawning – 'Eh? Who's there? What disaster?'

His sons are sent out with armies and fail to return. He sets out with a third army and finds in a narrow ravine among the mountains a silken tent; before it lie the slaughtered troops and his two sons who have killed each other. Then out of the tent appears a beautiful maiden, the Queen of Shemakha, and Dadon's lamentations come to an abrupt end.

> Как пред солнцем птица ночи,
> Царь умолк, ей гдядя в очи,
> Й забыл он перед ней
> Смерть обоих сыновей.

Like a bird of night before the sun the Tsar was silent, looking into her eyes, and before her he forgot the death of his two sons.

But he has promised the eunuch anything he may ask as a reward, and he claims the Queen. In vain he is asked to choose something else: he tries to hold the exasperated Tsar to his promise and is told to clear off.

> Старичок хотел заспорить,
> Но с иным накладно вздорить;

The old man wanted to argue, but with some people it is disadvantageous to pick a quarrel.

(Pushkin noted in his text his own original reading *No s tsaryami plokho vzdorit* (but it is a bad business to pick a quarrel with Tsars) and it is this which has led commentators to connect the poem with his own relations with Nicholas.) When the old man still attempts to argue Dadon strikes him dead. The maiden laughs.

> Вся столица
> Содрогнулась, а девица –
> Хи-хи-хи да ха-ха-ха!
> Не боится, знать, греха.

The whole capital shuddered but the girl – 'Hee, hee, hee!' and 'Ha, ha, ha!' Obviously she has no fear of the sin.

We hear the discordant sound in the sudden silence; it makes a curiously uncanny moment, an instant dramatic revelation like that of Dadon looking into her eyes; and its effect is not trivialised but enhanced by the pious platitude of the narrator. The cockerel flies down from the steeple and pecks the Tsar's head: he groans and dies, and the Queen vanishes.

It is not easy to describe the story without making it appear as lightweight as Pushkin's contemporaries found it, but the real achievement of the *Skazki* can only be measured by comparison with what was similar to them in the European literature of the time. Ballad, legend, and supernatural or uncanny verse tales were the stock in trade of contemporary romanticism, but nowhere – with a very few exceptions – do they rise above the mediocre when they are deliberately simple and naive: the poets of the Schillerian age strove to reproduce the naive but succeeded best when it became the starting point of reflection – ballads with a meaning, tales with moral depth. The 'meaning' and the 'depth' of *The Golden Cockerel* are natural aspects of its narrative function: they do not justify or implicitly patronise it; and *Tsar Saltan*, as a triumph of simple tale-telling, has no equivalent in European verse – only in the prose of Grimm and Hans Andersen.

A reason is the need of European poets who told such tales for paraphernalia, local colour. Though he enjoyed and admired Scott, Pushkin more than once comments on the excess of antiquarianism, the pleasure felt by author and readers in the properties of the past for their own sake He perceived that the romantic revival of the marvellous indulged itself in the properties of the genre instead of taking them for granted. When he lays marvels before us, as in the Prologue to *Ruslan*, the simple *tam chudesa* (wonders are there) holds in balance two opposite elements: the popular appetite for wonders, and the artist's sardonic knowledge that he himself is cut off from them by the self-imposed stringency of his art. He distrusted the extravagance of the French school and the cloudy Germanic ideology which it admired. He saw that the chief contemporary use of folk material was to touch off a process of free association and personal fantasy in the author's mind. Where the antiquarian left off the dreamer took over.

Matchless in themselves, his own narratives and ballads might almost be models (like those in Campion's *Observations on the Arte of Poesie*) to illustrate what he held to be the proper use of folk material.[1] As early as 1819, in a brief narrative poem entitled *Rusalka*, he showed his genius for the terse objective telling of a 'wonder': the water-maiden seen by an anchorite living by a lake, who tempts him for three days until he plunges in and drowns. Typically, though precociously, Pushkin manœuvres the action to avoid the bathos of a climax; on the third evening the distracted monk awaits the apparition, next morning he has disappeared:

> И только бороду седую
> Мальчишки видели в воде.

And only his grey beard was seen in the water by some boys. (I, 363.)

The ending replaces the hallucination of the monk with the factual observation of outsiders. The vision itself remains an open question – Pushkin's non-involvement complete. The poem combines a formal perfection of the picturesque with an almost Voltairean rationale – the *rusalka* who emerges from the lake and into the monk's mind is described simply as *zhenshchina nagaya* (a naked woman).

---

[1] Neither Pushkin nor Zhukovsky, who composed and translated many more ballads, wrote anything theoretical on the subject as did their contemporary Mickiewicz, and as Herder had done in Germany (*Stimmen der Völker in Liedern*) and Scott in the notes and introductions to his poems, and in his 'Essay on the Imitation of the Ancient Ballads'.

The avoidance of any incongruity in these poems is a remarkable feat. Zhukovsky, who translated so many romantic ballads, seems to have been sometimes aware of the pitfalls of romantic incongruity but could not – as an adaptor – always take evasive action. On the whole he improves on Scott's *The Eve of St John* in his version *Smaylhome Castle* (*Zamok Smalgolm*) by removing much of the mediaeval furniture which (as in an old-world teashop) is designed to compensate for the insipid brew of guilty passion. Adultery in Zhukovsky's poem is at least a dark and serious matter, and not, as in Scott, an excuse for local colour. The dialogue of Campbell's *Lord Ullin's Daughter* is likewise toned down by Zhukovsky from the engaging inadvertency of the original.

> 'Now who be ye would cross Lochgyle,
> This dark and stormy water?'
> 'O I'm the Chief of Ulva's Isle,
> And this, Lord Ullin's daughter.'

The stanza is an index of what goes wrong with many romantic ballads. The poet seems unaware that old and new conventions are at odds. Even the *Lyrical Ballads* are bedevilled by similar incongruities in dialogue, between the effectively commonplace and the unintentionally pompous.

Bürger's *Lenore*, which inaugurated the vogue of the romantic ballad in the seventies of the previous century, was responsible for a different kind of abuse. Inspired by the tradition of Anglo-Scottish balladry made fashionable by Percy's *Reliques*, *Lenore* begins with a superb rehandling, in a contemporary setting, of the *motifs* of *The Demon Lover* and *The Unquiet Grave*, but is carried away by its own enthusiasm into the excesses of the modern Gothic and the horrid. Scott paraphrased it in his *William and Helen*, and Zhukovsky rendered its metre accurately in his own version, which has no great merit but which enabled Pushkin (who was virtually without German) to naturalise the metre in his own ballad *The Bridegroom* (*Zhenikh*). This poem and *The Drowned Man* (*Utoplennik*) are his masterpieces in the form, recreations drawn not from Russian sources but from the modern fashion for ballads, and as perfect as Goethe's *Erlkönig* and *Es war ein König in Thule*, or Keats's *La Belle Dame Sans Merci*. All avoid the romantic ballad's tendency to show off its ancient lore, to put wild and passionate sentiments in stilted eighteenth-century dialogue, or to revel in the picturesque, the horrid or pathetic. As Zhirmunsky points out, Pushkin does not follow Zhukovsky's comparatively genteel renderings of fashionable modern balladry, but approved the emphasis another friend, fellow-author and theorist – Katenin – laid on the *prostonarodny* or 'folk-simple', and on an expressive 'simplicity and even crudity'.[1] Yet it is not the folk style for its own sake. Brevity is the keynote, but where the brevity of Keats and Goethe is deliberately stark and hallucinatory, Pushkin's is more comfortably functional. Concision is not for him an aid to feeling and atmosphere – an atmosphere that with the other two poets is very much in keeping with the *Zeitgeist* – but quite simply the best way to tell the tale.

The Bridegroom combines an oblique and dramatic narrative style with the *dénouement* of a good detective story. Natasha, the merchant's daughter, is missing for three days from home; she returns distraught, and though she soon recovers she will not say what has frightened her. Then, as she sits by the gate with her sisters, a *troika* flies by, driven by a young man:

> Он, поровнявшись, поглядел,
> Наташа поглядела,
> Он вихрем мимо пролетел,
> Наташа помертвела.

Drawing level he gazed – and Natasha gazed. He flew by like a whirl-wind: Natasha was like one dead. (IV, 411.)

Pushkin has combined Russian syntax with Bürger's metre to produce the most suggestive and matter-of-fact economy. There is no effort to be bloodcurdling: terror enters the poem abruptly but casually. Then the matchmaker arrives with a proposition:

> Она сидит за пирогом,
> Да речь ведет обиняком,
> А бедная невеста
> Себе не видит места.

She sits down to a pie, and engages in a lot of roundabout talk, while the poor bride-to-be does not know where to look.

The marriage feast is prepared; the bridegroom comes, and Pushkin contrives a dialogue in almost parodic relation to the exchanges of the demonic Wilhelm and the swooning Lenore in Bürger's ballad.

---

[1] V. M. Zhirmunsky, *Pushkin i zapadnye literatury* (*Vremennik Pushkinskoy Komissii*, III (1937).

'Why is my bride grieving?'; Natasha replies that she has had a dream, in which she walked into a dense forest:

> С тропинки сбилась я: в глуши
> Не слышно было ни души,
> И сосны лишь да ели
> Вершинами шумели.
>
> И вдруг, как будто наяву,
> Изба передо мною.
> Я к ней, стучу – молчат. Зову –
> Ответа нет; с мольбою
> Дверь отворила я. Вхожу...

I strayed from the path: In the forest depths one did not hear a single soul, and only the tops of the firs and pines rustled.

And suddenly, as if it was in real life, there was a hut in front of me. I go up to it, I knock – silence. I call out – no answer. With a prayer I opened the door. I enter...

The forest onomatopoeia here parallels the sound of the hoof-beats that echo through Bürger's poem:

> Und außen, horch! ging's trap trap trap,
> Als wie von Rosseshufen,
> Und klirrend stieg ein Reiter ab
> An des Geländers Stufen...
>
> Und hurre hurre, hopp hopp hopp
> Ging's fort in sausendem Galopp...

but instead of the gothic climax to which they lead, Pushkin produces an ominous quiet in which the tension rises as the chatter of the wedding feast is stilled and the bridegroom's interruptions of the tale become increasingly uneasy. In Natasha's dream the hut is filled with riches and as she looks round she hears horses. She hides, and a band of young men enter and with them a girl. While they feast the eldest takes out his knife, kills the girl, and cuts off her right hand. The bridegroom still protests that this is a good dream:

> Она глядит ему в лицо.
> «А это с чьей руки кольцо?»
> Вдруг молвила невеста,
> И все привстали с места.

She looks him in the face. 'And from whose hand does this ring come?' the bride said abruptly. And all began to rise from their seats.

The murderous bridegroom is apprehended and executed. Natasha is a practical heroine transposed into the world of modern balladry, and when she outfaces her demon bridegroom she makes a telling contrast with its languorous heroines.

Utoplennik (*The Drowned Man*) is also a *prostonarodnaya skazka* (a popular story) and its pungent flavour is in even greater contrast with the more insipid kinds of modern romantic ballad. No other nineteenth-century poem is so successful in achieving the colloquial directness, so often aimed at, without any suggestion of a contrived *simplesse*; the simplicity of the language does not seem a deliberate part of the poem's specification, as it so obviously is, for example, in Wordsworth's *Peter Bell*. The experience of Pushkin's *muzhik* is not the occasion for the poem – it *is* the poem. When his children find a drowned man by the river's bank and come rushing back in excitement to tell him, his reaction is not presented, like those of Peter Bell, inside the frame of the poet's attitude.

> Безобразно труп ужасный
> Посинел и весь распух.
> Горемыка ли несчастный
> Погубил свой грешный дух,
> Рыболов ди взят волнами,
> Али хмельный молодец,
> Аль ограбленный ворами
> Недогадливый купец:

> Мужику какое дело?
> Озираясь, он спешит;
> Он потопленное тело
> В воду за ноги тащит,
> И от берега крутого
> Оттолкнул его веслом,
> И мертвец вниз поплыл снова
> За могилой и крестом.

The shapeless corpse had turned a horrible blue and was all swollen. Was it some unhappy wretch who had destroyed his sinful spirit? Or a fisherman caught by the waves? Some drunken youngster or some slow-witted merchant robbed by thieves?

What does it matter to the peasant? He hurries along, throwing a glance round about, drags the drowned body by the legs to the water and pushed it away from the steep bank with an oar, and the dead man floated off again downstream, in search of a grave and a cross. (III, 74.)

Speculation is as alien to the poem as to the peasant. His impulse is to know nothing about the matter, in case questions should be asked later, and as he hurries towards where the corpse lies on the sand he looks not at it but all around him to see no one is about. That night there is a knocking at the window and a voice asking for the householder. Grumbling, the peasant looks out:

> Из-за туч луна катится –
> Что же? голый перед ним:
> С бороды вода струится,
> Взор открыт и недвижим,
> Всё в нем страшно онемело,
> Опустились руки вниз,
> И в распухнувшее тело
> Раки черные впились.

The moon rolls from behind the clouds. What is it? A naked figure confronts him. Water streams from its beard; the eyes are open and vacant; every part of it is horribly passive; the hands hang down, and black prawns have dug into the swollen body.

Wordsworth had set himself in *Peter Bell* to avoid the supernatural elements that Coleridge had used in *The Ancient Mariner*, explaining all the strange events that frighten Peter by natural means. As in *Rusalka*, whether the vision is real or unreal does not matter: simply the peasant is now compelled to *see* the corpse that he was concerned only to get rid of; and all night he must hear the knocking for admittance *pod oknom i u vorot* – under the window and at the gate. Each year, it is said, the visitor returns.

> Уж с утра погода злится,
> Ночью буря настает,
> И утопленник стучится
> Под окном и у ворот.

From morning on the weather rages; at night there comes a storm; and the drowned man knocks beneath the window and at the gate.

The thud of the repeated line closes the ballad. There is no moral, and there is no suggestion that the peasant, like Peter Bell or the Ancient Mariner, becomes a better man for his experience, though he must relive it again and again.

Where 'wonders' are concerned, only the sophisticated mind distinguishes between objective and subjective, real and hallucinatory. Pushkin's ballads carry the superstition of the common mind straight over, and without comment, into the most accomplished and sophisticated poetry. The self-interest and the superstitious terror of the *muzhik* are all of a piece: he must be the most

completely convincing peasant in a nineteenth-century ballad, and
the one to whose status the least attention is paid. But Pushkin also
used the ballad form for the opposite purpose: to examine and
analyse a particular kind of person, the kind of analysis that he
later perfected in the medium of the *Little Tragedies*. All the
ballads give the impression of being models, demonstrations without further comment of how the thing should be done. *Zhil na svete
rytsar bedny* (*Once on earth lived a poor knight*) goes further: it takes
the stock figure of the pseudo-mediaeval ballad – Coleridge's 'bold
and lovely Knight', Schiller's Ritter Toggenburg, Keats's knight-
at-arms – and relates him to a true mediaeval context of mystical
devotion to Our Lady. Pushkin wrote the poem in 1829 and included a version of it in *Stseny iz rytsarskikh vremen* (*Scenes from
knightly times*), a late dramatic work which was not completed but
which shows the interest he then took in problems of history and
historical development. Certainly the poem goes to the heart of its
matter, for the knight errant beloved by later romanticism is a
vulgarisation from the chivalric cult of the Virgin Mary.

> Несть мольбы Отцу, ни Сыну,
> Ни святому Духу ввек
> Не случилось паладину,
> Странный был он человек.

Never once did the paladin pray to Father or to Son or to Holy Ghost:
he was a strange man. (III, 116.)

Pushkin's knight is indeed a 'strange man' (the meditative line
beautifully echoes, for its own purposes of inquiry, the naive judgement of a mediaeval ballad) and not a cardboard figure who goes
about liberating damsels or wasting away for love of an elfin
mistress. His obsession is his life:

> Всё безмолвный, всё печальный,
> Без причастья умер он.

Still mute, still sad, he died without the sacrament...

but Our Lady intercedes for him at the last. The poem was a
favourite of Dostoevsky's, and Prince Myshkin in *The Idiot*
certainly owes something to Pushkin's conception. But the
haunting thing about the poem is the calm concentration and
meticulous sympathy with which it devotes itself to understanding
devotion. Dostoevsky's attachment to Myshkin, and Pushkin's
absorption in the poem life of his 'poor knight', illustrate two very
different kinds of inspirational process.

We should scarcely expect to find Pushkin using the marvellous, as Coleridge does in *Christabel* and *The Ancient Mariner*, to project on a sequence of wonders and excitements the inward *via dolorosa* of the poet. And yet one of his most remarkable poems, *Besy* (*The Demons*) does come close to the type of Coleridgean poetic narrative that is both objective and subjective. It was written in 1830, at a time when Pushkin was haunted by gloomy premonitions. He was always acutely superstitious and sensitive to popular omens – a hare on the left of the path or a priest seen when setting out on a journey – indeed his handling of folk material shows his instinctive solidarity with popular superstition; but in *Besy* Pushkin divides the response to superstitious terrors and introduces an 'I' into the poem:

> Мчатся тучи, вьются тучи;
> Невидимкою луна
> Освещает снег летучий;
> Мутно небо, ночь мутна.
> Еду, еду в чистом поле;
> Колокольчик дин-дин-дин...
> Страшно, страшно поневоле
> Средь неведомых равнин!

The clouds scurry, the clouds whirl; an invisible moon lights the flying snow; sky and night are overcast. I drive on and on in the open plain; ding-ding-ding goes the little bell...Despite oneself there is terror, terror in the unknown expanses. (III, 176.)

The blizzard is a real one, blinding the travellers, hypnotising and confusing them as they lose their way, until the wildly scurrying flakes suggest a multitudinous demonic presence, equivocating the whole nature of things. It is also a symbolic snowstorm, an obsession endlessly circling in the mind to the point of madness.[1] The first version had a traveller (*putnik*) instead of an 'I'.

> Путник едет в чистом поле,
> Колокольчик дин-дин-дин...

A traveller drives in the open plain.

The revision – *Edu, edu v chistom pole* – drops the literary 'traveller' and the repetition carries close to us the note of desperation, the storm within and without. The driver is the first to become convinced that their enemy is a single *he* – a vague object, dimly

---

[1] Its symbolism is elaborated by D. D. Blagoy, *Masterstvo Pushkina* (Moscow 1955), who emphasises the connection of *Besy* and other poems with Pushkin's hypothetical state of mind; and by V. V. Vinogradov, 'Yazyk Pushkina', *Akademia* (1935).

seen, which might be milestone, treestump, or wolf – a creature playing with them and leading them astray.[1]

> Посмотри: вон, вон играет,
> Дует, плюет на меня;

Look! There he is, over there – playing, blowing, spitting at me.

His idea of an external enemy is a simpler and somehow reassuring notion; but the 'I' of the poem is haunted by a vaguer multitude:

> Вижу: духи собралися
> Средь белеющих равнин.

I see them: the spirits assembled in the white expanses.

Where the driver sees one demon, his master feels the presence of many, though in the next verse he makes a kind of effort to feel the terror through the familiar medium of folklore, to externalise it in the comforting area of the early poems, 'where marvels are':

> Сколько их! куда их гонят?
> Что так жалобно поют?
> Домового ли хоронят,
> Ведьму ль замуж выдают?

How many there are! Where are they being urged? Why are they singing so plaintively? Are they holding the funeral of a *domovoy*? Celebrating a witch's wedding?

A *domovoy* and a witch's wedding are reassuring literary phenomena. But we can feel the attempt to folklorise the experience is useless: in the insane repetitive scurry the voice of the poem rises to a

---

[1] The driver, who sees the demon as his personal opponent, is a more realistic figure in the finished poem than in the early version, as if the promotion of 'traveller' to intimate 'I' had drawn him into an implied contrast with his passenger. Compare the first version:

> '*Poshel, poshel, yamshchik!*' – '*Net mochi,*
> *Dorogu snegom zameslo . . .*'

> 'Go, on, go on, driver!' 'Can't be done.
> The road's snowed up . . .'

with the second:

> '*Ei, poshel, yamshchik! . . .*' – '*Net mochi:*
> *Konyam, barin, tyazhelo;*

> 'Hey, go on, driver!' 'Can't be done. It's
> heavy for the horses, master;

which springs into a natural acoustic life based on the shrill note of the order, and the deep rumble of the reply. The first is acoustically as lifeless as most of the many dialogue exchanges in romantic ballads.

despairing wail (the sound of the fifth and sixth lines should be compared with the voices in the second stanza).

> Мчатся тучи, вьются тучи;
> Невидимкою луна
> Освещает снег летучий;
> Мутно небо, ночь мутна.
> Мчатся бесы рой за роем
> В беспредельной вышине,
> Визгом жалобным и воем
> Надрывая сердце мне...

The clouds scurry, the clouds whirl; an invisible moon lights the flying snow; night and sky are overcast. In the void without horizon the demons scurry in swarms, their plaintive shrieking and howling tearing my heart.

This superlative poem is the only one of Pushkin's narratives in which folklore is both dramatised and internalised, and the old ironic separation – the detached 'I' of the *Ruslan* Prologue – is quite lost. It is not surprising that Dostoevsky took its title for his great novel: the anguish of Shatov and Kirillov, the *nadryv* which tears their hearts, is implicit in its merging obsession of the inner and outer world, blizzard and nightmare.

It remains in this chapter to consider one other long poem of Pushkin's early years – *Gavriliiada*. Although it was written after his exile to the south it belongs in spirit to the poems of the Petersburg period, for it is a mock epic of the Annunciation, conceived in the style of Parny's *La Guerre des Dieux* and Voltaire's *La Pucelle*. Pushkin never admitted that he was its author, and in his later years resented any reference to it, although by then it had achieved an immense clandestine popularity.[1] It was not 'a part of his being' but an exercise in a genre which appealed to him; particularly, we may imagine, because it enabled him to show off his virtuosity anonymously. It could not be published, so there was no question

---

[1] In 1828, after a copy had been found by the police in the possession of a Captain Mitkov, Pushkin formally denied his authorship and his friends did their best to support his denial. The police and the Tsar were not convinced, and it seems likely that Pushkin saved himself from serious trouble by writing a secret confession of his authorship to Nicholas, who, characteristically, was pleased to assert his paternal power over the poet by accepting his act of contrition and calling off the inquiry. Pushkin would naturally have disliked any reminder of this episode, and his later revulsion against the poem may well have been chiefly against the circumstances in which he escaped the penalties of having written it.

of shocking the bourgeois and delighting the irreverent, as Voltaire had done with his squibs and satires under assumed names. The cheerful blasphemy of *The Gavriliiad* had more in common with the poems of Donne and the Cavalier poets, circulating by word of mouth – Pushkin's brother Lev was in the habit of reciting from memory passages of his brother's unprinted poems. Vyazemsky, Alexander Turgenev, and Alexeev, in whose lodgings in Kishinev Pushkin wrote most of the poem, were of course in the secret, and in September 1822 Pushkin wrote to Vyazemsky: 'I am sending you a poem of a mystical nature – I have become a courtier.' The reference was to the mysticism of Alexander I and his entourage, but Pushkin was not really setting out a counter-case for blasphemy against these *bien pensants*, as Baudelaire set out to shock the complacency of the French establishment.

Pushkin in fact treats the story of the Annunciation in much the same spirit as he treated the tale of Ruslan, Lyudmila and Chernomor. The approach is not satiric or mock-heroic but freely and ebulliently lyrical. Mary is an uncommonly attractive sixteen-year-old, described somewhat as Suckling described the bride in *A Ballad on a Wedding*; and Joseph, middle-aged, hard-working and respectable, is like a father to her.

> Он как отец с невинной жил еврейкой,
> Ее кормил – и больше ничего.

He lived with the innocent Jewess like a father, fed her – and nothing more. (IV, 135.)

God falls for her like a classical Jove, and sends Gabriel in the role of Mercury, a divine pander, to woo on his behalf.

> Царя небес пленить она хотела,
> Его слова приятны были ей,
> И перед ним она благоговела, –
> Но Гавриил казался ей милей...

She wished to captivate the Lord of Heaven; his words were agreeable to her and she worshipped before him – but Gabriel attracted her more.

But Satan also decides to take a hand in the game. Visiting Mary in serpent form he tells her how in the Garden of Eden he outwitted the jealousy of God, who felt about Eve as he now feels about Mary, and – by means of 'two apples, the seductive symbol of love' – instructed the previously innocent young couple in its pleasures:

И, не страшась божественного гнева,
Вся в пламени, власы раскинув, Ева,
Едва, едва устами шевеля,
Лобзанием Адаму отвечала,
В слезах любви, в бесчувствии лежала
Под сенью пальм, – и юная земля
Любовников цветами покрывала.

And not fearing divine wrath, all on fire, her hair disordered, Eve, barely moving her lips, returned Adam's kiss, with tears of love lay senseless in the shade of the palms – and the young earth covered the lovers with flowers.

The last two lines strongly suggest that Pushkin had already looked into a French translation of Milton, though it was not until 1836 that he read, and reviewed, Chateaubriand's word-for-word translation, *Le Paradis Perdu*.[1] Certainly Pushkin is able to combine something of the opulent Renaissance beauty of Milton's account of the lovers in the garden –

> And on their naked limbs the flowery roof
> Showered roses, which the morn repaired...

with the witty logic of love, as fallen mankind knows it, being envied by God and (according to his own account) a gift of Satan.

«Скажи теперь: ужели я предатель?
Ужель Адам несчастлив от меня?
Не думаю, но знаю только я,
Что с Евою остался я приятель».

'Tell me now: am I really a deceiver? Is it I who have made Adam unhappy? I think not, but I know one thing – that I have remained on excellent terms with Eve.'

Though he would hardly have appreciated the theological fascination and the mythological equivocation of the English poet, Pushkin would certainly have enjoyed his Eve. But he can also be – as Milton could not – as direct about action as about love: he contrives an epic encounter between the Prince of Darkness, who, transforming himself into a handsome young man, has just enjoyed Mary's favours, and the Archangel who arrives on God's business but with the same idea in mind. The ensuing tussle is a masterpiece of verbal high spirits.

---

[1] He may very likely have seen a version of *Paradise Lost* by A. G. Strogonov, which seems to have circulated among Russian *literati* at the end of the eighteenth century, as well as Parny's parodies of Milton.

Бес ахнул, побледнел –
И ворвались в объятия друг другу.
Ни Гавриил, ни бес не одолел:
Сплетенные, кружась идут по лугу,
На вражью грудь опершись бородой,
Соединив крест-накрест ноги, руки,
То силою, то хитростью науки
Хотят увлечь друг друга за собой.

The fiend gasped and blenched, and they rushed to grapple with each other. Neither Gabriel nor the Devil could get the upper hand. Interlaced, they circle over the field. Leaning chin against opponent's chest, arms and legs entwined criss-cross, each endeavoured by brute strength or scientific skill to drag down the other.

Having achieved victory by an underhand blow, Gabriel receives from Mary a victor's reward; and returning to heaven reports her readiness to comply with the divine will, whereupon God descends in his turn to possess her in the form of a white dove.

Он улетел. Усталая Мария
Подумала: «Вот шалости какие!
Один, два, три! – как это им не лень?
Могу сказать, перенесла тревогу:
Досталась я в один и тот же день
Лукавому, архангелу и богу».

Off he flew. 'What goings-on!' thought Mary, quite worn out. 'One, two, three! How do they keep on at it? One way and another I've had a hectic time. The Evil One, an Archangel and God have all possessed me in a single day.'

Beautifully constructed, the poem moves with lightness and grace, the alexandrines rhymed in free quatrains with a movement far more lyrical than the couplets of Boileau's successors, and packed with a verbal gaiety that transmits – like some of the mythic and sacred subjects in Tiepolo – a kind of participatory tenderness almost comically at variance with the scandalous events. Voltaire would have enjoyed the subject but he would also have gloated over it; he would have made it give his own views and reflect his own tastes. Pushkin, like Chaucer, writes in full confidence that everyone will share the joke. He liked obscenity – 'I should wish a certain biblical obscenity to remain in the Russian language', he wrote to Vyazemsky – and the Soviet editions of his letters remain peppered with asterisks and dashes; but he disliked the intimacy of the pornographic, of private satisfactions masquerading as public entertainment. About the same time as *The Gavriliad* he composed a wonderfully obscene little tale in verse, *Tsar Nikita and his Forty Daughters*, a version of which has been only transmitted to posterity through the memory of his younger brother. The forty daughters are all peerless beauties but unfortunately without *pudenda*, and the story of how they acquire them is as diverting as *The Gavriliad* and as stylishly told.

Pushkin's style in such matters has a flavour of its own, taking much from French models but substituting a native geniality for French elegance and self-esteem. It is also non-moral: Pushkin would not have cared for Goethe's *Das Tagebuch*, admirable poem though it is, because its shamelessness is the vehicle for the author's worldly wisdom. And yet this non-morality, or 'Parnassian Atheism', is merely an aspect of the collective vitalityof Pushkin's circle; it is not the individualistic aesthetic creed that Vladimir Nabokov – one of Pushkin's most sympathetic and enthusiastic disciples – has promulgated in the master's name. (Though we can be sure that Pushkin would have enjoyed much of *Lolita*, he might have had reservations about the conclusion, in which the slow-motion shooting of the villain seems to take place for the author's amusement rather than our own.) We shall be returning more than once to the question of Pushkin's views on art; but it is perhaps not too early to assert that *Ruslan and Lyudmila* and *The Gavriliad* are not composed in the context of 'aesthetic bliss' – writer and reader purring contentedly together in their private ecstasy – any more than in the fashion of romantic sexual dream: those dreams of persecuted maidens, demon lovers, and heartless *femmes fatales* which could be revelled in unashamedly by a public as yet unawakened by Freud. Pushkin does not encourage us to meet him in a private relation either aesthetic or sexual, or any combination of the two. He is an impersonal artist, not an impresario, *voyeur*, or exhibitionist.

His next attempt at a long poem after *The Gavriliad* was on a different tack altogether. Always goodnaturedly amenable to the views of the circle in which he moved and whose comradeship and encouragement he so much valued, he set out to compose the kind of narrative on a high national theme of which Ryleev the Decembrist was such an ardent exponent and practitioner. He chose the legendary figure of Vadim, the Slav hero of Novgorod who was credited in popular and patriotic story with a valiant resistance to Rurik and the Scandinavian conquerors. It was perhaps just this responsibility of an official topic, which offered no possibility of mixing the genres, of entering imaginatively into the characters concerned (as he was to do in *Poltava*) and of taking an attitude of his own, which led Pushkin to abandon *Vadim* before he had written two hundred lines.[1] The fragment shows the difference between his impersonal manner, in which much of his finest work is done, and the conventional one which he adopted in deference to topic and model. Another reason for dropping it, very likely, was his introduction, in South Russia, to the poems and personality of Byron.

[1] A fragmentary synopsis exists which suggests that Pushkin also thought of writing a tragedy on the subject, perhaps on the lines of Knyazhnin's *Vadim Novgorodsky*, published in 1793. He composed an opening scene before starting on the poem.

3

POEMS OF THE SOUTH

The Captive of the Caucasus (*Kavkazsky Plennik*) was written in the south late in 1820, a little before *The Gavriliiad*, but it is hard to imagine two more dissimilar poems. The second seems an eighteenth-century work, as dependent upon Petersburg and its intelligentsia as Pope is upon London: the first has travelled geographically into the wildest part of the Russian empire and stylistically into the nineteenth century. The sheer size of Russia is a factor in our sense of the distance between Pushkin's early poems, and the differences between them.

Discovering Byron gave Pushkin the *persona* of the hero who leaves the shallow society world for the stern freedom of the out-cast, and in *The Captive* and *The Gipsies* he makes a deliberate use of him; so deliberate, in fact, that such a hero for the first time becomes objectively seen by the reader, rather than unconsciously identified with. Though their previous history is left vague, and no attempt is made to give them a character, the captive of the earlier poem and Aleko of *The Gipsies* are observed with an almost scientific curiosity; surrounded as they are with romantic prop-erties they retain no romantic aura of mystery. Pushkin is the only poet of the time to present such a hero as psychologically interesting. Aleko, and even the Captive, are in some sense sketches of *Evgeny Onegin*, lacking the detailed background which gives an almost Marxian comprehensiveness to the later portrait. While the heroes of Byron's 'eastern poems' are localised and left behind, Pushkin's lead straight into the world of the nineteenth-century novel. He already treats the romantic hero in verse as Lermontov and Stendhal, Balzac and Emily Brontë treated him in their different ways in prose. Without their verse medium Byron's heroes could hardly exist: Pushkin's – even his earlier ones – are potentially intimate with the prose world and co-extensive with it. Tolstoy disliked *The Captive of the Caucasus*, but his sense of a story in it led him to recast its plot in simple prose; and when he first planned *The Cossacks* the precedent of Pushkin's poem even made him consider briefly the idea of writing it in verse.

Pushkin travels to the south, but he is still on duty, officially still a part of the Russian state machine.[1] The captive of the poem, who is taken prisoner by the Circassians, is attached in some unspecified capacity to the Russian army. For author as for character this lack of Byronic freedom is significant. When Byron and Childe Harold leave England it is to go where and do what they please; poet and hero are alike cut off from the necessities of nationality and environment. Byron cannot use Childe Harold to explore a situation different from his own, or to enlarge his range of imagination and understanding. By putting his captive into his romantic situation Pushkin is carrying out the most traditional method of creating character ('my first attempt at characterisation, which I mastered with difficulty') and exchanging his actual situation for a hypothetical one, to be explored by the artistic intelligence as the novelist explores it. We can if we wish see the captive's situation as a romantic analogue of Pushkin's own, irked as he was by his subordination to Vorontsov and the military authorities, but the precise observation of a Circassian village takes on the quality of a military intelligence or survey report; its objectivity is made possible because it is a self-imposed discipline, a means of escape from the routine of confinement; and so effectively did Pushkin imagine himself into this frame of mind that he later expressed surprise at how well he had described 'customs of the people and nature which I had seen only from a distance'. By choosing the right *conscience*, as Henry James would say, and interpreting through this focus what he had only caught a general glimpse of himself, he acquired authority over an environment. Belinsky noted the importance of the fact that the Caucasus was not made the occasion for a description by Pushkin, but formed part of 'the impressions and observations of the captive'.

By contrast Byron's picturesque Levantines are seen from boat or carriage; they are the free impressions of tourism, and the fact that they are accurately observed and accoutred in all the proper local colour only increases their essential unreality. Byron's best description, like the superb Italian impressions in the fourth book

---

[1] In the MS of *Kavkazsky Plennik* Pushkin provided an epigraph in Italian from a poem of Pindemonti, extolling the happiness of the man 'whose foot is never placed outside the dear soil of his own native land'. There may have been a concealed irony in the choice of quotation, which did not appear in the published version.

of *Childe Harold*, has the animation of an inspired guidebook –
the verse conveys with astonishing fidelity the nature of those land-
scapes and *objets d'art* which are best suited to it, like the Laocoön
group.

> Or, turning to the Vatican, go see
> Laocoön's torture dignifying pain –
> A father's love and mortal's agony
> With an immortal's patience blending: – Vain
> The struggle; vain, against the coiling strain
> And gripe, and deepening of the dragon's grasp,
> The old man's clench; the long envenom'd chain
> Rivets the living links – the enormous asp
> Enforces pang on pang, and stifles gasp on gasp.

Gigantesque, almost muscle-bound, wrenching itself free in the
spasm of the final rhyme, the verse is quite singularly fitted to its
job: it secures the exact poetic equivalent of the statuary admired.
The impressiveness of *Childe Harold* proceeds from this power of
diversified rhetoric, varying with each new object presented to the
tourist's gaze, and appropriate not only to the object seen but to the
sentiment it suggests. Lake Leman in a thunderstorm, the cataract
with its rainbow

> Resembling, 'mid the torture of the scene,
> Love watching Madness with unalterable mien...

the battles of long ago conjured up from their contemporary sites –
the whole dazzling guided tour enthralled Pushkin as it did
Byron's other readers. At Kishinev he was, he writes, 'mad about
Byron'.

As we have seen, Pushkin's early poems show a remarkable power
of absorbing and unifying discrepant material to produce symmetry
and form. Byron succeeds in *Childe Harold* by making no attempt
to unify, by leaving the various models he has drawn on to add to
the general variety of impression, often a comically and clumsily
incongruous assortment. The celebrated 'Last Goodnight' which
Childe Harold pours forth as the vessel leaves Albion's shore
combines a vague idea of the Elizabethan song fashion for amorous
or elegiac 'Goodnights' with a dialogue ballad in border style, both
superimposed upon the imitated eighteenth-century Spenserian
stanza. But in translation all these oddities disappear, together
with the sanguine vulgarity that so aptly reflects the *sehenswürdige*
objects singled out by Byron on his tour. In Pichot's version,
Harold's 'Good night' appealed to the whole of Europe, and not

least to Batyushkov and Pushkin in Russia.[1] Byron in French prose
sounded like an exciting development of *Atala* and *René*, and it is
singular that Dupont's French translations of Pushkin's eastern
poems, published in St Petersburg in 1847, raise as it were for the
second time the ghost of Chateaubriand, and in so doing succeed in
conveying at least something of the same quality; whereas a translation into English iambics can only appear to discredit Pushkin by
suggesting the echo of Byronic diction and rhythm. Disyllabic
rhymes in English always tremble on the verge of absurdity, and
Byron in his eastern tales seeks to produce an atmosphere in which
this incongruousness has no place, as it will have in *Don Juan*, where
Byron has found how to turn it to poetic account. It is instructive
to compare a characteristic clash of rhythm and sentiment in Byron:

> The faithless slave that broke her bower,
> And, worse than faithless, for a Giaour!

soon repeated as

> Who falls in battle 'gainst a Giaour
> Is worthiest an immortal bower –

with an equally characteristic piece from *The Captive*, which slips
into a supple nullity in which rhythm and sentiment are predict-
ably, but harmoniously, facile.

> Раскрыв уста, без слез рыдая,
> Сидела дева мододая:
> Туманный, неподвижный взор
> Безмолвный выражал укор;
> Бледна как тень, она дрожала:
> В руках любовника лежала
> Ее холодная рука;
> И наконец любви тоска
> В печальной речи излилася:

The young girl sat, sobbing without tears, her lips parted. Her fixed
and shadowy gaze expressed unspoken reproach; she trembled, pale as a
shadow; her cold hand lay in her lover's; and at length the anguish of
her love poured forth in sorrowful speech. (IV, 103.)

---

[1] It would be interesting to know what Pushkin thought of Byron's specific
rejection of Horace in his description of Rome. Not that Pushkin knew
Horace well: he had probably evaded 'the daily drug which turn'd my
sickening memory' more successfully at the Lycée than Byron had managed
at Harrow; but he would certainly not have upheld Byron's claim for
romantic rhetoric in description rather than classical restraint: his Russian
and his descriptive instinct in the Caucasus were for Soracte rather than 'the
Acroceraunian Mountains'. There is evidence from his library that Pushkin
later read Horace frequently and attentively, but in a French translation.

Even the most banal romantic formulae sound as right in Pushkin's verse as in Chateaubriand's prose. Though Pushkin often echoes a turn of phrase in Byron as well as a particular event, his rhymes are smooth, his language pure and unsensational, however full of commonplace poeticisms.[1] It is surprising that Pushkin's contemporaries (Pogodin was an exception) emphasised the influence of Byron on his eastern poems but disregarded the equally important inspiration of *René*, published twenty years earlier, and in which, by coincidence, the author had noted that the Caucasus was the only romantic place in Russia. Pushkin had appreciated the delicate prose-poem harmonies of *René*, the dying falls and languorous sentences of alternating length; and the still Gallic rather than Byronic texture of his eastern poems suggests a correspondence, audible in the plangent feminine rhymes with which the Russian language is so well stocked. In sentiment, too, *The Captive* is no less French. Though the Circassian maid is outwardly the sloe-eyed beauty of modern romance, she is really a sister of the white-muslined ladies who haunt the eighteenth-century novel of sentiment. Rousseau and the Abbé Prévost are in the background: Pushkin had not yet encountered Constant's *Adolphe*, but he curiously anticipates his own reading of it a year or so later; it too was in the line of a tradition already familiar to him, and the Captive and the Circassian maid, going hand in hand in speechless intimacy to their parting by the river bank, is prescient of Adolphe and Ellénore's last walk together. As well as admiring the exotic events of a Byronic tale we find ourselves unexpectedly on a different level of sensibility.

Writing to Vyazemsky from Kishinev in February 1823, Pushkin observed that their friend Chaadaev had found the Captive 'insufficiently *blasé*'. This is revealing, for it may show that the projected portrait of a disillusioned nineteenth-century hero had turned out rather differently. In an earlier letter to Gnedich Pushkin wrote that he wanted to depict 'the indifference to life and its joys, the premature senility of the soul, which is so characteristic of our younger generation'. Instead the Captive turned out to have a more old-fashioned sensibility, in keeping with the pure,

---

[1] See V. M. Zhirmunsky, *Bairon i Pushkin, Iz istorii romanticheskoy poemy* (Leningrad 1924). *The Corsair* (II, 490) 'Thou lov'st another then?...' and (II, 390) 'He slept in calmest seeming...' may well have suggested two similar moments in *Kavkazsky Plennik*. Other similarities which we shall notice later, particularly in *Bakhchisaraisky fontan*, are of more critical interest.

passionate, and abnegatory sentiments of the Circassian girl. She feels for the Captive all the involuntary ardour of first love: he, so far from being incapable of the emotion, has loved passionately but unrequitedly. It is an effective touch that the girl refuses to understand this and is convinced that he must have a sweetheart in his own country.

> Но кто ж она,
> Твоя прекрасная подруга?
> Ты любишь, русский? ты любим?...

'But who is she, your beautiful sweetheart? You love, Russian? You are loved?...'

Between her lofty sentiments the word *prekrasnaya* conveys a more realistic thrust of jealousy. Hopeless of gaining his love, she none the less sets him free, and overcome by her generosity the Captive swears that he will be hers for ever, and urges her to fly with him.

> Я твой навек, я твой до гроба.
> Ужасный край оставим оба,
> Беги со мной...» –

'I am yours for ever, I am yours to the grave. Let us both leave this horrible place – fly with me...'

No wonder Chaadaev thought him insufficiently *blasé*. In his first tentative attempt at a modern young man Pushkin naturally drew on an older and more familiar tradition of feeling and response, yet the significance of the Captive, himself the slightest of figures, is his connection with the more deeply studied creations of Aleko in *The Gipsies* and of Evgeny Onegin. All are half-way men, divided between two worlds of sensibility.

Much that is worked out by trial and error in Pushkin had come naturally to Byron: and in these poems we can see Pushkin's art profiting, as it were, from Byron's personality. More than once Pushkin comments on the all-devouring quality of Byron's egoism and its consequences in his works – the inevitable reappearance of the author as his own hero – 'as if' (as Pushkin puts it in *Evgeny Onegin*) 'we could no longer write long poems on any other subject than ourselves'. The most impressive feature of this egoism is the sudden revelation, in such a poem as *Lines on Hearing that Lady Byron was Ill*, of an emotion apparently outside the poet's control, and which all the resources of egoism and vanity do not seem quite able to overcome. Behind the pageant of the 'seeming marble heart', behind the even showier pageant of the bleeding heart, there are sensations and longings that even Byron cannot turn into an aspect of his displayed self. All Europe, and Russia in particular, had been absorbed by the drama of his relations with Lady Byron and convinced – on very little evidence – that a secret, wounded love for her had been buried under the pose of a flippant and callous indifference, a love for which he would face exile and death rather than reveal to her or to the world. However wide of the mark, this popular myth shows the enduring sources of the Byronic fascination, and Pushkin, like Stendhal, must have divined its artistic potentialities when treated as an objective case rather than suffered and expressed through an egocentric personality.

Certainly the Captive in his small way, Aleko and Evgeny, no less than Julien Sorel in *Le Rouge et le Noir*, all display the same characteristic symptoms. Julien murders the woman he loves, insensately abandoning the career he had schemed to make and the self he had determined to be. The French hero goes out on a note of high drama, Pushkin's disappears into the unspoken actualities of existence; but the Russian poet has as penetrating an insight into 'the hero of our time' as the French novelist, although the gaiety and artifice of poetry do not so much make the point as create its whole psychological and environmental atmosphere. The climate of his poetry makes Pushkin's heroes too complex to be vulgarised. We cannot trace them, as we can trace the Byronic archetype, to its feeble epigone – the strong silent man with the unexpected emotional vulnerability who still crops up in popular literature and film.

All the notable post-Byronic Russian heroes are seen objectively and presented with considerable narrative sophistication. Lermontov followed Pushkin, and the first episode of *A Hero of Our Time* is closely related in subject to *The Captive of the Caucasus*. It has of course been de-romanticised. Lermontov's hero Pechorin would not have incurred the charge of being insufficiently *blasé*: no one could be more so. Having abducted a beautiful Circassian girl he soon grows weary of her love for him, and when she is mortally hurt by a jealous rival from her tribe, and dies in agony, 'his face did not express anything unusual'. But in the next sentence we have the old formula in a new guise, as the narrator makes clear.

I wanted to comfort him, mainly for the sake of propriety don't you know, and started to speak; he lifted his head and laughed. A chill ran over me at this laughter.[1]

[1] V. Nabokov's translation.

The hero still feels in spite of himself. But his manner of registering the feeling is recorded by the simple-hearted and uncomprehending narrator, Maksim Maksimich, who is puzzled by Pechorin but cannot help liking him. He acts as an effective dramatic and distancing intermediary, though much of his account of Pechorin to the author follows with remarkable fidelity Byron's description of Lara.

> And those to whom he spake remembered well
> And on the words, however light, would dwell...
> You could not penetrate his soul, but found,
> Despite your wonder, to your own he wound;
> His presence haunted still; and from the breast
> He forced an all unwilling interest.

Lara, who 'half mistook for fate the acts of will' – one of Byron's most shrewdly expressive lines – is of course a self-portrait done by the poet with an extraordinary insight into the qualities he wished to be known by. (Even that laugh of Pechorin has a strange analogue in Byron's life: the howls of mirth uttered by him and heard by Leigh Hunt as they rode back through the Pisan pinewoods from Shelley's sea-shore cremation.) Yet it is impossible to take quite seriously so transparent a self-dramatisation as that of Byron as Lara. The point of these impersonations is our direct response to them, and so to their author. But no such response is possible to Lermontov via Pechorin. 'Those to whom he spake remembered well', and it is their accounts and the diary of the dead man which reconstruct him. What matters is the total effect – the interrelation of other characters and their views, the light falling from different angles – until there is no person left but only a work of art.

Byron supplied the hero, but Lermontov undoubtedly learnt the lesson in narrative from Pushkin, a lesson which Pushkin himself had learnt in the composition of *The Captive* at a time when he was 'mad about Byron'. 'The character of the Captive is unsuccessful', he wrote to Gorchakov, 'which proves I am not cut out to be the hero of a romantic poem.' The dissatisfaction he felt with his own relation to the poem appears in later remarks – 'Nikolai and Aleksandr Raevsky and myself have had a good laugh over it' – and in his comments in reply to Vyazemsky's objection that after his escape across the river the Captive makes no attempt to save the Circassian girl, who plunges in and drowns herself.

You say, my dear chap, that he is a brute because he does not grieve for the Circassian girl, but what do you want him to say? '*He understood everything'* expresses everything...There is no need to spell it out – that is the secret of narrative interest. Some readers may be cross that the Captive did not dive in to pull out my Circassian girl. Try jumping in yourself – I have swum in the rivers of the Caucasus...My Captive is an intelligent and sensible fellow. He is not in love with the Circassian girl and he did right not to drown himself.[1]

The defence is not wholly ingenuous, for Pushkin is defending on the grounds of realism a poem that in its nature must work, and does work, romantically. The Captive is *not* an intelligent and sensible fellow. If we follow the logic of Pushkin's claim it is clear that he would have made love to the girl, persuaded her to free him, and then either abandoned her or taken her with him to the Russian lines – where his comrades would have been properly envious – and discarded her, like Pechorin, when he tired of her. None of these things happens because the Captive is a romantic character in a romantic poem, which it does not help to discuss in terms of real experience. In fact he does not even ask the girl to free him – it is her own gesture of love – and when she drowns herself at the climactic moment it is technically vital for Pushkin to terminate the poem as quickly as possible. *Vse ponyal on* ('he understood everything') – the phrase that describes the Captive's only response to the situation – is not as Pushkin had implied to his friend an understatement, but a let-out.

It is the romantic proprieties and not the demands of realism that Pushkin observes in the poem, giving them proportion, simplicity, and detachment. The detachment indeed is part of the trouble, for a romantic theme works best when author, audience, and poem are all elevated together, and Pushkin stands back too far from the afflatus of his own work. He does not pile it on or 'spell it out' because of his artistic knowledge that this type of tale requires the suspension not only of our disbelief but of our common sense, our experience of actuality. *The Captive's* air of simplicity and naturalness ('perhaps it is even a bit too natural' commented Vyazemsky) misled the friends who did not realise that such queries as 'why didn't he try to rescue the girl?' can be allowed no cogency in the world of this kind of poem. No one supposes that the Canterbury pilgrims could really have told each other elaborate stories on their journey; or that Mark Antony turned all Rome against the conspirators by his speech over Caesar's body; or that Clarissa Harlowe found time at moments of crisis to write long

[1] Letter to Vyazemsky, 6 February 1823.

letters to her friends: no one complains that these conventions falsify the essential truth of the story. But the folly of romanticism, in Pushkin's view, was to take its own inflation too seriously, and hence lay itself open to parody. Parody of romantic art consists in saying: it was not really like this, it was like that; and none of Pushkin's poems after *The Captive* is vulnerable to such a parody.

Neither, of course, is *Don Juan*: Byron too learnt how to dissociate himself from his earlier romantic *personae*, but at the cost of making his hero null, a receptacle for satire and lyricism, sententiousness and fooling around. Pushkin's method is traditional and dramatic; by putting distance between his characters, and differentiating them one from another, he dissolves romantic unity and with it the sequence of romantic double-take – the feelings 'straight from my heart' followed by the 'good laugh' over them with friends. Byron, it might be said, solves the problem by becoming everything in his poem, not just its hero: Pushkin, by excluding himself from the poem altogether. Even in his next long poem, *The Fountain of Bakhchisarai*, he sets dramatic distance between its two heroines, as between Aleko and Zemphira in *The Gipsies*, Tatyana and Evgeny in *Evgeny Onegin*. The necessary incongruity and plurality of things declares itself from within. Each character confirms the truth of another's existence by an inability to understand it.

But the Captive and Circassian understand one another as if they were the same person, which in the working of the poem they are – hence the futility of commonsensical query which takes them to be acting as separate beings. Lermontov's Circassian girl, Bela, is as different from Pechorin as one species of animal from another. Their contact is disastrous because they are in every way incompatible, in race as in temperament. Before Bela's death Pechorin is bored with her and she, the daughter of a prince, is fiercely resentful at his indifference. In *The Cossacks* Tolstoy emphasises with equal thoroughness the lack of any understanding between his hero and the Cossack girl Mariula. And in his own story version of *The Captive* Tolstoy sets out to show in the simplest and baldest terms what might really have happened in the situation of Pushkin's poem. Both Lermontov and Tolstoy had already been shown the way by Pushkin's own later poems, and the use they made of the Caucasus story shows how deeply they were influenced by it. In the event *The Captive* proved as suggestive as Pushkin's other works.

In his first draft Pushkin put in the foreground of the poem a young Circassian brave who would have provided the *motif* for jealousy and a clash of arms. The opening shows him engaged in the kind of raid and ambush that in the final version are generalised and described as a part of the Circassian way of life, and kept significantly apart from the Captive's story. (Both Lermontov and Tolstoy use this jealousy *motif*, and in *The Cossacks* Tolstoy also adapts Pushkin's fine description of a native raider on a Cossack outpost floating across the river behind a log on which he has fastened his gear.) Action, in the completed poem, is reported and hearsay, elegiac in tone: even the Cossack on watch dreams.

> О чем ты думаешь, казак?
> Воспоминаешь прежни битвы,
> На смертном поле свой бивак.
> Полков хвалебные молитвы
> И родину?...Коварный сон!
> Простите, вольные станицы,
> И дом отцов, и тихий Дон,
> Война и красные девицы!
> К брегам причалил тайный враг,
> Стрела выходит из колчана –.

What are you dreaming of, Cossack? Are you remembering former encounters; your bivouac on the field of battle; the songs in praise of regiments; the homeland? Deceitful dream! Goodbye to the freedom of the camp, to your father's home, and the quiet Don, to war and pretty girls. A hidden enemy has moored by the bank, an arrow comes from his quiver.

Though full of life and detail the scene is strangely calm, a proper setting for the dreamlike encounters of Captive and maiden; like Wordsworth's solitary reaper they seem to inhabit a solitude peopled only by the ghosts of 'old, unhappy, far-off things, and battles long ago'. The Captive seems not so much brought by force to a savage place as transported back in time: his bondage appears almost self-induced, an impression increased rather than the reverse by the constant references to it. He seems to wake from dream to reality after his escape and the death of the girl, when the bayonets of the Cossack outpost glitter suddenly before him in the mist, and the poem is as suddenly concluded.

With its triumphant celebration of Russian conquest the epilogue makes almost brutally explicit the main reason for the dream-like retrospection of the poem.[1] In the face of the forces of progress the

---

[1] B. M. Eykhenbaum, 'Problemy poetiki Pushkina', *Pushkin – Dostoevsky*, ed. A. L. Volynsky (Petrograd 1921) comments that this heroic celebration, as in a patriotic ode, shows the way to the historic narrative of *Poltava* and *The Bronze Horseman*.

PUSHKIN

world it celebrates is already condemned to the past, where reality
and unreality have no quarrel with each other, and where a faithful
record of Circassian ways of life is quite compatible with a romantic
dream of pure and unrequited love. The Captive is not Pushkin, but
the heroic tones of the epilogue are equally compatible with the
Captive's return to duty and Russia. For the poet and his hero the
dream of romantic distance – *fuir, là-bas fuir* – is over, and both
return, the one in style and the other in the story, to public service
and official celebration.

I have discussed *Kavkazsky Plennik* at some length because it
shows Pushkin's success in a romantic mode which is basically un-
congenial to him. Belinsky first made the point, since echoed by
most critics, that the narrative 'eastern poem' (*Vostochnaya Poema*),
adapted by Pushkin from Byron, is predominantly 'lyrical' in tone.
Pushkin has sidestepped the story – and in particular the story's need
to take itself seriously, and to be so taken – by giving the whole
narrative an air of the lightness and simplicity of a brief lyric poem.
He shows the weakness of the 'heavyweight' eastern poem and also
how this weakness can be overcome, the Byronic melodrama trans-
muted, the absurdity of romance changed into the lyric impersonality
of a dream in which incongruity is inevitable and therefore cannot
be absurd. Moreover the incongruity between story and actuality,
which is the crucial point of his comments and exchanges with
Vyazemsky, is metamorphosed by Pushkin's instinctual craftsmanship into contrasts between one mode of relation and another –
the elegiac accuracy of the travel section on a brave and doomed
people and their way of life, the dream-like tenderness of the love
lyric, the terse and factual opening and ending. Whereas in Byron's
eastern poems we must respond simply to the excitement and
romance, and be drawn into it, the changes of key in Pushkin invite
a more detached and a more technically appreciative response.

The same process is at work in the stages of composition of *The
Fountain of Bakhchisarai*. The poem was begun in the conventional
epic form of five-stress iambics, and the first draft opens with the
Tatar Khan Girey sitting like Achilles in his anger, surrounded by
his silent retinue. In the final version he is as insubstantial as the
wreaths from his famous amber pipe, which is not a property of the
heroic world but an image of brooding reverie.[1] Unlike the pro-

[1] Herzen in his *Memoirs* mentions the kind of officer 'who cannot see a comrade
smoking without exclaiming "The amber fumed between his lips"' (*Yantar
v ustakh ego dymilsya*), an instance of how details in Pushkin's poetry became
part of the popular imagination and commonplaces of speech.

jected Circassian brave of *The Captive* he remains in the poem, but
only in a marginal and incongruous role. The hardbitten Tatar
Khan becomes an ineffectual romantic lover. After the death of the
Polish princess who is his captive and for whom he has pined in vain
he returns to warfare, but on the battlefield his sabre would often
droop in mid-swipe and he would turn pale. In *The Refutation of
Criticism* Pushkin made fun of the lines with the same defensiveness
with which he looked back on *The Captive*, observing that 'young
writers in general do not know how to depict the physical expres-
sions of passion'.[1] Though Belinsky thought him an admirably
picturesque figure of romantic love, Girey is certainly less convincing than Seyd in Byron's *Corsair*, but this in a sense is just the
point. Pushkin borrowed him from *The Corsair*, as he borrowed the
Gulnare/Medora theme, and even some of Byron's too confident
patter (the *Kislar* who guards the harem in both poems is really a
Turkish word meaning 'girl', a howler inherited by Pushkin via
Pichot's translation) and in the borrowing he has lost status but
acquired function.[2] He exists to bring about a dramatic encounter
between his former favourite, Zarema, and the virginal Polish
princess, and of this Pushkin observed in *The Refutation*: 'I do not
believe it has been criticised...it is dramatically effective.'

He was right. It is the first of many such confrontations in his
mature work, and its success lifts the poem far above the level of
Byronic local colour. While *The Captive* is an unacknowledged
dream poem, *The Fountain of Bakhchisarai* is a confessed one. As
Pushkin reveals in his conclusion, it was inspired by a visit to the
ruined palace, which an unquiet spirit seems to haunt. Is it the pure
spirit of Mariya, or the jealous and passionate Zarema? How did
Mariya die? – was Zarema drowned on suspicion of causing her
death? In the reverie induced by the sight of the ruin and the
abandoned garden this uncertainty is appropriate, whereas at the
end of *The Corsair* it is only a dismissive flourish: 'It was enough –
she died – what reck'd it how?' Pushkin has transformed the
Byronic evasion into the proper and harmonious climax of his poem.

---

[1] *Oproverzhenie na kritiki* (VII, 166). In the Boldino autumn of 1830 Pushkin
began an extended piece on the critical reception of his works. It remained
unfinished, but contains a number of recollections by him of comments by
his friends and enemies.

[2] B. V. Tomashevsky, *Pushkin*, Bk. 1 (1813–24) (Moscow–Leningrad 1956).
(The mistake was first pointed out by Dashkov in the *Russian Archive* 1868.)
Zhirmunsky in *Bairon i Pushkin* cites a quantity of parallels with *The Corsair*
and discusses Byron's and Pushkin's use of the historic present in the poems.

Twin foci of a nostalgic and erotic reverie, Mariya and Zarema come to life as Medora and Gulnare have no chance of doing; and by an exceptionally astute device, for the two girls themselves exist, like the poem itself, in terms of the past. Neither has a future, but their pasts are very different and determine the confrontation which makes them real to us. The proud and patriarchal seclusion of the castle of Mariya's upbringing is now dishonoured, as we learn in a terse phrase or two, by an owner who has come to terms with the extortionate Tatar. In her passionate plea to Mariya the childhood of Zarema appears in a vivid disconnected sequence.

> Родилась я не здесь, далеко,
> Далеко...но минувших дней
> Предметы в памяти моей
> Доныне врезаны глубоко.
> Я помню горы в небесах,
> Потоки жаркие в горах,
> Непроходимые дубравы,
> Другой закон, другие нравы;
> Но почему, какой судьбой
> Я край оставила родной,
> Не знаю; помню только море
> И человека в вышине
> Над парусами...

I was not born here but far far off...and yet the objects of those bygone days are still cut deeply in my memory. I remember mountains in the clouds, warm springs on the mountains, impenetrable woods; other laws and other customs. But why and under what destiny I quitted my homeland I know not. I only remember the sea, and a man perched up aloft, beneath the sails... (IV, 175.)

The childhood memory of the man seen on the mast touches as truly as good fiction. It seems right for this enterprising and adaptably animal nature that has found itself at home in the harem and set out with singleminded concentration to secure the affections of its owner. Now her fierce possessiveness is threatened by the captive who has no feelings left of her own. Zarema speaks of her past and we only hear of Mariya's; but at the climax of their encounter the past is decisive, for both have lost everything else – Zarema's happiness in the present, and her power over Girey, have been taken from her by the powerless ghost of Mariya.

As is typical of Pushkin's confrontations there is no comprehension between the two women: Zarema is asking something which her involuntary rival cannot understand and does not know how to answer. But the sense of two persons whose backgrounds are so different but whose predicament is the same is extraordinarily suggestive: Henry James as novelist and Shakespeare as dramatist created similar moments of pressure, and it would not be wholly absurd to compare Pushkin's two heroines with Charlotte Stant and Maggie Verver in *The Golden Bowl,* for in both cases it is environment that makes visible the drama of their competition. A romantic daydream has been penetrated by Pushkin with a curiosity which foreshadows the later 'dramatic investigations' of the *Little Tragedies.*

But Pushkin was probably not fully conscious of the potential of his own scrutiny – the form of the poem does not yet give him the chance to be, for it is in many ways naive, encumbered with the fashionably exotic, and revelling in a fluency of emotional expression which he was later to deprecate and disown. Even so he is curious about the essential truth of a fashionably picturesque subject – what must the harem guardian have been like, in his daily preoccupation and routine? – how did the girls live in the pathos of their arrested existence, children in the forms of women, taking 'a childish pleasure' in the fish swimming in the marble fountains? – in spite of his curiosity being compromised by the exuberance of the Byronic form and by Byron's facile eroticism, which is notably removed from the delicate and vivacious sexuality of *Ruslan and Lyudmila.* No wonder *The Fountain of Bakhchisarai* was his most popular poem, though by the standards of Pushkin's mature poetry it was not the best kind of success.

No great, or even very good, poetry has been written for the sake of the picturesque. Wordsworth does not describe mountains, he inhabits them; they are aspects of his imaginative life. But scenery poems had created a popular taste and every poet felt obliged to add his quota. Pushkin was no exception. The descriptive poems of Derzhavin and Zhukovsky had begun the fashion for Caucasian scenery, and 'pictures from the Caucasus' are as much a part of the function of *The Captive* as alpine and Italian views in Byron and Rogers. Over a number of years Pushkin produced lyrics – *The Avalanche, The Monastery on Mount Kazbek, Don,* and others – which have no true distinction or personal flavour, though they are well and simply made, without Byronic emphasis on the 'horridly beautiful', and with an implicit acknowledgement of spectacular nature as a world cold, austere, and apart: the 'froide nature' of

Vigny's *La Maison du Berger* rather than the anthropomorphic nature of the English romantics.

Pushkin never debated in his poems the sense of exclusion from nature, as Wordsworth did in the 'Immortality' Ode or Coleridge in 'Dejection', because he never felt, like them, the sense of unity with it. His imagination engages in brief pictures or visions of the natural world, pictures whose intimacy is of brief, sometimes intense, duration, but never reveal a prolonged and meditated relationship. And their precision never draws attention to itself, like the carefully worked details of Lamartine (whose *Méditations* were acclaimed in 1820 as a kind of new classicism.)

> Le mur est gris, la tuile est rousse,
> L'hiver a rongé le ciment;
> Des pierres disjointes la mousse
> Verdit l'humide fondement;
> Les gouttières, que rien n'essuie,
> Laissent, en rigoles de suie
> S'égoutter le ciel pluvieux,
> Traçant sur la vide demeure
> Ces noirs sillons par où l'on pleure,
> Que les veuves ont sous les yeux.[1]

Or in Tennyson's *Mariana*

> With blackest moss the flower-plots
> Were thickly crusted, one and all:
> The rusted nails fell from the knots
> That held the pear to the gable-wall...

In both poets detail is anthropomorphised into mood; a still life becomes a face 'folded in sorrow'. But this is as alien to Pushkin's sense of nature as Baudelaire's superbly definitional disillusion with its world of beauty.

> Pour l'enfant, amoureux de cartes et d'estampes,
> L'univers est égal à son vaste appétit.
> Ah, que le monde est grand à la clarté des lampes!
> Aux yeux du souvenir que le monde est petit!

Unlike all his contemporaries, Pushkin takes no attitude to the world of nature at all, and never concerns himself to make use of it.

Or rather he makes use of it in the same spirit that he makes use of other romantic properties. The poems about the Caucasus and the river Terek are at the same level of efficiency as *The Black*

---

[1] *La Vigne et la Maison.*

Shawl, *The Talisman*, *The Prisoner*, *Rodrik* (borrowed from Southey) and many other short poems which equably exploit the contemporary taste for brigands and assignations, love charms, fortune tellers, old Seville, and so on. His letters and his later prose account, *A Journey to Arzrum*, contain better descriptions of the wild scenery than his poems do, because the factual approach to these things suited him better. A declamatory landscape was best dealt with by the sobriety of prose, and by contrast, a sober landscape kindles his poetry. The flat sandy plains and forests of north Russia are the country of his finest short poems, *Winter Landscape*, *Autumn*, and of *Evgeny Onegin*, the 'other pictures' which are brought before us in Onegin's journey. And the flat Bessarabian steppe which is the background of *The Gipsies* helps to give the poem its spare geometrical outline and logic, even though, as we shall see, the individual gipsies are themselves as much out of literary tradition as the Circassian girl.

But there is one romantic landscape which really inspired Pushkin – the sea. Though *K moryu* (*To the sea*) is a romantically conventional poem with its salutation to Napoleon, engirt by the ocean at St Helena, and to Byron ('He was your bard O sea') it is full of the sound of waves, the magical sound that is even heard in the verses Pushkin wrote in 1830 for Karolina Sobanska's album.

> Что в имени тебе моем?
> Оно умрет, как шум печальный
> Волны, плеснувшей в берег дальный,
> Как звук ночной в лесу глухом.

What is my name to you? It will die, like the sad noise of a wave breaking on a distant shore, like night sound in deep forest. (III, 163.)

The place becomes instant and intimate to us through sound, as in Coleridge's simile in *The Ancient Mariner*.

> A noise like that of a hidden brook
> In the leafy month of June,
> That to the sleeping woods all night
> Singeth a quiet tune.

Or Keats's in *Hyperion*.

> As when, upon a trancéd summer night,
> Those green-rob'd senators of mighty woods,
> Tall oaks, branch-charméd by the earnest stars,
> Dream, and so dream all night without a stir,

Save for one gradual solitary gust
Which comes upon the silence, and dies off,
As if the ebbing air had but one wave;
So came these words and went...

The poem Pushkin wrote on his sea voyage to Gurzuf, soon after he had arrived in the south, uses sea onomatopoeia in a very different way, with a full rhythm and diapason which moves hypnotically in the background of his disturbed thoughts, its sighing heard as a faint undertone to them:

Минутной младости минутные друзья;

Transient friends of transient youth; (ii, 7.)

and three times breaking their erratic course with a deeper sound (*shum* embodies it in a single syllable) that drowns the past with its hypnotic presence.

Шуми, шуми, послушное ветрило,
Волнуйся подо мной, угрюмый океан...

Murmur, murmur, obedient sail; surge beneath me, sombre sea.

The acoustic opulence of this poem, *Pogaslo dnevnoe svetilo* (*The orb of day has died...*), recalls the movement of Hugo's *Oceano Nox*, which conveys in its irregular rhythms a still sea – 'such a tide as moving seems asleep' – running up a beach, now a shorter and now a longer way, reaching its furthest point in the smooth extended rush of its close.

Et c'est ce qui vous fait ces voix désespérées
Que vous avez le soir quand vous venez vers nous!

In Pushkin, as in Hugo and Tennyson, the sound may be rather too obviously an echo to the sense, but nothing shows more graphically than his sea images the extraordinary variety of Pushkin's descriptive effects. The language of the two nineteenth-century masters of opulent description has passed the point at which complete simplicity can still carry, for the reader, the most meaning of all. In Swinburne the need for sound rather than plain descriptive words is still more evident, and is not less so in the art of T. S. Eliot's *Four Quartets*.

The menace and caress of wave that breaks on water,
The distant rote in the granite teeth
And the wailing warning from the approaching headland...

But Pushkin's seascapes can turn back from the full-blown imported rhetoric of *K moryu* and *Pogaslo dnevnoe svetilo* to the word in itself, as if Pushkin – here as in so many contexts – had simply found and called the thing by its right Russian name, the name at the beginning of the *Ruslan* prologue, *U lukomore...*[1] or in the line from *The Covetous Knight* which Maurice Baring took as a keynote of Pushkinian simplicity.

И море, где бежали корабли.

And the sea, where ships were running. (v, 331.)

Or, most haunting of all, the two lines in the *Ruslan* prologue in which the land of wonders appears simply as the sandy shores of the Baltic.

Там о заре прихлынут волны
На брег песчаный и пустой,

There, at dawn, the waves come washing over the sandy and deserted shore...

At the end of *The Fountain of Bakhchisarai*, after the evocation of the Khan's harem and the fountain of tears, the traveller of today sees the southern sea turning from blue to green round the cliffs of the Crimea.

И зеленеющая влага
Пред ним и блещет и шумит
Вокруг утесов Аю-дага...

And the greening waves sparkle and sound before him around the rocks of Ayu-Dag.

The word *zeleneyushchy* (which can mean either 'green' or 'turning green') is typical of Pushkin's occasional use of colour adjectives, less striking in themselves than because of their positioning.[2] Their impact is not descriptive but dramatic and psychological. In *Poltava* the executioner, swinging his axe in practice on the scaffold, is noticed to have *white* hands: the possibilities of contrast are obvious but unstated. Here, not so dissimilarly, the sudden freshness, the living green of the sea, brings

---

[1] Literally 'By a curve of the sea'. Though the phrase in Russian is exactly and descriptively commonplace, Shakespeare's phrase in *Timon of Athens* 'the very hem o' the sea' surprises the mind into the reality of the place in a comparable way. It is tempting to render the phrase 'at bend of bay', after Joyce's phrase in *Finnegans Wake* 'from swerve of shore to bend of bay'.

[2] Compare *moy khladeyushchie ruki* (my hands growing cold) in the lyric *Dla beregov otchizny dalnoy*. The sense of neither could be rendered as a single word in a translation. As Pushkin himself remarked about Chateaubriand's word-for-word translation of Milton, the difficulty of translating Russian in such a way lies in its natural verbal economy.

back the life of the present which has been cut off from the poet's dream artifice of the past. (Shakespeare's dramatic use of colour makes the same kind of metaphor explicit in 'the multitudinous seas incarnadine'...) Lermontov's sea and shorescapes are markedly Pushkinian, and much superior to his mountain scenery, though as Nabokov points out, his use of the word 'lilac' (*sirenevy*), for the hue of a receding shore-line, was a new epithet at the time, and as such calls attention to itself. Pushkin's epithets are not only unoriginal but never give the impression of having been selected, in Yeats's phrase, as 'the right word which is also the surprising word'. That, none the less, is the effect they frequently make on us.

'The poem is simple and clear as a geometrical theorem' observes a recent critical study of *The Gipsies*.[1] Belinsky, on the other hand, commented on the depth of meaning which underlies the poem and suggested that this is achieved by the power of 'unconscious creations' (*bessoznatelnosti tvorchestva*), a power upon which critics are apt to fall back too easily in defence of works they admire but in which they sense contradiction.

If there is contradiction, where does it lie? *The Gipsies* is the most considered *poema* that Pushkin has so far written. As we have seen, *The Captive of the Caucasus* and *The Fountain of Bakhchisarai* begin as stories with certain epic features and in the process of composition they become more like dream poems. They undergo what seems an instinctual process of simplification and evasion of the problems of combining the romantic and epic genres in a long narrative poem. By contrast *The Gipsies*, and also *Poltava*, challenge these problems openly in the course of their construction. Instead of skilfully avoiding difficulties, Pushkin reveals them, making them almost solid and structural aspects of the narrative. Pushkin was working on *Evgeny Onegin* at the same time – completing the third canto as he wrote *The Gipsies* – and he was allowing the novel in verse to develop as it would. He expected it to be 'romantic', he wrote to Vyazemsky, and was surprised to find it becoming something else. Only in its final stages did he discern the 'distance of a free novel' which had been unclear to him when it first appeared in 'the magic crystal'.[2] Instead of this freedom, *The Gipsies* has from its beginning the air of strict and formal predestination.

[1] Slonimsky, *Masterstvo Pushkina*.
[2] *Evgeny Onegin* (8. 50) – the penultimate stanza of the completed novel.

Predestination on the one hand; on the other, feckless freedom, indifference to the future, the power of living solely in the present. These are the associations of gipsy life, and Pushkin had met in the environs of Kishinev the nomadic gipsy communities, had been fascinated by the kind of life they led, and according to one apocryphal account had actually spent some weeks living with them. But *The Gipsies* is far from being 'a gipsy poem'.[1] The gipsies of the poem are symbols in its geometry; they can hardly be allowed to exist, like the Circassians of *The Captive*, for the romantic and guidebook interest of their way of life. And it is here that dilemma and contradiction first appear. More than any other poem *The Gipsies* shows the problem of a poet as naturally classical as Pushkin in an epoch fashionably and self-consciously romantic, and there is much in the poem that is all the more banal and melodramatic for being expressed in lucid but earnest *cliché*. Gipsies were naturally romantic properties, like Corsairs, Circassians and Giaours. How can these compromised characters be acceptable *dramatis personae* for an austerely simple drama of fate and freedom?

In their various ways Pushkin's friends and contemporaries were aware of the paradox. Vyazemsky objected that the end of the poem was too much like Greek Tragedy: Ryleev, on the other hand, criticised the hero of the poem for his low occupations among the gipsies, and thus for not being more like the hero of a tragedy. Kireevsky, who of all Pushkin's contemporaries had the shrewdest idea of his problems, and for whose views Pushkin himself had a great respect, suggested in an article written in the year after the publication of the poem, that the reader would do better to ignore the Gipsy question altogether, and to regard the old Gipsy not as any kind of ethnic representative but simply as an abstract figure and a chorus on its tragic events.[2]

If this is indeed the answer it suggests something seriously wrong. Other poets and writers of the time had overcome the problem of making a morally typical figure at the same time typical of his environment, the very problem of realism which Lukacs was to explore in the context of the nineteenth-century novel and which Gukovsky has claimed as central to the nature of Pushkin's achievement.[3] We have already glimpsed Pushkin's

---

[1] As is Mérimée's *Carmen* (1847), which was avowedly based on it. Compare Zemfira's song with Carmen's.   [2] *The Moscow Messenger*, 1828.
[3] V. P. Gukovsky, *Pushkin i problemy realisticheskogo stilya* (Moscow 1957).

intuitive grasp of the thing even in the slight and romantic sketches of Mariya and Zarema.

The same point is at issue in Wordsworth's *Excursion*. Though Wordsworth's Pedlar, or his Leechgatherer, are in some sense figures of abstraction, through whom the poet explores the universality of human suffering and fortitude, they are also figures true to time and place, whose profession and way of life have made them what they are. We do not feel that Wordsworth has selected a suitable background and protagonists to work out his philosophy and reveal what he wants to say (though he does this in *The Borderers*). In Scott's tale *The Two Drovers*, the tragedy is of a Highlander compelled by his own sense of honour to take the life of his friend, an English drover who has offended him in a quarrel which seemed trivial by English standards. In these cases an understanding of history, locality, and environment justifies the writer's imagination, and combines the theme that has appealed to it with a background deeply sensed and loved.

But Pushkin in *The Gipsies* reveals himself not as the writer at home in the world he describes, but as the traveller, intrigued by the unfamiliar and the picturesque, and marrying it to ideas from his own background and culture. He is something like the eighteenth-century explorer, hoping he may find 'natural man'. Abstract queries present themselves; Rousseau, Montesquieu, and Madame de Staël are in the offing. Are primitive societies virtuous? Do they show that the passions and instincts of civilised man have become corrupted, that his assumptions are vain, arrogant, and selfish? Such questions count for little in the real world of Scott and Wordsworth, but they are the stock topics of the *Encyclopédistes*.

And they are relevant to connoisseurs of the picturesque. The Byronic traveller interests himself in local customs and conventions of love, courtship and adultery. Mérimée, who greatly admired Pushkin's work and helped to make it known in France, unites a dispassionate anthropologist's interest in customs and people with a gourmet's pleasure in strong flavours for their own sake. To the western reader the life of the gipsies as Pushkin describes it, the murder beside the ancient grave-mound, the tattered cart left behind after the tribe have moved on, seem to have a good deal in common with *Carmen* and *Matteo Falcone*. Zemfira's song *Stary muzh grozny muzh* (*Old husband, harsh husband*) is adapted from folk-song not so different from the kind that Mérimée had cleverly imitated in *La Guzla*.[1] Gipsy love has its own laws; gipsy women are different from other women. *The Gipsies* appears to summon up the atmosphere of ethnic melodrama, as it does the eighteenth-century dream of the noble savage, but neither is really central to its issue.

In fact they confuse it, and the poem suffers by their association. Its hero, Aleko, is a totally anonymous figure, of Byronic provenance, a fugitive from the civilised world who comes to live among the gipsy tribe and adopt their ways. Their mode of life is described by Pushkin briefly but with meticulous accuracy, and this realism is at odds with the stylised Byronism of the hero: we cannot really accept the picture of Aleko's life with his gipsy mistress and her old father, leading a performing bear to earn food and lodging in their wandering existence. Pushkin has shown how well he can harmonise contrasting genres, but this juxtaposition is too baldly incongruous. So at least it seemed to Pushkin's friends, Ryleev and Bestuzhev, who thought Aleko a much better romantic hero than the Captive, because he had a bitter soul carrying a dark burden of guilt, while the Captive was merely sentimental. But this significant improvement was nullified for Ryleev, as we have seen, by Aleko's low occupation of begging with the tambourine and bear – to have adopted a tinker's trade would have been more tolerable. Pushkin retorted that he might have been even better cast as a landowner or civil servant of the eighth grade – in that case, it is true, nothing at all would remain of the poem, *ma tanto meglio* – and mentioned in parenthesis that a lady of his acquaintance thought the bear the only honest person in the poem.[2] In the same spirit he replied in a letter to another friend, who asked what the aim of the poem was, that ' "the aim of poetry is poetry", as Delvig says – if he didn't steal the *mot*'.[3]

Naturally Pushkin could not and would not oblige with an analysis of the poem – it was done, and there was no more to be said – but the puzzlement of his friends and the questions they raised do reveal the poem's originality as a new departure. The critics tended to solve them then, and still do now, by a kind of

[1] Published in 1827, the same year as *The Gipsies*, it purported to be the work of an Illyrian folk poet. Most writers were taken in by it, including Pushkin, who later translated some of its poems as *Songs of the Western Slavs* (*Pesni zapadnykh slavyan*. (Mérimée guyed his own imitative skill in a later Lithuanian tale, whose folk-conscious narrator collects an ancient local poem which turns out to be by the modern Polish poet Adam Mickiewicz.)
[2] *The Refutation of Criticism.*   [3] Letter to V. A. Zhukovsky, April 1825.

reductive appreciation, leaving on one side the flesh and blood of
the poem and concentrating on its abstract meaning and its air of
a mathematical theorem. Kireevsky's advice is not untypical: to
forget the Gipsies and to see the old man simply as an embodiment
of folk wisdom and experience, contrasting with Aleko's self-
centred and impulsive violence. Belinsky's comment, that 'any
literature might be proud of the old Gipsy' reveals a similar
attitude. But we do not claim that any literature might be proud
of King Lear. Goethe may say that every old man is Lear, yet
he belongs only where he is: his reality is inside Shakespeare's play,
and there is no hiatus between his role in it and what he stands
for.

Kireevsky put the reasons for his attitude into schematic form.
Three periods can be traced, he says, in the development of
Pushkin's art – the 'Italian–French' of *Ruslan* and the early
poems; the Byronic, complete with exotic events and a disillusioned hero; and the properly Pushkinian and distinctively Russian
achievement of *Evgeny Onegin* and *Boris Godunov*. *The Gipsies* he
sees as a transitional poem between the second and third stage,
showing 'a strange struggle between Byron's idealism and the
lively *narodnost* of a Russian poet'. However artificial, these dis-
tinctions do correspond with the air of experiment in *The Gipsies*,
the drawing of diagrams that appear to cut off one *motif* and style
in the poem from another. Pushkin, who earlier had shown such
remarkable tact and skill in synthesis, does seem here deliberately
to demarcate and emphasise the disconcerting gaps, as if his
purpose were to bring into a revealing confrontation the modes he
had previously compounded together. In comparison with the two
previous 'eastern poems' the language of *The Gipsies* is uneven
and full of contrasts. The 'movements of the soul', as Tomashevsky
points out, are rendered as conventionally as in the earlier poems,
or even more so.

> И грусти тайную причину
> Истолковать себе не смел.
>
> Что ж сердце юноши трепещет?
> Какой заботой он томим?
>
> Но, боже, как играли страсти
> Его послушною душой!
> С каким волнением кипели
> В его измученной груди!

And he did not dare to explain to himself the secret cause of his sorrow. (IV, 203.)

Why does the young man's heart tremble? With what care is he oppressed?

But God! how passions played with his obedient soul! With what tumult they seethed in his tormented breast!

And yet, as if with Girey's romantic gesture on the battlefield in mind, Pushkin conveys Aleko's jealousy and its consequences in a way that is factual and flat as well as melodramatic.

> Он, с криком пробудясь во тьме,
> Ревниво руку простирает...
> Он с трепетом привстал и внемлет...
> Всё тихо: страх его объемлет,
> По нем текут и жар и хлад;
> Встает он, из шатра выходит,
> Вокруг телег, ужасен, бродит;
>
> Могила на краю дороги
> Вдали белеет перед ним,
> Туда слабеющие ноги
> Влачит, предчувствием томим,
> Дрожат уста, дрожат колени,
> Идет...и вдруг...иль это сон?
> Вдруг видит близкие две тени
> И близкий шепот слышит он...
>
> Алеко за холмом,
> С ножом в руках, окровавленный
> Сидел на камне гробовом.
> Два трупа перед ним лежали;
> Убийца страшен был лицом;

Waking with a shout in the darkness, he jealously stretches out his hand...Tremulously he sits up and listens...All is quiet – fear seizes him, both heat and cold pour through him. He gets up, goes out of the tent, and wanders round the wagons, looking terrible.

A grave by the side of the road shines white before him some way off... There he drags his weakening steps, tormented with foreboding; his lips, his knees tremble...on he walks...and suddenly...or is it a dream? Suddenly he sees two shadows near him and hears whispering close by...

Beyond the mound Aleko sat on the gravestone with a knife in his hand, covered in blood. Two corpses lay before him; the murderer's face was terrible.

The hero appears both objectively and subjectively. The 'cares that oppress him', and the language in which they are described, are conventionally romantic, but his actions and feelings are observed with impassive detachment. The most worn and ordinary words are used, and at the climax of the poem they sound almost as if a simple-minded witness was using them in the box to describe his impression of a maniac and murderer. In the bald line 'the murderer's face was terrible' the audience receive a more horrifying impression of the deed than if an educated person were giving evidence in chosen and considered terms. To continue the court-room analogy, we have the opposite impression of Aleko as murderer to that which Dickens gives us of Bill Sikes and Fagin. They are seen by the fascinated, verbally sensitive spectator, the reporter in court – Dickens himself. Pushkin gives the account not so much impersonally but as if these things were being described by someone else, by one of the Gipsies themselves, or any very simple man. To that extent the claim for his *narodnost* is true, though it might be more accurate to say that a dramatic impression of the simple is conveyed by sophisticated means, which assume the primitive setting and the violent emotion, and also alienate Aleko from us, making his action and sensations terrible because mechanical.

Together with this simplicity goes a different one, barely congruous with it, the air of 'a Greek play' that Vyazemsky objected to. The bear seen as 'the shaggy guest' (*kosmaty gost*), the dead lovers laid 'in the cold bosom of the earth', remind us of the eighteenth-century classic diction of Pope's Homer, and of Gnedich and Zhukovsky. So with the word *rek*, the archaic term for speech or announcement (Old English *mathelode*) which Ryleev thought too 'poetic'.

> Тогда старик, приближась, рек:
> «Оставь нас, гордый человек!

Then spoke the old man, approaching him: 'Leave us, proud man!'

In this speech the old Gipsy rises to the formal dignity of chorus. His primitive status, elsewhere dwelt on, is forgotten. And the Gipsies prepare in a murmurous throng to leave their encampment. The poem has come full circle and its opening lines are re-echoed, but now – the homely details of their nomadic routine unmentioned – they are compared to a flock of migratory cranes.

Сказал – и шумною толпою
Поднялся табор кочевой
С долины страшного ночлега.
И скоро все в дали степной
Сокрылось; лишь одна телега,
Убогим крытая ковром,
Стояла в поле роковом.
Так иногда перед зимою,
Туманной, утренней порою,
Когда подъемлется с полей
Станица поздних журавлей
И с криком вдаль на юг несется,
Пронзенный гибельным свинцом,
Один печально остается,
Повиснув раненым крылом.
Настала ночь; в телеге темной
Огня никто не разложил,
Никто под крышею подъемной
До утра сном не опочил.

He spoke – and in a murmurous throng the nomadic camp rose from the valley of the terrible night's resting place. And soon all was hidden in the distant steppe. Only one cart, covered with a tattered rug, remained in the fateful field. Thus sometimes before winter in the misty dawn, when a flock of belated cranes rises from the fields and with a cry flies swiftly southward into the distance, one, pierced by the fatal lead, stays sadly behind with its wounded wing hanging. Night came; in the dark cart no one lit a fire, no one beneath its folded hood fell asleep before morning.

The deliberately Homeric simile carries forward that transformation of tone initiated in the old Gipsy's speech, although some phrases contribute more to the self-consciously classical atmosphere than to the dramatic transformation itself. The Gipsy cart is isolated stylistically on the fatal field, a microcosm of the mode in which the components of the poem stand aside from one another. Their isolation is that of the solitude and distance which close round Aleko at the end. The abstract nature of Aleko is finally realised in his disappearance as a person, though his presence can still be inferred: the cart itself is the focal point of Pushkinian geometry and the vehicle of the Pushkinian art of distancing. The final touch, moreover, is not self-consciously but unobtrusively Greek – the 'whole truth' of Homer – for sleep does come in the morning at last, even to the killer in his solitude.

The fate of Aleko is as different as could be from that of Byron's heroes. He is stripped of the cloak of romantic mystery: they continue to wear theirs, as a reassurance to poet and reader, and because the poems they appear in are simply not capable of examining them as *The Gipsies* examines Aleko. And yet *The Gipsies* could only have been written in the epoch of romanticism. It stands beside the themes of its time, as the poem seems to stand beside its subject and style instead of coinciding with them, as separated as Aleko himself. In spite of its objective and classical appearance, it shows us more clearly than any other poem of Pushkin how far he is a poet of his time, of the romantic European idiom, and how far he is able to stand aside from that idiom instead of being unconsciously identified with it. *The Gipsies* makes use of romanticism from a position of detachment, as Aleko is with the Gipsies but not of them: the stance that Pushkin adopts is suited to the destiny he analyses and the tale he tells.

It is tempting to cite *Resolution and Independence* as an example of the way in which Wordsworth, probably without knowing it, makes a similar kind of virtue out of an incongruity of styles, combining them to present the old Leechgatherer in the various guises under which he appears to the poet's imagination. He is seen as a seer out of literature ('the sable orbs of his yet vivid eyes') and his speech comes

> With something of a lofty utterance drest –
> Choice word and measured phrase, above the reach
> Of ordinary men;

as a timeless landmark in the wild landscape,

> As a huge Stone is sometimes seen to lie
> Couched on the bald top of an eminence;

and as an actual and wretchedly poor old man, who tells the poet how he lives.

> And said, that, gathering leeches, far and wide
> He travelled; stirring thus about his feet
> The waters of the Pools where they abide.

It is an essential feature of these 'apparitions' of the old man that the different styles which suggest them remain in their separated state; they do not coalesce to form a unified style within the poem. Of course Wordsworth's imagination is far more deeply and continuously intimate with villagers, ancient leechgatherers, and pedlars on their rounds, than Pushkin was with a tribe of Bessarabian gipsies. Wordsworth's poems habitually grew like plants, shedding and proliferating, and his sureness was in this process rather than in the craftsman's manipulation of language.

> And I would give
> While yet we may, as far as words can give,
> Substance and life to what I feel.

The poet who writes that is far removed from Pushkin's delight in the power of language to convey not what he feels but what art can construct. Pushkin makes up for his traveller's detachment by his poet's confidence.

The Gipsies, and the old Gipsy in particular, have something in common with Wordsworth's Leechgatherer, though the use to which Pushkin puts a stock romantic hero and situation shows a detachment and an intellectual, almost chessboard sense of moves and pieces which suggests conscious manipulations. Just conceivably what I have called the 'metamorphoses' of the poem argue an equally deliberate kind of iconography. There is a possible connection between them and the figure of Ovid, who is very much a presence in the poem, and with whose exile at the classical Tomi Pushkin identified when he was living not far off at Kishinev. In a fine passage the old Gipsy tells Aleko how the legend of Ovid has been preserved among the people of the steppe – itself an indication just how far from being real nomads Pushkin's pastoral Gipsies are. It is of course most unlikely that Pushkin had Ovid's *Metamorphoses* before him, as a stimulus and a challenge to parody, as he had *Don Juan* and *Tristram Shandy* before him when writing *Evgeny Onegin*, but we know he had been reading Ovid in a French translation he borrowed at Kishinev in 1821 and did not return till some years later. In 1821, too, he wrote a poem in alexandrines *To Ovid*, recording that he himself was an exile in that barren Scythia so abhorred by the poet, and that though, as 'a stern Slav', he did not lament his own fate, he tendered his respect and sympathy to the illustrious shade. The poem does not take wings; it is a grave and graceful soliloquy in the André Chénier manner, and the old Gipsy's marvellous account of Ovid's life by the Danube – an account full of subtle ellipses which suggest the naive conception of the old man of Ovid as a kind of folk poet 'with a wondrous gift of song and a voice like the sound of waters' – is on a different level altogether. There is significance too in Aleko's comment on the old man's tale.

PUSHKIN

Певец любви, певец богов,
Скажи мне: что такое слава?
Могильный гул, хвалебный глас,
Из рода в роды звук бегущий
Или под сенью дымной кущи
Цыгана дикого рассказ?

Singer of love, singer of the Gods, tell me what kind of thing is glory? The tomb's resonance, the voice of praise, the rumour running from generation to generation? Or the tale of a wild gipsy under the bower of a smoky tent?

The clarity and grace of the Latin poet is changed into 'the tale of a wild Gipsy'; the classic *poema* is exiled and transformed into the primitive ballad and romantic tale: in the structure and tone of *The Gipsies* both might be said to be brought together.

The notion of *The Metamorphoses*, appealing in any case to Pushkin's protean genius, could have been the catalyst which precipitated the novel form of *The Gipsies* and replaced a dreamy enthusiasm for the denizens of the romantic 'eastern poem' by the objective study of the romantic hero. Ovid's mythologies are of men turned into stars, women into trees and birds. Transformed by the irruption of a classic image, the Gipsies forsake their passive status as romantic exemplars of the happy life, and are transformed into a flock of cranes; the old man (who once knew the 'difficult name' of the poet Ovid but has now forgotten it) becomes the wise judge vested with an authority that sentences and rejects the murderer Aleko. And Aleko, himself an exile pursued by the vengeance of 'an angry god', becomes a solitary and inhuman object, invisible in a tattered cart abandoned on the steppe. We remember that the 'crime' for which Ovid was banished remains obscure, and Pushkin never tells us what Aleko has done to compel him to flee from civilisation to life among the gipsies. Ovid himself, in the old man's account, was like a romantic hero – 'withered, pale, saying that an angry god was punishing him for some crime'.

If we accept in this way the gipsies' metamorphosis, and particularly that of the old man, we need not follow Kireevsky's advice and forget what they are supposed to be. The gipsies are metamorphosed into *The Gipsies*. Contradictions are an embarrassment to a geometrical proof but not to the fantasy of Ovidian art in which Pushkin can be seen as resolving 'the strange struggle between Byron's idealism and a lively *narodnost*', between the romance that ignores reality and the realism that finds romance ridiculous. The *sortilège* of the poem turns one into the other and then back again: the two are never united, but distinct and yet interchangeable. Is the gipsy life the golden age or a wretched poverty-stricken montony? Are the Gipsies wise, noble, and contented, or – as the final lines suggest – oppressed even more straitly than civilised men by the bonds of humanity? Is Aleko 'real' when he takes part in the picturesque routine of gipsy life, or is it real and he a romantic figment?

The kaleidoscopic mirage of reality and romance, of the character as he looks to himself and he looks from outside, is a dominant feature in the art of *Evgeny Onegin*, where parody and reality are blended and intertwined. In *The Gipsies* the process is diagrammatic and deadpan, and the reader is left to settle for himself the continuing significance of the abstractions which the poem has resolved on the level of art. Nor were the critics slow to help him. Thirty years after Pushkin's death *The Gipsies* had become a literary focus of the national self-consciousness, its dilemma and its destiny. It is understandable that Soviet critics take the line that Pushkin here demonstrates an objective and correct view of society, denouncing the individualism of Aleko and praising the collective virtue of the *narod*, but the same view had long been held by the populists and Slavophiles, notably Dostoevsky. For Dostoevsky Aleko is the archetypal Russian intellectual, while the Gipsies stand for the Russian people with its deeply instinctual and religious soul. Nezelenov, in 1882, echoed Dostoevsky's view of Aleko, but saw him as Byron personified, and his 'dispassionate but pitiless' treatment by Pushkin a final 'dethronement' of the fashionable Byronism of the earlier poems. Even Tomashevsky, the scholarly modern critic and editor of Pushkin, sees the poem as unquestionably didactic in form.

It is certainly true that *The Gipsies* is the first of Pushkin's 'open' masterpieces, which allow the reader to extract whatever he is capable of extracting, but this may be due not to a didactic purpose but a parodic one. Returning to our idea of metamorphosis, we might say that Pushkin deliberately turns the Byronic poem inside out. In *The Gipsies* the Byronic male becomes the female. The freedom for which he yearns becomes the routine of poverty, domestic cares, the casual infidelity of the spouse. It is Zemfira and not Aleko who has the qualities of will, determination, ruthless style. She takes him—

> Он будет мой:
> Кто ж от меня его отгонит?

He shall be mine: who shall drive him from me?

and she leaves him. Tired of him, she taunts him with her song:

> Ненавижу тебя,
> Презираю тебя;
> Я другого люблю,
> Умираю любя.

I hate you, I despise you; I love another; loving I die.

Yet Zemfira is not like Carmen, studied with a connoisseur's interest in her peculiar Gipsy seductiveness, her promiscuous vitality. She is too diagrammatic for that: she is a Haidée or a Zarema reversed, a Circassian girl who abandons her lover instead of being abandoned by him. Aleko has a dark past; 'desires seethed' in him once, 'and they will reawaken', but in the poem he is contented and passive, a model of connubial affection, satisfied with the conversation of his father-in-law and with his occupation of entertaining a gaping village audience. There is a remarkable contrast, probably not even intentional, between the familiar cliché in which Aleko is described and his actual situation in the poem. This incongruity produces more than a hint of the parody elements that run riot in *Evgeny Onegin*, and, as in the novel in verse, all suggestion of parody is abruptly dispelled at a climax of real and tragic violence.

The objectivity of *The Gipsies* is crude and rigid, but it is none the less compatible with parodic art; and the parodic in Pushkin, as in Shakespeare, opens up new and remarkable artistic perspectives. Despite their tragic fate, Aleko and Zemfira are more like puppets than fixed points in a geometrical theorem, and this too is the logic of parodic emancipation, for fate is not here a dark romantic *topos*, an artificial horizon to be gazed at with Byronic dignity, but a brutally indifferent process that reduces its victims to the status of mechanical dolls. Stabbed by Aleko, Zemfira utters as if by reflex the formula 'I die loving' (*Umirayu lyubya*) already familiar in a context of stock pathos in the poems of Karamzin and Gnedich;[1] and by contrast Aleko, after his crime, has not one more word to say. As the bodies are buried he sits in silence on an ancient gravestone, and when the job is finished he falls to the grass like a broken implement. No wonder Vyazemsky was bothered by this remarkable touch, so unsuited to any kind of current hero.

---

[1] V. V. Vinogradov, *Stil Pushkina* (Moscow 1941), Ch. 4, 'Sintez iskusstva i zhizni'. The author discusses the new features Pushkin gives to older stock phrases.

Another parodic reversal by Pushkin is the wordiness of romantic lovers, to which he had given its head in *The Captive of the Caucasus*. Instead of speaking for themselves with all the eloquence of fashionable feeling (of which there was a good deal more in Pushkin's early drafts) the relation of the pair is described in swift and equivocal strokes, in snatches of dialogue, in Zemfira's song, and in the nightmare of Aleko witnessed by Zemfira and her father. These rapid touches produce a dramatic tension which diverts us from any anomalies in the plot situation. Kireevsky, for example, not unreasonably pointed out that if the Gipsies really show no jealousy they can hardly be aware of 'the eternal affections', so that their claim to a primitive goodness and happiness, as of the golden age, is scarcely justified. He does not mention another and similar discrepancy, which ends the poem on a note which is conclusively perfect and yet unadmitted in the exposition.

> Но счастья нет и между вами,
> Природы бедные сыны!
> И под издранными шатрами
> Живут мучительные сны,
> И ваши сени кочевые
> В пустынях не спаслись от бед,
> И всюду страсти роковые,
> И от судеб защиты нет.

But there is no happiness even among you, poor sons of nature! Beneath your tattered tents live tormenting dreams, and your nomad shelters in the wilderness are not preserved from misery, and everywhere there are fatal passions, and from the fates there is no defence.

This is a truth that the diagram of the poem cannot recognise, for Aleko must be the sole disruptive element in the Gipsies' pastoral innocence. But now the play of metamorphosis has done its work; parody has become drama and ended in silence, a silence that is itself a comment on the conventional 'cast before the curtain' ending of romantic melodrama. This final metamorphosis of the Gipsies takes the leading characters out of existence. There is nothing more to be said about them, though much can be, and has been, said about the meaning that the poem leaves hanging in the air. In all the later long poems the characters have a reality which does not disappear with the ending, but here they have none. They are parodies who do not become people, as in *Evgeny Onegin*, for the classic finality of the Epilogue leaves them with no mode of survival in our minds.

The drama of *The Gipsies* is more searching than its melodrama: the queries planted in it are more dramatic than the cast. A key word, on which something like the same significances will be laid as are laid by Shakespeare in *King Lear* on the words 'nature' and 'nothing', appears in the fifth line. It is *volnost* (freedom, more particularly freedom of action), a common poetic word which Pushkin uses frequently, as he does the related word *volya* (the will and the freedom of the individual will). Gipsy life is 'like freedom'.

> Как вольность, весел их ночлег
> И мирный сон под небесами.

Like freedom, their nightly encampment is gay and so is their peaceful sleep beneath the skies.

When we first read the poem the phrase *kak volnost* may appear limp, a stock romanticism not uncharacteristic of *The Gipsies*, but in the course of the tale it is seen to take on a very precise meaning. To the outsider, to Aleko, gipsy life looks 'like freedom', but in fact it is free only in a special sense, the sense in which such a community is free because all its members unquestioningly accept its way of life and adhere to its customs. *The Gipsies* can be read in one sense as an extraordinarily graphic and economical dramatic commentary on the doctrines of Rousseau, whose pervasive influence is in the background of so much nineteenth-century Russian literature. Probably without having any very exact and coherent knowledge of them, Pushkin brings together in *The Gipsies* the doctrine of *The Social Contract*, the voluntary association of men for their mutual good, and the idea from Rousseau's earlier work *On the Origin of Inequality*, the idea of primitive man as naturally free in his native solitude. It is the Gipsies who exercise both the social contract and the virtues of the noble savage, while Aleko, the product of civilisation, is left in the utter solitude to which the bondage of egocentric passion condemns him.

But, as usual with Pushkin, the isolation and non-understanding between individuals is more eloquent than the working out of ideas. For Aleko, Gipsy life is 'freedom' because it is not the life of the society he knows, and he assumes that Zemfira will be faithful and virtuous because she must be different from the girls of that society. She, for her part, is amazed at his rejection of a society that seems far more attractive than her own.

Там игры, шумные пиры,
Уборы дев там так богаты!

There there are games and noisy parties, there the clothes of the girls
are so rich!

Aleko's life with the Gipsies is summed up in the demure line *Aleko
volen, kak oni* (Aleko is free, as they are). But when Zemfira is unfaithful he acts on an impulse as conditioned as her natural
promiscuity. He kills her and her lover, and the old man pro-
nounces the verdict and the key word.

«Оставь нас, гордый человек! –
Ты для себя лишь хочешь воли;

Leave us, proud man!...Only for yourself do you want freedom.

Pushkin first wrote *buiny chelovek* (violent man) and the change adds
the final touch to Aleko's case. He has been playing at being a Gipsy,
patronising their existence with his ignorant self-approval. He has
never understood the humility which would have accepted them
as they are. Pride is stupidity, the stupidity that Tolstoy analyses so
mercilessly in the hero of *The Cossacks*, who exhibits a naive conceit
in his 'understanding' of the Cossack girl and old man, and in his
conviction that they must love him for the interest he takes in them.

Even more than Evgeny Onegin, Aleko is a figure of suggestion
to nineteenth-century Russian intellectuals. He is a premise, a
hypothesis to which environment and personality can be added;
not a character himself but the reason why character is in others.
His ambiguous relation to the idea of freedom is returned to again
and again.[1] We see it in Dostoevsky's 'underground man', in his
Raskolnikov, Stavrogin and Ivan Karamazov. These great creations are in a sense parodies at two removes, descending as they do
through Pushkin from the Byronic hero. Like Hamlet, Aleko is
endlessly available both to fit new preoccupations and to perpetuate
a tradition of idea. (Hamlet, indeed, has the same parodic role as

---

[1] The old Gipsy's line – 'Only for yourself do you want freedom' – has been
used by Soviet spokesmen to condemn dissenting writers. By implication
they are selfishly demanding something which has no interest or meaning for
the Soviet masses, who are not concerned with themselves as individuals but
with their relation to what is by definition the just society. In fact the old
Gipsy is stating (though not probably with any intention of Pushkin's) the
cardinal point of the Anglo-Saxon political tradition: it is precisely for
myself that I want freedom, because I can be the only judge of what constitutes it for myself. It is not without irony that Catherine the Great
reversed the instruction in which she had stated – following Montesquieu
who had himself based it on the Anglo-Saxon tradition – that 'liberty is the
right to do whatever the law allows'.

Aleko himself: he brings to the revenge hero a new world of meaning by revealing that hero's very conventions and limitations.)

The relation of *The Cossacks* to *The Gipsies* is obvious enough, but Tolstoy's two great novels are as deeply related to Pushkin's dramatic investigation. We *are* what we take for granted; in becoming conscious of our needs we lose our instinctive social selves and the process may be tragedy or salvation. The complex structure of *Anna Karenina* depends on the equivocal balance of freedom and society, and the dependence of what the individual actively desires on his more profound, socially conditioned needs. Anna is isolated and destroyed by forces within her, and assumptions about the way she can live with Vronsky, that are recognisably akin to the 'pride' of Aleko. Both Pierre at the end of *War and Peace*, and Levin towards the end of *Anna Karenina*, appear as regenerated Alekos, discovering the proper nature of their unity with society; while the not wholly persuasive didacticism of the Karataev episode, or Levin's mowing with the peasants, seem to assert Tolstoy's determination to escape from the uncomfortable conclusion of the old Gipsy: 'you were not born for our way of life'.

Fate, the Greek *moira* much admired by Vyazemsky in the poem, is in fact a more conventional presence than the pregnant and subtle dramatic play on the idea of freedom; but it gives the structure a spare and classic symmetry. It is the formal statement of what is psychologically embodied in the poem's action.

> Теперь он вольный житель мира...
> И жил, не признавая власти
> Судьбы коварной и слепой;

Now he is a free dweller in the world...and he lived without acknowledging the power of blind and devious fate.

Aleko has virtually no character, and yet – ironically – it is as true for him as for Shakespeare's heroes that character is destiny. Disaster is brought about by his ignorance of himself and what he is capable of. And as Othello cries out, like a chorus on his own tragedy – 'Who can control his fate?' – so Pushkin places the particularity of his tale in the frame of generalised tragic commentary, joining the Gipsies to his hero and heroine in the universal lot of man.

> И всюду страсти роковые,
> И от судеб защиты нет.

And everywhere there are fatal passions, and from the fates there is no defence.

4

HISTORY AND THE HEROIC POEM

In the European literature of its time *The Gipsies* is a unique work, successfully dramatising and fining down a commonplace romantic form until it is taut with the pressure of idea. The ideas are not Pushkin's, they are part of the climate of his age, but nowhere else are they embodied in its art with such truth and assurance. What freedom means for the individual; what is the nature of the contract between the individual and society – these are problems about which the thought of the eighteenth and early nineteenth century had become increasingly self-conscious, but their exposition had taken a theoretical form. Wordsworth had failed to give the doctrines of Godwin dramatic life in *The Borderers*, and Godwin, like Rousseau himself, was in any case being left behind by the actualities of nineteenth-century social development. *The Gipsies* is above all a modern work, whose implications as a work of art are more prophetic than the ideas behind it: hence its inspiration for the Russian novel. To the ideas of freedom and of the individual's relation to society it adds a third, and for Russian literature the most potent of all – the alienation of the modern intellect, and its representative, from a society it can neither identify itself with, nor do without.

The alienation of Aleko, compared with the idealism of Schiller's and Goethe's heroes, is in some sense the result of his quasi-parodic status. Not only the dramatic economy of his presentation but his oblique relation to Byron's self-willed and brooding exiles leaves the impression of a colourless void, a cipher, one who – like Dostoevsky's Svidrigailov – is 'nothing in particular'. Byronism in reverse has not placed him but depersonalised him: in stripping him of all that is inessential Pushkin has left him, by a typically brilliant paradox of his art, with nothing but 'the superfluous'.

After this the next long narrative poem, *Poltava*, may seem a step backwards, and certainly seemed so to Pushkin's contemporaries. Romance, unparodied, is again in full flow, though now it is not the melodramatic travelogue of Byron but the 'storied romance' of

Scott. The poem does not exploit the weaknesses of romantic material and construct a brilliant variation on them. Instead it takes all the ingredients of the historical romance soberly and seriously, pares them down and rearranges their proportions to create a remarkable specimen of an otherwise undistinguished genre.

During the four years since *The Gipsies* Pushkin had been intermittently at work on *Evgeny Onegin*, but he had also set himself to consider the state of the Russian drama and to plan a model which he hoped might assist its future development. He had read a good deal of history, especially Voltaire and Karamzin; he had read Shakespeare with increasing absorption, and the result of these studies is as evident in *Poltava* as it is in *Boris Godunov*. Above all he had come to feel that fascination with the life and times of Peter the Great which was to retain its hold on him for the rest of his creative life. In the figure of Peter Pushkin saw the source of Russia's destiny and historical personality, the hand that was as heavy in the present as in his own lifetime, and whose immense achievement had nourished the pride of national culture and consciousness. For Pushkin, as for his contemporaries, Peter was still very much alive.

Peter's triumph at Poltava, not only over a foreign invader but over internal separatism and revolt, was as stirring a subject as the victory over Napoleon, with which it was freely compared. It was much more than a source of historical gratification: like most recent events in Russian history it has political implications for the present time. Views on contemporary issues could be expressed in poetry by means of events in the past; the censorship made the historical poem a possible vehicle for discreet propaganda. 'The history of a people belongs to the poet', Pushkin wrote to Gnedich in 1825, and went on to answer the lament of the translator of Homer that 'the shade of Svyatoslav is wandering yet unsung', by pointing out that the same was true of many other legendary Russian heroes. It is a tongue-in-cheek reply: Pushkin clearly had no intention of resuming *Vadim* or celebrating the shadowy heroes of the distant past. The history of the people belonged to the poet who could use it not as a fund of patriotic archaism but as a reality coterminous with the present.

Not that he wished to allegorise the present through the medium of the past. This would not be compatible with the 'dispassion' which – while he was working on *Boris Godunov* – he emphasised as the chief virtue of the historical dramatist. He perceived it in

Shakespeare. Did he realise the sense in which Shakespeare, in the English history plays, was endorsing the Tudor view of the state? It seems unlikely, though *Boris Godunov* suggests that Pushkin had understood Shakespeare's dramatic handling of the political counter-claims of national security and the dynastic principle. But more important were the similarities between the Shakespearean epoch and contemporary Russia. A growing national self-aware-ness, founded on recent victories and the emergence of the nation on the European scene; a vogue for the national past, as intro-ducing – and exemplifying – a present full of insecurity; problems of succession, threatened rebellion, an oppressed and often mu-tinous peasantry; a censorship – these things were common to Shakespeare's England and Pushkin's Russia.[1]

In contemporary England the case was different. Of course society never feels secure; change and catastrophe always appear imminent, and the England of 1825 was no exception. But literary fashion responded differently in an advanced and rapidly in-dustrialising society, and the typical literary use of the past in Post-Napoleonic Europe was as an escape from the present. The sub-title of *Waverley*: ''Tis Sixty Years Since' implied not the closeness of the past but its comfortably nostalgic distance. The Stuart rebellion had left the dynasty of the Georges undisturbed: in retrospect its disturbance seemed out of the question, and Bonny Prince Charlie not a dangerous portent, a prototype of today's or tomorrow's rebel, but a figure of pure Romance, of a chivalry whose disappearance could be regretted all the more in literature because it seemed no longer possible or relevant in modern society. The vulgar appeal of Scott, his predecessors and imitators, is summed up pretty fairly by Mrs Skewton in *Dombey and Son*.

'"Those darling bygone times, Mr Carker...with their delicious fortresses and their dear old dungeons, and their delightful places of torture, and their romantic vengeances, and their picturesque assaults and sieges, and everything that makes life truly charming! How dreadfully we have degenerated!"

'"Yes, we have fallen off deplorably", said Mr Carker.'

The irony of Dickens is directed to the unspoken fact that Mr Dom-bey's house *is* a dungeon, and the setting of his courtship of Edith

---

[1] Listening to a recitation of Pasternak's version of Shakespeare's Sonnets, a Soviet audience showed their awareness of this resemblance by repeated and pointed encores for Sonnet 66, with its line: 'and art made tongue-tied by authority'.

Skewton indeed 'a place of torture' for her. But historical romanticism appeals to any age of disintegrated industrial and urban growth from which the past seems to have vanished – indeed its appeal is still with us today. Pushkin's Russia was not like this: the past was still with it, politically and economically. The Russia of Nicholas I was in fact even closer to Petrine Russia than Shakespeare's England had been to the England of the late Middle Ages. And for Pushkin as for Shakespeare the past could afford powerful precedents. *Boris Godunov* is in many ways a historical play in Mrs Skewton's sense of the picturesque, and its theme returns to the epoch of old Muscovy, before the Romanovs came to power, an epoch cut off from the continuing political significance of Petrine and Imperial Russia. None the less the theme of a disputed succession was still dynamite, and the play's ending was modified on the direct order of a Tsar who had himself been involved in one. The soldiers on the Senate Square in Petersburg, who had obediently shouted that day of 14 December for 'Constantine and Constitution' had behaved like the Moscow populace at the end of *Boris Godunov*, who at the command of their betters hailed the pretender Dimitri as the new Tsar. Modification by censorship produced the now famous ending: 'The people are silent' – the crowd invested, by the irony of an Imperial command, with a discrimination, or at least a scepticism, which Pushkin's original version denied them.

Shakespeare would have enjoyed the joke. Pushkin probably picked up from him the dramatic presentation of a crowd's reactions; and he too had certainly experienced the unaccommodating demands of the great and their dangerous favours. We know that in the last years of Elizabeth's reign on the night before Essex's attempted *coup d'état*, his friend and fellow-conspirator the Earl of Southampton ordered that Shakespeare's company, who were under his patronage, should put on the play of *Richard II*. It was hoped that Londoners might take the hint from this revival (the play was already old and the company was bribed against the risk of a poor attendance) and acquiesce in the comparable deposition of a reigning monarch. When the plot failed their patron went to the Tower and the actors were in serious trouble, though they seem to have escaped without punishment; while at the trial the Lord Chief Justice repeatedly exclaimed – in reply to the plea of Essex that no threat was intended to the Queen's person if she were deposed – 'How long lived Richard II?'

Certainly neither *Poltava* nor *Boris Godunov* could be or was taken as this kind of object lesson in history, but rebellion is the background of each, as it is of Pushkin's prose tale, *The Captain's Daughter*. In all of them Pushkin is more interested in the psychology and personality of the rebel than in the divine and legal status of revolt, the aspect that probably had the greatest appeal for an Elizabethan audience. And the individual is studied with dispassion. Though he is seen *cherez istoriyu* (in his historical setting), Mazepa comes close to us as a human being, Dimitri and Pugachev still closer. Yet they are not, like Cassius and Macbeth, timeless subverters of order and seekers after power – they have a special significance for Russia and Russian history. None of them is safely encapsulated in a past to which there is no return. It is a curious feature of the Elizabethan historical play that even in its short span of popularity we can see history becoming romance. As the conditions and possibilities of power changed, after James I's peaceful accession, the old-fashioned rebel lost his contemporary charisma and fell out of history into popular sentiment. He is no longer right or wrong in terms of state and commonweal. The rebel of Ford's *Perkin Warbeck*, one of the last history plays of the period, has acquired the attributes of a Bonny Prince Charlie. He has no more in common with Shakespeare's Hotspur and Bolingbroke than Robin Hood has with Pugachev or Stenka Razin.[1]

Heroes do not fall so easily out of Russian history in this way, and certainly not in Pushkin's work. 'Not in vain', says Gukovsky, 'did Pushkin call his journal *Sovremennik* (*The Contemporary*). Usually one supposes a division between the past ('history') and the present ('politics'). Pushkin wanted to see them both together and in the same way.' For Gukovsky, Pushkinian 'realism' in narrative poetry means a process of seeing the past by means of the present and *vice versa*. Instead of ''Tis Sixty Years Since', we have both in *Poltava* and *The Bronze Horseman* the explosively vigorous

---

[1] In his *byliny*-type poem, *Songs of Stenka Razin*, Pushkin treats him as a legendary hero rather than a political portent; but in *Table Talk* (VIII, 103), an anecdote links him with both the founder Peter and the rebel Pugachev, who when a prisoner in Moscow had told the tale of Peter, on a campaign in the south, ordering the funeral mound of Stenka Razin to be opened, in order that he might gaze on the remains. Pushkin points out that Stenka Razin was in fact quartered and burnt in Moscow, but adds that this does not make Pugachev's telling of the old tradition any less significant, for the grave of Stenka Razin had become a legendary inspiration to revolt and class war. In November 1824 Pushkin wrote to his brother from Mikhailovskoye for 'the historical, dry information about Stenka Razin'.

phrase *proshlo sto let* (a hundred years went by) – the century since
Peter founded his capital and defeated the King of Sweden's
invasion – and this hundred years does not carry poet and reader
back into the past but seems to project them forward into the
future, a future that has not yet arrived.

Pushkin does not however use history as many of his contemporaries did – as Byron, for example, had done in *Marino Faliero*,
where the executed Doge becomes an early champion of the
liberties of the people and, inevitably, a projection of one of
Byron's images of himself. In his poem *Voynarovsky* Ryleev
presented Mazepa as an honourable and patriotic leader, seeking
to preserve the Ukraine from the despotic centralism of Peter, and
tragically compelled to realise his aim through the aid of a foreign
interventionist. Ryleev, an honourable man and a leading political
liberal, was hanged for his part in the Decembrist conspiracy. His
heroes naturally have some of his own features, and they move us
for reasons unconnected with the quality of the poem. For *Voynarovsky* has the worst of both worlds: in using Mazepa for political
ends it romanticises him as well, presenting a leader who is relevant
to the cause of contemporary revolt at the cost of misrepresenting
what history knows about the real nature of the Ukrainian Hetman.
As a sympathetic friend of Ryleev Pushkin admired *Voynarovsky*,
and noted that an incident from it suggested the plot for his own
Poltava. But he felt that both Byron and Ryleev had painted a
false picture of the historical Mazepa – Byron because he had based
his poem on a paragraph out of Voltaire's *History of Charles XII*.

The idea suggested to Pushkin was the tragic fate of Mazepa's
opponent Kochubey, his wife driven mad by their daughter's
infatuation for their political enemy. It is as melodramatic a theme
as Byron's poetic treatment of the apocryphal nightmare of
Mazepa's youth, bound to a wild horse by the jealous husband of
the Polish noblewoman he had loved. Byron's tale is told by the old
Mazepa to Charles after their defeat at the battle of Poltava, and
without any mention of the historical and biographical background
which Pushkin had carefully studied. Both begin with the idea of
'wild tale', but where Byron's had nothing more to offer, Pushkin's
can expand into the sober dimension of historical narrative. Some
years earlier, in 1821, he had begun a *poema*, *The Robber Brothers*,
suggested, as he told Vyazemsky in a letter, by an episode during
his stay at Ekaterinoslav. 'Two bandits, chained together, swam
across the Dnieper and escaped. Their resting on the little island,

and the drowning of one of the guards, was not my invention.'
Pushkin planned a 'wild tale' of southern Russia on this basis, with
robber bands and Volga merchants, madness, remorse, and
appropriate heroines. Pushkin thought well of the part he wrote, in
which the escape is rapidly and effectively described, but it proved
harder to elude the sensibility of Byron than his melodrama: a
remorseful bandit, urged by his dying brother to spare the aged, is
a *motif* to wring the heart in a way that Pushkin normally avoided.
'Certain verses', he observed wryly to Vyazemsky, 'remind one of
the translation of *The Prisoner of Chillon*. That is my misfortune –
I coincided with Zhukovsky accidentally.' The gentle Zhukovsky,
who did not care for the demonic side of Byron, had been much
moved by *The Prisoner of Chillon* and had made an excellent version of it. But to linger on such a situation was unnatural to
Pushkin. Mazepa's apocryphal ordeal, like that of the prisoner of
Chillon, could have been dealt with by him in a few pregnant lines:
to 'spell it out' for a whole poem would have been an indulgence.

Byron prided himself on his historical accuracy and always
preferred, as he said, fact to fiction. Some of his subjects, notably
the Venetian, are indeed well documented, and in his notes to the
poems he enjoyed pointing out the inaccuracies of other writers,
but *Parisina* (which Pushkin admired) has the history of what
really happened in the notes, and Byron's improvement on it in
the text. It is clear from the chroniclers that the Duke and his
natural son, whom he executed for adultery with his wife Parisina,
were very different in life from the standard Byronic figures they
become. But to distinguish one character from another is essential to
Pushkin's realism; there is no standard Pushkinian character as
there is a Byronic one, and *Poltava* is his first attempt in a *poema* to
study his characters as he had studied them three years before,
under Shakespeare's inspiration, in the drama of *Boris Godunov*.

The formula of the historical romantic poem is not Byron's but
Scott's, and in the Introduction to *Marmion* (1808) it is justified
with becoming modesty.

The present story turns upon the private adventures of a fictitious
character; but it is called *A Tale of Flodden Field*, because the hero's fate
is connected with that memorable defeat, and the causes which led to it.
The design of the Author was, if possible, to apprise his readers, at the
outset, of the date of his story, and to prepare them for the manners of
the age in which it is laid. Any historical narrative, far more an attempt
at epic composition, exceeding his plan of a romantic tale...

What makes *Marmion*, against all odds, still an impressive poem, is Scott's almost mystical enthusiasm for the past and a fine imagination which directly reflects the fineness of his nature, and which is quite missing in Byron. Scott's idea of conjuring up the past 'in the course of an interesting story' rests on a sound traditional basis. Dryden, he notes, planned to introduce supernatural machinery into an epic tale of Arthur and the Saxons, or Edward the Black Prince.

> The mightiest chiefs of British song
> Scorn'd not such legends to prolong:
> They gleam through Spenser's elfin dream,
> And mix in Milton's heavenly theme;
> And Dryden, in immortal strain,
> Had raised the Table Round again,
> But that a ribald king and court
> Bade him toil on, to make them sport.

Marmion shows how heavy a weight of tradition both inspired and embarrassed the romantic revival, for 'revival' often meant in practice the hopeful heaping together, in one large libertarian mixture, of every tradition and kind in the national poetry. The aim was liberation, but in the event poetic narrative is bowed beneath a load of heterogeneous material from the past.

No such load existed for Pushkin. He could refine out the promising elements as European poets could not – almost unconsciously they felt compression and cutting to be aspects of a sterile discipline. Nor was he concerned to 'prepare' his readers for 'the manners of a past age'. His technique in *Poltava* is not to mix the elements of romance and heroic history but carefully to compartmentalise them. There is a danger, clearly, that one will show up the other and that history will discredit romance as (in the view of some of his contemporaries) the accurate study of Circassian life revealed the insubstantial nature of the Captive, or that of the Gipsies, Aleko's. Pushkin avoids this by making his private characters in *Poltava* as convincing as the public ones – as Gukovsky says, they are not 'lyric emanations but independent strengths and objective realities'. Whereas Scott's heroine might be one of his own female readers taken on a trip to the past (the easy-going Scott even allows his Lady Clara to be present at the Battle of Flodden), Pushkin's Mariya belongs to her environment. Her infatuation with the aged Mazepa is not romantically typical but peculiar, almost monstrous; it isolates her in its own reality.

Isolated thus, she is ignorant of everything else in the poem, knowing and caring as little of what is happening as an actual girl of her historical situation would have done, and this separates her romance with Mazepa from what he is doing in the Ukraine. When the two themes meet she vanishes, and it is a misfortune that Pushkin succumbed to the demands of romantic atmosphere and brought her back at the end of the poem, where she acquires that quasi-supernatural freedom of action enjoyed by heroines of the period, who suddenly pop up, in wilderness or ruin, to confront their betrayers with mad laughter. Her mother receives this privilege earlier on, when she materialises before her daughter on the eve of her husband's execution and pleads with her to intercede with Mazepa and save him. But this is dramatically justified, for Mariya's stupefied exclamation '*Kakoy otets? Kakaya kazn?*' ('What father? What execution?') is the last touch, and the best, in the build-up of the kind of heroine she should be. Her words are as pregnant, as psychologically revealing, as – in Racine's *Andromaque* – Hermione's cry to Oreste, whom she has ordered to kill the man she loves: '*Qui te l'a dit?*' But after this the tension collapses and Mariya becomes merely a period heroine.

> Боже, боже!...
> Сегодня! – бедный мой отец!
> И дева падает на ложе,
> Как хладный падает мертвец.

God, God!... Today! My poor father! And the girl fell back on the couch as a cold corpse falls. (iv, 251.)

Slonimsky observes that Pushkin's other heroines do not carry on in this way, and as if making up for the flattest lines in the poem Pushkin hurries on to a remarkable description of the beheading of Kochubey, Mariya's father.

> Пестреют шапки. Копья блещут.
> Бьют в бубны. Скачут сердюки.
> В строях равняются полки.
> Толпы кипят. Сердца трепещут.
> Дорога, как змеиный хвост,
> Полна народу, шевелится.
> Средь поля роковой намост.
> На нем гуляет, веселится
> Палач и алчно жертвы ждет:
> То в руки белые берет,
> Играючи, топор тяжелый,
> То шутит с чернию веселой.

PUSHKIN

В гремучий говор всё слилось:
Крик женский, брань, и смех, и ропот.
Вдруг восклицанье раздалось
И смолкло всё.

Hats are motley. Lances shine. Drums beat. Horsemen canter. Regiments are ranged in ranks. Crowds seethe. Hearts beat fast. The road, filled with people, heaves like a serpent's tail. In the field appears the fatal scaffold. Strolling upon it, the executioner, animated, awaits with greed his sacrificial victims. In his white hands he grasps and plays with the heavy axe, jesting with the excited mob. All sounds mingle with a deep hubbub: women's cries, curses, laughter, and muttering. Suddenly there is an exclamation, and then everyone is silent.

The change is absolute. We have one prolonged and Shakespearean image of a given historical moment, a *tour de force* as sudden and startling as the gentleman's account in Henry VIII of the crowd at the coronation of Anne Boleyn.

> Believe me, sir, she is the goodliest woman
> That ever lay by man: which when the people
> Had the full view of, such a noise arose
> As the shrouds make at sea in a stiff tempest,
> As loud, and to as many tunes: hats, cloaks,
> Doublets, I think, flew up; and had their faces
> Been loose, this day they had been lost. Such joy
> I never saw before. Great-bellied women,
> That had not half a week to go, like rams,
> In the old time of war, would shake the press
> And make 'em reel before 'em. No man living
> Could say *This is my wife* there: all were woven
> So strangely in one piece.

Style could not be more different – the genius of each language showing its paces under a master hand – but the animation of a crowd at the prospect of a great man's death and of a royal birth are conveyed alike in the metaphor of explosive and organic movement. Individuality disappears, uniting Shakespeare's crowd in a sea of undifferentiated fertility, while the road in Pushkin's account 'stirs' (*shevelitsya*), an image proleptically joining the coiling of the crowd to the spasms of a dead body.

The life of language here has one parallel in Byron, though both Pushkin's and Ryleev's descriptions are certainly derived from *Parisina*. Writing to Vyazemsky in 1825, Pushkin says Ryleev 'has in his poem a hangman, with rolled-up sleeves, for whom I

would give a great deal'. It was a touch that echoed Byron's in
Parisina:

> The headsman with his bare arm ready,
> That the blow may be both swift and steady,
> Feels if the axe be sharp and true
> Since he set its edge anew:
> While the crowd in a speechless circle gather
> To see the son fall by the doom of the father!

Byron's account is crudely graphic and demonstrative; his indifference and insensitivity to the language appears not so much in
the self-cancelling rhymes as in the fact that even the word *bare*
has had its linguistic impact here nullified by a cliché used in the
previous couplet:

> Kneeling on the bare cold ground
> With the block before and the guards around.

Even Mariya's mad scene is an improvement on Parisina's –

> It was a woman's shriek – and ne'er
> In madlier accents rose despair

– and the wolf's head with which Mariya claims she has been
deceived and shown as her father's is a stroke not so much of
gothic horror as of Shakespearean grotesque.

Book II of *Poltava* should have ended with the two women
reaching the field after the execution is over.

> «Уж поздно». – кто-то им сказал
> И в поле перстом указал.
> Там роковой намост ломали,
> Молился в черных ризах поп,
> И на телегу подымали
> Два казака дубовый гроб.

'It's over', someone told them, pointing to the field. The fatal scaffold
was being dismantled and a priest was praying in his black vestments,
while two Cossacks were lifting an oaken coffin into a cart.

As it is, Mazepa's reaction on finding Mariya has vanished is
dangerously close to that of Girey in *The Fountain of Bakhchisarai*,
and the search party's spectacular foray to find her only emphasises
the implausibility of her disappearance.

It is possible that Pushkin might have cut out the passage,
'severing the connections' as ruthlessly as he had done in *The

Gipsies and as he was to do in *The Bronze Horseman*. Had he also cut out Mariya's reappearance she would have been as disciplined a heroine as Zemphira, who in the first draft of *The Gipsies* was almost as passionately fluent as the Circassian maid. (Pushkin had also cut a long reverie of Aleko over their sleeping child, leaving only the bare account of the routine of their two years together; while the eloquence of their original meeting was shortened into her laconic comment that he is hers; that it is late; that she is tired.) Instead of a 'spiritual relationship' the omissions imply one that is immediate and animal, with none of the elevated communication of romantic lovers. The relation of Mariya and Mazepa is far more dramatic but it is equally unelevated; and it would have been still more effective if Pushkin had left to the imagination Mariya's grief and madness over the death of her father.

Pushkin wrote *Poltava* in a fortnight, an astonishingly short time even by his standards, and he appears not to have submitted it to his usual protracted and rigorous process of revision. He may in any case have felt that for a poem of this kind too much pruning was not in place. Its failure with the reading public may have been due to the absence of mellifluous and romantic dream that had made *The Fountain of Bakhchisarai* so popular; but the vogue for narrative poems was in any case dying out, and *Poltava* – looking back as it did to Scott's *Marmion* written twenty years before – lacked appeal to the younger reader for whom the genre was already old-fashioned.

Pushkin's enemies, like the journalist Nadezhdin, attacked the poem in order to attack Pushkin himself; but even sympathisers were dubious, and Kireevsky, in an article which Pushkin himself thought perceptive, drew attention to the division between the heroic and the romantic themes.[1] I have suggested that if we are aware of the models Pushkin chose, and perceive what he made of them, this division is not a weakness, for both themes can enhance each other and acquire their own separate reality, as do the private and public scenes in a Shakespeare history. The real crack in the poem is perhaps not between history and romance but between two kinds of romance – which both Scott and Byron habitually mix – the modern melodrama and the traditional tragic ballad. The latter should work by distance: its heroine should be seen clearly but from far off, and Pushkin correctly and beautifully employs one of its devices in the last lines of the poem.

---

[1] *The Moscow Messenger*, 1828.

Лишь порою
Слепой украинский певец,
Когда в селе перед народом
Он песни гетмана бренчит,
О грешной деве мимоходом
Казачкам юным говорит.

Only the blind Ukrainian bard, at times when he plays the hetman's
songs before the village people, recalls in passing to the young Cossacks
the name of the erring girl.

That frames Mariya, and is proper to our ignorance of the girl who,
like a sleepwalker, brings disgrace upon her father without knowing
or caring until it is too late. As in a ballad there should be no
explanation; her relations with parents and lover should be guessed
at, not known; while her mother, too, should properly be seen like
the old wife in a ballad, scheming in the bedchamber and urging
her husband to avenge the wrong.] But Pushkin also makes us
see mother and daughter through the painfully powerful lens
of modern melodrama. In *Parisina* Byron had mixed the two
modes in the same way, but with much less taste. We are told
'Parisina's fate lies hid, like dust beneath the coffin lid' with a
dozen lines of further speculation, but the notes record that she
was executed along with her lover: the resort to distance and
mystery is merely a cynical invitation to enjoy fact and fancy side
by side.

Belinsky, we must remember, thought Mariya an admirable
character, more energetically *narodnaya* even than Tatyana in
Evgeny Onegin, and there is nothing romantically languorous about
her passion for the old hetman and her possessive jealousy. Does
Mazepa return her feelings? We are not told directly. He is *mrachny*,
obscure and devious, deep-set in guile. He has something of the
depth of a Shakespeare portrait – to Belinsky the poem smelt of
the Renaissance – and he also suggests qualities which we shall
find in their proper naturalistic setting in Pushkin's creation of
Pugachev. We can see why he is as dangerous as a force of nature,
and why he inspires devotion. He can be all things to all men the
more effectively because even his calculation has something irresponsible about it; his collectedness hides a coiled spring of impulse
and unreason. He schemes – 'he does not decide in a hurry what
can and what can't be done' – and yet the exercise of power is not
for him a process of cold logic. Pushkin analyses these contradictions in a passage of fine rhetorical concentration.

PUSHKIN

Как добродушно на пирах,
Со старцами старик болтливый,
Жалеет он о прошлых днях,
Свободу славит с своевольным,
Поносит власти с недовольным,
С ожесточенным слезы льет,
С глупцом разумну речь ведет!
Не многим, может быть, известно,
Что дух его неукротим,
Что рад и честно и бесчестно
Вредить он недругам своим;
Что ни единой он обиды
С тех пор как жив не забывал,
Что далеко преступны виды
Старик надменный простирал;
Что он не ведает святыни,
Что он не помнит благостыни,
Что он не любит ничего,
Что кровь готов он лить, как воду,
Что презирает он свободу,
Что нет отчизны для него.

Expansive among the greybeards at table, how piously that old man
sighs for the good old days; how he praises freedom with the licentious,
insults authority with the discontented, sheds tears with the embittered,
speaks sagely with the fool! To few, perhaps, is it known how indomitable
is his temper, with what joy he gets even with an enemy by fair means or
foul; that since he lived he has never forgotten a single insult, that the
arrogant old man has projected far and wide his criminal designs; that
nothing is sacred to him; that he remembers no kindnesses; that he
loves nothing, that he is ready to spill blood like water; that he despises
freedom; that he has no country of his own.

Mazepa has no country and freedom means nothing to him: he
cannot love. His self is in the part he plays; his reality in his
wrongs and his ability to avenge them.

Pushkin referred critics who objected that Mariya's love for
Mazepa was implausible and unnatural to Desdemona and her
'blackamoor'. *Boris Godunov* shows how he had studied Shakespeare's dramatic method, and *Andzhelo* and the *Little Tragedies* show
his deep interest in Shakespearean portraiture, an interest also
seen in *Poltava*. The reference to *Othello* is significant. It is only a
guess, certainly, but the heroic atmosphere of the play, and the
dramatic contrast between its two great protagonists, might have
entered Pushkin's mind. It is the tragedy of Othello to play a part
unsuited to him: he should lead us into 'the stately tent of war'

not to an intrigue in a marriage chamber; and yet the tented field is always in the background of the action and the decisions proper to it fatally determine the domestic issue. *Poltava* too makes war the background of love, and though the two have little dramatic interplay the dark figure of Mazepa is set against the brilliant Peter, duped by Mazepa as Othello by Iago. Duped, Peter betrays his loyal servants and the tragic consequence is the death of Iskra and Kochubey. It is an aspect of Pushkin's separations that the political failure of Peter, which resulted in the execution of the loyal pair and the triumph of Mazepa's plot in the Ukraine, does not diminish the glory of his victory and his god-like stature on the field of Poltava; yet it remains a shadow in the poem, a question mark in blood which suggests the equivocal relationship of the Tsar and his antagonist, not on the battlefield but in the dark background of power and intrigue.

In *Moy Pushkin* Bryusov devotes a chapter to the chastisement of a historian who had impugned Pushkin's historical principles in his account of Pugachev's rebellion, and criticised them for attaching too much importance to the influence of individuals on events, at the expense of historical necessity.[1] As we shall see, in *The Bronze Horseman* and in *Boris Godunov* Pushkin does indeed convey this necessity, but his sense of history, like Shakespeare's, is also concerned with men, and great men. Even Tolstoy contradicts his own theories about the forces that move nations and create history by the role that his imagination admits to such figures as Napoleon and Kutuzov. It seems clear that some periods of history are more determined than others, and also that the doctrine of necessity is never incompatible, even on the crudest *a priori* grounds, with the motives of remarkable individuals who may or may not have been the instruments of historical inevitability.[2]

Great art, in any event, takes men as the measure of the historical process, and sees public consequences in their private weaknesses and desires; the motivation of Kochubey and Mazepa is as psychologically revealing as that of Brutus and Cassius. Kochubey is Mazepa's old friend and comrade; he does not denounce him to the

---

[1] Professor Firsov, of the University of Kazan. The chapter in Bryusov's study is entitled 'Pushkin before the court of a learned historian', and is prefaced with a quotation from Ostrovsky: 'To judge me is to get me wrong.' V. Bryusov, *Moy Pushkin*, ed. N. K. Piksanov (Moscow–Leningrad 1929).

[2] The two doctrines were combined by P. L. Lavrov in his *Historical Letters* (1870), which strongly asserted the role of the individual in hastening the march of history, and were used as a text and justification by the terrorists.

Tsar out of public spirit but to revenge the disgrace of his daughter, and he finds a particular satisfaction in the hope that Mazepa will suffer at the hands of the public executioner in Moscow for the private wrong he has done. To gain one's ends indirectly is the supreme reward of power politics, and when the plot miscarries the final bitterness of Kochubey is to find himself in the position in which he hoped to place Mazepa. The undeclared motive behind the true denunciation has only strengthened the hetman's position, and Kochubey must die as an apparent traitor, without a chance of clearing his name and with his daughter's shame (as he feels it) still unavenged.

Despite his motives Kochubey in his last hours has a nobility denied to Mazepa, whose motives, like Iago's, lack any spontaneity of simple passion. On the night before the battle he tells his henchman Orlik the reason for his hatred of Peter – the quarrel long ago in Astrakhan when Peter had seized him by his moustaches. Pushkin says that what began as a poetic celebration of a great military victory was the unrelated family tragedy of Kochubey, and we may suspect that he was equally struck by the incongruous beginnings of the confrontation between Mazepa and the Tsar. He quoted with approval Pascal's remark that the history of the world might have been different if Cleopatra's nose had been shorter. Upon such things the fate of kingdoms – if not of historical necessity – may hang. Critics professed to find the use of the word *moustaches* low and ridiculous in a heroic context, and Pushkin replied, straight-faced, that for a Pole or Little Russian to have his moustaches pulled was as deadly an insult as tugging a Muscovite by his beard (he did not mention Peter's decree against beards). In fact he removes any real suggestion of the trivial by the subtlety with which he compounds Mazepa's psychology. His motives and their declaration, like Iago's, give the impression of having been thought up, cherished: they are a part of his general deviousness and the self-exculpation that makes him persuade Mariya – when he has already decided her father must die – into a confession that his life is dearer to her than her father's.

Mazepa's vengefulness may come from Byron where, like everything else in *Mazeppa*, it is spectacular and poetic. There is no reason to doubt Pushkin's admiration ('he creates a row of pictures – that's all – but what ardent creation! What a broad and stirring brush!') and he wished for that reason to distinguish his own poem from Byron's. To the imputation that he had not called it *Mazepa* in order to avoid comparisons, he replied that he had a different reason which was revealed in his choice – in English – of the Byronic epigraph.

> The power and glory of the war,
> Faithless as their vain votaries, men,
> Had passed to the triumphant Czar.

Whereas Byron described an apocryphal incident in Mazepa's youth, his poem would show the 'power and glory of the war' that was the climax of a historical career. Though many connections are cut we can see where they lead, and a single simile conveys the cosmopolite European forces against which Peter's national struggle is marshalled. Openly proclaiming himself leader of the insurgent Ukraine, Mazepa becomes young again.

> Согбенный тяжко жизнью старой,
> Так оный хитрый кардинал,
> Венчавшись римскою тиарой,
> И прям, и здрав, и молод стал.

Bowed down beneath a weight of years, like that cunning cardinal elevated to the Pope's tiara he grew erect, vigorous and young again.

With the image Mazepa suddenly appears to us in a different light, as he appeared to Moscow and to Peter – the embodiment of all things foreign and distrusted: Catholics, Jesuits, Poles. By contrast Peter is imaged not only as the *polubog* (half-god) but as the *pakhar* (ploughman); not – a point on which Soviet critics lay special emphasis – the autocrat, but the patriarchal leader and father figure. Mazepa is cut off from nation and history, disillusioned in his ally Charles and yet compelled to exile with that 'warlike wanderer' and 'mad hero' (*geroy bezumny*), phrases which connect the Swedish king with the extravagant world of romance, with Ariosto and Tom o' Bedlam.

Lyricism, too, does not exist for its own picturesque sake but as a part of the same linkage of revealing imagery.

> Тиха украинская ночь.
> Прозрачно небо. Звезды блещут.
> Своей дремоты превозмочь
> Не хочет воздух. Чуть трепещут
> Сребристых тополей листы.

Silent is the Ukrainian night. Clear is the sky. The stars shine. The air has no will to master its own drowsiness. The leaves of the silvery poplars hardly stir.

These phrases of tranquil beauty are twice repeated: the night and stars seen by the condemned Kochubey from his prison cell, and then by Mazepa as he walks in his garden outside.

> Тиха украинская ночь.
> Прозрачно небо. Звезды блещут.
> Своей дремоты превозмочь
> Не хочет воздух. Чуть трепещут
> Сребристых тополей листы.
> Но мрачны странные мечты
> В душе Мазепы: звезды ночи,
> Как обвинительные очи,
> За ним насмешливо глядят.
> И тополи, стеснившись в ряд,
> Качая тихо головою,
> Как судьи, шепчут меж собою.
> И летней, теплой ночи тьма
> Душна, как черная тюрьма.

Silent is the Ukrainian night. Clear is the sky. The stars shine. The air has no will to master its own drowsiness. The leaves of the silvery poplars hardly stir. But there are dark strange thoughts in Mazepa's mind; the night stars, like accusing eyes, gaze on him with mockery, and the poplars, ranged in a row, softly sway their heads, like judges whispering among themselves. And the darkness of the warm summer night is oppressive as a black dungeon.

Night, stars, and trees are seen by Kochubey for the last time; they are seen in and for themselves, objects of total tranquillity. But for Mazepa they are voluble and alive, a part of his own vigilant and unquiet consciousness. The trees are like a tribunal, and the open summer night a stifling prison. Like Clarence and Macbeth he sees nature populated by accusing spirits and symbols of judgement.

Imagery exerts a dramatic leverage throughout the action of *Poltava*, but its operation is objective and formal: the characters do not have the acoustic individuality which we can detect even in the spare dialogue of *The Gipsies*. There we can hear the voice of Aleko dissociating himself from the Gipsies' permissiveness – the tone of '*Ya ne takov*' ('I am not that kind of man') catches the sullen conviction of his personal right to jealousy and revenge – while a simple and unselfconscious resignation is in the old man's voice as he describes his desertion by Zemphira's mother.

> Тоскуя, плакала Земфира,
> И я заплакал!...

Pining, Zemphira wept, and I wept too!

The spoken drama of Poltava is developed in appropriately impersonal tones; in Kochubey's vindictive monologue, in Mazepa's last formal utterance on the eve of battle, in the blank incomprehension of Mariya's '*Kakoy otets?*' ('What father?'), most of all in Peter's sudden cry on the field of Poltava '*Za delo, s bogom!*' ('To the business, with God's aid!'). In this brief and rapid sweep of history Pushkin is right not to bring us close enough to hear his characters' voices. He has not the leisure that Shakespeare has in his histories to produce the authenticity of irrelevance, the confidence of real actors on the stage impersonating kings, queens and clowns. He may possibly have noted (for Pichot's translation conveys something of it) Byron's spirited but not wholly successful attempt to give a voice to his Mazeppa –

> I think 'twas in my twentieth spring –
> Ay, 'twas – when Casimir was king –
> John Casimir – I was his page...

a voice to convey the garrulous recollections of the old man, which send Charles to sleep, and which the actual narration of 'the wild tale' has to set aside in favour of its 'row of pictures', to resume at moments with un unavoided incongruity. The historical narrative of *Poltava* is not brought close, in the painstaking romantic fashion, but distanced; and its figures are all the more meaningful historically because they are not dressed out in the attempted intimacy of local colour.

The battle is the set piece and climax of *Poltava*, and yet the best of the poem is over before it. A battle scene does not suit Pushkin's instinct for precision. The duel between Onegin and Lensky in *Evgeny Onegin* can be seen in every detail and followed in the exactest sequence; but a panorama of bayonets, regiments and cannon smoke allows no opportunity for the accuracy that follows events each moment viewed with the eye. Stendhal observed that since poetry must generalise it cannot describe what really happens in a battle, which is seen by a number of excited and isolated eyewitnesses. Homer would have agreed, for he recounts only single combats. Shakespeare too may have felt the same, for his memorable battle sequences are always told by such a witness, ranging from the rhetoric of the sergeant in *Macbeth* to the astonishing description of a counter-attack in *Cymbeline*, a metrical *tour de force* that conveys the actual mix-up in all its strenuous irrationality. Pushkin's generalisations do a conventional job, in a mode in which convention is at a disadvantage.

Швед, русский – колет, рубит, режет.
Бой барабанный, клики, скрежет,
Гром пушек, топот, ржанье, стон,
И смерть и ад со всех сторон.

Swede and Russian stab, hack and cut. Drum-beats, yells, grinding of teeth, the boom of cannon, hoof-beats, neighing, groans; and death and hell on every side.

Slonimsky notes that Pushkin first wrote

Гром пушек, топот, ярый стон –
И ад и смерть со всех сторон...

The boom of cannon, hoof-beats, furious groans; and hell and death on every side...

and observes how the change improves the movement. Yet in such a context the sound, instead of echoing the sense, serves to deprive it still further of meaning. We can see the same thing happening in Chaucer as in Scott, drawn from a whole tradition of battle scenery.

> Up springen speres twenty foot on highte;
> Out goon the swerdes as the silver brighte,
> The helmes they to-hewen and to-shrede;
> Out brest the blode, with sterne stremes rede.
>
> (*The Knight's Tale*)

> The stubborn spear-men still made good
> Their dark impenetrable wood,
> Each stepping where his comrade stood
> The instant that he fell.   (*Marmion*)

In such cases the poetic art removes actuality to the level of incantation: not vision but excitement is intended, and this is good for romance but less good for the heroic, and still less for that distinguishing accuracy which is native to Pushkin and from which the Russian novel learnt its business. Poltava is no Borodino. But it is the finest example of a battle piece in Russian poetic style before prose takes over.

Though Pushkin's descriptions may be standard his organisation of them is not. He divides the battle scene into four parts, introducing the first with the line

Горит восток зарею новой

The east burns with a new dawn

that recalls by symbolic contrast the *tikha ukrainskaya noch*, and ending it with the lull at noon when Peter appears before the troops.

> Далече грянуло *ура*:
> Полки увидели Петра.

A Hurrah rolled round from afar: the regiments have seen Peter.

This is the signal for the introduction of individual leaders on both sides, which gives excuse in its turn for a moment of single combat: the young Cossack who had loved Mariya from afar rushes sword in hand on Mazepa, is shot down by his entourage, and dies with her name on his lips. Like Mazepa's final encounter with the mad Mariya it is a jarring interlude, and not less so because the story needs it, but Pushkin disposes of both as expeditiously as he can, and the final sequence and climax is the triumph of Peter as god of war.

> Его глаза
> Сияют. Лик его ужасен.
> Движенья быстры. Он прекрасен...

His eyes shine. His face is terrible. His movements are rapid. He is beautiful...

The two epithets, *uzhasen* and *prekrasen*, suggest in their positioning that 'abyss of space' which Gogol – in one of his moments of insight – noted as characteristic of Pushkin's simplest adjectives.[1] For it is not only Peter who is 'terrible and beautiful' but the face of war itself, and the summation of it here is that which Tolstoy's soldiers feel as they go into action. '*Nachalos! Vot ono! Strashno i vecelo!' govorilo litso kazhdogo soldata i ofitsera* ('It's begun! That's it! Terrifying and exciting!' said the face of every soldier and officer).

II

Poltava sees history in terms of personality, *The Bronze Horseman* in terms of historical determinism, though such a generalisation does little to indicate the remarkable difference in 'feel' between the two poems.

> Богат и славен Кочубей.
> Его луга необозримы;

Kochubey was rich and famous, and his estates immense.

---

[1] Two lines in the MS draft that were afterwards omitted show how Pushkin pared down the metaphorical associations to give simple images with the starkest contrast:

> *Ego glaza*
> *Goryat, kak bozhiya groza,*
> *Ego chelo blestit pobedoy.*

His eyes burn like the wrath of God; his brow is resplendent with victory.

With *Poltava* we know at once what sort of poem we are dealing with – a romantic and recreative poem, the opening taste of which subtly corresponds to the cosiness in the idea of recreation. There is a world of difference between Kochubey, 'in his habit as he lived', and Peter at the beginning of *The Bronze Horseman*.

На берегу пустынных волн
Стоял *он,* дум великих полн,
И вдаль глядел.

On a shore of desolate waves stood *he*, full of high thoughts, and gazed into the distance. (IV, 377).

In the first draft of the poem Peter was named, placed as a person in the past like Kochubey. In the final version there is only *he*, almost *it* – history personified, as in *Poltava* he was war personified – *mogushch i radosten, kak boy* (powerful and joyful, like battle). The superhuman size of Peter is common to both poems, but in *Poltava* it is only incidental. In *The Bronze Horseman* Peter is the vast *kumir*, the image of the poem as of the city and destiny.

Yet Peter had been very much a personality, and one studied by Pushkin with always increasing fascination; his extraordinary nature, his omnivorous interests and colossal energy, were aspects of a god who might none the less be represented in all his humanity. Just before *Poltava*, Pushkin had begun a historical novel about Peter, *The Negro of Peter the Great*, in which the Tsar appears as the friend and patron of Pushkin's African great-grandfather.[1] He is introduced as a homely figure: 'a tall man in a green peasant coat and with a clay pipe in his mouth...leaning his elbows on the table and reading the Hamburg newspapers'. He talks 'with such gaiety and good nature that no one could have suspected this kind and hospitable host of being the hero of Poltava and Russia's mighty and formidable reformer'.

Belinsky says it would have been a great novel, but we may doubt this, and so clearly did Pushkin, for he wrote no more than a few chapters. Lively enough when it is dealing with Gannibal's adventures in France, the writing becomes flat and almost embarrassed when the action returns to Russia: it is the only occasion in Pushkin when an air of unnaturalness creeps in, as if the author were an *enfant terrible* constrained to behave with dull decorum in the presence of a feared and respected father. There is a kind of family duty in the account of Peter's qualities, which emphasises

[1] VI, 7.

the conventional historical novelist's duty of describing for us the local colour and customs of Peter's court and of the newly founded capital. Yet had Pushkin completed it, he would certainly have obtained the kind of success which Zagoskin had in the following year (1828) with his novel *Yury Miloslavsky or The Russians in 1612*. Zagoskin and others exploited the fashion that Scott translations had begun, and offered the pleasures of patriotic retrospection as well as costume romance. Nor was the success undeserved, as Pushkin was the first to admit: he enjoyed Zagoskin's novels as much as Tolstoy was to do. But in singling out Peter for his own experiment in the genre he went to the heart of the matter and discovered – as Tolstoy also did – that Peter could not be made the subject of a historical novel.

The technique was sacrilegious: the method compromised by the safeties of nostalgia: to describe Peter's homely ways was a vulgarisation, and respect itself became almost patronising. Peter could not be seen by a Russian author with the kind of affectionate objectivity with which Scott in *Ivanhoe* had portrayed Louis XI. Kochubey's grief and rage over his daughter's defection was a theme, as Pushkin observed, from which 'a poet might make something'. It could be observed with the sympathy of dispassion and its link with a historic drama implied, but how – for example — to record Peter's rage over his son Alexis, and the dark episode of the Tsarevitch's death? When he had finished *War and Peace* Tolstoy himself was tempted to go further back and write a novel on Peter, but the fragment he produced on the conspiracy of the bodyguard, at the beginning of Peter's reign, remained far slighter even than Pushkin's.

Up to the time of his death Pushkin was accumulating notes for a history of Peter, but he was not hopeful for its outcome; he told the actor Shchepkin that there were too many things about Peter which he could not reconcile with his respect for him. And in *The Bronze Horseman* Peter does not have that personality which historical reconstruction confers on great historical figures who are manufactured after their deaths. Napoleon only becomes Napoleon in all kinds of histories, memoirs, retrospections. In Mallarmé's words about Poe: 'Tel qu'en lui-même enfin l'éternité le change.' However controversial the evidence, we accept the composite picture bestowed on us from the past. In order to create finished portraits fiction must turn its head backward; if it does not, the people it treats of remain modern, as they do in *Le Rouge et le Noir*,

The Castle, or *Women in Love.* Not for nothing did Stendhal claim that he would begin to be read towards 1900. Hamlet and the heroes of Dostoevsky are not the selves that we place in the past as 'characters': it is because they are never defined by the past that they continue to have meaning for each new age.

Shakespeare's *Troilus and Cressida* treats the most famous of ancient legends as if it was at that moment taking place in the hugger-mugger of the stage. Caught in the contingent moment, its actors cannot do or want anything that has time to make sense. In contrast to the other historical plays, which cherish the past 'that unmasks falsehood and brings truth to light' *Troilus* is an anti-history play: it makes what has occurred as essentially meaningless as what is going on. And in a rather different and yet related sense *The Bronze Horseman* might be called an anti-historical poem. It too brings the past into the present, instead of presenting us with what is hallowed because accomplished – the silent battle, the tale told by a Cossack singer or a Gipsy in his tent – the past that Pimen records in *Boris Godunov.*

> Минувшее проходит предо мною –
> Давно ль оно неслось событий полно
> Волнуяся, как море-окиян?
> Теперь оно безмолвно и спокойно.

The past unrolls before me. Is it long since it swept by, full of happenings, surging like the ocean sea? Now it is silent and tranquil. (v, 217.)

We may suspect that Pimen was intended by Pushkin as an embodiment of history, and history in the Shakespearean sense, for *Boris Godunov* was deliberately made on the Shakespearean model. Like *Poltava, Boris Godunov* is a deliberate investigation of the possibilities of a genre, while *The Bronze Horseman* seems by contrast to appear with the inevitability of a work of nature: although it was written out in a mere three weeks it had been growing for a long time and nourished from a number of oddly different sources, and it was never definitively completed.

The most important of the sources was Mickiewicz's poem, *Forefathers' Eve.*[1] In 1826 the Polish poet had been in Petersburg, where he had met Pushkin, and in spite of their political differences the two poets had remained friends – indeed in 1828 Pushkin had

---

[1] The connection of Mickiewicz's poem with Pushkin's is discussed by W. Lednicki in 'Pushkin's "Bronze Horseman": The Story of a Masterpiece', *Slavic Studies, University of California Publications,* I (1954).

been among those who had petitioned without success that Mickiewicz should be allowed to return to Poland. Mickiewicz had admired
such early revolutionary poems of Pushkin as *The Dagger*, which
had been popular in army circles and among the Decembrists, but
like many of Pushkin's friends he had been disturbed by the
apparent *rapprochement* with Nicholas's regime.[1] Konrad Wallenrod of *Forefathers' Eve* is Mickiewicz himself, and the *Digression* in
the poem describes the journey of the exile to the capital and what
he sees there. It is a satire, the vigour of which only partially re-
deems its crudity, but circulating in secret among the Petersburg
intelligentsia it created a sensation, and there is some evidence that
Pushkin thought of translating it.[2] Everything about the poem
must have outraged his aesthetic sense, but like the grit in the
oyster it worked in him until the final casting of the pearl at
Boldino in 1833. *The Bronze Horseman* is not a reply to Mickiewicz's poem, but it might not have been written without it.

In both poems Falconet's great bronze statue of Peter the Great
is a symbol of the city and of the autocrat who built it. For Mickiewicz the statue is an occasion for homily; for Pushkin it is the
central feature of a tragic tale, a tale based on accounts of the
great Petersburg flood of 1824.[3] Konrad Wallenrod meets beside
the statue the 'Russian bard', who may have been based on
Ryleev but more probably on Pushkin himself, and the pair dis-
course on liberty and despotism and even on the general theory of
equestrian statues. The bard points out that while the statue of
Marcus Aurelius in the Campidoglio at Rome is extending his
hand in protection and blessing, Peter's is raised in a threatening
and possessive gesture. In fact (though this was probably not
known to Mickiewicz) Falconet had intended a close parallel
between his creation and the statue of the Roman emperor, though
he declined to fall in with the wishes of Catherine II and Diderot
and provide a mere imitation of it. His statue was a romantic and

---

[1] Particularly by the short poem 'In hope of all the good and glory...'
(*V nadezhde slavy i dobra*) (II, 342), in which Pushkin celebrated the accession
of Nicholas and compared the Decembrist conspiracy with the mutiny of the
Moscow *streltsy* at the beginning of Peter's reign.

[2] It is not without interest that Conrad's novel *Under Western Eyes* is flawed
artistically by an equally unremitting irony and disgust directed by a Pole
against everything Russian.

[3] In his note at the beginning of the poem Pushkin refers 'the curious' to the
account of the flood 'composed by V. I. Berkh'. He meant V. N. Berkh's
A Detailed Historical Account of all the Floods that occurred in St Petersburg
(1826).

localised version of the generalised classic pose.[1] Peter is treading down the swamp serpent whom he overcame to build his city, raising his hand to show the upward path to his emergent people. In his pleasant townscape poem *Walks to the Academy of Fine Arts*, Batyushkov had commented on the resemblance between the two statues, and patriotically observed that he preferred the Russian stance to the Roman. And yet despite the sculptor's intention the rider's gesture does remain equivocal – in his *Soirées de St Pétersbourg*, which was known to both Mickiewicz and Pushkin, De Maistre had observed that the bronze hand might be lifted in either protection or menace.

Such a sculpture is as subject as poetry and other art may be to the interpretation of the audience; and the point is of some importance, because it is by exploiting the enigma that Pushkin's poem achieves its dispassion and its universalising force.

> Ужасен он в окрестной мгле!
> Какая дума на челе!
> Какая сила в нем сокрыта!
> А в сем коне какой огонь!
> Куда ты скачешь, гордый конь,
> И где опустишь ты копыта?
> О мощный властелин судьбы!
> Не так ли ты над самой бездной,
> На высоте, уздой железной
> Россию поднял на дыбы?

Terrible was he in the surrounding gloom! What thought was in his brow! What strength was hidden in him! And in this steed what fire! Where are you galloping, proud horse, and where do your hoofs fall? O mighty master of fate! Was it not thus, aloft on the very edge of the abyss, that you reined up Russia with your iron curb? (IV, 377.)

As in *Poltava* Peter is both splendid and terrible, but now the epic simplicity of the hero on the battlefield has given place to a vision that is shot through and through with deliberate equivocation.

---

[1] Though it would require a lengthy analysis to define in what sense, if any, Falconet could be called a 'romantic' sculptor. In *Réflexions sur la Sculpture* (1761) he advanced the heretical view that the plastic softness of the human body was better rendered by his contemporaries than by the ancients. His own and Clodion's nymphs, compared with the Korai or the Aphrodites, show the obvious if misleading truth involved, and it is arguable that the figure of Peter also shows the influence of this theory. It is naturalistically bulky, not to say dumpy, and the outstretched hand all too easily appears to the eye as a gesture of recovery, as if the weight of the Emperor was slipping backwards off the horse.

'Where are you galloping, proud horse? And where do your hoofs fall?' Where indeed. The aesthetic and the political are cunningly blended, for the poet's open admiration is for the statue, whose qualities *qua* statue are never lost sight of.

Bryusov claims that the last line can only mean that Peter has pulled Russia back from the brink of anarchy and barbarism. He mentions – to reject – the possibility that Peter is *driving* Russia to the abyss rather than saving her, pointing out that all the MS readings have the word *podnyal*, and that this can only mean a gesture of restraint. In Mickiewicz's *Digression* the Tsar is seen as checked at a precipice over which he is attempting to urge the Russian steed. Symbolism of Peter and Russia as rider and horse, explicit in Mickiewicz and indeed more than a trifle grotesque when we begin to follow up all the permutations of the relation, is in Pushkin equally explicit but uninsistent. The statue remains a statue, for the really important contrast is not between the possibilities of interpretation suggested by the romantic dynamism of its design, but between the rhetoric that this design inspires, and the actual and solid presence of the bronze figure in the darkness.

и того,
Кто неподвижно возвышался
Во мраке медною главой,

...and him who motionless held his bronze head aloft in the darkness.

The heavy lines are decisive. Where Mickiewicz, through Konrad and his friend the bard, engages in homiletics about freedom and tyranny, justice and injustice, Pushkin converts all to drama and to the dramatic confrontation of his two protagonists, statue and clerk. Through the crazed mind of his hero Evgeny is already running the fantasy of the bronze horseman, and the responses that the statue might evoke, and yet the poem all the time keeps steadily before us the giant unresponsiveness and immobility of the thing. It is as indifferent to what we make of it as – outside the mad climax in his own mind – it is heedless of Evgeny himself.

И, обращен к нему спиною,
В неколебимой вышине,
Над возмущенною Невою
Стоит с простертою рукою
Кумир на бронзовом коне.

And with its back turned to him, on unshakable eminence above the rebellious Neva, stands the Image on his bronze horse, with outstretched arm.

133

In the summer after he wrote *The Bronze Horseman*, when he was working desultorily in the capital on his biography of Peter, Pushkin wrote to his wife: 'I'm accumulating materials, bringing them into order and all at once I'll cast a brazen monument that cannot be dragged from one end of the city to the other, from square to square and street to street.' He may have intended an oblique reference to the preparations for the erection of the Alexander column, but it is also possible that he had his own *Bronze Horseman* in mind and what contemporaries and critics would make of it. Andrei Bely, the symbolist poet, thought so, and he and his fellow symbolists certainly dragged Pushkin's statue from street to street, making it one of the common properties of their poetic world.

And yet *The Bronze Horseman* remains outside that world, because it does not display its private meanings, meanings which begin and end with the poet and his friends. Pasternak observed that Blok's vision of Russia's sufferings remains basically a private affair, its terrors not real terrors, but terrors in poetry.[1] His vision of the twelve Red Guards, or of the Tatars on the field of Kulikovo, are as inward as those of Yeats and belong to the same epoch. History for the symbolists is, in the phrase of Yeats's spirit counsellors, 'metaphors for poetry'; it cannot draw its material from the same accepted and external realities which Pushkin used in *The Bronze Horseman*, the realities of a recorded flood and a tutelary statue.

Nor could anything be less proper to the doctrine of symbolism than a poem which 'answers' the contention of another poem, a poem which turns back on its rival the uses of satire and polemic. It is almost as if Pushkin had said to Mickiewicz: 'You call that a satire on what the capital stands for? I will show you how such a thing should be done – by a native who really knows.' He was not going to dispute with the Polish poet and defend Peter's creation, but make the most effective reply of all, an agreement that would

---

[1] The Russia of *Dr Zhivago* is itself, we might note, a private Russia, insulated in the vision and technique of the Symbolist era; and that is indeed the source of its moving appeal, for in the modern era there is a positive heroism about this insistence on the authenticity of a private vision. Yet the technique of the Russian Symbolists is the logical expression of their complete alienation from the Russia they lived in, and their preoccupation with symbolising her (as in Pasternak's last play fragment *The Blind Beauty*) in fact emphasises all the more strongly their artistic isolation. Ironically, history gives this isolation a central importance and integrity under the Soviet regime, but it cannot wholly enliven and universalise an enclosed and esoteric method.

reveal the crude *parti pris* of his *confrère*. His reply is subtly patronising, in that it is from the citizen of a great country to the outsider from a little one. 'Of course I despise my fatherland from head to foot' he exclaimed in a letter to Vyazemsky. 'However, it makes me angry when a foreigner shares my feeling.'[1] Russians can afford the luxury of self-denigration, and can make fun of their own contrariness: Pushkin's letters are full of such humour. He can also make fun of his own pride in his ancient family, though any mockery on the subject from outsiders like Bulgarin and Polevoy incurred his implacable indignation.

This attitude lies behind the lyrical vivacity of the Prologue to *The Bronze Horseman*. Pushkin is not celebrating the capital in a straightforward sense. Instead he enlists the reader as 'one of us', one of *les Nôtres*, the *beau monde* of Peter's city, to whom it is life and nature itself. Even the figure of Peter is drawn into this participatory intimacy: it is here – most unexpectedly – that he becomes briefly but completely human to our imagination, whereas in *The Negro of Peter the Great* he had remained wooden. Here he too is one of us, the charmed circle of the poet's genius, and with gigantic relish he acts his part as destiny's executor, brooding in the soughing forest by the deserted shore, ignoring with us the insect traces of the wretched Finn. His reflections sound less like the echo of Petriadic destiny than some unscrupulous and energetic landowner, delightedly scheming how to do down his neighbour, enlarge his property and increase his possessive pleasures. (In his historical notes Pushkin commented on the contrast between Peter's works and institutions, designed for perpetuity, and his 'outbursts of a despotic proprietor'.)

> И думал он:
> Отсель грозить мы будем шведу.
> Здесь будет город заложен
> Назло надменному соседу.
> Природой здесь нам суждено
> В Европу прорубить окно,
> Ногою твердой стать при море.

[1] 27 May 1826. Pushkin, in exile in Mikhailovskoye, had heard that the French writer Jacques Ancelot was in Petersburg, and probably (as indeed turned out) taking notes for a travel book on the outlandishness of Russia. Pushkin's love-hate relation with his country comes out strongly in this letter. 'You, who are not held on a lead, how can you remain in Russia? If the Tsar gives me *liberty*, I won't stay a month. We live in a gloomy age, but when I imagine London, railways, steamships, English Journals – or Paris theatres and brothels – then my godforsaken Mikhailovskoye fills me with boredom and rage.'

Сюда по новым им волнам
Все флаги в гости будут к нам,
И запируем на просторе.

And he pondered: From here we shall threaten the Swede, here a city shall be founded to spite our haughty neighbour. We are destined by nature here to cut a window through to Europe, to stand with firm foot on the sea. Hither, on waves unknown to them, ships of every flag will come to visit us, and we shall have space enough for our revels.

We can hear the grating glee in the first line, the sensual trumpet tone of the last. And we feel a complete solidarity with this Peter. It seems a privilege to be partners in crime, one of his family, and to participate in the building of the new city before which (and again we hear the undercurrent of hilarity beneath the resounding phrase) the old capital of Moscow will appear like a dowager in purple widow's weeds before a new Empress. In Pushkin's lifetime only the Prologue was published under the title *St Petersburg*, and even so the dowager and Empress simile had to be cut out. Did Nicholas and Benkendorf hear the levity behind the superbly eulogistic rhythm? It is unlikely: they were concerned only with superficial proprieties, but even as a separate poem, an apparent paean of praise, the Prologue makes the point that Mickiewicz laboured with such venom, and in doing so makes its point against Mickiewicz himself. We know, the Prologue says, what tyranny and suffering accompany the decreed foundation, but it is a great achievement; it is ours, and we love it. 'The love of one's native land', Pushkin had written in 1830 to Kutuzov's daughter, 'such as it can be in a Polish soul, has always been a gloomy feeling. Look at their poet Mickiewicz.' To the Russian, patriotism is not a gloomy feeling, because it is not a reaction against external, but a relief from internal tyranny. Its atavism is irresponsible and gay, and has no need of reverence and justice to support it.

So the Prologue implies, and is sharpened by specific reference to incident and description in Mickiewicz's *Digression*. Mickiewicz commented that in the savage climate of the capital the girls' cheeks become mottled with cold, are 'white as snow and red as a lobster'. Pushkin answers this in four lines.

Люблю зимы твоей жестокой
Недвижный воздух и мороз,
Бег санок вдоль Невы широкой,
Девичьи лица ярче роз.

I love the stirless air and the frost of your cruel winter, the sledge course along the broad Neva, girls' faces brighter than roses.

Roz rhymes with *moroz* (frost), as it should do and as the reader of *Evgeny Onegin* expects.

> И вот уже трещат морозы
> И серебрятся средь полей...
> (Читатель ждет уж рифмы *розы*;
> На, вот возьми ее скорей!)

And now already the frost crackles and is silver in the fields...(the reader is of course now expecting the rhyme *roses*, so here, quick with it!)

Less expected but equally to the point are the words *lyublyu* and *zhestokoy* ('I love' and 'cruel') that begin and end the opening line, a discreet stylistic parallel to Mickiewicz's gibe. The appeal is to gaiety and to the civilisation that delights poetic art. Everyone knows that girls' cheeks are like roses in poetry, and that is why we – but not, apparently, our Polish friend – like poetry and like girls. Everyone knows that balls at the Anichkov are a bore (Pushkin with Natalia had certainly found them so) but that is why we celebrate balls in poetry, and in the same breath remember the drunken feasts among our bachelor friends.

> И блеск, и шум, и говор балов,
> А в час пирушки холостой
> Шипенье пенистых бокалов
> И пунша пламень голубой.

...and the sparkle and hum and din of voices at balls, and at the hour of the bachelor's feasting, the fizz of foaming glasses and the blue flames of the punch.

Mickiewicz gives an extraordinarily vivid and harrowing account of the great winter parades on the Field of Mars. The day after one a valet was found frozen stiff and still holding the coat which his master had left with him. He had not dared to put it on, and his master could not do so either, for the Emperor had worn no great-coat. The passage is full of grotesque conceits. Green uniforms seem to grow like a lawn out of the snow, and a gun crouches like a tarantula, its crew preparing it 'as a fly alternately washes its front and back legs'. Again, Pushkin turns this grotesque violence back against the other poet, excluding him from 'our' sense of what goes on, isolating him in the eccentric bitterness of his single vision.

> Люблю воинственную живость
> Потешных Марсовых полей,
> Пехотных ратей и коней
> Однообразную красивость,

PUSHKIN

В их стройно зыблемом строю
Лоскутья сих знамен победных,
Сиянье шапок этих медных,
Насквозь простреленных в бою.

I love the warlike animation of the diversions on the field of Mars, the symmetrical beauty of the troops of horse and foot, those tattered flags of victory dipping in orderly formation, the gleam of those brazen helmets riddled through in battle.

By traditional hyperbole and this gracefully nodding onomatopoeia, Pushkin pulls off the delicate feat of making the martial spectacle seem at once stirring, beautiful, and slightly ridiculous: with him we both admire and smile. The regiments at Poltava were in heroic action, these are merely performing, and the difference is in the fact that here we are *all* taking part. In the Prologue the heroic and the lyrical are not separate elements of style but interchangeable: each can do the work of the other because we are at one with Pushkin in the familial mood.

This sense of family understanding which Pushkin conveys in the Prologue is echoed in the great writers who follow him. We have it in the family scenes at the end of *War and Peace*, in the Tolstoyan certainty that in the family there is no need for fine sentiment, in the balance of creative genius between joyful acceptance and profound disquiet. 'It is quite possible to live without political liberty,' Pushkin wrote to his wife in the summer of 1834, but 'without the inviolability of the family it's impossible.' The Prologue is a hilarious family gathering to which Mickiewicz has not been asked: there is no conflict, no hostility, but no invitation. That is how Pushkin's Prologue deals with his poem. But just as we might begin to be thinking that this intimacy is too complacent, and wondering whether we want to belong after all, Pushkin abruptly breaks up the gathering. After this unanimity we are now to experience alienation and disquiet. For the last time Pushkin calls on us, his friends in the poem.

Была ужасная пора,
Об ней свежо воспоминанье...
Об ней, друзья мои, для вас
Начну свое повествованье.
Печален будет мой рассказ.

There was once a terrible time, the memory of it is still fresh...I will begin my narration of it for you, my friends. Mine will be a sad tale.

The *Digression*, it might be said, has been seen off in one way and will now be seen off in another. Pushkin will leave the family and become as much of an outsider as Mickiewicz himself. And in doing so he will show how he can write from the outside, objectively and impassively, without indignation and without comment. And yet the change of tone from Prologue to story does not seem unduly deliberated. Unlike his prose, where an artificial reticence and simplicity are evident, Pushkin's poetry never loses the easy freedom of the speaking voice. Poetic celebrants of Petersburg – Batyush-kov, Gnedich, Vyazemsky – had been many: indeed it was their idylls which were partly responsible for Mickiewicz's attack on the 'Petropolis' cult, and it is possible that one function of the tone of Pushkin's Prologue is to imply that only an outsider would take this cult seriously, that 'we ourselves' do not. In the tale this circle has broken up; only one voice speaks, and its audience is mute. Pushkin turns the familiarity of friendship into the different familiarity of the accomplished story-teller touching in the preliminaries.

> В то время из гостей домой
> Пришел Евгений молодой...
> Мы будем нашего героя
> Звать этим именем. Оно
> Звучит приятно;

It was then that young Evgeny came home from visiting friends...We will call our hero by this name. It sounds agreeably;

The name sounds right: it is congenial to me: the surname does not matter though it could be an ancient one, celebrated in the past by other narrators. By sailing so close to his own well known preoccupation with his own name and descent, Pushkin paradoxically avoids giving the impression of avoiding it. And the narrative convention, too formal to seem deliberately deadpan, enables him presently to describe Tsar Alexander's grief at the flood disaster and to record his words: 'Tsars cannot have mastery over the divine elements' – even to refer to the poet Count Khvostov, who had described the disaster 'in deathless verses'. Such ironies seem a part of the *Skazochnik*'s expressional repertoire, neither personal nor sugges-give but flicked off in passing for the professional appreciation of the bystanders.

'This is how tales are told in Russia' might have been the tacit moral for Mickiewicz, who in *Forefathers' Eve* had availed himself of the accepted European and Byronic identification of author with romantic hero figure. Oleszkiewicz, whom Konrad meets in

Petersburg in the final section (Part Three) of *Forefathers' Eve* was a Polish painter, mystic and freemason, living in the capital during the time of Mickiewicz's enforced residence. The convention employs them, like Shelley's Julian and Maddalo, as the poet and friend discovered in a picturesque setting and discoursing upon high topics (Pushkin briefly uses the same device near the beginning of *Evgeny Onegin*). Discovered by the poet at night by the Neva, Oleszkiewicz foretells the destruction of St Petersburg, and then goes off with his lantern to address in soliloquy the Winter Palace. Tsar Alexander, he says, is not asleep. He was once a man but is now a tyrant, and like all tyrants is consumed with cares. Then, sensing the presence of the listening hero, he blows out his lantern and vanishes in the darkness.

The darkness, the lantern, the dramatic denunciation are as much a part of contemporary European fashion as Oleszkiewicz's status as mason, seer, and amateur scientist – he is found measuring with his instruments the height of the Neva. *The Bronze Horseman*, and its hero, are deliberately cut off from this fashion; the poem achieves its profound and universal political meaning through having no truck with the liberal ideals and assumptions of its time. By a curious irony this could only happen with a poet as cosmopolitan and European in his outlook as Pushkin was. The 'defence' of Petersburg would be nothing if it were the mere defensiveness and xenophobia characteristic of many Russian authors, not excluding Dostoevsky, and commonplace in the provincial and proletarian ethos of Soviet writing. Only a poet with Pushkin's instinctively European outlook could have written a masterpiece as universal and yet as deeply and subtly nationalistic as *The Bronze Horseman*. The greatest political poem of the nineteenth century rests on the paradox which Pushkin threw off with typical lightness and accuracy in that comment in his letters – 'Of course I despise my fatherland from head to foot. However it makes me angry when a foreigner shares my feeling' – a paradox which Tolstoy would have understood, and which relates to his own great creative division between war and peace, the pride of the flesh and the logic of pacifism.[1]

Pushkin's hero Evgeny is naturally the opposite of Konrad Wallenrod. He is indifferent alike to the injustices of the present

---

[1] In his old age Tolstoy expressed indignation at the surrender of Port Arthur in the Russo-Japanese war, and recalled the defence of Sevastopol, in which he had taken part.

and the glory of the past. He would rather not be poor, and he is honest enough to wish he had more brains, but he will work hard to make up for these things and for the rewards of a happy married life with his Parasha. Pushkin, as we shall see later, had some difficulty in deciding how to fill in his background. Unobtrusively he should give the impression of being a sensible straightforward young Russian, as opposed to all these modish and romantic young Europeans and Poles. But Pushkin avoids any combativeness in the contrast by being as cursory and noncommittal about him as he can.

We must remember, however, that Pushkin can be as violently didactic in his poetry as Mickiewicz himself. In his ode *To the Slanderers of Russia* (III, 222) he hurls defiance at western criticism of Russia's Polish policy, and his letters make it clear that he is not merely speaking as a Russian patriot but giving his own opinion on what he called the 'new European principle of non-intervention' (both phrase and attitude may not unreasonably remind us of Czechoslovakia in 1968). It is worth taking a close look at what Pushkin is saying in this poem, and saying as trenchantly as a good political journalist. Out of the elaboration of its form the ode creates an impression of spontaneous indignation. In their terse sarcasm, queries hurled at Russia's western critics are fitted with such cunning into the metrical form that they sound more immediate and more colloquial than if they were in prose. 'You hate us. And for what?'

> За что ж? ответствуйте: за то ли,
> Что на развалинах пылающей Москвы
> Мы не признали наглой воли
> Того, под кем дрожали вы?...
>
> Иль нам с Европой спорить ново?
> Иль русский от побед отвык?
> Иль мало нас?

And for what? Answer! Is it because in the ruins of blazing Moscow we did not recognise the insolent will of him under whom you trembled?... Is it new for us to dispute with Europe? Is the Russian grown unused to victories? Are there so few of us? (III, 222.)

The ode's first line (*O chem shumite vy, narodniye vitii?* (What are you clamouring about, bards of the people?)) parallels more forcefully and crudely the tone of *The Bronze Horseman*'s Prologue. The sarcasm is directed at the whole gamut of Gallic political and artistic posturing. *Vitiya* suggests the afflatus of a demogogic bard, and *shumite* the sonorousness of poetic cant as well as the hubbub of a meeting. Pushkin contrives to make the elevation of the ode suggest hard down-to-earth commonsense, the commonsense of the family which (like the Rostovs in *War and Peace*) instinctively distrusts fine feelings. (It is a singular thing that Pushkin, and the Russian establishment for whom he speaks, dismiss as typically European the kind of ideological jargon in which contemporary Soviet xenophobia habitually expresses itself.)

> Уже давно между собою
> Враждуют эти племена;
> Не раз клонилась под грозою
> То их, то наша сторона.
> Кто устоит в неравном споре:
> Кичливый лях иль верный росс?
> Славянские ль ручьи сольются в русском море?
> Оно ль иссякнет? вот вопрос.

For ages these peoples have been feuding among themselves. Not once but many times has their side or ours been worsted in the tumult. Who will survive in the unequal conflict, the swaggering Pole or the true Russian? Shall the Slav streams merge in the Russian sea? Or will it dry up? That is the question.

The so-called Polish question is as simple as that. In fact, of course, Pushkin's summing-up of the situation is as disingenuous as Swift's seemingly blunt good sense – 'We have been bribing our neighbours to fight their own quarrels' – in *The Conduct of the Allies*. Why, in fact, should the 'Russian sea' dry up if the Slavonic races do not mingle in it? Pushkin contrives to suggest that in this private quarrel of the Slavs among themselves the national existence of Russia is somehow threatened by Polish recalcitrance.

To the Slanderers of Russia pays the penalty of good journalism. We can see the flaws in the argument and we can see they derive from Pushkin himself, but the strength of the poem is in the way this rush of strong personal feeling is concentrated by the artifice of the form. Technically it is one of Pushkin's maturest performances, but its sentiments did not please the establishment as much as they shocked many of Pushkin's friends and former admirers. It is easy to see why. *The Dagger, To Licinius,* and other early liberal utterances are compliant rather than heartfelt: they oblige in sentiment while they exercise in technique. *Klevetnikam Rossii* throws the full force of genius into feelings that Pushkin at the time held very strongly. In 1834 Count Stroganov sent Pushkin a number of the *Journal de Francfort* which contained an account of the Polish politician Lelewel reading, amid applause, some of Pushkin's early revolutionary verses; and the article went on to point out that Pushkin had now become a man of the Court and a writer of anti-Polish poetry. 'I am sorry to be paying the penalty for the vain fancies of my youth', Pushkin wrote in reply. 'Lelewel's accolade seems harsher than exile to Siberia.'

'One really cannot blame him', Pushkin wrote to his wife of the Tsar – 'if you live in a privy you get used to the smell of shit.' Even the Tsar's hateful paternalism, like the enchanted seashore of the *Ruslan* Prologue, 'smelled of Russia'. In his youth Pushkin wrote an epigram on Karamzin's *History of Russia*, which his later admiration for the author made him regret. The *History*, concludes the epigram, 'showed simply and impartially the necessity of despotism and the pleasures of the knout'. That 'impartiality' and those 'pleasures' had now taken on other kinds of meaning. But Pushkin could never have been a government poet, nor could he have written, as Marvell did in his *Horatian Ode* to Cromwell, a poem of subtle and reasoned diplomacy, in which compliments are proffered in the foreground of a meditation on power.

> But thou, the War's and Fortune's son,
> March indefatigably on;
>   And for the last effect
>   Still keep the sword erect:
>
> Besides the force it has to fright
> The spirits of the shady night,
>   The same arts that did gain
>   A power, must it maintain.

Marvell turns the artifice of the Horatian ode as admirably to his purpose as Pushkin uses for his the quasi-Pindaric one. But *Klevetnikam Rossii* is neither a patriotic poem to order nor a balanced weighing up of the distressful claims of right and might. It is an instinctive outburst, and Pushkin showed more than once a natural exasperation at the belief that he had sold himself to the forces of reaction.[1]

---

[1] Much more impetuous and less detached, we night note, than Yeats's poem on the Irish rising, *Easter 1916*, with its superb central meditation and metaphor:

> Hearts with one purpose alone
> Through summer and winter seem
> Enchanted to a stone
> To trouble the living stream...,
>
> Too long a sacrifice
> Can make a stone of the heart...

The Bronze Horseman was not his first parable about power and injustice.

> Но человека человек
> Послал к анчару властным взглядом:
> И тот послушно в путь потек
> И к утру возвратился с ядом.

But with a glance of authority a man sent a man to the upas-tree; and obediently he set out on his way and returned at dawn with the poison. (III, 82.)

Neither *Prorok* (*The Prophet*) nor *Anchar* (*The Upas-Tree*), from which this stanza comes, is an allegorical poem; nor is their meaning dependent on a generalised symbolic structure. In both, a stereotype is endowed with all the weight and concentration of which language is capable. In *Anchar* it is taken from contemporary romantic mythology, the sinister and exotic poison tree of travellers' tales, but Pushkin does not dwell on the horrific associations. His account sounds almost scientific in its objectivity.

> Яд каплет сквозь его кору,
> К полудню растопясь от зною,
> И застывает ввечеру
> Густой прозрачною смолою.

The poison oozes through its bark, melting in the midday heat and hardening at evening into a thick transparent gum.

'*Transparent* gum' – any romantic poet who treated the legend would try to do better than that, but Pushkin's description is all the more sinister from its air of botanical accuracy,[1] as if in the word *prozrachny* we were seeing through the myth to the thing in itself. The first five stanzas are dominated by the desert solitude where the tree grows, but then the tone of the poem abruptly changes: the decisive human relation erupts in a single line. *No cheloveka chelovek poslal k ancharu...* (But man sent man to the anchar...) There is a stylistic parallel in Suetonius's famous line: *Titus reginam Berenicem...ab urbe dimisit invitus invitam* (the Emperor Titus sent away Queen Berenice against his will and hers). In both phrases the possibilities of economy in an inflected language are taken to their limit, and in both the motive for the economy is the same.[2] The words touch the centre of power; they say as little

---

[1] The botanical term *anchar* (Latin *antiaris*) also sounds better than the familiar romantic 'upas'.

[2] In his essay on Pushkin (Paris 1868) Mérimée observes that only Latin and Russian could achieve the concise syntax of these two lines. He even translates the verse into Latin: 'At vir virum misit ad anchar superbo vultu', etc. See also V. M. Zhirmunsky, *Pushkin i zapadnie literaturi*.

as they do because there is no more to be said. Pushkin, like
Suetonius, implies a fated and irreducible situation. The slave who
goes to collect the poison does not die *for* his master. He is obedient
in the same sense as the arrows which his master dips in the poison,
and his master does not recognise his sacrifice. Master, slave, and
poison, are alike under the destiny of power.

To this destiny Pushkin gives incomparable expression in *Anchar*,
as in *The Bronze Horseman*. He does not give his own 'views', as in
a sense he did in the early revolutionary poems – or at least the
views of his set. He gives a voice to Russia's historic and fatalistic
acquiescence in absolute rule. Even his fascination with the
phenomenon of Peter the Great reveals not only his own emancipation and quick intelligence of insight, but also the deeper and
almost superstitious awe and admiration of Russia for her most
dynamic tyrants – a Peter or a Stalin. The oriental setting
of *Anchar* is not merely, one feels, a picturesque convention,
and yet the poem's sober and factual accuracy has nothing allegorical about it – Pushkin was contemptuous of the censor's office
for trying to find specific meanings for 'arrows', 'poison' and so
forth.

Where *Anchar* condenses its apprehension of power in a few
heavy drops, *The Prophet* pours it out like a stream of molten lava.
It is a poem of inner power, the inspiration of an Old Testament
prophet compressed into a few lines of visionary fervour. Power has
been conferred upon the speaker, the power to 'burn the hearts of
men', but it is not by his own will. The intensity and concentration
of both poems may remind the English reader of Blake – *Anchar*
might be compared to *A Poison Tree*, and *The Prophet* with the
first poem in *Songs of Experience*, 'Hear the Voice of the Bard!'
But there is an important difference. Densely meaningful as they
are, Blake's poems often require a further elucidation of meaning
outside themselves. Like most poems of the great English romantics
they are part of the complex and yet continuous life of the poet's
consciousness, and must be understood in its total dimension. The
reverse is true of Pushkin's. Inherently dramatic, each poem is
complete in itself: to read it in the light of others will not extend or
modify its meaning. In *The Prophet* Pushkin incarnates himself as
prophecy, not as the message a prophet brings.

> Как труп в пустыне я лежал,
> И Бога глас ко мне воззвал:
> «Восстань, пророк, и виждь, и внемли,

Исполнись волею Моей,
И, обходя моря и земли,
Глаголом жги сердца людей».

Like a corpse I lay in the desert, and the voice of God called out to me:
'Arise prophet, and see, and hear, be filled with My will, and journeying
over sea and land, set the hearts of men on fire with the word.' (II, 338.)

In something of the same way, the year before, Pushkin had re-
incarnated in himself not only the style but the temperament of
André Chénier in the melodious and moving poem which is called
by his name. Chénier's gentleness and fineness of temper, his ardent
political idealism and also his hatred of revolutionary tyranny, are
alive in the poem. We can feel Pushkin's feeling for them, but they
are not his, and they cannot be identified with him.

Four lines written by Pushkin at the time of *The Prophet* have
sometimes been taken as an additional or alternative ending to it:

Восстань, восстань, пророк России,
Позорной ризой облекись,
Иди и с вервием вкруг выи
К убийце гнусному явись.

Arise, arise, prophet of Russia, clothe yourself in a shameful garment,
go with a halter about the neck, and appear before the abhorrent
murderer. (II, 437.)

It has been suggested that the lines refer to Pushkin's interview
with Nicholas, which could have resulted in punishment or exile
instead of forgiveness. No doubt they do, but Annenkov's view that
they represent Pushkin's summation of his poetic calling seems as
wide of the mark as the opposite view, taken in 1898 by Chernyaev,
that they could not have been written by Pushkin at all.[1] They
belong to his life and not to the poem, and they are the clearest
possible indication of the distance between the two.

Another remarkable short poem, *Arion*, which in point of time
comes between *Prorok* and *Anchar*, most certainly does refer, and
in a figurative allegory, to the poet and his former Decembrist
companions. But the handling of the allegory sets the greatest
possible distance between the events that actually occurred and the
way they are here imaged. *Nas bylo mnogo na chelne*...the syntax
of the first line ('nous étions nombreux') sets the tone of detached
and reflective understatement. The vessel sank in a sudden tempest

---

[1] A discussion of the fragment and of the attitudes to it of Pushkinists occurs
in N. O. Lerner, *Rasskazy o Pushkine* (Leningrad 1929).

and the poet alone survived, drying his garment on a rock and
singing his songs as before.[1] The measure and concentration of
movement, as in a Greek frieze, lifts the action out of the realm of
contingency. We do not ask who the steersman was, whether
Ryleev or another – what matters is his sculptured posture, commemorated on the *stele* of the poem, and the kind of being it
reveals:

В тишине
На руль склонясь, наш кормщик умный
В молчанье правил грузный челн;

Calmly leaning against the tiller, our sage steersman conned in silence
the loaded vessel; (III, 15.)

Silence, effectiveness, calm: these by implication are the qualities
not possessed by the singer who is saved. We remember that
Pushkin was not taken into the Decembrists' confidence because
he was thought too impetuous and indiscreet; and it is ironic that
nothing could reveal less of either failing than the tone in which
Arion is conceived and written. All Pushkin's traits – his excitability
in talk and friendship, his incontinent pleasure in social life – are
resolved into their opposites; and this achievement is in itself the
poetic embodiment of a profound sorrow and respect.[2] Sentiment
and overt grief are not necessary: the poet accepts the destruction
and disappearance of his friends as simply as he accepts his own
survival.

Arion should be compared not only with the warm and immediate solicitude of the short 'Lycée' commemoration poem of that
year (1827) – *Bog pomoch vam, druzya moi* (God preserve you, my
friends) – but also with another short poem of the same period,
addressed to the Decembrist exiles in Siberia. It exhorts them to be
patient and keep up their hopes in the knowledge that their high
endeavours have not been in vain. It is a fine bit of rhetoric, but it
is none the less a curiously insensitive poem, and when smuggled

[1] Pushkin uses for 'garment' a Church Slavonic word, *riza*, whose primary
meaning is a priest's vestment (as in the quotation from *Poltava* given above,
page 117). The application to the poet, as the priest of Apollo, is obvious, and
there may be an equally pointed application of the word in the 'Prophet'
fragment – 'clad in a shameful garment' – for *riza* also once had the meaning
of a formal robe worn by the Tsar. Pushkin does not in general use such words
with point or method but in harmony with his general sense of style, as in
Prorok. Detailed discussion of Pushkin's linguistic sources is outside the scope
of this study, but see Chapter 5 for further reference to his use of archaisms.
[2] Pushkin substituted the first person singular and plural, 'I' and 'we', for the
'he' and 'they' of the original draft, a change that paradoxically distances
and stylises still further the setting of the poem.

into Siberia by one of the exiles' wives it was coolly received, and a reply in verse was composed, thanking Pushkin for his words of encouragement but intimating that they were not really needed. Though it seems the more indifferent and egocentric poem, *Arion* is really a more moving testament – it accepts the situation without trying to take it over. Shedding both the ordinary commonplace of a personal response, and the Bardic personality donned to address the exiles, it presents a view of the poet which is closer to Pushkin's genius than either.

Bryusov says that *The Prophet* incarnates two ideas of the poet – the mortal fallible man, and the immortal vessel of inspiration. We could say this, if we wished, about the contrast between the poems – *Anchar, Prorok, Arion* – that incarnate what I have called 'opposites', and the occasional poems that express Pushkin's own immediate and contingent feelings. The unique and endearing appeal of Pushkin lies not so much in the fact that he is 'Protean', as in the many relations which his genius of opposites has with his own briskly straightforward and unpretending personality (there is a parallel in English poetry with Keats). No one, not even his closest friends, needed to take Pushkin very seriously; no one revered him. Mickiewicz, on the other hand, who might well have written the poem to the Siberian exiles or *To Licinius*, was treated by his fellow-countrymen with awe and reverence. And he expected to be. Herzen in his *Memoirs* records seeing the Polish national poet calmly accepting the slavish worship of his entourage, a sight that Herzen, who was as subject to anti-Polish – and anti-German – prejudices as many other liberal Russians, found repellent. Pushkin's vanity, by contrast, was the most commonplace of weaknesses. He was proud of his name, of his beautiful wife, of being a Russian and a gentleman, and of being a poet. In several poems he writes about the status of poethood, and the claims that he makes for it, not on his own behalf but for all Russian poets, are completely ordinary, unoriginal, and unexceptionable. The poet should care nothing for the applause of the crowd; his own exacting judge, he ignores alike the patronage of the great and the censure of self-appointed critics. To these prescriptions in *To the Poet* he adds, in the *Dialogue of Poet and Bookseller*, that the poet's inspiration is without price but his works are not, and he should get the best bargain he can for them.

His prose contains a number of more penetrating and more cursory insights, such as that on the isolation of the poet, who does not cease to be a poet as he grows older, though most of his readers have ceased to respond to poetry and merely recall the verses they knew when both they and the writer were young. But it is remarkable how unilluminating for his own poetry are most of Pushkin's general pronouncements on the art. *To the Poet* describes a different world from the one we really meet in his poems, a world of art in which the Parnassians and the symbolists lived. Only in *The Egyptian Nights* and in the twelve-line *Echo* (1831) does he give an intimation of how his own poetry works. The *improvvisatore* in *The Egyptian Nights* fragment produces *to order* – like a poetic craftsman of the Renaissance – a fine piece of rhetoric on the same theme as *To the Poet*: the artist's godlike independence and right to choose his own subject! And, like Echo, the poet answers the voice of everything in nature, but to his own voice there is no echo: his words end in themselves, complete in their own achieved finality.[1]

This is in striking contrast to the nineteenth-century poet's increasing absorption in the sources of his own art as his own main poetic theme. The mysticism of a Blok or a Yeats, the seemingly deliberate extravagance of their imaginative and notional structures, often strike us as attempts to engulf the world in their own creative process, to twist reality into 'metaphors for poetry', history into cycles of personal emblems, Red Guards into followers of the poet's Christ. Beside these attempts at unity the simple dualisms of Pushkin's poetry between the created and the expository, the personal statement and the impersonal embodiment, may strike us as the very height of sanity and good sense.[2] The unique strength of nineteenth-century Russian literature lies in its indifference to bogus ideals of artistic 'wholeness' and unification, its ability to speculate and analyse in theoretical terms while engaging simultaneously in prodigies of primary creation. Tolstoy and Dostoevsky have this in common: the massive strands of theory that intertwine in *War and Peace* with the natural growth of family and fable, are paralleled in *The Brothers Karamazov* by debate and discussion on power and human ideals and necessities – Dimitri on Schiller, Ivan on the Grand Inquisitor and the entrance

---

[1] There is probably also a note of deliberate irony in the conclusion of *Echo*: the poet receives no response from the dull public. (Possibly, too, there is the added twist that he does not deserve any if he *only* echoes the voices of nature?)

[2] Blok's comment in his later years: 'in the poetic exerience of the world there is no rift between the individual and the general' would scarcely have made any sense to Pushkin.

ticket – which coexist with the monastery and the town, Poles and Gipsies, and the Shakespearean portrait of old Karamazov himself. The reflective and the naive (in Schiller's terminology) could not work together and enhance each other in European nineteenth-century literature as they did in the Russian. We have a Dickens, Balzac or Hugo on the one hand; Hegel, Comte, Mill or Arnold on the other. 'We are lucky', wrote Belinsky, 'that Pushkin's nature did not succumb to reflection. That is why he is a great poet.'

But in his poetry there is a simple and natural distinction between the distance of the creator, the *tainstvenny pevets*, and the familiarity of the commentator and friend. As a 'mysterious singer' he does not, like Blake, inhabit an arcane system which runs beneath its outbreaks in poetry, alternately illuminating and confusing them; still less does his creative intelligence defend itself by creating a para-world like that of the symbolists. As with his great successors Tolstoy and Dostoevsky, the creative and reflective sides of his genius are on the best of terms with each other.

In *The Bronze Horseman* we see the combination at its most masterly. The Prologue: genial, personal, appealing; the Tale: the climax and masterwork of Pushkin's 'opposites'. We have seen how in such poems as *Anchar*, *Prorok* and *Arion*, the fable of the poem is used to secure a total objectivity, exploring a theme in ways quite different from anything Pushkin himself wrote in poem or letter. The bronze statue and the Petersburg flood are the most distanced and the most elaborately treated of these fable materials. Pushkin's own reaction to the news of the great flood of '24 was a joke in a letter, '*Voilà une belle occasion à vos dames de faire bidet*' and afterwards a request to his brother to make an anonymous donation of some of the money from *Evgeny Onegin* for any relief scheme that was being organised. Six years later he was considering going on with *Onegin*, and his first tentative ideas about the poem that afterwards became *The Bronze Horseman* ('I cannot get the flood out of my mind') involved the use of the hero on whose story he had spent eight years, and who had become so familiar to him.

Too familiar perhaps. Evgeny Onegin was certainly not an *alter ego*, but neither was he in any sense an 'opposite'. Nor was he, like Byron's Don Juan, a passive cipher who could be the hero of any new adventure. Pushkin, and his friends, may have thought Onegin could be continued, but it became clear that he was a hero inseparable from the drama in which he figured. Moreover Pushkin required a new hero for a particular purpose, a purpose that came close to a kind of apologia for himself. Bulgarin and the journalistic set were attacking him continually, and the gibe that most hurt was at his family pride. In the spirited poem *My Pedigree* he employs a cruder variant of the technique of rebuttal he used against Mickiewicz in the *Bronze Horseman* prologue. Bulgarin was a Pole, an outsider, but that was nothing against him, as Pushkin observed in an epigram of the same period (1830):

> Не то беда, что ты поляк:
> Костюшко лях, Мицкевич лях!
> Пожалуй, будь себе татарин, –
> И тут не вижу я стыда;
> Будь жид – и это не беда;
> Беда, что ты Видок Фиглярин.

It's no disgrace that you're a Pole – Kosciuszko and Mickiewicz are Polaks. Become a Tatar if you please, and I would see nothing shameful in that; become a Jew, and even that would be no disgrace. The disgrace is, that you're Vidocq Figlyarin.[1] (iii, 192.)

You say that I am 'a bourgeois nobleman' (*Ya vo dvoryanstve meshchanin*) says Pushkin in *My Pedigree* – I am proud to be a *meshchanin* when I see where the present-day aristocracy comes from, just as I am proud to be descended from Peter's Negro.

Pushkin does not, like Pope, distil the finest poetry out of quarrel and vituperation; rather, as Tennyson does, he shows himself on occasion an admirable exponent of the laconic and devastating retort. Critically speaking, however, the important thing is the evolution, under these personal attacks, of a new kind of 'opposite' hero, an essentially peaceable fellow but one to whom society and circumstances were indifferently or cruelly hostile, a *victim* in fact. Such a hero would be very different from Onegin, who (as in all great fictions) develops both under the pressure of environment and through his own actions. The new hero would be acted on only, and hence the poem in which he moves would be radically different, a *rasskaz*, possibly a satire, even something closer to *Don Juan* than Onegin ever begins to be. Juan, after all, is a gentleman in distressed circumstances, whose adventures and misfortunes can be

---

[1] Vidocq was the detested head of the Paris secret police, Bulgarin was a spy and informer for its Russian equivalent. *Figlyar* – the Russian word for toady and fraud. Bulgarin was also married to an ex-prostitute, a fact referred to by Pushkin at the end of *My Pedigree* with a pun on the name of the Petersburg brothel quarter: *On v Meshchanskoy dvoryanin* (He is a nobleman of Bourgeois Street).

used at the author's whim to satirise warfare, court life, or high society. So there began to evolve in Pushkin's mind the notion of a Petersburg Tale, some stanzas of which were published in *Sovremennik* in 1836 entitled *The Genealogy of My Hero* (*A Fragment from a Satiric Poem*). A larger version also exists to which Zhukovsky gave the title *Ezersky*, the name of the new hero, who in numerous variants is also referred to by other names.

Echoing the tone and the graceful stanza of *Onegin*, *Ezersky* does little more than give the details of the hero's pedigree *ab ovo* from the days of the Varangian followers of Rurik, but it opens with a fine stanza on autumnal Petrograd, and the return of Ezersky, 'my neighbour', from his work as a civil servant. Pushkin's printed version breaks off there after a disdainful reference to his enemy Bulgarin, but the longer variant goes on to query rhetorically the choice of so commonplace a hero, and sweeps up to a magnificent climax (stanzas 13 and 14) echoed later by Pushkin in *The Egyptian Nights*, which proclaims that the poet will go where he pleases, ignoring fashion and public demand. The last stanza returns us to Pushkin's hero:

> Скажите: *экой вздор*, иль *bravo*,
> Иль не скажите ничего –
> Я в том стою – имел я право
> Избрать соседа моего
> В герои повести смиренной,
> Хоть человек он не военный,
> Не второклассный Дон Жуан,
> Не демон – даже не цыган,
> А просто гражданин столичный,
> Каких встречаем всюду тьму,
> Ни по лицу, ни по уму
> От нашей братьи не отличный,
> Довольно смирный и простой,
> А впрочем, малый деловой.

Say: 'What rot' or 'Bravo' or say nothing at all. I maintain that I had the right to choose my neighbour as the hero of my humble tale, though he is not a warrior or a second-class Don Juan, nor a demon – not even a gipsy; but simply a citizen of our capital, of the kind we meet everywhere in thousands; and not distinguished in our society by wit or good looks, but just quite mild and simple, and furthermore a solid sort of young chap. (IV, 339.)

This is far from reassuring. Ezersky was seemingly to be built up in the same way as Onegin, an appearance followed by an explanatory flashback, but here the process would have been more stylised and far more tendentious. Onegin develops; when he is fully created his story is over, but we have the impression that Ezersky was to be first invented and documented and then used, a very different thing. With the eventual hero of *The Bronze Horseman* all connections have been cut; his reality is achieved within the brief compass of the poem's happenings.

We can distinguish between the dramatic hero, who is fully realised without background or explanatory antecedents; and the fictional hero, who is built up on the basis of these things. Only the greatest writers can use the dramatic method within the fictional density of the novel, and it is a striking thing that both Tolstoy and Dostoevsky create their most memorable characters in the same way that Pushkin finally presents his hero in *The Bronze Horseman*. Pierre, Prince Andrew, Prince Myshkin, Anna Karenina most remarkably of all – they have no previous life filled in retrospectively: they exist entirely in the actions which the novelist is immediately describing, but so real do they become in these, particularly with Tolstoy, that we understand intuitively how they have grown into what they are and why they act as they do.[1] The supreme advantage of the dramatic method is that it avoids all impression of a *study*, the kind of study that Balzac, George Eliot and most great nineteenth-century novelists make of their big character creations, the kind of study that Lukacs and other Marxist critics rightly describe as the method of social realism.

In Pushkin's work, as we might expect, both methods are projected, but in his supreme poetic masterpiece it is the dramatic method which finally wins, after what might be described as a prolonged fictional gestation. Ezersky was to be used as the exemplar of Pushkin's thesis on the old nobility and its decay. The newmade Petrine aristocracy would belittle him, and he in his turn would ignore them; he would not 'belong' to the court life of Petersburg, but be living of necessity in the capital. There would be a relation, and one not so deeply buried, between Pushkin's own predicament and that of his hero. For by 1833 Pushkin was an outsider in the capital, hating the court, the balls, and the pretensions and intrigues of new favourites. In the fictional construction

---

[1] As we do with Shakespeare above all other writers, where the unknown previous existence of Hamlet, Macbeth, Othello, Lear, to say nothing of more minor characters, is all the more potent for being undocumented. So too with Dickens, after Shakespeare the greatest creator in English of dramatic characters (even when, as with David Copperfield or Pip in *Great Expectations*, we meet them first in early childhood).

of *Evgeny Onegin* he had been 'a friend' of the hero, and yet he could not be identified with him. He claimed similarly to be 'a neighbour' of Ezersky, but the personal connection was all too clear.

Pushkin's instinct is straightforward: either he is the kind of 'I' which a chosen form requires, without self-consciousness or self-dramatisation, or he must be invisible. Yet from 1830 onwards the relationship between himself and his fictions does become a more devious one. It can take the form of a deliberate and even slightly arch invitation to the reader, as in the introduction he wrote in 1830 to a projected but unwritten story:

My friend is a very simple and ordinary man. When the 'silly fit' (as he calls his inspiration) takes hold of him, he locks himself in his room, goes to bed and writes from morning to night, dresses hurriedly to have dinner at a restaurant, goes out for a walk for an hour or so, and goes back to bed and writes till morning. This goes on for two or three weeks, at most a month, and once a year, always in the autumn. My friend assures me that only then does he know true happiness...My friend derives his descent from one of our oldest families and is proud of it...Except for this little weakness which we attribute to his wish to imitate Lord Byron (who also sold his works for a good price), my friend is *homme tout rond* as the French say...He dislikes the literary crowd with a very few exceptions...he prefers the society of women, and men of good social position who...do not indulge in literary conversations with him.

This was afterwards used on the account of Charsky in *The Egyptian Nights*. Both Charsky and the 'friend' here are Pushkin himself, as we are clearly intended to recognise. There is an equally obvious connection between Pushkin and the heroes of some of his unfinished prose stories. The clearer the resemblance the more sardonic the presentation ('his wish to imitate Lord Byron') and yet the suggestion of an apologia is never far off. The vigorous opening of *Ezersky* has a simile which Pushkin afterwards used in *The Bronze Horseman*:

Над омраченным Петроградом
Осенний ветер тучи гнал,
Дышало небо влажным хладом,
Нева шумела. Бился вал
О пристань набережной стройной,
Как челобитчик беспокойный
Об дверь судейской.

An autumn wind drove the clouds over sombre Petrograd, the sky breathed a dank chill, the Neva muttered. Waves broke against the shapely embanked quays like an unquiet suppliant at the judge's door.

Here the image of suppliant and judge might have been proleptic.
For in *The Bronze Horseman* it occurs later in the poem when the
mad Evgeny is wandering through the city, and its significance is
already plain.

> И бьясь об гладкие ступени,
> Как челобитчик у дверей
> Ему не внемлющих судей.

...and beating against the smooth steps, like a suppliant at the door of
judges who have no ear for him.

Though modelled on the *Ezersky* opening, the beginning of *The
Bronze Horseman* has a different simile:

> Над омраченным Петроградом
> Дышал ноябрь осенним хладом.
> Плеская шумною волной
> В края своей ограды стройной,
> Нева металась, как больной
> В своей постеле беспокойной.

Over darkened Petrograd November breathed its autumn chill. With
muttering waves beating against the verge of her shapely embankments
the Neva tossed about, like a sick man on his unquiet bed.

Both show something new in Pushkin's narrative poems – the use
of metaphor which refers by indirection not only to the hero but to
the author himself. The first image of the city in the story (in
marked contrast to the Prologue) is of sickness and unquiet, but the
patient tossing in his bed, the petitioner vainly waiting on the
law's delays – *Ne day mne Bog soyti s uma* (God grant I don't go
out of my mind) and *Pora, moy drug, pora! pokoya serdtse prosit*
(It's time, my dear, it's time! The heart begs for peace) – these are
images with an unmistakable echo from Pushkin's later lyrics.
Pushkin's division of himself (if we may call it that) between the
happy native son of the Prologue and the outcast of the Tale is
already foreshadowed, moreover, in the invention of Ezersky. Two
variants present him as a rich young Petersburger, sitting in his
luxurious study or returning to his fine house, but a third sketches
him as a penurious clerk, a man in love, living in a garret. Both
might be said to find their final form in *The Bronze Horseman*, the
first the celebrant of the Prologue, the second the victim of the
Tale.

Annenkov, one of Pushkin's first and best biographers, thought
that *Ezersky* would have been the first part of a long poem, of which
The Bronze Horseman, as we have it, is a much modified version of

155

the conclusion originally planned. Evgeny's protest against the Tsar's effigy, and the disaster of the flood which brought it about, have been substituted for the armed revolt of the Decembrists against Peter's successors, the climactic event in which Ezersky would have taken part. This must remain speculation, and in any case such a poem could never have passed the censorship. Pushkin hoped *The Bronze Horseman* would do so, and so the censorship might have played its part in transforming the local themes of *Ezersky* into the universal one of *The Bronze Horseman*. Certainly the Decembrists are in the background of the poem, but their relation to it is ambiguous, so much so that Lunacharsky, the first People's Commissar for Education, pronounced that Pushkin had invoked the Decembrists in order to pass judgement on them: for Peter was historical necessity enthroned, and his dynamic autocracy a necessary stage on the road to the communist state.[1] Like the Kronstadt mutineers against the Bolsheviks almost exactly a hundred years later, the Decembrists were guilty of what Lenin termed 'infantile disorders', pitting their libertarian instincts against the majestic progress of the dialectic.

An earlier generation of liberals saw Evgeny's protest as equally symbolic of the Decembrist uprising: 'voiceless and will-less' Russia crying out that it was 'even now' going to settle its own fate; and all historical and ideological interpretations of the poem echo the original insight of Belinsky that its tragedy resides in the conflict between the individual and the collective will. Even Merezhkovsky follows this pattern of interpretation, seeing the confrontation as 'the Christian stand against heathen idealism', with Evgeny representing the patient goodness of the peasant against Peter's atheistic modernity.[2] The poem has an enduring fasincation for intellectuals and theorists, and their ideologies – often of great interest and subtlety – feed on its art and produce interpretations which the very perfection and inclusiveness of that art make quite compatible with one another.

But to the student of poetry detail is more important than generality. Why, when he cut the connections and made Evgeny

---

[1] A. V. Lunacharsky, *Sobranie Sochinenii* (1963), vol. I. Although his dogmas are the orthodox ones of early Soviet society, Lunacharsky was in fact a cultivated and sympathetic literary critic.

[2] D. S. Merezhkovsky, *Vechnie Sputniki* (St Petersburg 1897). Merezhkovsky links the basic confrontation in the poem with that in *The Gipsies* and in *Evgeny Onegin*. The Evgeny of *The Bronze Horseman* is thus the Old Gipsy to Peter's Aleko, and the Tatyana to his Evgeny Onegin.

the anonymous hero (*Prozvanya nam ego ne nuzhno*) did Pushkin none the less retain the references to his ancient lineage? Why is he not quite simply a *chinovnik*, like Gogol's Akaky of *The Overcoat*, one of Petersburg's vast clerical proletariat? It may of course be mere whim or oversight on Pushkin's part, and the consequence of the poem's complex gestation. But a more inherently artistic explanation is also possible. Pushkin always avoided the fashionable literary figure, the facile type, whether it was the Byronic hero, the persecuted heroine exemplified by Karamzin's 'poor Liza' (sardonically detypified by Pushkin in his story *The Station Master*) or the 'little man', one of the insulted and injured. Evgeny's elaborate family tree and all genial Ezersky-style documentation must of course be cut out, yet he need not become such a simple type-figure. Nor does he. As we have seen, he is created dramatically, endowed with an obliquely conceded individuality, as decisive in effect as Shakespeare's equally cursory and often equally moving suggestion of a personality where a type might seem to be all that is required. Though Gogol's Akaky is also created by the dramatic method, he is presented as a kind of creaturely grotesque: defined in his face, his food, his speech, and of course his overcoat, as a dog might be by the movement of its tail and the look in its eyes. Akaky is almost literally what Pushkin's Evgeny in his madness becomes: *ni zver ni chelovek* (neither beast nor man). What are the irrelevant human parts of his history? Whom has he loved or failed to love? What goes on in his head? Gogol does not need to provide an answer, as Dickens does not in the case, say, of Quilp or Traddles. The difference between Akaky and Evgeny is the difference between a Dickensian and a Shakespearean reality.

It is worth stressing this because most appraisals – especially Soviet ones – tend to lay emphasis on the 'little man' aspect of Evgeny, the helpless and pathetic clerk driven mad by his misfortunes. In fact the character of Pushkin's hero owes much to the *Little Tragedies*, written two or three years earlier, and to the understanding of Shakespeare that had helped to inspire them. Pushkin had been struck by such figures as Shylock, whose ruling passion, that of a miser, was less important in the plot than his possessive love for his daughter and his passion for revenge.[1] Evgeny is all the more effective a casualty because he is not just a 'little man' but the bearer of a once famous name whose immediate and

---

[1] *Table-Talk* (VIII, 90), notes written by Pushkin at various times and unpublished in his life-time. The English term for them is his own.

sufficient concern is to hold down a steady job, marry his sweet-heart and raise a family. The common happiness and common fate he desires is all the more convincing because he might be expected to be a dissatisfied cynic nurturing a hopeless *folie de grandeur*, an embittered exile from the past. In fact, like Hardy's Tess, he bears the burden of the past while concerning himself only for the present and the future. Fate hangs over them both, but neither would have their individuality and their power to move us if they merely exemplified the power of fate, and were types of the anonymous mass of mankind.

It seems clear from Pushkin's alterations that he wished to remove from the portrait of Evgeny the impression of any stylised generalisation.

> Каких встречаете вы тьму,
> От вас нимало не отличный
> Ни по лицу, ни по уму.
> Как все, он вел себя нестрого,
> Как вы, о деньгах думал много,
> Как вы, сгрустнув, курил табак,
> Как вы, носил мундирный фрак.

You can meet a thousand like him, and there's nothing distinguishes him from you either in face or intellect. Like everyone else he was not very strict in his conduct, like you he thought a lot about money, smoked when he felt low and wore like you a uniform coat. (IV, 531.)

There is a marked difference between the comparative familiarity and facility of this early draft and the remoteness of the later version. But if remoteness was what Pushkin was aiming at it is arguable that he went too far. Though *The Bronze Horseman* was never definitively completed, a late revision cuts out Evgeny's soliloquy as he lies in bed listening to the storm and worrying about his future:

> «Жениться? Мне? зачем же нет?
> Оно и тяжело, конечно;
> Но что ж, я молод и здоров,
> Трудиться день и ночь готов;
> Уж кое-как себе устрою
> Приют смиренный и простой
> И в нем Парашу успокою.
> Пройдет, быть может, год-другой —
> Местечко получу, Параше
> Препоручу хозяйство наше

И воспитание ребят...
И станем жить, и так до гроба
Рука с рукой дойдем мы оба,
И внуки нас похоронят...»

Get married? Me? Well and why not? It would be hard going of course, but then I'm young and healthy and ready to work day and night. Somehow or other I'll fix up a simple modest little place for Parasha to settle down in. After maybe a year or two I'll get myself dug in with a job and be able to delegate the household and the kids' education to Parasha...and so we'll live, and so we'll go down hand in hand to the grave, and our grandchildren will bury us. (IV, 538.)

So good is the passage that many editions, even the most modern ones, ignore the MS cancellations and retain it. Yet scholars emphasise that Pushkin had already cut this paragraph before the poem was submitted to the censor, and that he did not restore it after publication of the poem as a whole had been refused. For Bryusov, this confirms that Pushkin intended wholly to depersonalise the poem, removing all traces of Onegin-like familiarity; and he compares the emphasis on the anonymity of the hero with the excision, at a much earlier stage, of the name of Peter himself from the first two lines of the Prologue, and the substitution of the bare monosyllable *on* ('*he* stood, plunged in vast thoughts'). But we have noticed that Peter's thoughts are not those of a monolithic and impersonal potentate but of an ebullient and self-satisfied landlord, and Evgeny's meditation is equally sanguine and preoccupied. 'Marry? Me? Well and why not?' It is vitally important that Evgeny's reflections should not appear to be for the audience's benefit, and that there should be no placing, through what he dreams, of his function in the poem as little man, proud of his small home and his simple amenities. Pushkin's first attempt overdid it, creating the diary of a nobody with a certain pastoral patronage. After the idea of a small home for Parasha and himself, Evgeny's reflection continued:

Кровать, два стула; щей горшок
Да сам большой; чего мне боле?
Не будем прихотей мы знать,
По воскресеньям летом в поле
С Парашей буду я гулять;

A bed, two chairs, a pot of soup – there I'd be my own master, what more would I need? We wouldn't have grand ideas. On Sundays in summer I'd take Parasha out for a stroll in the country.

Pushkin wisely omitted the furniture, and moved the Sunday outing to the end of the poem, generalising it among the tribe of clerks to whom Evgeny had once belonged.

> Остров малый
> На взморье виден. Иногда
> Причалит с неводом туда
> Рыбак на ловле запоздалый
> И бедный ужин свой варит,
> Или чиновник посетит,
> Гуляя в лодке в воскресенье,
> Пустынный остров.

A little island can be seen offshore. Sometimes a fisherman out late after a catch will moor there with his nets and cook his meagre supper; or some clerk, out boating on a Sunday, will visit the deserted island.

Only the fisherman and the *chinovnik* on an outing, seen appropriately now in their pastoral setting, visit the island where the little house in which Parasha and her mother had once lived is washed up by the flood, and where Evgeny's body is found.

Pushkin's problem was to avoid any trace of sentimentality in his presentation of Evgeny's future hopes, the sentiment that would come from our contemplation of him rather than from an oblique dramatic glimpse. The final presentation is almost pedantic – *O chem zhe dumal on?* (What, then, did he think about?) and *On takzhe dumal...* (He also thought...) – phrases which give a silent irony to the point in Evgeny's stream of consciousness where he falls to dreaming, *kak poet*. '*Like* a poet': the point is that he is not one. Pushkin avails himself again of the distancing technique. *Were* Evgeny a poet he would not dream as he does, and the point is made again unobtrusively when he fails to return home after the flood and the landlord lets his lodgings to 'a poor poet'.

Both Annenkov and Chernyshevsky[1] agreed that too many detailed outlines would detract from the stark contours of the poem, but the latter felt none the less that Evgeny's dream was needlessly sacrificed. It is certainly something quite new in Pushkin's poetry and quite unlike the comic or witty passages which recalled the manner of *Evgeny Onegin* and *Ezersky* and were rightly removed. The tragic and the comic-grotesque were perfectly compatible, as Pushkin well knew from his dramatic experiments, but the new poem required a new style, and facetiousness could only bring back the tone of the previous one. An early draft contains a

---

[1] *Sovremennik* (1856), vol. LXX, no. 12.

senator, who sees a general in a boat outside the window and thinks he must have gone mad, but finding his servant sees the same thing too he is greatly relieved, and ordering a cup of tea dismisses the matter from his mind. The anecdote is in deadpan style, but its tone is quite unlike that of the completed poem, and the most startling proof of the transformation that took place during its growth. Earlier on, too, there was a longer statement of intent at the end of the Prologue, chatty in the *Onegin* style, which was finally condensed into five lines, the last of which states simply that 'mine will be a sad tale'.

Pechalen budet moy rasskaz – it is this that sets the tone of what is to come, and strangely enough it is a line that Pushkin first used in a draft of *Bakhchisaraisky fontan*, that nostalgic dream of a romantic harem tragedy. The line that would there have been languorous is here brusque, full of the cryptic and almost explosive animation that controls the tale. It is not, in its timing and context, a simple line. It implies, among other things, that even the anecdotal aspect of what follows will have an undercurrent of bitterness, the sombre hilarity that is buried under the account of the Tsar's reaction to the flood.

> В тот грозный год
> Покойный царь еще Россией
> Со славой правил. На балкон,
> Печален, смутен, вышел он
> И молвил: «С божией стихией
> Царям не совладеть».

In that dread year the late Tsar still reigned over Russia with glory. Sad and troubled he came out on to the balcony and said: 'Tsars cannot master the divine elements.'

Peter had superbly assumed that a Tsar *could* master 'the divine elements'. But beneath the gravity of the words there is no hint of satire making its neat snap of demonstration. The tyrant's helplessness is not mocked: art accords it the same attention as the helplessness of the slave. As in *Anchar* there is no hint of why the Prince (or Tsar in the uncensored version) behaves as he does, so Alexander's reaction to the disaster is somnambulistic. There can be no warmth of sympathy, no intimacy of grief; though the generals are sent to help the people it is plain why nothing as engagingly human as the story of the senator and the boat can be left in the poem. Neva and Tsar, statue and Evgeny, are held apart like the corners of a quadrilateral. 'There is in this city', said

Ansiferov, 'the pathos of space.' Across those wide streets and squares, the broad river, the slender isolation of the gilded spires, nothing can touch, nothing can join.

But the vision of the poem extends far beyond Petersburg and beyond Russia. More than any other comparable work of the modern literary imagination *The Bronze Horseman* includes the experience of modern man, urban animation and urban solitude, the images of which are more vivid and more haunting even than those of the statue and Evgeny, power and the personal fate. They are proffered with no persistence and no sign of deliberate attempt – the positive in Pushkin's 'opposites' seems unaware of the negative leverage, and the solitude of the tale is equally unconscious of the gaiety and acceptance of the Prologue. In its 'abyss of space' every object in the poem denies its fellows. Beside this vision the Paris in the flux of Baudelaire's *Andromaque*, the *fourmillante cité, cité pleine de rêves*, seems as intimate as the 'waste land', the London townscape of T. S. Eliot which Baudelaire inspired. They are a Paris and London belonging solely to the poet, the literary towns that Petersburg itself was to become for the Russian symbolist and acmeist poets. And the fragments that these poets 'shore against their ruins' are those of tradition and past poetry, the linkage that enables the poet to make sense of his alienated world, to connect by art the disparate experiences that seem to have no coherence in modern life. Pushkin in *The Bronze Horseman*, it seems to me, gives us modernity in poetry before it has come to give this characteristically modern representation of itself.

In the world of the poem nothing comes out of the past but power, in the shape of the bronze statue, and in the inhuman world it has created life is sustained as Evgeny in his madness sustains it.

> И так он свой несчастный век
> Влачил, ни зверь ни человек,
> Ни то ни сё, ни житель света
> Ни призрак мертвый...

And so he dragged on his miserable life, neither beast nor man, neither this nor that, neither dweller in this world nor ghost from the dead.

The irony of the poem's comprehensiveness is that 'all human life is there' but appears only in its absence, the absence even of human speech, for the removal of Evgeny's dreaming soliloquy means that he utters only five words in the poem:

> Он мрачен стал
> Пред горделивым истуканом
> И, зубы стиснув, пальцы сжав,
> Как обуянный силой черной,
> «Добро, строитель чудотворный! –
> Шепнул он, злобно задрожав, –
> Ужо тебе!...»

Lowering he stood before the proud effigy and clenching his teeth, clenching his fists, as if possessed by some black force, he whispered, trembling with fury: 'All right then, miracle-builder! – you've got it coming to you!...'

The solitary madman has found his voice and established a kind of human contact. And the effigy, who ignored the waves that were inundating his capital, now seems abruptly to react as one human being to another.

> Показалось
> Ему, что грозного царя,
> Мгновенно гневом возгоря,
> Лицо тихонько обращалось.

It seemed to him that – lit with a flicker of rage – the face of the dread Tsar was slowly turning...

Evgeny has two human contacts in the poem, with the heroine we never see, and with the statue itself. Parasha and Peter are not present in human form but in places, the local habitations of Evgeny's day-dream and his nightmare.

> ...Почти у самого залива –
> Забор некрашенный, да ива
> И ветхий домик: там оне,
> Вдова и дочь, его Параша,
> Его мечта...

...almost by the gulf itself is an unpainted fence and a willow and a shabby little house: there they are, the widow and her daughter, his Parasha, his dream...

Yet there is no explicit contrast between the unpainted fence, the little house and the willow, and Peter's square and monument, with its vast rock and iron railing. And Evgeny has no further contact with the statue. If he passed the square in his deranged wanderings he would remove his cap without raising his eyes. But his body is found on the island where the cottage, like a black bush, has been washed up by the flood. In the final lines of the poem the brief sentences interrupt the rhythm, placing a full stop in the centre of almost every line; after the sonorous onomatopoeia of the charging horseman the effect is almost like Shakespearean prose following on the rhetoric of verse. Not only is the rhythm prosaic; it dies away into the mutter of the last line, with its feminine ending:

У порога
Нашли безумца моего,
И тут же хладный труп его
Похоронили ради Бога.

By the threshold my madman was found and in that very place his cold corpse was buried, out of charity.

– an ending which contrasts most obviously with the two triumphant concluding syllables of the Prologue's demand:

Вражду и плен старинный свой
Пусть волны финские забудут
И тщетной злобою не будут
Тревожить вечный сон Петра!

Let the Finnish waves forget their old enmity and bondage, and let them not disturb with their vain rancour Peter's eternal sleep!

And that is all. Lear does not die with Cordelia in his arms. Peter is exalted and Evgeny laid low, and each epiphany seems unconscious of the other. Yet the needs of tragedy are fulfilled, and we are moved, as only the greatest art can move us, that in a poem of absence, of utter separation, Evgeny's body should be found where it is. Characteristically the tragic dismissal is buried far back in the poem when the flood subsides, the people walk in the streets again 'with cold unfeeling', and 'everything returned to its former order' (*V poryadok prezhny vce voshlo*), a line that twins and locks into place the last line of the Prologue: *pechalen budet moy rasskaz*. But one thing has not returned. Tragedy is human, and the corpse of Evgeny is left by its own free and final will outside the prison of power.

The Bronze Horseman is the most remarkable of nineteenth-century poems in that it achieves the goal which the most ambitious of them set themselves without recourse to any structure of mythology or meditation, legend or symbol. It does not – like *Faust* or *Prometheus Unbound* – create a world of its own to image man's condition and the forces that determine it. It brings the past into the present, using history and fantasy to give a yet sharper reality to an actual place and event. It is the last wholly comprehensive work of literature to present itself to us in the form of a poem, and to make that form not the *chose préservée* that for Valéry poetry in the nineteenth century had necessarily become, but a medium that is meaningful on the same terms as the novels that came after it.

5

THE DRAMA

In the draft of a projected introduction to *Boris Godunov* Pushkin wrote that he did not care about the reception of the successive books of *Evgeny Onegin*. 'But I shall admit quite frankly that I should be upset by the failure of my tragedy, for I firmly believe that the popular tenets of the Shakespearean drama are better suited to the Russian theatre than are the courtly habits of the stage of Racine, and any such failure might slow down the reformation of our stage.' *Boris* was Pushkin's most carefully executed work. He took much more trouble over it than he did with *Onegin*, the *Little Tragedies*, or *The Bronze Horseman*, and he felt that as a model for a future Russian drama it would be the corner-stone of his reputation. Shakespeare may quite possibly have felt the opposite – taking pains over his long poems but writing his plays rapidly and caring little what became of them – for to Shakespeare's contemporaries the long poem had the same august status that historical drama on the Shakespearean model had acquired by 1830. The form that will seem of decisive importance to posterity seldom shows it at the time. *Onegin*, not *Boris*, was to be the inspiration of Russian literature, because it was a novel, though a novel in verse; while the dramatic element in Dostoevsky's novels owes less to Pushkin's play than to his poems.

Pushkin's theories and ideas about drama in his day were perceptive and unportentous, but they were ideas, they were theories. Where the drama was concerned he could not follow the instinctual path that had enabled him to make use of and discard other writers: Parny, Voltaire or Byron. Shakespeare could not be used in this way. Moreover the things in his art which seemed most inspiring for a new model drama were not the essentials. No more than his contemporaries could Pushkin be expected to grasp, still less to profit from, the secrets of Shakespearean unity. What appealed was the impression of careless mastery – endless scenes, rapid transitions, the formal and informal, the tragic and the comic – 'as if the mask of human history itself had been put on the

stage'. Moreover Shakespeare seemed to authorise the free adaptation of a historical source, and Pushkin had already decided to take
one from Karamzin's History. 'You want a plan', he wrote to
Vyazemsky when he had completed the first half of *Boris*; 'take
the end of the tenth and all the eleventh volume of Karamzin's
history, and there is a plot for you.' 'What a marvel they are!' he
exclaimed of these volumes in another letter to Zhukovsky, '*C'est
palpitant comme la gazette d'hier*'.[1]

Shakespeare's plots were not drawn from Plutarch or Holinshed
in quite this fashion. After his apprentice work in the first two parts
of *Henry VI*, his stagecraft achieves unity by emphasis on one or
two characters or groups of characters and the confrontation
between them. The confrontation of Richard II and Bolingbroke
dramatises in action their respective natures. In *Henry IV*, as in
Antony and Cleopatra, the pattern is triangular: power and weakness contending in different shapes; to secure it Shakespeare
transformed Plutarch's Cleopatra from an enigmatic political
figure into a marvellously and monstrously human one, and he
transforms in the same way the sources of both *Lear* and *Othello*,
isolating and enlarging his main protagonists and letting the action
flow from the collision between their natures.

Poltava shows a deeper reading of this aspect of Shakespeare's
stagecraft than does *Boris Godunov*. Though the opponents do not
meet, Mazepa's hatred of Peter points up Peter's imperial preoccupations; it is because his activities are multifarious and god-
like that the lower nature can deceive him. But between Boris
Godunov and the Pretender Dimitri there is no dramatic relation
at all. Not only do they never meet but each is absorbed in his own
affairs, and their historical antagonism is not transposed into
psychological terms but left in the realm of the accidental – or of
the historically determined, for as we shall see, Soviet critics are
quick to translate this dramatic weakness into a display of true
historical insight. This history is not dramatised by the clash of
personality. Shakespeare confronts Cleopatra with Octavius, a
meeting that may indeed have taken place, in order that the truth
of their natures should be finally revealed in their incompatibility.
Schiller confronts Elizabeth with Maria Stuart, a meeting we know
did not take place, so that the play's spiritual dimension should be
enhanced by their union, at the sacrifice of their historical and
plausible selves. Neither unifying course is open to Pushkin, and,

[1] September and August 1825. Written from Mikhailovskoye.

dramatically speaking, Boris and the Pretender remain chronicle characters.

'*Est-elle une tragédie de caractère ou de costume?*' asked Pushkin rhetorically in a letter in French to the younger Raevsky, which was not sent off and which may have been kept by Pushkin as a memorandum of his ideas on drama and dramatic verisimilitude, ideas more easily expressed in the French literary vocabulary than in Russian.[1] *Costume* has the sense, originally Italian, of manners or habits, and Pushkin comments that though he has chosen this easier genre he has tried to unite both. Yet it is clear he knew he had not achieved the historical character who is also universal; and that he was concentrating on the sober and localised historical account. 'I had been looking at Boris from the political point of view, without observing his poetic side' he wrote to Vyazemsky, acknowledging a comment passed on from Karamzin. The latter had suggested that there was a fine dramatic contradiction in the combined piety and ferocity of the Tsar, who constantly searched the scriptures for justification for his deeds. Pushkin, who alone of the playwrights of the time had the Shakespearean gift of linguistic *seizure* of the core of a personality (as we see in the *Little Tragedies*, *The Gipsies* and *Rusalka*), was inhibited in his most ambitious play from the instinctive use of it. He relied instead on rhetoric and demonstration. Boris's speech beginning *Dostig ya vysshey vlasti* (I have reached the height of power) records his disillusion and his sense of the people's ingratitude –

> Живая власть для черни ненавистна.
> Они любить умеют только мертвых.

Living power is hateful to the mob. They are only capable of loving the dead.

[1] Written during his Mikhailovskoye exile in July 1825, the letter expresses commonsense views about dramatic convention remarkably similar to those of Dr Johnson's Preface to his edition of Shakespeare. Since all theatre is artificial, why should some conventions be accepted and others not? 'The true geniuses of tragedy have never troubled about verisimilitude' writes Pushkin. 'Look how boldly Corneille managed *The Cid*. You wish the rule of 24 hours? So be it – and he piles up enough events for four months. There is nothing more vain than small changes of the accepted rules. Alfieri is profoundly struck with the absurdity of the *aside*. He does away with it..., lengthens the monologue, and thinks he has made a revolution in the system of tragedy.'

The letter fragment ends with an illuminating comment on the different problems involved in play writing. 'Most of the scenes require only the reason; when I arrive at a scene which demands inspiration I wait for it, or I skip the scene – this way of working is quite new for me.' *Boris* was clearly not written with the headlong speed of the narrative poems.

in comments which join up with his death-bed instructions to his son. But this is not Boris in himself: there is no dramatic spark across the gap between speaker and sentiment. The famous line *Okh, tyazhela ty, shapka Monomakha* (How heavy art thou, crown of Monomakh!) is a regal commonplace like Henry IV's 'Uneasy lies the head that wears a crown'. Compare the conscience of King Claudius, in whose voice we can hear the vulnerability and incongruity of feeling ('All may be well'...) which make up an individual response to the same situation of kingly power, guilt and remorse. It shows the depth of Pushkin's insight into Shakespeare that this freedom his heroes have from the characteristic aspect of their situations struck him more forcefully than anything else. As he put it, *il ne craint jamais de compromettre son personnage, il le fait parler avec tout l'abandon de la vie, car il est sûr en temps et lieu de lui faire trouver le langage de son caractère.*[1]

But Pushkin could not give this freedom to Boris: he is too tied to historical conception. And even so there is some inconsistency between two concepts. Karamzin's treatment of Godunov's rule emphasises poetic justice: Boris had murdered the true heir, and the offence must be expiated by the killing of his own son and the succession of the Pretender. Historically there is no evidence that Boris did kill the Tsarevitch: he profited from what seems to have been the accidental death of an epileptic child. But when affairs in the state went badly and he lost popularity it was remembered that he had no true claim to the throne. Pushkin makes some play with the Tsar's guilt, but the whole tendency of the play is to show that it has only the most indirect connection with the march of events. The boyars spread and exploit the rumour that Boris had attempted but failed to kill the Tsarevitch, who is now coming to claim the throne; for their own ends they make use of the Pretender and are as indifferent as his Polish supporters to the actual authenticity of his claim. They are carried forward by the rising tide of popular feeling which they have helped to manipulate, and it is

---

[1] Pushkin, as he may well have known, was here joining issue with the central neo-classic canon on the portrayal of character in drama. Rymer, an admirer of Rapin, had censured Shakespeare in his *Tragedies of the Last Age Considered* for the very quality that Pushkin admired. Iago, for example, belongs to the military profession, which values honour, and so could not – according to Rymer – have stooped to low trickery and deceit. Yet Pushkin seems to have been the only writer of his age to see the issue clearly and to profit from his perception. The romantic playwrights who so much admired Shakespeare did not discern the real importance of this freedom – its field for precise psychological inquiry. See the further references on pages 183 and 187.

ironic that the Pushkin who is a boyar character in the play, and the poet's ancestor, can claim with perfect truth to Boris's general Basmanov that it is useless for him to struggle any longer against popular sentiment, the instinct of the *narod*.

Boris's death, though opportune for his opponents, is merely an incident, not a climax. History gives the impression of not being interested in drama. And this, according to Pushkin's Marxist and determinist critic Gukovsky, is precisely the play's strength.[1] For Gukovsky, realism in art is above all the correct understanding of the historical process, and *Boris Godunov* establishes Pushkin's claim to be the first European realist. In its implicit vision of how things work out, *Boris* is certainly a remarkable conception, but neither its form nor its overt dramatic interest is anything but conventional and old-fashioned, and the many Russian history plays that followed it copied its form without understanding its equivocal idea of history. In any case this idea can perhaps rightly be intuited, but not demonstrated: when Gukovsky observes that Boris's contempt for the people shows that he is unfitted to be 'the agent of history', we can only wonder if he is seriously suggesting that Pushkin himself thought this and put it in; but it is possible that Gukovsky, who was more of a literary critic than a Marxist, was paying tribute here, as in other contexts, to the party line.

The costume drama could not keep pace with the nineteenth-century advance in historical awareness – only the novel could do so. The novelists of social realism were conscious historians and were capable of falsifying history by theorizing about it; Shakespeare may change history for dramatic purposes but he does not use the play as a vehicle for his own historical theories. Yet in Shakespeare history lives on the stage as in the nineteenth century it can live only in the novel. Büchner's *Danton's Tod* is perhaps the only other play of Pushkin's epoch to present historic events on the stage with something of Shakespeare's simplicity and 'pointlessness' – Danton is no more of a hero than Boris Godunov, and much less of one than in Carlyle's history – but the French Revolution was a different matter from seventeenth-century Muscovy. Since Schiller, the best historical plays had become virtually the starting-point of query and transformation. Schiller's *Und im Abgrund wohnt die Wahrheit* contradicts the Shakespearean world of primary creation. Hebbel wishes to make the historical poetic drama the vehicle for solving 'the riddle of the world'. Taking from the

[1] V. P. Gukovsky, *Pushkin i problemy realisticheskogo stilya* (Moscow 1957).

Apocrypha the story of Judith and Holofernes he observed that the simple revengeful nature he found there 'was not worthy of its success. The fact that a cunning woman long ago cut off a man's head left me cold.' Schiller did not wish to see Joan of Arc as a peasant girl playing a remarkable part in the Hundred Years War, but as a manifestation of the human spirit – almost the categorical imperative – in action; and such a manifestation cannot wear trousers and be burnt at the stake. Up to our own day the chronicle origins of the history play have shown themselves to be incongruous with the sophistication of many authors who have used the form;[1] and Pushkin wisely does not attempt any sophistication. With *Boris Godunov*, as with Shakespearean drama, it is we who debate the phenomenon and not the author who appears to explore it.

Idealistic Zhukovsky, the chief populariser of Schiller in Russia, translated *Die Jungfrau von Orleans*, and there is an irreverent reference by Pushkin to 'the maidenhead of Orleans' in a letter written from Kishinev to his brother in 1822.[2] He knew Schiller's plays (including probably the *Demetrius* fragment, whose hero is the pretender Dimitri of *Boris Godunov*) but their peculiar splendour, which was to have so profound an influence on Dostoevsky, was alien to him. It is an illuminating instance of the way in which great writers respond or fail to respond to their predecessors. In spite of his admiration for Shakespeare, Dostoevsky's understanding of him was nothing like so intuitive or so just as Pushkin's – Dostoevsky calls Stavrogin of *The Devils* his Prince Harry, seeing both as men of mystery whose secret the drama will reveal – but Pushkin could not of course transform Shakespeare in the astonishing way that Dostoevsky was able to transpose the sympathetic genius of Schiller. The characterisation of *The Brothers Karamazov*, with its five main figures as aspects of a single whole, is clearly founded on that of Schiller's plays, whose *dramatis personae* 'elucidate each other', in Benno von Wiese's phrase, in an undivided vision of the human spirit. The lofty Schillerian soul becomes the Russian family, grotesquely unified in evil and good, soul and flesh, exaltation and despair. In Dmitri Karamazov (a

---

[1] Hochhuth's play *The Soldiers* continues the nineteenth-century German tradition of the history play into an interpretation of our own times – the war of 1939–45.

[2] Cf. E. K. Kostka, *Schiller in Russian Literature*. See also Eykhenbaum's suggestive essay 'O tragedii Shillera v svete ego teorii tragicheskogo' in the collection *Skvoz literaturu*.

Russian Karl Moor who is constantly quoting Schiller), and in his father, the ideal is reconciled in art with actual human horror and degradation; the great court scene is the German intellectual drama transformed into Russian comedy.

The weakest aspect of *Boris Godunov*, by contrast, is its literal resemblances to Shakespeare. The Moscow friends who, as Pogodin records, listened enthralled to Pushkin reading the play, were struck by the bold originality of the comic scenes, then quite novel in serious Russian drama, though Pushkin noted sardonically that Petersburg enemies afterwards claimed they were all copied from Victor Hugo's *Cromwell*, for whose interminable ebullience he felt impatience and contempt.[1] Hugo's example, however, did to some extent help to create the enthusiasm with which comic sequences and contrasts were received; the days were long past when Schiller found it necessary to substitute for Shakespeare's porter in *Macbeth* a porter who enters chanting an invocation to the dawn. The crowd and battlefield scenes in *Boris*, and the use of popular rhyming puns during the comic business in the tavern on the Lithuanian frontier, are admirably done, but they are too close to the Shakespearean model to have a true indigenous vitality.

Though he helped to pioneer comic business in Russian poetic drama, Pushkin was by no means the first to take the subject of Boris and the Pretender. It was already the favoured historic dramatic subject and Pushkin's idea may well have been to provide a copy-book drama by selecting an obvious theme. As if by policy he seems to dissociate it from the metaphysical interest in pretenders as such that previous dramatists had shown. The Romantic drama was naturally fascinated by *identities* and the dramatic realisation of individuality – Byron's *Werner* and Kleist's *Amphi-*

---

[1] In an article written in 1836 (VII, 487) and published in *Sovremennik* in 1837, Pushkin joined in the controversy that had been taking place in English and French reviews over Chateaubriand's literal translation (how do you translate the English *how do you do* – French *comment vous portez-vous* – *word for word* into Russian, he wonders). He takes the occasion to berate Hugo for the vulgarity with which he brings Milton into his *Cromwell*, whether he is portraying him as the butt of Cromwell or being received with compliments by Corneille and Descartes. He also deflates the notion that *narodnost* requires the choice of subjects from Russian history. No author is more *narodny* than Shakespeare, who sets his plays in Italy, Denmark, Bohemia etc. (Dostoevsky, as we have noticed, was later to remark in his Pushkin lecture that Shakespeare's foreigners are really all Englishmen, whereas Pushkin's – in *The Stone Guest* and elsewhere – really are like inhabitants of the country he portrays. Like many of Dostoevsky's claims in the lecture it should be taken with a grain of salt.)

tryon are typical examples – and combining as he did the man of mystery with the local colour of the past, the kingly pretender was a highly favoured conception.[1]

As long ago as 1771 Sumarokov had written *Dimitri Samozvanets*, and Kotzebue, in Petersburg at the time, was probably influenced by it in taking up the same theme. Significantly he made Dimitri the true and rightful heir, and not the *obmanshchik*, the impostor of the Russian sources, thus initiating a series of European plays on the Demetrius theme. It took the genius of Schiller to perceive that a dramatic and philosophic focal point could be made of the Pretender's uncertainty about the truth of his own claim, but the very effectiveness of this challenge made it correspondingly difficult to devise a *dénouement* that would not be anti-climax or – worse – mere 'theatre'. The unfinished plays of both Schiller and Hebbel keep history wholly in the dramatist's hands, juggling with it as drama and philosophy require. Hebbel's preoccupation is with the hero made or unmade by his role, how the office has made the man and the Pretender the Prince.

In Schiller's Demetrius fragment the Pretender, doubly confident by reason of his legitimacy and his European success, despises Russian backwardness and barbarism; and the 'kernel' of the tragedy as Schiller saw it is the irony that this civilising confidence is in fact that of a man who is stateless and illegitimate. He has no deep inborn national being and national sympathy. His political ambitions may be noble, but they proceed from a technical ignorance of himself which must also be an ignorance of what Russia requires. Unlike Perkin Warbeck, also an absorbing dramatic subject to Schiller, his confidence in his claim and himself can be destroyed by what seems certain proof that the claim is false: when the man who claims to have murdered the true Dimitri reveals himself, the Pretender kills him. His claim is now unchallengeable, but the crime has revealed to himself his own lack of certainty, and like Macbeth, he dies inwardly. He comes to hate Marina, to whom he is betrothed, and falls in love with Axenia, Godunov's daughter. But as with Thekla and Piccolomini in *Wallenstein*, the love interest (Axenia detests the Pretender and loves the imprisoned Romanov, who unaware of her feeling worships her without hope) is merely the accepted convention of such a drama, and without internal pressure.

---

[1] A fascination that finally expires in the formalism of Pirandello and in Sartre's play *Kean*.

The same cannot be said of the relation between Marina and the Pretender in *Boris Godunov*. As we shall see, that has a significance in the play's context which bears out its general meaning, even though that meaning is the reverse of Schiller's: it cannot be seen taking shape in the author's mind, and its relation to Pushkin's avowed purpose – to create a model for local drama – can only be guessed at. Some indications exist however. In his notes on Pogodin's *Marfa Posadnitsa*, a historical play about the free town of Novgorod, Pushkin commented that 'the dramatist must be as dispassionate as fate. He must not be adroit, and lean to one side, avoiding the other. His task must be to resurrect the past in its truth.' The same idea is expressed by the old chronicler Pimen, in conversation with the young monk who will afterwards become the Pretender Dimitri and who himself sees in Pimen the impartial recorder:

> Спокойно зрит на правых и виновных,
> Добру и злу внимая равнодушно,
> Не ведая ни жалости, ни гнева.

Calmly he looks alike on the just and the guilty, impartially noting evil and good, and observing both without wrath or pity.

In dramatic terms such a conscious policy of dispassion is reductive, cutting motive and connection: we can *see* Pushkin not manipulating the past as we can never see Shakespeare. Hence the distancing of Boris and Dimitri, with whom we are never intimate. (Compare Shakespeare's very unchronicled presentation of Richard III who speaks the opening lines of the play, drawing the audience at once into the genially amoral world of 'I am myself alone', and whose consciousness is the index of the play's events.) It is significant that Pushkin wrote, and afterwards cut, a scene in which Dimitri laments in trochaic metre his tedious life in the monastery and in which he is prompted by an evil monk to take upon himself the role of Pretender. In the final version we have no hint of his intention until he appears on the Lithuanian frontier. Instead we have the admirable scene with Pimen, the ideal Russian chronicler who is indifferent to flattery or gain and who betrays neither thought nor passion.

> Ни на челе высоком, ни во взорах
> Нельзя прочесть его сокрытых дум;
> Всё тот же вид смиренный, величавый.

Not on his high forehead nor in his looks can his hidden thoughts be guessed at; his air is at once humble and sublime.

But Pimen has himself been a warrior in time past, as Dimitri reminds him, and when Dimitri tells the dream that presages his rise and fall, the old monk admits that his own sleep is disturbed by dreams of the passions and struggles of his youth. The resonance of past and future is audible in the cloistral quiet; the Dimitri who talks with Pimen is very different from the adventurer in Poland who accepts a court poet's tribute in Latin verses and quotes *Musa gloriam coronat, gloriaque musam.* And the Boris who plotted the death of the Tsarevitch at Uglich is unrecognisable in the careworn ruler advising his son on his death-bed, ignorant whether or not the dynasty he has founded will survive. There are neither endings nor beginnings, and the principle of absolute differentiation governs the presentation of both character and history, a principle that Pushkin certainly did not find in Shakespeare, who in his mature histories no less than his tragedies is always careful to reveal causality and continuity by dramatic demonstration. The dying Henry IV is still the usurper Bolingbroke, and his son Prince Hal explains his own present conduct and future policy, to be corroborated by time and event; the surefootedness which is his most effectively ambiguous characteristic is shown to the audience by his own awareness of it.

This discontinuity between the successive reports on, or appearances of, the protagonists is excellent as history but less so as drama, and Pushkin's real weakness is in stage sense. He does not recognise, as Shakespeare always did, how much an audience needs to be helped, and it is no wonder that his friends were puzzled by what they considered the play's lack of point (*Qu'est-ce qu'il prouve?* Katenin wanted to know). But his instinct has its advantages, though they could scarcely reveal themselves on the stage. Dimitri in Poland is no longer a Russian monk but a western soldier of fortune, a *vert galant* (Pushkin compared him to Henry of Navarre) who will lead Europe into Russia. His passion for Marina is an aspect of the Renaissance gallantry that he has acquired from his new environment. He wishes to appear to Marina not in his role as Tsarevitch but in the new guise of confidence and chivalric spirit which he has created for himself. She, on the other hand, has no interest in what he is himself but only as the Tsarevitch, the instrument for her own ambition. In terms of history love is fashion, folly, or – above all – *policy*, as Marina makes clear when he asks her if she would have loved him if he were not the true Dimitri.

Димитрий ты и быть иным не можешь;
Другого мне любить нельзя.

You are Dimitri and cannot be another; it is not possible for me to love another.

The scene inverts the obligatory love scene of romantic historical drama and is almost – as occurs not seldom in Pushkin – a parodic trap that here may remain unsprung by an audience not unnaturally failing to grasp the hidden irony. The assumptions of romantic love as a *sine qua non* of plot and personality, the nemesis of other plays,[1] are avoided by Pushkin; though the Pretender's confession to Marina makes it a *scène à faire* in the contemporary French style, the clearly recognised precedents of the love scene are Richard III and Lady Anne, Henry V and Katherine.

In the comic scenes Shakespeare is merely copied; here he is virtually parodied, and the scene is all the better for it. The echo of Richard III is repeated even more broadly when Dimitri, defeated in battle, is discovered lamenting the death of his horse, and is reminded by a follower that a horse is less important than a kingdom lost. This is the last we see of the Pretender, who has apparently suffered a climactic reverse, and yet a few minutes – as it were – later, Russia has submitted to him and his name is proclaimed in the Red Square. In the two intervening scenes Boris has died and his general, Basmanov, has been persuaded to join the Pretender. In the scale of history the drama of a battle is far less important than the slow fruition of chance and intrigue. It is as if Shakespeare had shown the military successes of Brutus and Cassius after the murder of Caesar, and then abruptly ended the play with the triumph of Octavius. The conventional sequence of dramatised history is reversed; the emphasis is taken from willed and successful action and laid on passivity. Instead of a conqueror Dimitri is indeed shown to be 'the agent of history'.

For the stock expectations of an audience, history's gain is drama's loss; there seems no doubt that in the last scenes Pushkin was deliberately concerned to emphasise a growing sense of the protagonists' helplessness, of their waiting for the inevitable to take place. In Karamzin's account Basmanov decides on his own initiative to become a traitor, and his defection spells the downfall of Boris's son Feodor. In the play the boyar Pushkin, emissary from the Pretender, blandly admits to Basmanov that he holds every

---

[1] For example Baron Rosen's *Pyotr Basmanov*, a five-act blank verse play of 1835, in which the hero has long been in love with Boris's daughter Kseniya.

military advantage, that all the cards are in his hand, but if he persists in playing them he will lose the game; and Basmanov, paralysed, gives in.

Boris Godunov is the only history play of its time which does not depend on an artificially dramatic conclusion only marginally related to history, and accepted by the audience like any other dramatic convention.[1] The projected climax of Schiller's *Demetrius* was a confrontation between the Pretender and his supposed mother, the widow of the last true Tsar. If she recognises him as her son the conspiracy formed against him will collapse After a moment of dramatic tension she refuses to recognise him and he falls dead, pierced by the conspirators' swords. Scenically admirable but historically quite impossible: by requiring such a suspension of our disbelief this ending would have surrendered history wholly to the conventions of the theatre; and this would have been inconsistent on Schiller's part, for in the earlier and completed part of the play the great scene in the Polish diet, with the significance of the antagonisms it reveals, is more than worthy of that mastery as a historian which Schiller had displayed in his history of the Thirty Years War. It is admittedly unfair to judge an uncompleted work, but *Demetrius* seems likely to have moved from the historical to the purely theatrical, while *Boris Godunov* comes at its end to the bare bones of event and makes the impersonal forces of history almost visible.

The ending required by the censor's office has an odd felicity, but the silence of the populace (*Narod bezmolvstvuet*) contradicts that logic of passivity which the final scenes have more and more deeply underlined. Having announced the deaths of Boris's widow and her son Feodor, the boyars demand why the crowd is silent and order it to shout 'Long live Tsar Dimitri Ivanovich!' In Pushkin's original version the reply comes like a great echo: *Da zdravstvuet tsar Dimitri Ivanovich!*, – as if the people incarnated the impersonal status quo of history and cannot withhold their recognition of its accomplishment.[2] Although it is clear that Boris's wife and son

---

[1] In the Raevsky letter Pushkin drew a distinction between the so-called verisimilitude of tragic convention (the unities) and verisimilitude of situation and speech. ('Verisimilitude of situations and truth of dialogue – here is the real rule of tragedy'.)

[2] Several critics have pointed out the similarity between the original ending and *Richard III*, III, vii:

Buckingham Then I salute you with this royal title –
Long live King Richard, England's worthy King!
All   Amen.

have not poisoned themselves but have been murdered, what matters is that they are dead. The last few lines of the play have a hidden subtlety, for in the boyar's proclamation the odiously false is juxtaposed with the palpably true: to the first statement the *narod* responds with the silence of horror (*narod v uzhase molchit*), to the second with a cry of assent.

It is no wonder that *Boris Godunov* has never been a success on the stage, for its best effects are both too obvious and too unexpected to be easily taken in by the spectator. It regards itself with a professional interest rather than looking out into the auditorium, yet there is nothing immodest or narcissistic in this – indeed Pushkin's approach could not be more modest, as if he felt that any attempt at originality or the spectacular was the last thing required. In his notes on Pogodin's *Marfa Posadnitsa*, which he thought of as a similar pilot work, he commented that the new folk drama on a Russian theme required a small circle to form the taste by which to judge it and to help 'overcome and change the customs, tastes and understanding of a whole generation', the generation that understood by tragedy the work of Voltaire and his successors and their Russian imitators. (Comedy, thanks to the far superior model of Molière and its use by Fonvizin, and especially by Griboyedov in *Woe from Wit* (*Gore ot uma*), was in much better shape.) Curiously enough, Pushkin's enemy Bulgarin had written in 1825 in the *Russian Thalia* on the question of folk drama, maintaining that the Russian chronicles were a better model than 'Schiller, Shakespeare, Goethe, Racine, and Voltaire', a wholesale denunciation of foreign influence (far from uncommon in reactionary circles) which made Katenin scoff and no doubt amused Pushkin, though it was from the *Thalia* that he got the idea of giving *Boris Godunov* its affectedly antiquarian sub-title: 'A Comedy of the True Tribulations of the Russian State' – 'Comedy' in the old sense of any chronicle play.

Apart from the proper use and treatment of chronicle material, literary opinion was divided on the question of contemporary references and allusions in plays. The *Thalia* which Pushkin was sent in 1825 also contained the third act of Katenin's *Andromaque*, adapted from Racine, which Pushkin had already heard read and which was generally accepted to be full of political references, Alexander I figuring as Agamemnon. Küchelbecker's *Argives* and Zhandr's adapted *Wenceslas* (which Pushkin borrowed from extensively) were similarly seasoned with topical references on the method known as 'the second plan', inherited from the post-Voltaire tragedians of the Napoleonic empire. Katenin, who wished to get back to the purity of Racine, deplored these allusions, blaming Jouy, who put Napoleon into his *Sylla*, and Ozerov for the patriotic references in *Dimitri Donskoy*, which had aroused great enthusiasm at the time of the Battle of Eylau. Pushkin agreed. He felt that a true 'romantic' tragedy would present history dispassionately, without any of these neo-classic hints and nudges, and yet such a presentation was bound to suggest some contemporary application for, as he put it defensively in a letter about *Boris* to Benkendorf: 'tous les troubles se ressemblent'.[1]

Karamzin's history 'is as full of life as yesterday's newspapers', but it was the life of its own age and not of the modern scene. The actor should not, in the French fashion, court the audience's response by modern allusions, but should 'cut out of his performance everything not completely subdued and harmonised to the age that was being represented'. Pushkin's friends were somewhat dashed by this purism, and dismayed to find, when the Pimen scene was published in the *Moscow Messenger*, that the aged chronicler appeared to point no moral except that of submission to God and the Tsar, for Pushkin had appended in a note that Pimen embodied 'something youthfully naive and wise at once – his submission to the power of the Tsar, given from God'. Historically Pushkin must be right about this, though the incident shows how self-consciously political the atmosphere of dramatic theory had become. In any case, the strength of the scene lies not so much in the antiquarian reconstruction of Pimen as in the contrast between him and his disciple the Pretender: the tranquil old man reviewing history and the young one who is going to make it for himself. Naturally, too, the crowd scenes are drawn as much from first-hand observation (as must be the case with Shakespeare's histories) as from historical reconstruction. In Moscow at the time of Nicholas's coronation, Pushkin noted that the crowds were more interested in the free vodka than in sharing the solemn feelings of

---

[1] April 1830. It is of some interest that another of Pushkin's comments anticipates an argument of the defendants at the Sinyavsky–Daniel trial: that 'the author is not responsible for what his character may say'. None the less Benkendorf and Nicholas still thought the play potentially subversive, and in forbidding its production the Tsar gave Pushkin his celebrated advice to recast it as a novel on the model of Walter Scott. Considering Boris's shortcomings in stagecraft, the recommendation is perhaps not so ludicrous as it has usually been taken to be, though it is certainly unlikely that the Imperial wish was based on any critical discernment.

the occasion, a perception that appears in the talk of the townsfolk when Boris is being petitioned to accept the office of Tsar. A critic has pointed out that the crime on Boris's conscience would certainly have been taken to refer to Alexander I, who had connived in his father's murder.[1] Pushkin himself commented on the Pretender Dimitri's resemblance to Peter the Great and called him a westerniser who came before his time. It would be remembered that when the Pretender himself succumbed to intrigue and was murdered, his ashes were fired from a cannon towards the west – a symbolic purgation of European influence.

Indeed it is here that the real dramatisation of history occurs, and Pushkin must have planned it with conscious but unobtrusive care. Annenkov first noted the clash of two cultures, Russian and Western – more specifically, Polish – in the play. And Gukovsky has emphasised the schematic paralleling: a Russian poet (though he does not know he is one) Pimen, and a court poet of Cracow; we have two feasts, two priests (a Jesuit and the Russian patriarch), even two kinds of love: the romantic wooing, at once courtly and politic, of Dimitri and Marina, and the simple and touching devotion of the Tsarevna Kseniya to her dead betrothed. Over all there is Boris, the mature and responsible but historically fated ruler, and the adventurous Pretender with all the appeal of youth and change.

Gukovsky's emphasis on the dialectic does not affect the insight with which he describes the dynamic nature of contrast and opposition. Pushkin, he says, did not make the mistake of his contemporaries in supposing past and present can be equated: 'he did not see the people of the past as people in general, but understood their special characteristics and how they link with the present and also with the future'. By artistic instinct Pushkin understood the correct dialectical method of making history continuously meaningful, and he brings out the clash of thesis and antithesis with all the resources of human feeling and poetic style. However much he imputes to Pushkin an impossible degree of Marxian foreknowledge, Gukovsky's interpretation is if anything strengthened by the

[1] In his commentary on this play, 'Kommentary k "Borisu Godunovu"', in *Pushkin, Collected Works* (Moscow 1935), vii, G. O. Vinokur refers Boris to Macbeth, Richard III and Henry IV, and also to Napoleon's judicial murder of the Duc d'Enghien and Alexander's complicity in his father's assassination. As Pushkin put it, all these troubles certainly resemble each other, but it can hardly be by chance that a note in his MS refers to his own *Imaginary Conversations with Alexander I*, an earlier unfinished piece which shows his interest in the workings of an autocrat's conscience.

bafflement of Pushkin's contemporaries. Even the censor in 1826 had observed that whereas in 'Anglo-German drama' there was always a connection and a point, Pushkin's play was just 'bits of Karamzin divided into scenes and conversations' – 'Chinese shadows' as an anonymous critic put it in 1831.[1]

The interest of the censor's remark is that in Shakespeare and Schiller there is indeed 'a connection and a point', that of theatrical need as opposed to historical truth. Remove the hero, the climactic death, and the audience will not know where they are ('In this piece nothing is complete' complained Bulgarin). Although Gukovsky's thesis has the disadvantage of imposing a kind of unity by hindsight on the play – the *narod* is for him its true hero – it does draw attention to an underlying symmetry and structure as invisible to the first audience as the far more massive and complex symmetry of *War and Peace* was invisible to the reader of 1870.[2] In both play and novel the basic antithetical stance is the same: Europe and European ways as against Russia and Russian ways. The trouble is that Pushkin cannot give this shape a dramatic form as Tolstoy – by means of the novel's devices of coincidence, love and marriage, different kinds of family etc. – can give it the leisurely and extended one of fiction.

Hence the comparative failure of the play against the triumph of the novel. Gukovsky's interpretation really does help to make sense of the play, but cannot invest it with the status of a masterpiece. His insistence on its position as a pioneer work of historical realism leans too heavily on what came after. Since realism must have started somewhere let it start with *Boris Godunov*; and though his schematic comparisons with Racine (classic) and Shakespeare (romantic) do show how and where Pushkin's play differs from both in its avoidance of dramatic heroes and dramatic solutions, they do not really justify the application of the third label, realistic. The limitations of Boris evade the pattern, as the immense individuality of *War and Peace* evades the category of social realism in which Lukacs places it.

[1] Quoted by Slonimsky, '"Boris Godunov" i dramaturgiya 20kh godov', *Sbornik Statei*.
[2] It is an odd coincidence, if it is no more, that the title of Tolstoy's novel appears in a line of Pimen's speech on the task of a chronicler to record

> *Vse to, chemy svidetel v zhizni budesh:*
> *Voinu i mir, upravu gosudarey...*

All the things which you shall meet in life: war and peace, the government of Sovereigns...

The verse and poetic vocabulary are created with the same conscious deliberation, and in terms of a model, as the plot structure. As verse it lacks the full individuality and inevitability of Pushkin's poetry and of the blank verse he afterwards wrote in the *Little Tragedies* and *Rusalka*. The caesura after the second foot, after the French pattern, makes for monotony; and the lines have something abstract and insubstantial about them, a lack of full-bodied succulence, which, as in the different cases of Schiller and of Shelley, seems sometimes to arise from a kind of bloodless paraphrase of Shakespearean phraseology.[1] And yet the verse is by no means lacking in variety and range of effect. As Gukovsky points out, parallelism extends to the use of different and appropriate styles for Boris and the Pretender, Russia and Poland. The Pretender's love scene is in the language of western love poets, verging again on parody: the Tsarevna's lament for her dead betrothed is in a simple and touching prose with the aura of Russian folktale.

Pushkin intended to make a stylistic mixture. In the Raevsky letter he observed that the French dramatists had added a fourth unity to the classic three, 'the unity of style'. Russian tragedy, he felt, was still imprisoned in the *krepost* of the high style from which the English, Spanish and German playwrights had all freed themselves in their time. And though Ryleev, Küchelbecker, and Katenin had all been anxious in their own ways to liberate Russian drama from fashionable European influences, they wanted a unified Slavic style, a high Russian vocabulary that would combine the purity of Racine with the choral and lyric declamation of Schiller's German. In the old but still current forms of Church Slavonic the Russian language possessed what seemed an admirable instrument for this purpose. Pushkin had nothing against Church Slavonic, but he declined to employ it as a special *Kunstpoesie*. He used it to expand and enrich the writer's vocabulary in any context, and together with idioms of ordinary speech and the Gallicisms which the French-speaking Russian upper-class imported consciously and unconsciously into the language. He was all for incorrectness provided it was idiosyncratic. He wrote to Pogodin in November 1830 that in *Marfa Posadnitsa* the language was treated 'as Ioann [Ivan III] treated old Novgorod. Yet...more freedom

---

[1] For example Boris's speech to Shuisky about dead men rising from their graves to challenge him echoes Macbeth's words on the murdered Banquo. (Schiller, too, in *Maria Stuart*, paraphrases Macbeth's thwarted wish to be 'as broad and general as the casing air'.)

must be given our language (of course in keeping with its spirit) and your freedom is more to my liking than our prim correctness.' He thought Pogodin's play had 'a high, a European merit'. The adjective is significant. The better Russian national drama became, the more it would join Russian to European literature; no carefully segregated linguistic tradition could produce great art.

In his study of the play's language Vinokur points out that Pushkin combines in Pimen's speeches the imagery of his own lyrics combined with a flavour of archaism.[1] The sea to which Pimen compares the turbulent events he has recorded is the sea apostrophised in *K moryu* and *Pogaslo dnevnoe svetilo*, but the voice is that of the old chronicler himself, formed in the hours of scriptural study and intoned liturgy. Vinokur compares this 'multiform style' (*raznoobrazny slog*) to 'a laboratory in which the elegance, passion, sweetness and simplicity of Pushkin's lyric manner are mixed with the bookish elements of eighteenth-century cabinet drama and the chronicle'. Mixed – not compounded – that is the drawback. The style of *Evgeny Onegin* and *The Bronze Horseman* is not *raznoobrazny* in this sense, for its energy has burned up and transformed the elements it contains.[2] The styles in *Boris* harmonise with each other but exhibit in slow motion their archaic, pseudo-archaic, and contemporary romantic components.

It would have been logical for Pushkin to use these linguistic elements to make congruous dramatic patterns, Gallicisms for the Pretender and Poland, Church Slavonic for Boris and Moscow. But, whether deliberately or not, he avoids consistency here. He salts his mixture with Church Slavonic throughout, only occasionally concentrating it in a suitable context. It is to be found in Marina's speeches as well as those of Boris and the Patriarch. Nor does Pushkin seem perturbed by incongruity and anachronism. Bulgarin objected that some courtly European, 'a Ritter Toggenburg', might have compared the disillusionment of supreme power with a young man's disillusion in love, but not a seventeenth-century Russian Tsar.

The point is interesting for the light it throws on contemporary

---

[1] G. O. Vinokur, 'Yazyk *Borisa Godunova*', *Sbornik Statei*, ed. K. N. Derzhavin (Leningrad 1936).

[2] Compare the soliloquy of Pimen with that of Evgeny in *The Bronze Horseman* beginning *Zhenitsya? Mne? zachem zhe net?* (Marry? Me? Well why not?). For all its qualities the former remains consciously a fine speech in a poetic drama, while Evgeny's line – with its marvellous acoustic and mimetic suggestiveness – appears as unaware of itself as poetry as do similar effects in Shakespeare's plays.

attitudes to historical accuracy – Bulgarin himself produced historical novels – but it was this kind of insistence on 'getting things right' which helped to make the nineteenth-century history play so barren a form. Pushkin's 'verisimilitude of situations and truth of dialogue', and 'style suited to characters and events' never becomes an anxious search for the appropriate. Even through Letourneur's translation he may have guessed at the vitality that Shakespeare's dialogue can derive from the unexpected and the incongruous. Soldiers and peasants in Shakespeare do not necessarily speak like soldiers and peasants. The conscript Feeble's utterance has a prince's heroism, and in the heat of narration the Sergeant in *Macbeth* coins hyperboles like a courtier, as does the blunt soldier Enobarbus in his account of Cleopatra; while the conversation of Cleopatra herself and her ladies would be more appropriate to the Boar's Head in Eastcheap than the palace at Alexandria.

Of course *Boris* cannot show the vast dimension of reality which these examples imply, but in creating a *raznoobrazny* style Pushkin clearly intended to use it so that his characters should not become 'characteristic':

When a character is conceived, all that he is made to say, even the most random things, bears his essential stamp (like the pedants and sailors of Fielding's old novels). A conspirator says 'Give me a drink' conspiratorially – and that's ridiculous. Look at Byron's Hater [Loredano in *The Two Foscari*]...this monotony, this affectation of the laconic, this continual rage – is this nature? Thus we get this self-consciousness and timidity of dialogue. Look at Shakespeare. Read Shakespeare – he is never afraid of compromising his character...[1]

In a short article, *O Narodnosti v Literature*, Pushkin observed that though Shakespeare, Calderón, and Racine do not necessarily bother about their own country and people, they have *narodnost* in the definitive sense that they are both national and popular, and this is more important than writing *Petriads* and *Rossiads*.[2] He connects the tendency to be 'characteristic' with the self-conscious wish for a national literature.

Despite his indifference to stagecraft, Pushkin may have adopted from Shakespeare the device of 'signposts', indications which reveal the dramatically vital aspect of a key character unmistakably to the audience and prevent confusion when he does not necessarily speak or behave 'in character'. Isabella's lines in

[1] The Raevsky letter. (The first draft in French, July 1825.)   [2] VII, 38.

Measure for Measure: 'Then Isabel live chaste, and brother, die: /
More than our brother is our chastity', or Iago's self-explaining
couplets in soliloquy, are of the same order of indication as Boris's
Da, zhalok tot, V kom sovest nechista (Yes, pity him whose conscience
is unclean). Dimitri's complementary utterance, his proud declaration to Marina, is put in a quatrain:

> Тень Грозного меня усыновила,
> Димитрием из гроба нарекла,
> Вокруг меня народы возмутила
> И в жертву мне Бориса обрекла.

The phantom of the Terrible has adopted me; from the tomb he has
given me the name of Dimitri, stirred up the peoples around me and
consigned Boris to me as a victim.

Pushkin may have had the formal Shakespearean couplet in mind
here, but he is more likely to have been influenced by the lyric
declamation of Zhukovsky's *Orleanskaya deva* and Katenin's
Argives. Omitted drafts suggest that the Pretender's speech was
frequently to be in rhyme, and in another omitted scene Marina's
maid Ruzya, while arraying her mistress, celebrates her conquest
of the Tsarevitch in irregular rhyming lines, a chant which makes
an effective formal contrast between the loquacity of the servant
and her mistress's curt preoccupation. But to suggest role and
character by metric variations would have been too rigid a device;
in fact, as Vinokur points out, *Boris* is the first Russian tragedy
in which declamation is not artificially controlled by metrical
stops. Within the limitations of his fixed caesura Pushkin
secures naturalistic dialogue by half-lines expressing query and
repetition.

Naturalism can betray him, however, into a fault not found in
Shakespeare. The decisive characters in such a history should not
reflect on the historical process. In the Pretender's 'signpost' lines,
when he claims that the shade of Ivan the Terrible has adopted him,
he reveals the significance of such a claim but does not *think* it for
himself – indeed the adoption that he impetuously claims is grimly
ironic: he is the instrument who in his turn will become the victim.
On the other hand when Basmanov in his last speech reflects on the
nature of his historical dilemma, the moment misses fire – we see no
longer the character but the playwright. The concluding line *No
smert...no vlast...no bedstviya narodny...* (But death...but
power...the people's miseries...) may be exculpatory – he betrays

Boris's son because he has the interest of the whole state at heart – but the over-obvious attempt of the broken, too naturalistic line to convey the struggle at work in him is not only a short cut to what such a man of action would in fact be undergoing mentally at a crucial moment (compare Macbeth's soliloquy before Duncan's murder), but also makes articulate in a single line the groundswell of history which should only be audible in the background throughout the play.

The portrayal of 'human destiny and national destiny' – Pushkin's definition of the true tragic aim – is achieved at least partially in Pushkinian ways, but there are moments when each comments too obviously on the other. In writing such a play he could not follow what he called 'the accepted custom of literature' – experiment in form and language had had to reveal itself as such – and his own verdict on *Boris* remains the most perceptive. 'A writer should possess his subject without looking at the difficult working of it; just as he possesses his language without looking at its grammatical structure.'

In the Boldino autumn of 1833 Pushkin tried out a different sort of Shakespearean experiment. *Measure for Measure* had long fascinated him, and he had begun a translation of it of which twenty-two lines exist in manuscript. Abandoning that, he now composed a dramatic poem, in alexandrines, in which he sought to isolate the character who most intrigued him, Angelo. He uses Shakespeare not as a model but as a point of departure, as he uses the Don Juan legend in *The Stone Guest*. 'Dramatic investigations', one of the titles Pushkin had thought of for the *Little Tragedies*, would also fit *Andzhelo* – the poem belongs by nature to the genre of the four short plays he had written three years earlier.[1] The use of alexandrines is curious, for in the *Little Tragedies* Pushkin had developed a blank verse as completely his own as his four-stress rhyming iambics, and the unfinished *Rusalka*, written the year before, shows an even richer and more relaxed mastery of the medium. But it is possible that while paraphrasing the story of *Measure for Measure* Pushkin wished to substitute for Shakespeare's broad dramatic treatment a deliberately neo-classical one, a remarkable experiment in transposition – much more remarkable, indeed, than his modern version of the tale of Lucrece in *Count Nulin*.

---

[1] I retain the Russian transliteration to distinguish more conveniently Shakespeare's characters from Pushkin's.

Andzhelo, perhaps for this reason, has no flavour. It is an international poem with all Pushkin's logic, clarity and precision, but without the *russky dukh* that accompanies these qualities in the other poems. And the bubbling corruption that outruns the stews of Shakespeare's Vienna – London, that is – also disappears. As in a *novella*, Pushkin's setting is a stylised Italian town: *V odnom iz gorodov Italii schastlivoy* (In one of the cities of fortunate Italy). There is no Pompey, Elbow, or Mistress Overdone – no Barnardine or Abhorson. Lucio's activities are confined to those of go-between and friend. All is subordinated to the nature of the confrontation between Angelo and Isabella. In his 'Table Talk' (Pushkin gave the English title to this collection of jottings) he echoes the point made in the Raevsky letter on the heroes of Shakespeare whose leading characteristics can always be *compromised* by their author. Molière's hypocrite Tartuffe cannot be: he is the archetypal hypocrite. Shakespeare's Angelo, on the other hand, is proud and just; he beguiles innocence with powerful and impressive sophistries, not with a comic mixture of devoutness and lechery; none the less he is a hypocrite because his public actions contradict his secret passions. 'And what depth there is in that character!' concludes Pushkin.

Andzhelo offers us the unique spectacle of one great poetic genius interpreting the creation of another through a different poetic medium. By concentrating attention on a character whom Shakespeare (we may infer) threw off in his stride, Pushkin's poem throws more light upon Shakespeare's conception than criticism can. Shakespeare's Angelo is not 'compromised' because he is not isolated and studied. He lives not only in his own motives and temperament but as a part of the swarming comedy life of the play: his dramatic effect lies in the way so fastidious and withdrawn a character is compelled by the action to enter that life, to be ground in the mill of common human nature. By removing the comedy, Pushkin shows how greatly the dramatic unfolding of Shakespeare's Angelo depends on it. Andzhelo is necessarily a different conception because his weakness is analysed, not acted out in the sprawling incongruous field of comedy and plot. Pushkin shows us just how, in art, a different form means a different man; even though he puts his finger, at the end of the poem, on the heart of Shakespeare's matter. Pleading for Andzhelo's life, Maryana cries: *On chelovechestvu svoyu prines lish dan* (He has only paid his tribute to human kind). His weakness and falsity have been revealed and thus expiated; her line sums up in classic fashion the tenor of the poem and is capped by the swift judgement of the final line:

Прости же ты его!»
И Дук его простил.

'Forgive him!' – and the Duke forgave him. (IV, 349.)

Andzhelo is Pushkin's subject: his Duke is mere mechanism. There is no reason to suppose, as some critics have done, that the poem has an occult political meaning, that the Duke is Alexander I and Andzhelo his hated minister Arakcheev, called in to exercise the tyranny the ruler cannot bring himself to employ directly.[1] Shakespeare's Duke, as we know, displeased Pushkin. The curious ambiguity of his role as 'power divine' and as eccentric human ruler jarred on him, and he makes his Duke merely a Haroun al Raschid figure who enjoys wandering among his people in disguise. The religious as well as the comedy aspect of the story is omitted. As Angelo must be seen as a part in a Shakespearean comedy, not in isolation, so the Duke in *Measure for Measure* must be understood as providence and 'power divine' whose workings are not subject to the judgements human beings pass upon each other, even though the irrepressible and irreverent man, Lucio, may see God in his own image and with his own failings.

The many unfavourable comments which have been made on the behaviour of Shakespeare's Duke are thus beside the point.[2] But both inclination and discretion must have kept Pushkin away from the religious theme that is so natural a part of Shakespeare's play. The allegory of divine and human justice could have had no more appeal for him than a political allegory (and had he intended the latter he could not have found in his own portrait of Andzhelo any convincing parallel with the vices of Arakcheev). What mattered to Pushkin, as in the *Little Tragedies*, was the complex and incongruous psychology of an individual.

The comedy that is the setting of life in Shakespeare is replaced in Pushkin's poem by the topography of dramatic convenience,

[1] Notably N. I. Chernyaev, *Kriticheskie stati i zametki o Pushkine* (1900).

[2] The shrewdest, but also the most misleading, is Hazlitt's: that the Duke 'is more tenacious of his own character than attentive to the feelings and apprehensions of others'. The Duke, in fact, illustrates Pushkin's comment: he is not 'compromised' because he is a divine agent as well as the mainspring of a comedy plot. He has the 'freedom' that Pushkin considered the final gift of Shakespeare to his characters. Detractors of the Duke should bear in mind the proleptic significance of Lucio's comment near the beginning: 'Grace is grace, despite of all controversy'.

mere occasions for scene liaison that make us realise that – as brothel and prison are the setting of grossly fulfilled natures –so the denied natures of Angelo and the two women are made equally vivid and visible in Shakespeare's convent, garden-house, and moated grange. Omitted from the poem are Angelo's reported directions to Isabella:

> With whispering and most guilty diligence
> In action all of precept he did show me
> The way twice o'er...

and Mariana's reply to the query of the disguised Duke: 'You have not been enquired after: I have sat here all day.' Omitted too is Isabella's brief but significant dialogue with the nun:

Isabella And have you nuns no further privileges?
Francisca Are not these large enough?
Isabella Yes, truly: I speak not as desiring more
But rather wishing a more strict restraint
Upon the sisterhood, the votaries of St Clare.

Angelo's words reveal the essential ludicrousness of the obsessed man, for whom nothing is now as serious as lust; Mariana's, the pathos of an arrested life, a pathos all the more effective because it is not romanticised but discontented, achingly commonplace; while Isabella's dialogue with the nun gives us a hint of something more fully revealed in the scenes with her brother and with Angelo: the strength of a nature in which desire has become centred on restraint, sensuality on abnegation. But all these examples, and especially the first, are instinct with Shakespearean drama, revealing the gesture and expression of the stage even if the words are read in the study.

Unlike Angelo, Andzhelo is an unconscious hypocrite: that is his dramatic effectiveness and the feature that absorbs Pushkin. Like many men in public life he lives by an idea of himself, not knowing of what his nature may be capable. And the shape and compass of the poem permits him to retain his dignity to the end and remain a tragic figure in the limiting sense. An accident has revealed his weakness, and though he cannot expiate it tragically the Duke's forgiveness is a substitute for such expiation. Andzhelo is closer to Othello than to Angelo, and indeed Pushkin's adaptation draws attention to a criticism frequently but erroneously made of *Measure for Measure* – that Angelo is a tragic figure who has strayed into comedy. But Angelo's fall is not only horrible but pathetic and ridiculous as well, his fantastic tricks those that all men – openly or in secret – play before high heaven to make the angels weep. He is at one with the unregenerates he felt himself fitted by nature to condemn. Though Shakespeare wisely distracts us from too close a look at Angelo in his abasement, he must listen as we do to Mariana's valiantly uxorious plea on his behalf:

> They say, best men are moulded out of faults,
> And, for the most, become much more the better
> For being a little bad...

The man who has ordered the secret execution of the brother he condemned for the offence he himself committed with the sister, in return for that brother's life – this man must now hear the affianced wife he abandoned plead for him as if he had committed some childish peccadillo! Like Parolles of *All's Well that Ends Well* he must learn to say: 'Simply the thing I am shall make me live' – and the bitterness of this must be for him a total, as it is a comic, expiation.

Nusinov claims that the 'great Russian humanist' extends and clarifies the conception of the 'great English humanist'. In fact Pushkin's version shows the full significance of Shakespeare's by putting it in a different artistic frame and concentrating attention on a small part of it. He avoids comedy and its confusions not only by direct simplification but by omitting what one character says of another – his poem confines itself to exposition, soliloquy, duologue. Lucio does not say of Andzhelo that he 'was begot between two stock-fishes', nor does the Duke – more decorously – observe, as in Shakespeare, that Angelo 'scarce confesses that his blood flows'. Pushkin, moreover, alters as well as omits. Andzhelo is already married to Maryana and separated from her because of gossip; he is indifferent whether it is true or false, but her reputation, like that of Caesar's wife, must be as above approach as his own. Angelo jilted Mariana, though contracted to her, because she lost her brother and with him the money for her dowry. Not loving her he was unmoved by her predicament – 'left her in her tears and dried not one of them with his comfort'. Shakespeare suggests here the insistence on legal proprieties which would accompany imperviousness to ordinary human and sexual feeling; as he also suggests, in Angelo's behaviour during the examination of Pompey, the judge who is concerned with the image of uncompromising rectitude which he enforces, but who is repelled by the complications and incongruities of evidence in the actual hearing, and abandons them to his deputy, 'hoping you'll find good cause to whip them all'. Furthermore, the bed deception, common to both authors, receives only in Shakespeare the full point implicit in his title. By bedding inadvertently with the girl to whom he is pre-contracted but not married, Angelo commits exactly the same offence as Claudio, who also has a betrothal contract with Juliette and is awaiting the terms of a settlement.

Andzhelo is not revealed, like his namesake, in all the disarray of human meanness before his great test takes place. And it is here that Pushkin's concentration begins to gather significance. For Andzhelo is really noble and upright: he is not compromised, like his namesake, by so many discrepant and incongruous human traits. Angelo is already a 'seemer', as the Duke divines; he has already shuffled with himself; he knows in his hour of trial of 'my gravity, in which – let no man hear me – I take pride': Shake-spearean intimacy and collusion imply that he can see himself and approves what he sees, before the true convulsion of self-revelation shakes him. Angelo, in fact, is close to us all in the sense that Leigh Hunt so aptly noted:

> For so much knowledge of ourselves there lies
> Cored, after all, in our complacencies.

But Pushkin is concerned with Andzhelo as a singular man, to be examined from the outside and revealed, as in the *Little Tragedies*, by the dramatist's objective art and not by what seems to be the character's self-awareness. And the objectivity of Pushkin illuminates what he himself called the 'freedom' of Shakespeare – the genius in not 'compromising his characters' – all the more clearly by not attempting it. The irony of *Andzhelo* is that in abandoning comedy Pushkin also abandons the very thing he so much admired, the freedom that is an aspect of Shakespeare's natural and essential comic genius.

Did he get anything in exchange? Only one thing, perhaps, but for him an important one. Pushkin compromises Andzhelo and Izabela by clearly implying what in Shakespeare is no more than a dramatic possibility: that their relation is one of mutual passion, a passion that reveals them to themselves and to each other. In fact Shakespeare cannot afford to license the possibility, for the pattern of *Measure for Measure* requires not the recognition of each in the other by Angelo and Isabella, but her *forgiveness* of Angelo when

she still thinks he has killed her brother, and her final union with
the Duke, the union of forgiveness with divine justice. Pushkin
alters this. Having always known her brother safe, Izabela's plea
for Andzhelo takes on a hidden dimension of dramatic pathos
nearer to Racine than to Shakespeare. Her final words both
recognise and renounce him.

> «Он (сколько мне известно
> И как я думаю) жил праведно и честно,
> Покамест на меня очей не устремил.
> Прости же ты его!»
> И Дук его простил.

'He (so far as is known to me and as I think) lived uprightly and honour-
ably in the time before his eyes encountered me. Forgive him!' – and the
Duke forgave him.[1]

I kak ya dumayu is full of Pushkinian meaning; a passage emotionally inert in Shakespeare comes alive with dramatic possibility,
at once cut off by the impassive swiftness of the close. Andzhelo
is united with his wife and Izabela returns to the convent; we are
left to infer the extent to which each has had to recognise a new
self in the close psychological relationship which has begun and
ended between them. Pushkin modernises the Shakespearean hint
here to include the dramatic world of Racine on the one hand and
Henry James on the other.

Those worlds, significantly, rely on hints and scenes – the unspoken knowledge in confrontation – and *Andzhelo* has little more
than these to offer us. Pushkin seems to have subdued his poetic
genius to render only what is essential and formal. His lines

---

[1] Here is the parallel passage in Shakespeare. Compare the judicial hesitation
of 'I partly think':

> *Isabella* Look, if it please you, on this man condemned,
> As if my brother lived: I partly think
> A due sincerity governed his deeds
> Till he did look on me; since it is so,
> Let him not die. My brother had but justice
> In that he did the thing for which he died: for Angelo
> His act did not o'ertake his bad intent
> And must be buried but as an intent
> That perished by the way...

It is moving that in her supreme act of forgiveness Isabella uses only the bald
terminology of crime and punishment. None the less the passage has no trace
of the dramatic and forensic power of her earlier scenes with Angelo and with
her brother, and though we should recognise its decisive importance in
Shakespeare's *dénouement* we may still find it theatrically and emotionally
null.

actually *sound* like a translation, but – because of the alexandrines – a translation from the French rather than the English. In rejecting the grand Shakespearean flux of language – comic, bawdy, suggestive, tormented – he had to rely on a sense of scene alone, and this strengthens his rendering of the one confrontation which clearly fascinated him. Shakespeare suggests Isabella's equivocal relation with the flesh by words alone, like those she uses to Angelo:

> The impression of keen whips I'd wear as rubies,
> And strip myself to death as to a bed
> That longing have been sick for, ere I'd yield
> My body up to shame.

The baroque ambiguity of this is lost in the Russian, even though the idea is presented. But the formality and simplification of Pushkin's approach makes the confrontation of the pair much more like a love scene of a peculiar intensity. We see, what is less clear in Shakespeare, that Andzhelo's passion becomes more ungovernable with each new sign of Izabela's ignorance of it. Pushkin places a real distance and incomprehension between them, and it is this that paradoxically increases the tension, dissipated in Shakespeare by the verbal fencing which has already brought them together. With sophistication and even perversity, Shakespeare mimes in this black comedy a 'white' comedy flirtation (Benedick and Beatrice are in the background) in which argument and equivocation appeal to an audience schooled in comedy exchange. Isabella may be innocent but her language is not:

> *Isabella* I have no tongue but one: gentle my lord,
> Let me entreat you speak the former language.
> *Angelo* Plainly conceive, I love you.

Sexual innuendo here undoes the drama of naturalism and the contrast that made so strong an appeal to Pushkin – the honourable man totally mastered by his desire for the saint who gives no sign of understanding it. He achieves that contrast by the simplest means.

> *Изабела* Тебя я не могу понять.
> *Анджело* Поймешь: люблю тебя.

Izabela I cannot understand you.
Andzhelo Understand this: I love you.

Belinsky thought *Andzhelo* a cold exercise, a mere experiment in translation, and his opinion has usually been accepted, with various reservations, by later critics. Pushkin himself wrote that 'our critics do not give their attention to this piece and think it one of my weak works, whereas I have written nothing better'. For him perhaps the great challenge, which he felt he had met, was to extract its true shape and meaning from a diffuse, extravagant, and contradictory piece. But the riches of *Measure for Measure* are not susceptible to this treatment in the way that John Wilson's contemporary dramatic extravaganza, *The City of the Plague*, certainly was. Belinsky admired Pushkin's adaptation of a scene from it as much as he depreciated *Andzhelo*, and exclaimed 'this Wilson wrote a great work!' *The City of the Plague* is not a great work, *Measure for Measure* is: but Pushkin's purpose in his handling of the two pieces was clearly quite different. *Andzhelo* really looks back to his *Scene from Faust*, written at Mikhailovskoye in 1826, in which the spotlight is directed on one small aspect of Goethe's vast canvas. In both cases Pushkin focuses attention on a point which the genius of the whole creation has left undetermined, which has been lost sight of in the general scope of the drama.

II

Pushkin observed that Byron had wrestled with Goethe like Jacob with the angel, and received a throw, for in *Manfred, Cain* and *The Deformed Transformed* Byron had imitated Goethe and sought to emulate him. His Faust figures, like so many others of the time, are crippled by their obvious derivation from the great poem. Pushkin, by contrast, appears to slide into it, adding a page that opens up a disquieting perspective which the animation of Goethe's dialogue had rushed past without a glance; and adding to Goethe's myth a touch of mundane psychological reality.

In 1823 Pushkin had written a short poem *Demon*. It was printed in *Mnemosyne* the following year and his friends saw in it a reference to the 'demonic' character of A. N. Raevsky, who had impressed Pushkin so deeply in Odessa and who was the elder brother of his friend and regular correspondent, Nikolai. Küchelbecker incorrectly titled the poem *My Demon* and Pushkin (who had by that time broken off relations with the elder Raevsky) objected to this so much that he wrote a commentary on the poem as if by an anonymous critic, who observes that 'not for nothing did the great poet Goethe call the enemy of man "the spirit of denial"', and that Pushkin clearly had it in mind to personify this spirit in a brief sketch. The incident shows how much he disliked the assumption of autobiography in his poems and in this case justly: for the tone of *Demon* is impersonal, it contains no trace of private animus or hidden feeling but sums up the contemporary persona of Goethe's Mephistopheles.

> Не верил он любви, свободе;
> На жизнь насмешливо глядел –
> И ничего во всей природе
> Благословить он не хотел.

He did not believe in love, freedom; he looked mockingly on life, and nothing in the whole of nature had he any desire to praise. (II, 159.)

Pushkin was always non-committal about Goethe, and in the *Scene from Faust* he seems to oppose a certain deliberate realism to the idealism of the sage of Weimar: it is the only instance in his works where 'realism' does have the air of being deliberate. Pushkin's Mephistophel is a shabbier devil than Goethe's *Geist der stets verneint*, a corrupted valet rather than a power from hell – Dostoevsky's Devil in *The Brothers Karamazov* may owe something to him. For all that he is the spirit of denial, Goethe's Mephisto is a creature of immense gusto. Like Iago he enjoys all the pleasures of disguise; clowns, drinks and swaggers, as at home in a beer cellar as on the Brocken. A very German devil, he arranges everything with efficiency and zest, infecting Faust with his own *joie de vivre* and teaching him how to live.

> Damit du, losgebunden, frei,
> Erfahrest, was das Leben sei.

So that you, released and free, may experience what life can be.

It is significant that Faust draws these gifts from Mephisto without suffering any loss of innocence or the power to enjoy. He gives the impression of using Mephisto without being corrupted by him, as if he were the stronger character. And so indeed he is, for he is Goethe, with all Goethe's immense powers of using life without remorse or regret. Mephisto is thus both an aspect of Faust and the means by which he fulfils himself. He is not a separate being, nor is Gretchen: there is no dramatic distance between the three of them – the distance that Pushkin suggests in his Faust scene.

Pushkin puts back into the Faust legend the idea of evil that Goethe omits, the evil that, as for Dostoevsky and Gide later, is not the opposite of good but merely 'the rumination of the brain'. Where Goethe's Mephisto liberates Faust to live life to the uttermost on one condition – that he is never satisfied with the moment as it passes but is always impatient for the next experience – Pushkin's shuts Faust behind the *huis clos* of his own consciousness and compels him to face not only *accidie* itself but its consequences, the harm done by the individual in his search for distraction.[1] Faust's boredom is the immediate opening stroke:

Фауст	Мне скучно, бес.
Мефистофель	Что делать, Фауст?
	Таков вам положен предел,
	Его ж никто не преступает.
	Вся тварь разумная скучает:
	Иной от лени, тот от дел;
	Кто верит, кто утратил веру;
	Тот насладиться не успел,
	Тот насладился через меру,
	И всяк зевает да живет –
	И всех вас гроб, зевая, ждет.
	Зевай и ты.

Faust I am bored, fiend.
Mephistopheles What's to be done, Faust? Such is the limit set for you, and none may exceed it. Every thinking creature is bored: this one by idleness, that one by work. One has faith, another has lost it; some have failed to enjoy themselves, others have done so to excess. And everyone yawns and lives on, and the grave waits, yawning for you all. And you yawn too. (II, 283.)

Goethe's Faust is ideal man: Pushkin's, the average man as he really is, disillusioned by the present but compelled to feed on illusions from the past, on the purity and innocence of his love with Gretchen. But Mephisto remorselessly exposes this as an illusion. He slyly asks if Faust remembers what went through his mind at a time which he now recalls as one of innocent happiness:

Фауст	Говори. Ну, что?
Мефистофель	Ты думал: агнец мой послушный!
	Как жадно я тебя желал!
	Как хитро в деве простодушной
	Я грезы сердца возмущал!

---

[1] Goethe's Faust makes the famous pact with Mephisto:

> Werd ich zum Augenblicke sagen
> Verweile doch! du bist so schön!
> Dann magst du mich in Fesseln schlagen,
> Dann will ich gern zu Grunde gehn!

Should I ever come to say to the passing moment: 'Stay! You are so beautiful!' then you can have have me in your fetters, then I will gladly be done for!

Любви невольной, бескорыстной
Невинно предалась она...
Что ж грудь моя теперь полна
Тоской и скукой ненавистной?...
На жертву прихоти моей
Гляжу, упившись наслажденьем,
С неодолимым отвращеньем:
Так безрасчетный дуралей,
Вотще решась на злое дело,
Зарезав нищего в лесу,
Бранит ободранное тело;
Так на продажную красу,
Насытясь ею торопливо,
Разврат косится боязливо...
Потом из этого всего
Одно ты вывел заключенье...

Фауст Сокройся, адское творенье!
    Беги от взора моего!
Мефистофель Изволь. Задай лишь мне задачу:
    Без дела, знаешь, от тебя
    Не смею отлучаться я –
    Я даром времени не трачу.

Faust Tell me now – what?

Mephistopheles You thought: 'My obedient lamb, how avidly I desired you! How cunningly in a simple girl I stirred up tender dreams! Innocently she gave herself up to helpless and selfless love... Why then is my breast now full of gloom and hateful boredom? Having enjoyed the draught of pleasure I look on the victim of my whim with unconquerable disgust.' Thus a reckless fool, committed to some evil, unprofitable deed, curses the mangled body of the beggar he has killed in the forest. Thus vice casts a squeamish glance sidelong at the bought beauty on whom he has hastened to take his pleasure... and so from all this you drew one conclusion...

Faust Hide yourself, hellish creature! Get out of my sight!

Mephistopheles At your pleasure. But appoint me some task. Without work, you know, I do not dare to separate myself from you – I do not waste time for nothing.

The last lines reveal the mean collusiveness of the pair: the valet is as dependent on distraction as his master.[1] The scene ends with

---

[1] This atmosphere of meanness was almost certainly the inspiration of Sologub's novel *Melky bes* (*The Petty Devil*), published in 1907, in which the odious hero is attended by a shapeless being, the *Nedotykomka*, as negative, joyless and meaningless as himself.

Faust ordering Mephisto to sink a ship laden with modish offerings, including 'the fashionable disease' (the pox) which Mephisto slyly intimates has lately been presented to Faust.

The brief, brutal scene is not only a tacit comment on the spacious idealism of Goethe: it is also more objective and more realistic than Goethe can afford to be on the nature of the Faust–Gretchen relationship. The innocence of Goethe's Faust is invincible. He is not compelled to think about his relation to Gretchen, and the fact that he tires of her – must tire of her if he is not to lose his bargain with Mephisto – is passed over. His return to her is not psychologically convincing but melodrama, and the *dénouement* of *Faust Part I* is necessarily facile. It has to lead to the immense metaphysical apologia of *Faust Part II*, which Pushkin knew nothing of, and which was only completed in 1832, a few months before Goethe's death.

Pushkin's scene was first published in 1828, under the title 'A New Scene between Faust and Mephistopheles', and takes place by implication in the limbo after the end of *Faust Part I*. Goethe's Faust may be led into darkness and error but he is saved by effort and endeavour, toil in the world's business and for the world's good. Pushkin's appears as a 'superfluous' young man of fashion in Petersburg, not an industrious employee of the model Duchy of Weimar, and this solution is not open to him. Not unlike Aleko, he is destroyed by the emptiness and isolation which is all the freedom that Mephisto's gifts bring. Goethe's Faust is, if we like, a survival from the optimism of the eighteenth century: Pushkin's a nihilistic child of the nineteenth: yet they are far from being the same kind of archetype. Goethe's is not one of the types of the age, *vekovye obrazy*, which, like Byron's Cain or Rousseau's Saint-Preux, lead us back to their creator through the very success of their contemporary significance: he is large enough to be timeless. Pushkin's much slighter sketch has by contrast the more local anonymity of a fictional situation. Bored and disillusioned, his Faust needs to feel that he was once happy with Gretchen, and his damnation is in the pitiless reminder from Mephisto that even with her he could not stop scheming and reflecting. He never has been nor could be a child of nature, and her love repelled him by the very innocence and wholeheartedness which distinguished it from his own, so that revulsion compels him to destroy it like a murderer.

The case and the image are haunting, and were not lost on the

great novelists. In *Anna Karenina* Vronsky finds himself looking
with horror on Anna after they have first made love:

He felt what a murderer must feel when looking at the body he had
deprived of life...but in spite of the murderer's horror at the body of the
victim that body must be cut in pieces and hidden away, and he must
make use of what he has obtained by the murder.

The resemblance between the images of poem and novel is not
likely to be coincidental. Levin, in *Anna Karenina*, quotes from
Pushkin's short poem *Vospominanie* (Remembrance) which had
always haunted Tolstoy.

И с отвращением читая жизнь мою,
Я трепещу и проклинаю,
И горько жалуюсь, и горько слёзы лью,
Но строк печальных не смываю.

And reading the chronicle of my life with loathing I tremble and curse
and complain bitterly and shed bitter tears, yet I do not wash away the
sorrowful lines. (III, 60.)

The 'I' of *Vospominanie* is seen as objectively as Faust and the
figure in *Demon*, and Pushkin's discovery in the *Little Tragedies* of
the dramatic form that best suited him enables him to use there his
own self-awareness. The genial 'I' of *Evgeny Onegin* is used by
Pushkin as a barrier against self-revelation. There is no 'I' in the
Little Tragedies but there is much more self-revelation, and yet no
mechanism is required to shut it out.

Except, it may be, a purely formal one. In a perceptive essay on
The Stone Guest, Anna Akhmatova points out that it alone of the
Little Tragedies was unpublished by Pushkin in his lifetime, and
suggests that the reason may be the same as in the case of *Vospominanie*, *Net ya ne dorozhu*, and the poems connected with
Amalia Riznich – not because of the censorship but for personal
reasons.[1] The chief reason may be Pushkin's infatuation with
Natalia Goncharova and his determination to marrry her, for an
equivocal theme in *The Stone Guest* is that of the rake who is
caught – caught by a woman whose conduct is determined by
motives he cannot fully understand; who is not swept away by his
passion and his will to win her; who remains calm and collected,
virginal, statuesque. We can see the same preoccupation in his

[1] A. Akhmatova, '"Kamenny gost" Pushkina', *Pushkin, Issledovaniya i materialy*, II.

treatment of Angelo three years later – a man undone by a woman quite unlike what he safely assumes women to be.

Pushkin's Don Juan is not the compulsive and undiscriminating seducer of the legend, but a man who has loved many different women in different ways and who finds himself at last helpless before Donna Anna – or professes to do so – because she possesses some quality that deprives him of his adroitness. Though he still sees himself as the seducer, he may now be the victim, the seduced, a climactic sensation which is also – unknown to him – a terminal one. There is no more erotic moment in Pushkin's works than the kiss he begs from Donna Anna at the end: *odin, kholodny, mirny* (one cold, peaceful embrace). The tranquillity of the passage is like an eternity of domesticity compressed into a few words, and the word *mirny* suggests the reciprocal finality of the moment as well as its peacefulness.

The stone guest is the agent of fate, but fate of an unexpected kind. He is the dead husband of Donna Anna (Pushkin's is the only version of the legend in which the *Komandor* is Donna Anna's *husband*) come to view his living successor; and the grasp of his hand might be taken as condemning Don Juan to an eternity of marriage rather than to perdition. In any event the old Don Juan is no more.[1] He and Donna Anna sink into the ground as if undergoing in a moment that decline into the vale of years that would have awaited Lensky had he survived the duel, the fate so touchingly dreamed for himself and Parasha by Evgeny in *The Bronze Horseman*. Don Juan's exclamation in the final line: *Ya gibnu – koncheno – o Dona Anna!* (I'm perishing – it's finished – Donna Anna!) could almost be a cry of consummation, of final pleasure. Or a consummation taken from him at the moment he accepted his new self and the life it offered.

For the *Little Tragedies* are investigations with no conclusion, which sharply distinguishes them from the pre-formed situation of *Andzhelo*; and they define only by differentiating, setting clear Pushkinian distance between one person and possibility and another. *The Stone Guest* achieves the remarkable feat of demythologising Don Juan and giving him the immediate simplicity of a mere human being. Pushkin is the only author to treat the legend who does not present a new image or interpretation of its

---

[1] Pushkin's is also the only version in which Don Juan and his final conquest are destroyed *together*, though in Dargomizhsky's opera, based on *The Stone Guest*, retribution seems to befall the hero alone.

hero. He is not the free man whom Tirso de Molina first imaged and perhaps secretly admired, the hedonist outside the moral order and wholly happy without God. He is not Molière's aristocrat, the supreme incarnation of privilege, assuming his right to the possession of all he sees, and his sole duty to be true to himself and treat all others as a *means*.[1] Still less is he the appetite in action of Mozart and Da Ponte, the harmonised *brio* of sexual will. There is nothing in him of de Musset's thwarted idealist or Mérimée's thwarted scientist. For Pushkin the Mozartian Don Juan is clearly the most important, and *The Stone Guest* shows itself conscious of the great opera as it does of the many other Juan figures. But Pushkin's hero resembles these meaningful predecessors as little as he does the amiably passive hero into which Byron could project the vitality of his poem.

We first see him entering Madrid in disguise, or what he supposes to be disguise:

> — скоро
> Я полечу по улицам знакомым,
> Усы плащом закрыв, а брови шляпой.
> Как думаешь? узнать меня нельзя?
>
> *Лепорелло.* Да! Дон Гуана мудрено признать!
> Таких, как он, такая бездна!

Soon I shall be striding through the well-known streets, moustaches hidden under cloak, brow under hat. What do you think? Impossible to recognise me?
Leoporello O yes, a tricky business to recognise Don Juan! There's a whole crowd just like him! (v, 369.)

Leporello's joke is very much to the point. Don Juan could be recognised anywhere because he might be any young man of his class and provenance. The cloak that disguises him is as much a part of him as his own moustache. In the opening lines Pushkin has removed the aura of solitary and diabolical distinction that set previous Don Juans apart. And a few lines later, as the pair near the convent, he remembers a former conquest in the same neighbourhood:

> Бедная Инеза!
> Ее уж нет! как я любил ее!

Poor Inez! She's dead now! How I loved her!

---

[1] Cf. Henri Gouhier, 'L'inhumain Don Juan', *La Table Ronde* (November 1957). (This is a 'Don Juan' number, containing several interesting essays on the varieties of the hero in literature.)

As Nusinov points out, no previous Don Juan has said such a thing.[1] How we take it is another matter. Don Juan not only remembers a previous woman but recalls her attraction in detail:

> В июле...ночью. Странную приятность
> Я находил в ее печальном взоре
> И помертвелых губах. Это странно.
> Ты, кажется, ее не находил
> Красавицей. И точно, мало было
> В ней истинно прекрасного. Глаза,
> Одни глаза. Да взгляд...такого взгляда
> Уж никогда я не встречал. А голос
> У ней был тих и слаб – как у больной –
> Муж у нее был негодяй суровый,
> Узнал я поздно...Бедная Инеза!...

In July...by night. I used to find a curious pleasure in her sad gaze and her bloodless lips. An odd thing. But you, it appears, did not think her much of a beauty. And just so, there was small trace of real beauty about her. Her eyes, just her eyes. And her expression...such a look as I've never met with since. And her voice was soft and weak, like that of someone ill. Her husband was a tyrannical wretch, I found that out too late... Poor Inez!

No caesura controls the reflective and colloquial ease of the verse, and from a first setting in two words of time and season the eleven lines give us an astonishing amount of information, presented through the tone of the voice but not determined by it. We seem to see Inez both as she was and as Don Juan saw her. She was not seductive, but her peculiar individuality expressed itself in her lassitude, her appeal in her lack of any will left to appeal. And Don Juan not only recalls all this but by implication blames himself for her unspecified fate. 'I realised too late...'

The tone of recall is a peculiar one. Some Russian critics have called Don Juan a deliberate study in sexual morbidity. 'The one specifically novel thing about Pushkin's Don Juan', says Blagoy, 'is his romantic pleasure in death', his *sladostrastny kharakter*.[2] He

---

[1] I. M. Nusinov, *Pushkin i mirovaya literatura*. Nusinov discusses the relation of Pushkin's Don Juan to his predecessors and concludes that he is a good man condemned by the nature of pre-revolutionary society to misuse his virtues and to 'find no way to unite the hedonistic with the social'. Gukovsky finds in him the emancipated spirit of Renaissance man. These historical impositions are not without interest and justification, but they seem far more incongruous with the psychological immediacy of *The Stone Guest* than are Marxist historical interpretations of Pushkin's other works. See also Nusinov's *Vekovye Obrazy*, a study of the relation of literary figures to their age.

[2] D. D. Blagoy, *Masterstvo Pushkina*.

remembers with love the victimised and dying Inez; he makes love
to Laura over the corpse of her previous lover, whom he has just
killed; he summons the dead husband to keep watch at the door
behind which he woos the widow, and he cries out her name with
his last breath as he stiffens in the grasp of the *Komandor*. This
sets him apart from what Veresaev calls the normal and 'healthily
instinctual' Don Juan of the tradition. Certainly a fashionably
romantic element of love and death is made use of by Pushkin in
the drama – but it is made use of. It does not dominate the action,
much of the dramatic depth of which comes precisely from our
sense of the simple reality of Don Juan and his women in situations
which are traditionally theatrical, and which Pushkin makes
deliberately even more melodramatic. The kinship with Shakespeare is again of the first importance. 'Must I think that insubstantial death is amorous?' demands Romeo in Juliet's tomb,
and the declamation does not label him as a morbid dreamer, but
on the contrary heightens even more our sense of the youthful
intensity and vulnerability of his love. With the same 'sanity of
true genius', in Lamb's phrase, Pushkin heightens with contemporary romantic colour the Don Juan legend of seduction and
retribution in order to reveal in it what is most immediate and
human.

The three women in *The Stone Guest* are all sharply differentiated.
Their lack of contact, even of knowledge of one another, underlines
their separate and peculiar realities. It is possible they bear some
relation to women Pushkin knew; and likely, too, that Mozart's
Zerlina may be in the background of the contrast between Laura
and Donna Anna. But where such a contrast has no effect on
Mozart's Don Giovanni, and the serio-comic notation of his list, it
is vital to the psychology of Pushkin's hero. Like every man, he
feels differently about the different women in his life, and Pushkin
graphically and accurately distinguishes these feelings. Inez he
recalls with nostalgic affection and regret; Laura is the friend and
comrade – almost the female *alter ego* – with whom he is on terms
of complete understanding; Donna Anna represents the unknown,
the unfamiliar challenge of virtue and compassion. Pushkin contrives to make it plain that there is no sexual hypocrisy in Donna
Anna: she is moved by Don Juan for what he is, or at least by how
he behaves, not because she is ready for an affair.

Her distance and her incalculability subject him to a wholly
novel and unexpected emotion – jealousy – which again unites him

with all ordinary men. He is helplessly jealous of the dead husband
he has himself killed, and whom he tries vainly to exorcise by the
act of bravado which destroys him. Pushkin's real stroke of
originality is to make the stone guest the object of jealousy, the
personification of its irremovable pangs. The dead man whose
widow he loves now haunts Don Juan, as so many living husbands
have been haunted by him. In vain he hears that she was married
against her will: he can think only of the dead man's happiness in
loving her first, of Donna Anna's daily visits to his tomb, and of her
conviction that had she died first he would always have remained
faithful to her memory. Don Juan has become the most vulnerable
of men, and it is the dead man who is unassailable, huge in stone
where in life he had been small and puny.

> Какие плечи! что за Геркулес!...
> А сам покойник мал был и щедушен.
> Здесь, став на цыпочки, не мог бы руку
> До своего он носу дотянуть.

What shoulders! What a Hercules! While the buried man himself was
so small, a puny creature! – standing on tip-toe here he would not be
able to reach his own nose.

But the comforting conceit does not help Don Juan to dismiss the
statue; he imagines him still potent, still endowed with human
anguish and desire:

> Без нее –
> Я думаю – скучает командор. –

The Komandor – I think – must be having a tedious time without her. –

and this is underlined by his hopefully flippant comment to
Leporello:

> Ты думаешь, он станет ревновать!
> Уж верно нет; он человек разумный
> И верно присмирел с тех пор, как умер.

You think he will be jealous! Surely not; he's a sensible fellow, and he
must have calmed down a good deal, since he died.

Leporello's reply, that the statue none the less looks angry, shows
that he understands his master's state of mind and leads to the
fateful invitation – Don Juan's last effort to rid himself of the
jealousy that has come with the new love and promises to be its
eternal companion. He invites the husband to come and stand like
a porter before the door while he makes love to the widow within.
The stone guest is not a portentous monolith of retribution but a

character like the others and – as befits the supreme object of jealousy – even more physically realised than they are (the image of the man reaching up to touch the nose of his own statue).[1]

Certainly there is both autobiography and prophecy here, for Pushkin's jealousy of his wife's admirers – the Tsar included – was to become more and more obsessional and lead straight to the duel that killed him. Some of his letters hint at his anguish at the thought of what she might do after his death. Yet as Akhmatova observes, the element of autobiography does not touch the dramatic objectivity of *The Stone Guest*. The characters are completely realised, but (except for Laura) they are not *known*, by themselves or us. Between Laura and Don Juan there is such easy familiarity that neither is jealous of the other: on the contrary, one of the pleasures of their reunion is to give each other the news of their intermediate affairs. Because Don Juan knows Laura so well, he does not love her with passion and jealousy as Don Carlos does (for Carlos she is *mily demon*, for Don Juan *mily drug* – dear friend), and when he interrupts her and Don Carlos together it is not he who provokes the fight in which Carlos dies.

But in his wooing of Donna Anna Don Juan *may* be cynical: the disclosure of his true identity (which echoes Dimitri's to Marina and Shakespeare's scene of Richard III and the Lady Anne) may be a calculation which he senses will prove irresistible. Some critics have taken his aside *Idet k razvyazke delo!* (The *dénouement* approaches!) as evidence of cool and expert timing, though the idealistic Belinsky stoutly maintained that he really has fallen in love with virtue, and is determined to throw himself on Donna Anna's mercy by revealing his real identity. In fact consummate guile and passionate feeling can be close together, are indeed the hallmark of the lover's psychology. The Don Juan who gambles on revealing himself to the widow of the man he has killed (and there again we learn he was not the aggressor) is also the Don Juan who exclaims to Leporello that his feeling for Donna Anna makes him 'happy as a child' and 'ready to embrace the whole world'. And Donna Anna perceives the contradiction: she is not taken in by the subterfuge but is moved and at least partially won by the nature it reveals. *Tak eto Don Juan* (So this is Don Juan) she exclaims, and again *Kto znaet vas?* (Who knows you?). To the coarse perception of

---

[1] Incidentally one of the very few instances in Pushkin of a possible sexual *double-entendre*. One or two others – of a more evident and less Elizabethan kind – occur in *Evgeny Onegin*.

Leporello it is a case of 'widows are all alike': in fact she is involved in a much more subtle appeal to her vanity and also her tenderness. Who knows Don Juan? – perhaps she begins to, or to think she does.

Like a play in three acts the action of *The Stone Guest* concerns in turn each of the three women. The first is retrospective and nostalgic – the memory of Inez – the last looks forward with a child's excitement to a future that never comes. The centre of the play is the present moment, and its celebrant and symbol is Laura. She is closely identified with Don Juan, but she is a Don Juan of a purely feminine kind. As gaily promiscuous as he, she would not keep a list of her lovers (as Pushkin did, though there is no mention of his Don Juan doing so) and would not set herself to add to it. She is as excited by violence as Don Juan is by chastity, coldness, and reserve; and when Carlos responds violently to her mention of Don Juan: *moy verny drug i vetrenny lyubovnik* (my true friend and fickle lover) she responds at once to him:

Лаура	Ты, бешеный! останься у меня.
	Ты мне понравился; ты Дон Гуана
	Напомнил мне, как выбранил меня
	И стиснул зубы с скрежетом.
Дон Карлос	Счастливец!
	Так ты его любила?
	[*Лаура делает утвердительный знак.*]
	Очень?
Лаура	Очень.
Дон Карлос	И любишь и теперь?
Лаура	В сию минуту?
	Нет, не люблю. Мне двух любить нельзя.
	Теперь люблю тебя.

Laura You, mad thing! Stay here with me. You've taken my fancy; you reminded me of Don Juan when you scolded me and gritted your teeth and ground them.
Carlos Lucky man! So you loved him. [*Laura gives an emphatic nod*] Very much?
Laura Very much.
Carlos And you love him now?
Laura At this minute? No, I don't love him. One can't love two at once. Now I love you.

Carlos is gloomy, upright, and honourable (there is an indication that he is the brother of the dead *Komandor*) and like that between Don Juan and Donna Anna the attraction between him and Laura is one of opposites. In his ponderous way he is bewitched by her animal acceptance of the present.

> Ты молода...и будешь молода
> Еще лет пять иль шесть. Вокруг тебя
> Еще лет шесть они толпиться будут,
> Тебя ласкать, лелеять, и дарить,
> И серенадами ночными тешить,
> И за тебя друг друга убивать
> На перекрестках ночью. Но когда
> Пора пройдет, когда твои глаза
> Впадут и веки, сморщась, почернеют
> И седина в косе твоей мелькнет,
> И будут называть тебя старухой,
> Тогда – что скажешь ты?

You are young...and will be young for another five or six years. They will swarm around you for another six years, flatter, caress and reward you, divert you with serenades by night and kill each other for you by night at street corners. But when the time has gone, when your eyes are sunken, and your eyelids wrinkle and grow dark, and grey hair gleams in your tresses, and you begin to be called an old woman: then – what will you say?

The word *moloda* here takes on the utmost of itself, in timing, sound, and significance. In all of Pushkin's works the *Little Tragedies* show most clearly a language realising the full potential of its simplest words. It encloses both the heavy sententiousness of the speaker and the careless animalism of the girl, for in *The Stone Guest* Pushkin reaches the summit of poetic drama where such a speech can be abstracted and read as a superb essay in the commonplace, while at the same time its context exactly transmits the tone of the speaker and the quality of the listener's attention. Characteristically, Carlos conceals the violence of his infatuation in the measured tones of headshaking solicitude, and her reply shows a mischievous awareness of this before expanding into her own lyric certainty of existence:

> *Лаура*   Тогда? Зачем
> Об этом думать? что за разговор?
> Иль у тебя всегда такие мысли?
> Приди – открой балкон. Как небо тихо;
> Недвижим теплый воздух, ночь лимоном
> И лавром пахнет, яркая луна
> Блестит на синеве густой и темной,
> И сторожа кричат протяжно: «Ясно!...»

А далеко, на севере – в Париже –
Быть может, небо тучами покрыто,
Холодный дождь идет и ветер дует.
А нам какое дело? слушай, Карлос,
Я требую, чтоб улыбнулся ты...
– Ну то-то ж! –

Then? Why think of it? Why this homily? Or do you always have such thoughts? Come out on the balcony. How calm is the sky, the air is still and warm – the night smells of lemon and laurel, the bright moon shines in the deep dark blue – and the watchman cries from afar: 'All's well!...' But a long way off in the north, in Paris, the sky may be covered in clouds and a cold rain falling and the wind blowing. – But what's that to us? Now listen, Carlos. I order you to smile. That's right!

Even in Shakespeare and Racine we would hardly find an exchange as abstract as this and yet as alert with the peculiar individuality of the speakers. The Duke's counsel for mortality in *Measure for Measure* ('Be absolute for death...'), and Claudio's ensuing outburst of terror at the thought of it, may conceivably have been at the back of Pushkin's mind, but they do not confront one another in an exchange of such graphic incongruity.

Events overtake the resolution of the two opposites, foreshadowing the climax of the play when the Stone Guest interrupts the consummation of Don Juan and Donna Anna. Carlos's disquisition on the mortality that awaits careless youth is that of a man himself to die within the minute. And his *mily demon* is at once transformed into Don Juan's *mily drug*. Delighted to see Juan, Laura shows no trace of embarrassment that she was about to make love to one of his successors, and he no sign of jealousy – the stone guest that awaits him in the next scene. Their intimacy instantly renewed, they are at once like brother and sister, poet and muse, for Laura has sung that night to universal applause a song composed by Don Juan himself. And the genius of dramatic parody is at its height in the scene – the body of Carlos is not so much an invitation to graveyard love as an unwanted guest whose presence can be comfortably ignored by an old married couple. Laura's scolding exasperation at the inconvenience of a killing in *her* room

Убит? прекрасно! в комнате моей!
Что делать мне теперь, повеса, дьявол?
Куда я выброшу его?

He's killed? Well, really! Charming! In my room! And what do I do now you rascal, you devil? Where am I to get rid of him?

soon subsides into a mixture of archness and practicality.

> *Лаура*   Друг ты мой!...
> Постой...при мертвом!...что нам делатьс ним?
> *Дон Гуан*   Оставь его: перед рассветом, рано,
> Я вынесу его под епанчою
> И положу на перекрестке.

Laura   My darling!...Wait...before the corpse! What are we to do with him?
Don Juan   Leave him – before daybreak, early, I'll carry him out under my cloak and leave him at the crossroads.

Don Juan's words confirm the forecast in the last speech of Don Carlos: they also emphasise the parody contrast between this present domesticity and the traditional world of Don Juans to which they relate. The problem disposed of, the pair settle down to exchange news of each other's affairs, postponing a more leisurely discussion of them until after they have made love.

> *Дон Гуан*   А признайся,
> А сколько раз ты изменяла мне
> В моем отсутствии?
> *Лаура*   А ты, повеса?
> *Дон Гуан*   Скажи...Нет, после переговорим.

Don Juan   But confess – how many times have you deceived me in my absence?
Laura   And you? you rogue!
Don Juan   Tell me...no, we'll talk about it later.

There is nothing here to hint at the retribution to follow; it is as separate from it as Laura is from Inez and Donna Anna, and as the Don Juan in her room is from the Don Juan who can be haunted by regret and tormented by jealousy.

The Stone Guest was the last of the *Little Tragedies*. All three were written in three weeks at Boldino in the autumn of 1830, though *Mozart and Salieri* was probably begun earlier, when Pushkin jotted down at Mikhailovskoye in 1826 some notes and subjects for this kind of dramatic treatment. Even by Pushkin's standards this speed of composition was extraordinary; in a few days the idea of the dramatic sketch, adopted by Pushkin from Barry Cornwall, is elevated to the status of a master genre, culminating in the achievement of *The Stone Guest*, a climax of perfection which had no successors in Russian drama, and which Pushkin himself may have regarded as realising the full potential of the form. For he attempted nothing else of quite the same kind. The last dramatic work of that autumn, *The Feast in Time of Plague*, adapted from a scene in John Wilson's lengthy melodrama *The City of the Plague*, is of a different order of experiment, as are the later dramatic or partially dramatic explorations: *Andzhelo*, the unfinished *Rusalka* and *Egyptian Nights*, and the fragment entitled by Zhukovsky 'Scenes from Knightly Times' (*Stseny iz Rytsarskikh vremen*) when it was published posthumously in *Sovremennik* in 1837.

Barry Cornwall, the pseudonym of Bryan Proctor, was a man of letters in the forefront of the literary fashions of his day and popular with all his London contemporaries, including Byron, Keats, and Leigh Hunt. In 1819 he published his *Dramatic Scenes*, which had a vogue with readers who had seen Kean on the stage and had learned to share Lamb's enthusiasm for the diction and scenic effects not only of Shakespeare but of the minor Elizabethan tragedians. The *Scenes* make no attempt at dramatic point and coherence but aim simply at an immediate emotional appeal, either by exoticism and violence or by 'illuminating' dialogues between great artists of the past. In *Michael Angelo*, the painter of 'ante-diluvian Adam' – 'with limbs *dawning* into sinewy strength' – is compared with the gentle and feminine genius of Raphael, fresh from painting his 'Galatea'. Raphael is a child of nature, whose art is an aspect of his love of women: when he asks Michelangelo what he loves the latter replies resoundingly: 'MINE ART!' This amiably facile and rather comic contrast might none the less have given Pushkin a hint for *Mozart and Salieri*. In one of the wilder pieces, *Juan*, Don Juan has secretly murdered the old husband of the woman he loved:

> The impudent dotard laughed,
> Boasting he had outschemed a younger man,
> Me, – *me*...

Now married to her, he remains madly jealous, and stabs his wife for a suspected affair with another man, who, as she informs Juan with her last breath, is in fact her brother! (In the Elizabethan tragedies Proctor imitated this would have been a highly equivocal confession, but in his own scene it is of course a guarantee of purity and innocence, as in the music hall song 'After the Ball'.) Again, however, the idea of a *jealous* Don Juan might have suggested something to Pushkin if he read the piece.

Like many of his contemporaries Proctor had a real love of

Elizabethan plays and some skill in imitating them, but both he
and his readers were quite content with sensationalism for its own
sake, and what passed for fine writing. Despite their comparative
feebleness the *Dramatic Scenes* have an originality which a greater
writer could profit from – Browning as well as Pushkin – and
although they represent theatrical decadence (as did Kean's acting)
in their shirking of build-up in favour of the emotional moment,
their brevity is a real potential asset in an age of interminable
poem-plays. In a sense, the scenes attempt to make a virtue out of
the romantic weakness: where other more talented writers
(including Keats) left uncompleted dramatic fragments, they are
at least what they set out to be; they cater with logic and
honesty for the contemporary pleasure in the speech and the grand
moment; they attempt to provide exposition and climax in a
package deal without the working out of a plot or the building up
of characters.

As we have seen, one of Pushkin's tentative titles for the *Little
Tragedies* was 'dramatic investigations', and this indicates an
artistic purpose, perhaps too clearly, which may have been why
the less revealing title was chosen. The secret of the three pieces is
in the way they investigate without coming to conclusions, and the
potential of undissipated meaning which is built up by the form.
When, in *Andzhelo*, Pushkin confronted Shakespeare directly, he
cannot help revealing the difference between primary creation – the
character whose 'interest' is not for the creator but for the audience
and for posterity – and the secondary creation that is a deliberate
inquiry by the artist into a psychology that interests him. Shakespeare's Angelo is not, like Pushkin's, a conception: he is part of a
play. But in the *Little Tragedies*, and above all in *The Stone Guest*,
Pushkin achieves the total realisation of form and language which
cuts the connections with the author's intention and removes from
the completed work any suggestion of an individual study. Pushkin's Don Juan seems no more 'compromised' by his creator than
Hamlet is by Shakespeare. The play's the thing, and the area of
illumination which its enactment reveals.

It may none the less be true that Pushkin's friends and contemporaries would have seen him in his hero, as they saw Raevsky
in *Demon*. They might also have identified Don Juan with the
legend of Byron, in whose personal life Pushkin, like all his age,
had taken the greatest interest (a prose article of his on Byron
stresses the poet's ancestry and the influence of his early life on the

contradictions of his personality.[1] Pushkin cannot have known the details of Byron's relations with his wife and with his half-sister Augusta, but Don Juan's relation with Laura and with Donna Anna reveals a remarkable intuitive understanding of the Byronic need for different kinds of women, and the complex simultaneous attractions of the comrade figure and the cool aloofness, even priggishness, of virtue.

It certainly seems likely that in the first of the *Little Tragedies*, *The Covetous Knight*, Pushkin resorted to a piece of mystification to forestall the possibility that his own father, a notorious miser, might be assumed to be the model of the miserly Baron. Its sub-title, 'Scenes from Chenstone's Tragi-Comedy', seems not to refer to anything by the English poet Shenstone; and the corruption of his name – whether in error or deliberately – has usually been taken to mean that no connection exists. And yet there may be a tenuous one, as has recently been persuasively argued, for Shenstone's didactic poem *Economy*, though less popular in England than his *Schoolmistress*, was extensively translated after his death in 1763.[2] Shenstone emphasised that the poet's true freedom is money ('This perishable coin / Is no vain ore, it is thy liberty'), a sentiment with which Pushkin would have been in complete agreement, and himself states in the *Dialogue between Poet and Bookseller*. In *The Covetous Knight* the Baron and his son are both prisoners – the father to his gold and the son to his lack of it. ('It fetters misers but it must alone / Enfranchise thee': so Shenstone admonishes his poor poet.) Knowledge of the power the gold gives him is enough for the Baron. He does not wish to use it but only to feel it is there to be used.

> Я выше всех желаний; я спокоен;
> Я знаю мощь мою; с меня довольно
> Сего сознанья...

I am above all wishes; I am quiet; I know my power: and this knowledge is enough for me...

---

[1] vii, 316. Probably written in 1835 and published posthumously in 1841. It is only the opening of what may have been intended as a long article on Byron and his influence on literature. Characteristically, Pushkin commented in a letter that he was glad Moore had destroyed Byron's Memoirs. 'He would have been caught in the act, as Rousseau was, and spite and slander would have triumphed again...Moore's deed is better than his *Lalla Rookh*. We know Byron well enough.' Pushkin to Vyazemsky, November 1825.

[2] See R. A. Gregg, 'Pushkin and Shenstone: The Case Re-opened', *Comparative Literature*, xvii (1965). It also seems to me possible that Pushkin had one of Horace's odes in mind, perhaps No. 16, Book iii.

There is irony in the fact that the Baron lives in and by the imagination – his is the most spiritual nature in all Pushkin – and a corresponding irony is his son's fearless bravery in the lists – prompted not by desire to win repute with knights and ladies but by anxiety to hide the shortcomings of his equipment – and his rage if an opponent's blow puts it in jeopardy.

> когда сама Клотильда,
> Закрыв лицо, невольно закричала,
> И славили герольды мой удар, –
> Тогда никто не думал о причине
> И храбрости моей и силы дивной!
> Взбесился я за поврежденный шлем;
> Геройству что виною было? – скупость.

When Klotilda herself, hiding her face, could not restrain a cry, and the heralds praised my blow, – none of them then thought of the reason for my valour and marvellous strength! I was driven mad by the thought of my broken helmet. Was it heroism that did it? No, meanness.

Apart from the Shenstone possibility, Molière's Harpagon and Shakespeare's Shylock were the types of miser certainly Pushkin had before him, and in 1834 he noted how a kind of choice between them had been made. 'In Molière the *avare* is avaricious, and nothing else. Shylock is avaricious, resourceful, revengeful, a devoted father, a man of wit and sharp intelligence.' The point echoes what Pushkin had long thought about dramatic character. Though the Baron and his son are locked in their family antagonism – the one scheming to keep his gold, the other to get some share of it – neither sacrifices his whole nature to this end. When the Baron is summoned by his overlord, the Duke, he hastens to Court and announces his readiness to take the field in the Duke's defence whenever the command should come. His son is prepared to make any arrangement with a Jewish moneylender to borrow against future expectations, but when the Jew suggests that the Baron may live long, and that there may be a quicker way to come by his inheritance, he is filled with incredulous rage.

Their separateness puts them in that state of mutual ignorance so typical of Pushkin's dramatic exchanges. The Jew knows that he can trust Albert's word but he does not realise what Albert lives by. Of the three, only the Jew takes it for granted that men will do anything for money, and yet Pushkin does not imply that the 'standards' of the Baron and his son do them any credit. Both have conditioned reflexes that are more powerful than any ruling passion.

They are representatives of their age and class and prisoners of its assumptions, more important to them than poverty or avarice. Like some Renaissance monster the Baron dreams of the luxuries he might get with his wealth and the crimes he might commit with it, but in fact he will do nothing of the sort, for his position and up-bringing would not permit him, though he has no hereditary scruple about grinding the last ounce out of his tenants and dependants. At Court the old man recollects the Duke's grandfather in a speech which is like Gaunt's or Nestor's: his true unconscious pride is in his status, which the chests in his cellar are powerless to alter or improve. And the Duke knows him, not as a miser, but as his grandfather's old friend:

> Я помню,
> Когда я был еще ребенком, он
> Меня сажал на своего коня
> И покрывал своим тяжелым шлемом,
> Как будто колоколом.

I remember when I was a child he would seat me on his horse and cover me with his heavy helmet, as if it was a bell.

The old man's tragedy manifests itself in the increasingly shifty excuses (as incomprehensible to the Duke as were the Jew's hints to Albert) with which he seeks to evade the command that his son should come to court. When he at last brings out the accusation that his son has plotted to kill him, Albert springs out to confront him, whereupon the pair – father-and-son relation in abeyance to the stronger instinct – challenge one another like two *knights*. Albert's comment as they are separated – *Zhal* (A pity) – shows that though he could not as a son have planned his father's death, as a knight he could have slain him in formal combat. The Duke, as chorus, is scandalised both by the father's accusation and the son's eagerness to take up the challenge, and his concluding com-ment *Uzhasny vek, uzhasnye serdtsa!* (What dreadful times, and dreadful hearts!) has an unconscious irony behind its pious horror. The miserly father and his spendthrift son are perennial types; but the behaviour the Duke has just witnessed, with all its tragi-comic contradiction, could only take place in the feudal age in which the scene is set.

Marxist critics have interpreted *The Covetous Knight* as a kind of deep fable of finance and its effects on the human spirit. Gukovsky points out that Pushkin had been reading with interest in the chron-icle history of the Dukes of Burgundy, and like many cosmopolitan

Russians was highly conscious of the slow change in the pattern of Russian society, compared with the rapid changes in the west brought about by the growth of wealth. Though the Baron, a product of his age, does not conduct his affairs like a capitalist, he has already the mentality of one. In imagination he enjoys the insulation from the human state that wealth gives: 'All things obey me – none do I obey.'[1] He desires 'freedom for himself alone' and hence (for the Marxist moralist) money has poisoned his moral nature at its source. Like most capitalists he is not personally odious or inhumane but, as Nusinov observes, 'cruelty for the Baron is a terrible necessity'. He has none of the ferocious full-blooded enjoyment in the lawless power of money imagined in those two great Elizabethan dramatic conceptions: Marlowe's Barabbas and Jonson's Volpone. He is embittered by the knowledge that his son thinks he has no desires, no heart and no conscience. He has all these things, and they co-exist with his avarice in tragic incongruity.

The Merchant of Venice also has the power and significance of money in its background, and it is Antonio and Bassanio, rather than Shylock, who are its moral victims.[2] Shylock is a natural man – 'If you prick us do we not bleed...and if you wrong us shall we not revenge?' – and Antonio, by contrast, is emotionally paralysed by the possession of wealth. He is repelled by Shylock's enjoyment of it and respect for its breeding powers; he values it for the help it can give to his friend Bassanio. But money has its revenge. Bassanio, who takes it to win a wife, cannot save his benefactor by offering to pay the debt to Shylock three times over – he must be saved by the magic of Belmont and by Portia as *dea ex machina*. Shylock, who prefers revenge to repayment, has in a sense more human dignity than Bassanio, who seeks only to degrade that human impulse by offering more gold. The pathos of Antonio and the conditioned self-seeking of Bassanio have often been commented on, and it is possible that they impressed Pushkin as much as the figure of Shylock. His characters do not resemble Shakespeare's, but it could be said that all alike are victims of the cash

---

[1] Nusinov compares Balzac's banker Gobseck, who exercises the power of his wealth in society in order that society should have no power over him. Just the same points could be made of Marlowe's and Ben Jonson's tyrannical misers, whom Pushkin had probably not heard of, but who would do equally well as examples of pre-Marxian insight into the power of money. Cf. L. C. Knights, *Drama and Society in the Age of Jonson*.

[2] See W. H. Auden's essay on the play in *The Dyer's Hand*.

nexus, which places them in false and perverted relations. And yet all are primary characters, who do not exist as vehicles for authorial speculation although – and indeed because – the freedom of their absolute existence offers an endless perspective of meaning to the reader.

For obvious reasons the later Russian critics emphasise Pushkin's understanding, in *The Covetous Knight*, of the role of capital in history; but their comparison with the great nineteenth-century money themes in the novels of Balzac, Dickens and Dostoevsky ignores the fundamental difference in the kind of art involved. Pushkin's art-forms, like Shakespeare's, exist: those of the novelists expound, explore, argue and symbolise. Besides, money was there before Marx, and we can accept Pushkin's use of it in his art without claiming that he anticipates *Das Kapital*. If Pushkin did find a hint in Shenstone, it was that money, like law, is historically a cornerstone of *personal* freedom, a kind of freedom not much emphasised in the Soviet state. We must remember that the dramatic premise of *The Covetous Knight* is that money enslaves the miser but the lack of it enslaves his son. Moreover, in their pursuit of realism and capitalism in the play Soviet critics tend to ignore the humour with which Pushkin creates a dramatic balance between realism and romantic historicism. The young knight who unhorses his opponent, in a burst of rage because his valuable helmet has been damaged, is as comic a conception as that of the aged Baron – torn between avarice and obedience to his overlord – is a tragic one.

The speeches of the Baron, and of Salieri in *Mozart and Salieri*, are the most sustained feats of rhetoric in Pushkin's work and without question the finest blank verse written in the nineteenth century. Acting at once as apologia and exposition, they both reveal the speaker and embody him, making audible in his words a whole background of history and culture. The Baron is a figure in the foreground of a huge canvas, portraying court and camp, swarming armies and seascapes, grandees in satin and beggars in rags. Salieri's speech is like a feat of classical architecture, a structure massive and elegant, whose symmetry is both severe and self-absorbed. Their tone determines the shape and body of each drama, giving it the compact unity which is the secret of the genre as Pushkin developed it, and far removed from the insipid freedom of the scenes he found in Barry Cornwall.

The three *Little Tragedies* are almost as different from each other as they are from any other drama of the period. But the unity of each is not that of dramatic monologue. Browning's monologues are, by contrast, deliberately cluttered and aggressively diversionary, aiming to enrich by their variety of words and objects the message in applied psychology which they drive home. As a study, Salieri is the most Browningesque of Pushkin's conceptions, but where Browning's obsessed characters all soliloquise in the same standard idiom, Salieri's speech is uniquely and originally of the man. The Baron falls naturally into the images and exposures of rhetoric:

> Как молодой повеса ждет свиданья
> С какой-нибудь развратницей лукавой
> Иль дурой, им обманутой, так я
> Весь день минуты ждал, когда сойду
> В подвал мой тайный, к верным сундукам.

As a young rascal awaits his meeting with some wanton deceiver or with some silly girl he has deceived, so I await all day the moment when I come down to my secret cellar, to my faithful chests...

In cheating the world he is cheating himeslf, and there is unconscious irony in the image of the youth who may be the thief or the victim of love, as there is boundless satisfaction for the mind which has achieved its goal not in the world of men but in its own idea of itself.

> Не много, кажется, но понемногу
> Сокровища растут. Читал я где-то,
> Что царь однажды воинам своим
> Велел снести земли по горсти в кучу,
> И гордый холм возвысился – и царь
> Мог с вышины с весельем озирать
> И дол, покрытый белыми шатрами,
> И море, где бежали корабли.
> Так я, по горсти бедной принося
> Привычну дань мою сюда в подвал,
> Вознес мой холм – и с высоты его
> Могу взирать на все, что мне подвластно.
> Что не подвластно мне? как некий демон
> Отселе править миром я могу;
> Лишь захочу – воздвигнутся чертоги;
> В великолепые мои сады
> Сбегутся нимфы резвою толпою;
> И музы дань свою мне принесут,
> И вольный гений мне поработится,
> И добродетель и бессонный труд
> Смиренно будут ждать моей награды.

THE DRAMA

Я свистну, и ко мне послушно, робко
Вползет окровавленное злодейство,
И руку будет мне лизать, и в очи
Смотреть, в них знак моей читая воли.
Мне всё послушно, я же – ничему;
Я выше всех желаний; я спокоен;
Я знаю мощь мою: с меня довольно
Сего сознанья...

It does not seem much, but it is by trifles that treasures grow. I have read somewhere that once a Tsar ordered his army to take handfuls of earth and throw them in a heap, and a proud hill arose – and from its height the Tsar could gaze in pleasure on the valley, covered with white tents, and on the sea where ships were running. So I, bearing each poor handful, have schooled myself to bring hither my tribute, and erected my hill, and from its summit can gaze on everything over which my power extends. And where does it not extend? Like a demon I can rule the world from here. I've only to wish, and palaces will rise, and nymphs in lively throng dance in my splendid gardens. The muses will bring me tribute, and free genius make itself my slave; and goodness and unsleeping toil humbly await my pay. I whistle, and to me, obediently, timidly, bloodstained villainy will crawl and lick my hand, and look in my eye and read there the sign of my desire. Everything is subservient to me, I – to nothing. I am above all desires; I am quiet; I know my power: and this knowledge is enough for me...

In Salieri's meditation fantasy has no place. For him everything is logical and simple; his thought progresses step by step, as the musician from one note to the next:

Все говорят: нет правды на земле.
Но правды нет – и выше. Для меня
Так это ясно, как простая гамма.

All say: there is no justice on earth. But there is none on high either. This is as clear to me as a simple scale. (v, 355.)

Sometimes the pace is quickened by emotion for the love of his art, but this only serves to bring out the persistent underlying monotony, the plodding determination of dedicated talent.

Что говорю? Когда великий Глюк
Явился и открыл нам новы тайны
(Глубокие, пленительные тайны),
Не бросил ли я все, что прежде знал,
Что так любил, чему так жарко верил,
И не пошел ли бодро вслед за ним
Безропотно, как тот, кто заблуждался
И встречным послан в сторону иную?

217

PUSHKIN

Усильным, напряженным постоянством
Я, наконец, в искусстве безграничном
Достигнул степени высокой.

What do I say? When the great Gluck appeared and revealed to us new
secrets (deep captivating secrets) did I not throw away all I had learned
before, all I had loved and ardently believed, and did I not walk bravely
behind him, uncomplaining, like one lost who receives the direction to
turn back and take another road? By vigorous, tense persistence I at last
in boundless art reached a high place.

In *Mozart and Salieri* Pushkin certainly portrays his knowledge
of the nature of a genius like his own. But Mozart is not a dramatic
figure: he says little and there is little to be said about him. Such
genius is simple, inexplicable, and in psychological terms uninteresting. Pushkin seems sardonically conscious of this; there is
no concealed complacency in his portrait of Mozart. To Salieri goes
both the interest and the poetry; Mozart's speeches are notably
less 'harmonious' and his speech on art is the flattest in the play

Когда бы все так чувствовали силу
Гармонии! Но нет: тогда б не мог
И мир существовать; никто б не стал
Заботиться о нуждах низкой жизни;
Все предались бы вольному искусству.
Нас мало избранных, счастливцев праздных,
Пренебрегающих презренной пользой,
Единого прекрасного жрецов.

If only everyone could feel the power of harmony as you do! But no:
then the world would not exist; no one would be concerned about the
needs of ordinary life; all would give themselves to art alone. We are a
chosen few, happy idlers, despisers of vulgar utility, the priests of
beauty alone.

No doubt Pushkin did not intend it to be flat, but the happy idler
and priest of beauty announcing the fact is neither edifying nor
dramatically felicitous. The point is, or should be, that neither
Mozart nor Pushkin was a happy idler: both were men of immense
intelligence, fully aware of what they were doing and fascinated by
the theory and techniques of the art they practised, but this was
not the impression they made on many who knew them. We
should not see Mozart as he saw himself, but as Salieri saw him,
and for the rest of the piece we do.

We can, of course, suppose the Pushkin makes Mozart speak as
he does from motives of perceptive delicacy, sensing Salieri's envy

and drawing him into the self-deprecating band of genius; or that the speech is deliberately intended to reveal Mozart's child-like *naïveté*, but both hypotheses are dramatically superfluous, and have the feel of critical ingenuity determined to save every appearance. What matters is that Salieri is not in the ordinary sense envious: he himself clearly speaks the truth here. He does not hate Mozart because he, Salieri, is judged inferior beside him – as was clearly the case in the story of the real Salieri hissing an *aria* in *Don Giovanni*, the story from which Pushkin drew his idea. Pushkin applies the principle which he more than once stated theoretically: in true drama a hypocrite, a miser, an envious man must not be just that and no more. A miser may demonstrate other affections, passions and loyalties; and a seemingly envious man may be driven by an impassioned and impersonal sense of justice.

The dramatic climax of *The Covetous Knight* is the moment when Albert accuses his father the Baron of lying. And from his own point of view, rightly. He has just heard his father, driven to desperation by the Duke's insistence that the son should be given a proper allowance to maintain himself at court, claim that he has planned his death, or at least desires it, and has attempted to rob him. The scene is typical of Pushkin's dramatic sense of psychology, for the Baron will not admit to himself that he *can* lie, even though the miser does so in an attempt to avoid parting with any of his gold. As we have seen, in his final cry of rage the Baron reveals that in his own estimate he is a knight, not a miser:

> Я лгу! и перед нашим государем!...
> Мне, мне...иль уж не рыцарь я?

I lie! And before our Sovereign!...At me, me...am I no longer a knight?

In the revelation of Salieri's psychology there is no comparable climax, only the slow unfolding of his decision to poison Mozart in the cause of art. For the man himself Salieri feels not only reverence but friendship and love. He would not dream of exploiting Mozart's confiding lack of professional caution, or stealing his ideas. But Mozart's existence is an affront to justice and to art, and he must be eliminated in order that the decorum of art may be preserved. His murder is a duty, as A. C. Bradley observed that murder becomes a 'terrible duty' for Macbeth, and as Nusinov comments that 'cruelty for the Baron is a terrible necessity'. In both these *Little Tragedies* human weakness is raised to tragic proportions.

Like Brutus about Caesar, Salieri might say: Not that I loved Mozart less but that I loved art more.

Relating the play to his general critical position, Gukovsky sees its conflict in historical and cultural terms as between classic and romantic. Musically I suspect this makes little sense, but it does suggest the forces of conservatism and propriety which Salieri represents. Mozart feels that both of them are 'priests of beauty' and that 'genius and villainy are two incompatible things', but to Salieri he is like a modern heretic who has discredited the traditions of the Church. When he has administered the poison Salieri for the first time can shed tears of pleasure over Mozart's music, but after Mozart's departure Salieri returns to the point in his concluding speech:

> Ты заснешь
> Надолго, Моцарт! Но ужель он прав,
> И я не гений? Гений и злодейство
> Две вещи несовместные. Неправда:
> А Бонаротти? или это сказка
> Тупой, бессмысленной толпы – и не был
> Убийцею создатель Ватикана?

You will sleep long, Mozart! But can it be that he is right, and that I am not a genius? Genius and villainy are two incompatible things. Not true: what of Buonarroti? Or is that a fiction of the dull unthinking mob – and was the architect of the Vatican not a murderer?

With the sleep-walking unease of these final lines another idea glides onstage. The identification that Salieri implies reveals the madness in him but also summates the whole structure of his thought. Michelangelo was rumoured to have killed the model to achieve the realism of his crucifixion. Salieri identifies himself not with Michelangelo the painter and sculptor but with the architect of the Vatican, the supreme edifice of the Church in whose name so many crimes have been committed. From such high motives Salieri has committed a crime in the cause of art, and yet the possibility that such a crime is not justified, and may not be one with so august a precedent, is not quite dispelled in the majesty of the final line. The High Priest of tradition, who has sacrificed his life to an idea of the dignity and unity of his calling, is left facing the possibility that it is he, and not his victim, who is the *bezumets*, the mad eccentric who has destroyed art.

Their endings are a touchstone of the Little Tragedy method, and they reveal the technical difficulties the method emphasises. It cannot afford the relaxation into a valedictory formula which is at the disposal of Shakespearean drama. The short pieces must not fade away, but they must not end with too much of a bang either. The ending of *The Covetous Knight* is neat but over-pointed: it too noticeably winds up and comments on the tale, while those of the other *Little Tragedies* both round them off and tacitly prolong their perspective of meaning. In *The Feast in Time of Plague* Pushkin, as we shall see, achieves this prolongation without words but by means of a stage direction, and the action of *Rusalka* – conceivably by intention – breaks off when the audience can see what is going to happen but before the *dénouement* is reached.

Pushkin's formula of psychological diversification is sometimes a little too evident. From Albert's exchange with his servant about his last bottle of wine being sent to a sick blacksmith, we are rather too obviously meant to infer that he is a young man with a kind heart who thinks of other things than inheriting his father's money. The same with Mozart's remark that before dining with Salieri he will step home and tell his wife not to expect him. Genius is considerate. These inert indications have disappeared in *The Stone Guest*, where every word has an instant dramatic compulsion, but they do reveal the difficulty of using dramatic conventions in the swift and naturalistic medium of the *Little Tragedies*. The leisurely expositions and Shakespearean 'signposts' that Pushkin employed in *Boris Godunov* are not feasible here. And his later dramatic experiments, *The Feast in Time of Plague* and *Rusalka*, turn away from naturalism, using songs and ceremonies to reveal character and situation instead of conversational exchanges for an audience's benefit.

Yet in the *Little Tragedies* Pushkin is a complete master of the art – long vanished from European drama – of making interjections, comments, and single lines at once 'inevitable' as poetry and completely unselfconscious as uttered speech. Don Juan's *Tak zdes pokhoronili komandora?* (So it was here they buried the Komandor?), Laura's *A ty, povesa?* (And what about you, you rogue?), Salieri's

Ты, Моцарт, бог, и сам того не знаешь;
Я знаю, я.

You are a god, Mozart, and do not know it yourself. I, I know it.

– all such comments seem in their context the only way to say the thing, like Shakespeare's 'Look where she comes!' or 'Nay answer me, stand and unfold yourself'. Such lines would live in the actor's mouth, though the *Little Tragedies* are not intended for stage presentation. Apart from technical difficulties – Mozart's playing is for the ear of the imagination and could not be synchronised with dialogue – the long rhetorical speeches of the first two plays are, as it were, a visible and on-the-page emanation of the man, rather than an acoustic representation. Even Don Juan, dramatic as his role is, would present an actor (as he does not the reader) with the impossible task of pinning him down, and deciding how to interpret a role whose immediate effect consists in not being open to interpretation.

By contrast, the unfinished *Rusalka* might well be as impressive on the stage as in the study, and *The Feast in Time of Plague* would make a moving spectacle. It was the last of the dazzling dramatic series in the Boldino autumn of 1830, adapted from a lengthy poetic melodrama published in France in 1829 in a miscellany which also included work by Bowles (whose views on nature poetry were the object of a famous attack by Byron which was known to Pushkin), Milman, and Barry Cornwall. Its author, John Wilson (who afterwards became the Christopher North of *Blackwood's Magazine*) had first published *The City of the Plague* in 1816, at the same age as Pushkin when he wrote the *Little Tragedies*, and he had hoped to score a success with a piece that was as romantically wild in tone as it was conventional in moral sentiment. Up to a point he succeeded. His drama is really a dramatic fragment of the Barry Cornwall kind, padded out to inordinate length and embellished with every kind of sensation – duels in graveyards, prostitutes penitent and golden-hearted and a multiplication of dead mothers whose memories are invoked with tears by their dissolute progeny. The male characters are sea-officers, home from the fleet in the plague year (patriotic naval references recall more recent glories by reference to the Dutch wars) and the hero's name, Walsingham, aptly adds two further touches of local colour, the religious and Elizabethan. For good measure one of the prostitutes, Mary Gray, is Scottish, and sings a lengthy ballad in the fashionable romantic border diction.

'This Wilson wrote a great work' wrote Belinsky, who knew his play only through Pushkin. 'The fundamental idea is an orgy in time of plague, and the more terrible the more gay – a truly tragic idea.' 'In Wilson', objected Carlyle, 'the central tie-beam is wanting always' and indeed in *The City of the Plague* any central idea is lost beneath an orgy of emotional incident. Wilson is scarcely to blame. Irrespective of their length the European romantic dramas had no

centre – Shakespeare misunderstood is as usual the reason – and
writers like Hugo, who were far more talented than Wilson, had
failed as obviously as he. But even so Belinsky seems to miss the
significance of Pushkin's adaptation. None of the *Little Tragedies*
gives the impression of exploiting 'a truly tragic idea', and *The
Feast in Time of Plague* is no exception. Like that of its predecessors, its unity comes from a created world in which 'the tragic idea'
– avarice, envy, the legend of Don Juan, an orgy in time of plague –
loses its insistence to gain a greater diversity and scope of meaning.
Wild gaiety in the face of death is indeed the theme. But by re-
writing the two songs which are buried in Wilson's text and making
them the main features of his own, Pushkin creates a further dimension of drama expressed through them, and through their contrast
with one another.

There is no rhetorical exposition, as in the first two *Little Tragedies*,
and no dramatic exchange as in *The Stone Guest*. Walsingham's
song embodies the masculine attitude to death by plague; Mary's
that of a woman, and a woman in love. Yet the contrast is wholly
unobtrusive and unsymbolic, and there is nothing *ewig weiblich*
about Mary. Her femininity is conveyed wholly through the *form*
of her lyric, as the male attitude is through Walsingham's.

> *Мери [поет]* Было время, процветала
> В мире наша сторона;
> В воскресение бывала
> Церковь божия полна;
> Наших деток в шумной школе
> Раздавались голоса,
> И сверкали в светлом поле
> Серп и быстрая коса.

Mary [sings]   There was a time when our land flourished in peace; God's
church was full on Sundays; in the clamour of the school rang out our
children's voices, and in the sunlit field flashed the sickle and the swift
scythe. (v, 411.)[1]

---

[1] With its conscientious Scottish lilt, Wilson's version is not so much bad as
self-indulgent, indefatigably picturesque through sixteen stanzas, two of
which are enough to give the flavour:

> I passed by the schoolhouse – when strangers were coming –
> Whose windows with glad faces all seemed alive,
> Ae moment I hearkened, but heard no sweet humming,
> For a night of dark vapour can silence the hive.
>
> I passed by the pool where the lasses at dawing
> Used to bleach their white garments wi' daffin and din;
> But the foam in the silence of nature was fa'ing
> And nae laughing rose loud thro' the roar o' the lin.

PUSHKIN

Walsingham's song has the masculine energy of the Horatian tradition and the 'Tribe of Ben' – 'born in the foaming wine-cup' – an energy as incisive as it is robust, but also exclusive and egocentric:

Председатель [*поет*]   Когда могущая Зима,
Как бодрый вождь, ведет сама
На нас косматые дружины
Своих морозов и снегов, –
Навстречу ей трещат камины,
И весел зимний жар пиров.

Master of Ceremonies [*sings*] When mighty winter, like a doughty warrior, leads her shaggy guard of frosts and snows in person against us, then the crackle of the hearth joins battle with her, and the cheerful warmth of winter feasting.[1]

The plague is a challenge and calls for the resolution and zest which alone make life worth living and which are found only in danger:

Есть упоение в бою,
И бездны мрачной на краю,
И в разъяренном океане,
Средь грозных волн и бурной тьмы,
И в аравийском урагане,
И в дуновении Чумы.

Всё, всё, что гибелью грозит,
Для сердца смертного таит
Неизъяснимы наслажденья –
Бессмертья, может быть, залог,
И счастлив тот, кто средь волненья
Их обретать и ведать мог.

Итак, – хвала тебе, Чума,
Нам не страшна могилы тьма,
Нас не смутит твое призванье.
Бокалы пеним дружно мы,
И девы-розы пьем дыханье, –
Быть может...полное Чумы.

[1] Though cruder in finish, the anonymous English drinking-poem of the seventeenth century has something of the same boisterous precision and gives an idea of the syllabic 'attack' of the Russian:

When as the chill Charokko blows,
And winter tells a heavy tale;
When pyes and daws and rooks and crows
Sit cursing of the frosts and snows:
    Then give me ale...

Ale, that the absent battle fights,
And frames the march of Swedish drum,
Disputes with princes, laws, and rights,
What's done and past tells mortal wights,
    And what's to come...

There is intoxication in battle, and on the brink of the dark abyss, and on the wild ocean among dread waves and stormy murk, and in the Arabian hurricane, and in the breath of the plague.

All, all that threatens disaster cherishes an inexpressible delight to the hearts of mortal men – a pledge, it may be, of immortality – and happy is he who, among the tumult, can find and discern it.

Therefore, praise to you, O Plague. The gloom of the grave holds no terrors for us, your summons does not confound us. Together we raise our foaming goblets, and we drink in the breath of girls like roses – though it may be...laden with the plague.

The strong melodious logic of the lines recalls the seventeenth century in a way that is almost uncanny, for there is no likelihood that Pushkin knew its lyrics or attached the flavour of Walsingham's song to the century in which the Feast is supposed to take place. In fact he drops Wilson's naval and historical associations, retaining only the Scottishness of Mary; but whereas his version of Walsingham's song has a true and tough poetic logic, Wilson's has an emotional vagueness typical of its time:

> Two navies meet upon the waves
> That round them yawn like op'ning graves.
> The battle rages; seamen fall
> And overboard goes one and all.
> The wounded with the dead are gone
> But Ocean drowns each frantic groan
> And at each plunge into the flood
> Grimly the billow laughs at blood.
>
> Then what although our plague destroy
> Seaman and landsman, woman, boy?
> When the pillow rests beneath the head
> Like sleep he comes and strikes us dead.

Wilson's attempt at a demonstration ('*Then* what although...') does not follow from the proposition but is merely associated with it, whereas Pushkin's *Itak – khvala tebe, Chuma!* (Therefore – praise to you, O Plague!) has been earned by the logical steps of each stanza.

Mary's song is the seventeenth-century tradition in its feminine guise – half ballad, half lover's lament. Wilson's Mary sings her border ballad in the first person, but Pushkin's is made impersonal. A girl called Jenny implores her lover Edmund not to approach her body if she dies of the plague, but only to visit her grave:

PUSHKIN

Если ранняя могила
Суждена моей весне –
Ты, кого я так любила,
Чья любовь отрада мне, –
Я молю: не приближайся
К телу Дженни ты своей,
Уст умерших не касайся,
Следуй издали за ней.

И потом оставь селенье,
Уходи куда-нибудь,
Где б ты мог души мученье
Усладить и отдохнуть.
И когда зараза минет,
Посети мой бедный прах;
А Эдмонда не покинет
Дженни даже в небесах.

If my spring days are fated for an early grave – you, whom I love so, whose love is my delight, do not I pray come near the body of your Jenny; do not touch her dead lips, follow her from afar.

And then leave the village; go away and rest in some place which may soothe the anguish of your soul. And when the plague passes, visit my poor dust; and even in the heavens Jenny will not forsake Edmund.

Dostoevsky exclaimed that in the song 'Pushkin discerns the anguish of British genius...its suffering presentiment of its future'. However that may be, he certainly summons up a potent and vanished spirit from English poetry. What Blagoy calls the 'morbidity' of the images in the two songs has the true Jacobean flavour, not that of its contemporary romantic revival in writers like Beddoes, Darley, and Wilson himself. And it is both humanised and made Pushkin's own by the dramatic meaning embodied in these two significantly different responses to the terror of death by plague.

So much do the songs convey that the blank verse dialogue has only the function of bridging sections, giving context to the dramatic situation. Partly for this reason, partly no doubt because it is a fairly close rendering of Wilson, it has none of the superlative distinction of the blank verse of the *Little Tragedies*, almost as if Pushkin had deliberately nullified it in order to throw the songs into greater relief. Pushkin's few touches of alteration in the single scene that he adapts from Wilson are inconspicuously distancing, eliminating the facetious, the personal, and the over-emphatic.

When the dead cart comes by, driven by a negro, the second prostitute Luisa faints away. Mary's words to her when she comes round show the difference between the two conceptions, though Pushkin only omits a few words:

> *Mary* O sister of my sorrow and my shame,
> Lean on my bosom. Sick must be your heart
> After a fainting-fit so like to death.

> *Мери* Сестра моей печали и позора,
> Приляг на грудь мою.

Sister of my sorrow and shame, lean on my breast.

The change gives Pushkin's Mary true feeling, and reveals the extent to which her original is merely histrionic.[1]

At the end of the scene a priest enters and deplores the revels, urging Walsingham to remember the tears he shed for his dead mother three weeks before. Wilson's reader is invited to thrill with religious horror at the blasphemous behaviour of the unfortunate man. Here Pushkin begins to cut. He removes the priest's account of Walsingham's behaviour at the funeral. The latter speaks quietly, asking the priest to leave, and separating himself both from the consolations of religion and from the wild irreverence of his companions. When he speaks of his dead wife, a female voice cries: 'Fool, thus to rave about a buried wife!' Pushkin translates the verb but alters the tone.

> *Женский голос* Он сумасшедший, –
> Он бредит о жене похороненной.

> *Female voice* He is mad – he raves about his buried wife.

In Pushkin's version Walsingham and Mary have no further communication; their songs have both brought them together and set them apart. But the inexorable Wilson continued to pile on the agony. Having looked towards heaven and imagined his dead wife there ('Most glorious star! Thou art the spirit of that bright innocent!') his Walsingham goes on to patronise Mary with righteous indignation on her and his own behalf:

> On the breast
> Even of this prostitute (why should I fear
> That word of three unmeaning syllables?)
> I now will seek and seeking I will find
> The open-eyed sleep of troubled happiness...(etc.)

---

[1] This point is well made by H. Gifford, 'Pushkin's "Feast in Time of Plague" and its Original', *American Slavic and East European Review*, VIII (1949).

It would be interesting to know what Pushkin felt about this. He breaks off the scene with the priest's departure and a single stage direction:

Председатель   Отец мой, ради бога,
          Оставь меня.
Священник   Спаси тебя господь.
          Прости, мой сын.

[*Уходит. Пир продолжается. Председатель остается погружен в глубокую задумчивость.*]

Master of Ceremonies (Walsingham)   My father, for God's sake, leave me.
Priest   May the Lord preserve you. Farewell, my son.

[*He goes out. The feast continues. The Master of Ceremonies remains sunk in deep reverie.*]

The Feast in Time of Plague is the most remarkable instance in Pushkin of inferior work made use of and transformed. Its substance is not rejected or parodied (parody in Pushkin is a very different matter) but purified. In *Rusalka* a different kind of transformation takes place, not of an inferior work of literature but of a cliché situation – a humble girl who is abandoned by a princely seducer and drowns herself. In fact Pushkin had in mind a Viennese *opéra comique, Das Donauweibchen,* which had been translated by Krasnopolsky and enjoyed a success in Petersburg, but it provided him with a starting-point rather than a scenario. In 1831 Zhukovsky had begun to turn into Russian hexameters De la Motte Fouqué's romantic tale *Undine,* and it is also possible that Pushkin meditated a Russian equivalent of this sentimental story of a water nymph divided between her native element and her love for a human being. *Rusalki,* who are met with in many Slav tales, are seductive beings in the south, but in northern Russia they were malignant and horrible creatures who haunted river banks by night to catch and drown men and women. In early folk tradition they are elemental beings like the *Domovoy* and the *Vodyanoy,* but in later tales they become girls who have drowned themselves for love and seek revenge. Pushkin also combined themes from two folksongs: the betrayal of a girl who drowns herself and is revenged by her brothers, and the motif of a wedding-feast blighted by remorse. The scenes he had projected much earlier were determined by these folk patterns and they underlie the contemporary romantic plot with which Pushkin combined them when he wrote the play. *Ruslan and Lyudmila* is a parallel case, but in *Rusalka* the disparate

elements combine with Pushkin's now perfectly developed blank
verse to produce a tragedy of a unique sort, as original as the *Little
Tragedies*, but less theoretical in scope and on a larger scale.

In *Hamlet* and *King Lear* Shakespeare compelled an oft-told tale
to reveal its fullest potential of human significance – the significance
of a son urged by his father's ghost to avenge his murder; of a king
who finds the meaning of his previous life taken from him by the
children among whom he thought to divide his kingdom. The story
of the faithless prince, and the miller's daughter who drowns herself and becomes a revengeful *rusalka*, is likewise intensified by
Pushkin's dramatic poetry to a point where we are compelled to
experience what such a drowning and such a revenge might actually
mean. *Rusalka* reveals the distance between the inherent cosiness of
a folk tradition – however fateful and supernatural – in which
expectation is satisfied by the recounting of what is already known,
and the kind of truth which great art can impress upon the
situation which folk-tale takes for granted. Belinsky truly observed
that Pushkin enriched the work with elements half fantastic and
half sober and factual. Fantasy discloses a simple meaning, all the
more terrible for being commonplace.

In folk-tale the miller's daughter must be a type, on whom the
situation imposes itself. In Pushkin's tragedy it is her individual
nature which determines the strength of her love and the danger
implicit in its self-abandoning energy, the energy that after her
transformation into a *rusalka* becomes utterly cold, collected, and
determined. Though she is a miller's daughter she is not the
Gretchen the prince expects her to be: he seduces a type and finds
she is a person. He is not unkind but he is without sympathy, and
again we have Pushkin's infallible feeling for the conditioned
response. Relaxed and supple dramatic verse is used to point the
difference between spontaneity and *mauvaise foi*: the ardour of the
girl is trapped between the calculation of her father and the dis-
honesty of her lover.

The tone is set by the miller's opening speech:

> *Мельник* Ох, то-то все вы, девки молодые,
> Все глупы вы. Уж если подвернулся
> К вам человек завидный, не простой,
> Так должно вам его себе упрочить.
> А чем? разумным, честным поведеньем;
> Заманивать то строгостью, то лаской;
> Порою исподволь обиняком

PUSHKIN

> О свадьбе заговаривать – а пуще
> Беречь свою девическую честь –
> Бесценное сокровище; она –
> Что слово – раз упустишь, не воротишь.
> А коли нет на свадьбу уж надежды,
> То всё-таки по крайней мере можно
> Какой-нибудь барыш себе –

Oh you are all fools, you young girls. If an eligible high-class chap comes sniffing round you, it's your duty to make sure of him. And how? By clever, prudent conduct: entice him now by severity, now with a kiss; and all the while bring the situation round to the idea of marriage – but always keeping safe your maidenhead, your irreplaceable treasure. It's like a word – once uttered, never recalled. But if there's no hope of marriage, at least take care to get something out of him...

Shakespeare also has this counterpoint (an aspect, it may be, of the 'freedom' Pushkin saw in him) between a sound commonplace universalised in poetry, and the unadmitted personal intent of the person who utters it. In laying on his daughter the weight of ancient precepts the miller exonerates himself; he regrets only that she has not got anything out of the liaison – his motive for permitting it. Like Claudius's speech to Hamlet ('For you must know, your father lost a father...') what he says is all the more false in the particular for being so true in general.

More bland and more cunning, the Prince is aware, like Ulysses in *Troilus and Cressida*, of his own reasons for sage generalisation.

> *Князь*   Зачем мне медлить? чем скорей, тем лучше.
> Мой милый друг, ты знаешь, нет на свете
> Блаженства прочного: ни знатный род,
> Ни красота, ни сила, ни богатство,
> Ничто беды не может миновать.
> И мы, – не правда ли, моя голубка?
> Мы были счастливы; по крайней мере
> Я счастлив был тобой, твоей любовью.

Why linger? the quicker the better. 'My dear one, you know there is no lasting happiness in this world. Neither high rank, nor beauty nor strength, nor riches – none of these can avoid misfortunes. And we – isn't it true my dove? – we were happy; at least I was happy with you, in your love.'

He goes on to reverse in words what has occurred, and to claim that she is free and he is not.

> Что делать?
> Сама ты рассуди. Князья не вольны,
> Как девицы – не по сердцу они
> Себе подруг берут, а по расчетам
> Иных людей, для выгоды чужой.

What to do? Judge yourself. Princes aren't free like girls – they can't engage themselves as they want to, but by the calculation of others, for the good of strangers.[1]

How far she is free she reveals:

> сегодня у меня
> Ребенок твой под сердцем шевельнулся.

Today your child stirred beneath my heart.

He promises to look after her, but the confession only increases his wish to get away.

> Ух! кончено – душе как будто легче.
> Я бури ждал, но дело обошлось
> Довольно тихо.

Ouf! It's over – I feel a bit better. I expected a storm but the business went off quite quietly.

The reflection as he escapes shows how little he understands her. He has been playing with fire – or with water – and her calm is not that of acquiescence but despair.

> Не верю,
> Не может быть. Я так его любила.
> Или он зверь? Иль сердце у него
> Косматое?

I don't believe it. It can't be. I loved him so much. Is he a beast? Is his heart covered with hide?

The violence of her love and its sense of natural justice emerge in the beast images. Her child has stirred within her like a young animal (*shevelnulsya*). She will claim justice of his bride.

> Я доберусь. Я ей скажу, злодейке:
> Отстань от князя, – видишь, две волчихи
> Не водятся в одном овраге.

I will go there. I'll say to her, the wretch: Leave my prince – look, two she-wolves don't live in one lair.

---

[1] Just possibly an actual recollection by Pushkin of Laertes' words to his sister in *Hamlet*:

> For he himself is subject to his birth;
> He may not, as unvalued persons do,
> Carve for himself...

They are creatures of hot blood – or at least she is one until her transformation. As *rusalka* her nature does not change, but everything passionate and warm in it becomes cold without losing its passion. With an uncanny change in tone and tempo, the verse conveys this in the penultimate scene, her last words before the play breaks off:

> С той поры,
> Как бросилась без памяти я в воду
> Отчаянной и презренной девчонкой
> И в глубине Днепра-реки очнулась
> Русалкою холодной и могучей,
> Я каждый день о мщенье помышляю,
> И ныне, кажется, мой час настал.

From that time when I threw myself without remembrance into the water, a girl despised and out of her mind, and in the Dnieper's depths was transformed into a cold and powerful *rusalka*. I have thought every day of my revenge, and now, I think, my time has come.

The prince too has changed, and this is revealed with a force equally simple and strange in one line spoken by the hunstman whom his young wife sends to find him:

> Остался
> Один в лесу на берегу Днепра.

He has remained alone in the forest by the banks of the Dnieper.

It has the force and timbre of a line in Racine. Nothing needs to be said of conscience, of the misery of an unanticipated change of heart, or of his indifference to his wife and obsession with the memory of the love once given him.

Though the tone of these lines is so different, they blend none the less with the ritual of the wedding scene, when the chant of the young girls is disturbed by a mysterious voice, the cold *rusalka* measure interrupting the rustic gaiety of the marriage chorus.

Хор	Сватушка, сватушка,
	Бестолковый сватушка!
	По невесту ехали,
	В огород заехали,
	Пива бочку пролили...
Один голос	По камушкам по желтому песочку
	Пробегала быстрая речка.

Chorus Matchmaker, matchmaker, stupid matchmaker! We have been to the bride, been to the garden, drunk a barrel of beer...
A single voice Over the pebbles, over the yellow sand, ran a swift river...

These contrasts succeed one another in dramatic alternation. The next scene, between the young princess and her *mamka*, takes us to the world of *Evgeny Onegin* and of Juliet and her nurse. After we have seen him through the huntsman's words, we find the prince on the banks of the Dnieper, and his romantic melancholy, subjective where it is objective, adds to the cold fact his attempted fulfilment of feeling.

> здесь она,
> Обняв меня, поникла и умолкла...
> Возможно ли?...
> Что это значит? листья,
> Поблекнув, вдруг свернулися и с шумом
> Посыпались как пепел на меня.
> Передо мной стоит он гол и черн,
> Как дерево проклятое.

Here, embracing me, she inclined her head and was silent...Is it possible? What does this mean? Faded leaves suddenly contract and fall rustling on me, like ashes. Before me he stands dark and naked, like a blasted tree.[1]

The bluff, cunning miller is now a broken and mad old man. He also is transformed, and this is a real madman, very far removed from the romantic apparition of Mariya at the end of *Poltava*.

The dramatic confrontation of romance and brute fact requires all Pushkin's habitual discipline and his instinct for terseness. The first *Rusalka* sketches of 1826 show how Pushkin must have learnt his dramatic technique by refusing every opening for poetic indulgence. The theme seems to cry out for graphic illustration of all the suggestiveness of cold *rusalka* sexuality, and Pushkin seems to have got it out of his system in his first draft of the prince's soliloquy as he awaited on the bank the appearance of the *rusalka*.

> Как сладостно явление ее
> Из тихих волн, при свеге ночи лунной!
> Опутана зелеными власами,
> Она сидит на берегу крутом.
> У стройных ног, как пена белых, волны
> Ласкаются, сливаясь и журча.
> Ее глаза то меркнут, то блистают,
> Как на небе мерцающие звезды;
> Дыханья нет из уст ее, но сколь
> Пронзительно сих влажных синих уст
> Прохладное лобзанье без дыханья.

---

[1] The onomatopoeia of the falling leaves, unselfconscious as are all Pushkin's sound-effects, cannot be suggested in translation.

How ravishing her appearance out of the quiet waters, in the light of the moon! With green tresses tangled she sits on the steep bank. Lapping and murmuring, the ripples caress her graceful feet, white as foam. Her eyes now darken, now shine out like the stars twinkling in the sky. There is no breath in her mouth, but how shrill on her moist blue lips is the cold whisper of a kiss without breath.[1]

It is fine, if lax, description, but dramatically it would not do. The 'cold and powerful' *rusalka* must remain human, changed not externally but in the psychological vision of the tragedy. In the first draft of the wedding scene, the apparition of a girl streaming with water is seen by the matchmaker and the prince, and this again would be too explicit an indulgence. In poetic drama a voice is all that is needed.

And it is the need to reduce and refine which may have led Pushkin to break off the play before a *dénouement*. Hard to see how he could have avoided anti-climax, for the *rusalochka*, the daughter he has begotten and the instrument of her mother's revenge, may be a feasible agent of retribution in terms of plot, but carries us fatally back to the atmosphere of operetta and of *Undine*. The play breaks off as the prince meets her on the river bank. In a sense it is a highly Pushkinian ending, to leave the rest to our imagination, yet it is unlikely that Pushkin could really have meant to leave the play – which he did not attempt to publish – in this condition, unless he saw it as appropriately complete in its form as a fragment, like the marvellous poem *Osen*, and thus forgoing any claim to stage presentation. Certainly it remains the most haunting of nineteenth-century romantic tragedies, achieving with apparent effortlessness what so many plays (Coleridge's *Remorse*, which *was* acted, is one) attempted so earnestly.

As usual with Pushkin, it had no descendants except in prose. Whether Tolstoy was conscious of the connection or not, the central theme of *Resurrection* breaks through to the same kind of disturbing insistence, and the novel makes explicit what is implicit in Pushkin's poetry – the transformation that takes place in the relations of seducer and victim, and in their natures. Tolstoy's Prince Nekhlyudov stands by the river at night, a prey to conflicting emotions; and when he pursues her with his repentance and his desire to make amends, the servant girl Masha meets him with cold malignity and with a strength and awareness which reverses their

[1] Bilibin's well-known illustration of a *rusalka* rather resembles this description.

previous roles. Prostitution, crime and exile have made a kind of *rusalka* out of her, and the pair can never meet again on the old terms, no matter how much the Prince may will it. In *Resurrection* a sense of personal guilt and anguish lay deep, and the knowledge that the past can never be brought back or forgotten.[1]

[1] At the beginning of May 1826 Pushkin wrote to Vyazemsky asking him to befriend the bearer of the letter, Pushkin's serf-girl Olga Kalashnikova, whom he had got with child. She was married and afterwards lived at Boldino, but nothing is known of the fate of the child. Pushkin's references to her are kind and business-like but not particularly remorseful. Whatever he felt he kept to himself.

6

'EVGENY ONEGIN'

I

Evgeny Onegin occupied Pushkin intermittently for more than eight years. He began it at Kishinev on 9 May 1823, and at Tsarskoe Selo in 1831 he added Onegin's letter to Tatyana to the final chapter. The creation of the novel in verse thus extends over the period of most of his other narrative poems – *The Gipsies, Poltava, Count Nulin,* and *The Little House in Kolomna,* and the time in which *Boris Godunov* and the *Little Tragedies* were written. I have postponed a detailed discussion of it to this chapter, because it is best considered against the background of Pushkin's work as a whole, and in conjunction with the poems that are most closely related to it.[1]

Evgeny Onegin is a triumphant hybrid; the most glitteringly poetic of poems, and yet as full of 'felt life' as the most richly conceived work of fiction. Before examining how it works, and analysing one of its chapters in detail, it is worth looking for a moment at the idea of the verse novel, and its relation during the nineteenth century to the novel in prose. In his essay 'Is Verse a Dying Technique?' Edmund Wilson suggested that Flaubert, Joyce and Virginia Woolf were in a sense poets who wrote in prose because at the time they were writing only a prose form seemed to offer the freedom and the authority for the kinds of fictional

---

[1] Particularly since *Evgeny Onegin* is widely known in the west – the only work of Pushkin that is widely known – and is often assumed to be the only work that justifies his reputation. The several verse translations, notably Oliver Elton's, are all spirited; and though they can only give a crude and sometimes misleading idea of the original, they hardly deserve the measureless contempt of V. Nabokov, whose own translation *Evgeny Onegin in Verse* (Routledge 1964), though admirably literal and full of subtle art, sports a highly eccentric vocabulary that can give an equally misleading impression of the words that Pushkin uses. But both his translation and his admirable and copious notes do convey the sheer density as well as the delicacy of the novel.

Of the many commentaries in Russian, N. L. Brodsky's (Moscow 1932) is the most comprehensive, and by no means deserves Nabokov's cosmopolitan contempt. Also helpful is D. Chizhevsky's shorter commentary in his edition of *Evgeny Onegin* (Harvard University Press 1953).

experiment they wished to attempt. Such novels resemble the kind of poetry which keeps our attention fixed on its medium, and embodies in its physical identity what it says and the nature of the world it creates. By contrast the evolved realistic prose novel takes its medium for granted in the interest of its exposition and narrative viewpoint – the authority of the novelist as a 'man speaking to men' both assumes and overrides the mode of presentation. The 'poetic novel', on this showing, is at least as old as *Tristram Shandy*, which, as we shall see, is more closely related to the form of *Evgeny Onegin* than is the more obvious parallel of Byron's *Don Juan*.

The significant kinship of the novel in verse is thus with new kinds of novel in prose, rather than with traditional long poems. And the comparative failure of most verse novels of the nineteenth century is usually due to the author's inability to rid himself of the instinctive assumption that he is writing a long poem. The epic or narrative poem cannot by nature easily adopt the relative form. Arms and the man it sings, or man's first disobedience, or the growth of a poet's mind; and for all the ingenuity of its composite and relative presentation, Browning's *The Ring and the Book* is really as straightforwardly didactic as Wordsworth's *Excursion*, Cowper's *Task* or Crabbe's *Borough*. The claims made for Browning's development of the relative viewpoint are in fact disallowed by the very medium he uses – blank verse exposition – for through Bishop Blougram or Andrea del Sarto, whatever their merits in monologue, we can see the author manipulating the case and preparing the *dénouement*. (This is very evident in the role of the Pope in *The Ring and the Book*, which Henry James, though an admirer of the poem, significantly felt to be superfluous.) Moreover the medium of *The Ring and the Book*, as of *The Excursion*, seems to invite us like a prose novel to get used to it and take it for granted, so that we may concentrate on what the author is saying, just as we come to take for granted the exposition of Balzac and George Eliot or of Tolstoy and Dostoevsky.

By contrast the medium of *Evgeny Onegin* – as in their differing ways those of *Tristram Shandy*, *Dead Souls*, *Don Juan*, *Finnegans Wake* or *The Waves* – is continually brought to our notice by the author: Byron and Pushkin lay it before us in the repetition of every fresh stanza, and we may note that the most successful verse novels employ a highly idiosyncratic and demanding stanza form. The impression is one of constant and brilliant improvisation, problems and contingencies recurring in endless permutation, and being solved and disposed of with an ever renewed cunning, labour, and expertise, which masks itself (particularly in the case of Byron) under the guise of a dazzling helplessness. The author is far too busy to be detached and authoritative: he cannot be expected to *know*, for he escapes at every moment into the new patterns of the structure he is creating. Hence the relative viewpoint is really built into the exigence of such a work, and is virtually the consequence of each fresh and yet ever recurrent crisis, compromise, and solution.

The form of Pushkin's stanza lends itself perfectly to this process. Its regularity holds endless permutations of tone, stress, and flow; and yet at the same time the unchanging metrical co-ordinates of its fourteen lines, rhyming *ababeecciddiff*, lead us with each verse to new contemplation and appraisal of what it achieves. *Ruslan and Lyudmila* is a traditional narrative poem in that the freely rhymed paragraphs eventually distract the reader – as with couplets or blank verse or the prose of an ordinary novel – from this kind of renewed awareness: he falls in with the medium and begins to take it for granted as he concentrates on the tale. Pushkin seems to have hit on his new stanza form by regularising a more or less chance arrangement that occurs not infrequently in the *contes* of La Fontaine, from which Pushkin, like other Russian poets before him (Dimitriev was one) had derived the irregularly rhyming tetrameter measure of their narrative poems.

In the introduction to his edition of *Evgeny Onegin* Nabokov has admirably suggested the characteristic movement or pulse of the Onegin stanza:

The *abab* part and the *ff* part are usually very conspicuous in the meaning, melody, and intonation of any given stanza. This opening pattern (a clean-cut sonorous elegiac quatrain) and the terminal one (a couplet resembling the code of an octave or that of a Shakespearean sonnet) can be compared to patterns on a painted ball or top that are visible at the beginning and at the end of the spin. The main spinning process involves *eecciddi*, where a fluent and variable phrasing blurs the contours of the lines so that they are seldom seen as clearly consisting of two couplets and a closed quatrain.

The process, which can be punctuated as flexibly as prose, is thus one of fairly predictable advance, a blurred and variable 'spin', eddy, or equilibrium, followed by another more or less predictable resolution or withdrawal.

The parallel with the sonnet sequence is instructive; and it is tempting to suggest that the fascination and dramatic elusiveness of Shakespeare's Sonnets, which have provoked so many inadequately schematic and 'non-relative' interpretations, are also the logical result of a medium comparably handled. The poet appears to commit himself, plays with that appearance, withdraws, modifies his approach, introduces and repeats with variations another theme; again reveals himself, and again compounds the revelation with a change of tone and the introduction of a further set of variations. The process lends itself to a seeming irresponsibility which is both justified and transfigured by the verbal dexterity and psychological adroitness of the poet. When we think we have him we find he is no longer there, and his words open out an ambiguous glitter of perspective, the very opposite of a poetic *paysage moralisée*. A sequence of intricate stanzas can be ideally suited to the debatable ground of emotion, individuality, and social relations, and it is no accident that later in the century Tennyson in *Maud* and Meredith in *Modern Love* achieve tales in verse in which other and more equivocal meanings and possibilities seem to appear mutely in the pauses between each successive metrical enactment of the speaker's feelings and passions.

In such works even the proper span and *dénouement* of the tale seem to wait upon the medium, and the form of *Evgeny Onegin* only gradually became clear to Pushkin during its composition, as he tells us in the penultimate stanza:

> Промчалось много, много дней
> С тех пор, как юная Татьяна
> И с ней Онегин в смутном сне
> Явилися впервые мне –
> И даль свободного романа
> Я сквозь магический кристалл
> Еще не ясно различал.

Many many days have passed since that time when young Tatyana, and Onegin with her, in a blurred vision first appeared to me – and the distance of a free novel I did not then clearly discern through the magic crystal. (8. 50.)[1]

[1] The expression 'a free novel' probably corresponds to the 'free poem' – freed, that is, from conformity to the rules of a single genre – which for Pushkin and many of his Russian contemporaries in literature was the only really worthwhile aspect of 'Romanticism'. Byron's poems were 'free' in this sense, and so were Shakespeare's plays. In his prefatory dedication, Pushkin offers his 'collection of parti-coloured chapters, half-funny and half-sad, ideal and folk-simple' (*prostonarodny*). In his essay (1825) 'On Classical and Romantic Poetry' (VIII, 32) Pushkin maintains that all forms of literature

The developing shape of the poem is associated with its slow growth over a comparatively long and eventful period of Pushkin's life. Even with Tolstoy we feel that the novel is moving and that the author is standing still, directing its movement; but Pushkin himself appears to be changing and developing parallel to his own work and its own progress. It ended with his own marriage, as so much fiction ends with that of the hero and heroine; and though he made efforts to continue it, embarking on a new chapter in the same Boldino autumn that saw the composition of the *Little Tragedies* and the *Tales of Belkin*, its proper life span was over. Had Onegin, like Byron's Don Juan, been a kind of passive *alter ego*, Pushkin might with facility have thought up further adventures for him. His friends thought he could and should, and as late as 1835 Pushkin played with the notion of doing so. But paradoxically it was the care with which he had separated Onegin from himself, in spite of having lived with him for so long and shared so many comparable experiences, which determined the proper period of Onegin's existence in art. Pushkin had to 'read life's novel to the end': his creation had already completed his separate course.

He himself probably did not bother to consider what kind of hero he had created. All his other compositions are planned with care; their limits are foreseen and every effect is carefully gauged within given terms of reference. *Evgeny Onegin* was allowed to grow and take its own way. But in the upshot this free unplanned work acquired the same proportions and the same air of inevitability as the considered masterpieces. Even when he allowed himself to do so Pushkin could not 'ramble on', like Byron; his unconscious came up with the same artistic solutions that he achieved in his conscious art.

In 1829 he told a friend that 'Onegin will either perish in the Caucasus or join the Decembrist movement'. But the prediction proved wrong. Travelling about Russia (Pushkin wisely demoted Onegin's journey from the text to an appendix) or turning up on the Senate Square as a Decembrist, would have been equally

which were not known to the ancients, and whose forms are constantly changing, are 'romantic'; and that all attempts to distinguish the two kinds in terms of subject-matter are fruitless. Pushkin's solution is typically incisive and unmetaphysical, and shows why he considered Shakespeare *the* Romantic Writer *par excellence* and why, writing to Bestuzhev in November 1825, he expressed his fears for *Boris Godunov*: 'our timid taste will not swallow true romanticism'. A question of form, true romanticism was not for him connected with the taste of the time or the *Weltanschauung* of a particular epoch. See note, p. 278.

impossible for Onegin. Not only can Pushkin put no conviction into his hero's afterlife, the reader too cannot face him further without a sense of aesthetic irritation amounting almost to embarrassment. He has departed as finally as Lensky, whom he had shot in the duel.

> Теперь, как в доме опустелом,
> Всё в нем и тихо и темно;
> Замолкло навсегда оно.
> Закрыты ставни, окна мелом
> Забелены. Хозяйки нет.
> А где, бог весть. Пропал и след.

Now, as in a deserted house, all there is still and dark; it is silent for ever. The shutters are up, the window-panes whitened with chalk. The mistress has gone. But where, God knows. The trace is lost. (6. 32.)

The novel turned out to be one of sentiment and not of picaresque episode and adventure. As with Jane Austen (whom Maurice Baring perceptively invoked in connection with Pushkin) we are poised between two centuries and their fictional expectations. The eighteenth-century novel retains much of the bravado of opera, stage, and poem; and D'Arcy and Elizabeth Bennet are happy relations of Onegin and Tatyana on the same kind of stage. It would be ridiculous to follow them to Pemberley: excited by the glitter of the novel's crescendo we play with the idea, only to dismiss it with a smile and a shrug. And yet Jane Austen's earliest critics were struck, and not always favourably, by her faithful imitation of daily living. Pushkin's novel has it too, though neither he nor Jane Austen was concerned to record life in the methodical fashion of the nineteenth-century novel, the novel of realism and naturalism. The stylisation of their art conveys the real as part of its *insouciance*. Later in the nineteenth century when Flaubert set out to shed the heavy weight of the prose novel by an immense stylistic effort, and to rediscover the tone and artifice of poetic form, it was necessary for him to remove all traces of his heroine and her husband before he could call *Madame Bovary* finished, and their disappearance is painfully and meticulously prolonged. Pushkin's hero and heroine vanish like harlequins from the stage, and yet their significance as living beings is every bit as resonant as that of Madame Bovary or Julien Sorel.

The episodic novel of the eighteenth century grew naturally into the climate of realism: the novel of sentiment did not. In terms of her own art Jane Austen was conscious of the gap between them. *Mansfield Park* she fully intended to be weighty, and in a sense complete, for *Pride and Prejudice* she felt had 'wanted shade', the shadow of mundane actualities. In terms of endings, Fanny Price must live outside the novel; it is part of her unsatisfactoriness that she must continue into an external world of controversy, which expresses the difference between the sentimental pattern and Jane Austen's moral image of her. Fanny must come out of the novel into a debate which is wider than the sphere in which she moved, even though this extension implies a kind of artistic failure. She can and must embody evangelical principles outside the novel, though a part of it. But Onegin could not possibly have embodied Decembrist principles, because the Decembrist world is outside the 'magic crystal' of the novel whose boundaries Pushkin had come to discern by the time he wrote the eighth chapter.

Even *War and Peace* is obedient to the same discovery. Pierre was also to become a Decembrist and undergo exile, but as its shape became clearer to him, Tolstoy realised that even the wide space of his story could not take in such a development. No less than Onegin, Pierre moves inside artistic limitations which fully reveal themselves as the novel draws to its end. Like Onegin he is essentially an eighteenth-century hero, one of whose main functions is to give a greater reality to the more solid social characters. The concluding idyll, in which we take leave of the happy married couples, resembles the end of *Evgeny Onegin* in one important respect: nothing more can happen to *these* people, only to their author, who has already begun to detach himself from them. The disquieting intimations of the future, which are so much a part of the atmosphere of the epilogue, are the preoccupations of Tolstoy himself, who is beginning to look beyond the boundaries of the book and into his own future. They correspond to the repeated and stylised farewells to his hero – 'for a long time, for ever' – into which Pushkin draws his readers.

Onegin's victim Lensky, killed in the duel at the end of Chapter 6, is immortalised by death where Onegin is consigned into the limbo of non-being. As a poet, he is crowned with the laurels that can be awarded by a novel in poetry. It does not matter that he might never have written anything that was any good: this itself becomes the grounds for his survival in the author's verse.

Быть может, он для блага мира
Иль хоть для славы был рожден;
Его умолкнувшая лира
Гремучний, непрерывный звон

В веках поднять могла. Поэта,
Быть может, на ступенях света
Ждала высокая ступень.
Его страдальческая тень,
Быть может, унесла с собою
Святую тайну, и для нас
Погиб животворящий глас,
И за могильною чертою
К ней не домчится гимн времен,
Благословение племен.

А может быть и то: поэта
Обыкновенный ждал удел.
Прошли бы юношества лета:
В нем пыл души бы охладел.
Во многом он бы изменился,
Расстался б с музами, женился,
В деревне счастлив и рогат
Носил бы стеганый халат:
Узнал бы жизнь на самом деле,
Подагру б в сорок лет имел,
Пил, ел, скучал, толстел, хирел,
И наконец в своей постеле
Скончался б посреди детей,
Плаксивых баб и лекарей.

Perhaps he was born for the world's good, or at least for glory. His lyre made silent might have roused a sonorous unending chord throughout time. A lofty stair perhaps awaited the poet on the staircase of the world. His martyred shade has perhaps carried away with him a sacred mystery; for us a life-creating voice is dead, and the blessing of nations, the hymns of the ages, will not ascend to him beyond the confines of the tomb.

And then again, perhaps, a more customary fate awaited the poet. His youth would have gone and the fire of the spirit grown cold in him. He would have changed in many ways; have parted with the muses, married, have worn in his country place a quilted dressing-gown; and been cheerful and a cuckold. He would have come to know life as it is, had the gout at forty, eaten, drunk, been bored, got fat, gone to pieces; and died in his bed at last among children, weeping women, and doctors. (6. 37, 38.)

A third stanza was removed by Pushkin from between these two, which speculated in much more factual terms and with obviously ironic intent about Lensky's future. He might have become an influential journalist, one of the kind who were to dominate the world of Russian letters in mid-century. He might have become as famous as Nelson or Kutuzov, if he had not died in exile like

Napoleon or on the gallows like Ryleev. The stanza breaks off here, but it reveals what Pushkin had to keep *out* in order to keep his characters *in* the poem.[1] Lensky must remain a figure of the vaguest and most touchingly ideal potential. His pathos is only enhanced by the contrast between the pantheon of Chénier and the destiny of a Russian country gentleman: it must not be impugned by ironic authorial speculation.

The complex tone of the novel is kept in continual balance between objectivity and confiding personal engagement. Each has its sphere precisely allotted, and the many cancelled stanzas almost always reflect a temporary loss of balance or a collision between the two, for the dramatic relation of characters is seldom directly exposed to what is known to Pushkin only – his personal interventions do not directly impinge on them. This again is an aspect of the novel in poetry, whose unique form makes it possible. The eighteenth-century novelists whom Pushkin depends on most – Sterne, Richardson, Rousseau – and in whose climate *Evgeny Onegin* began to live and take shape, offer no corresponding contrast between the objective tale and the authorial presence.

In them the consciousness of the writer is the world of the novel. Rousseau's claim to uniqueness and to the possession of an individuality 'such as no one else has had since the creation of the world', acted as an intoxicant upon the reader of fiction, and the writer of it. Everyone perceived instantly how to be unique, and the result was the immense crop of imitations which followed the appearance of *Clarissa* and *Sir Charles Grandison*, *La Nouvelle Héloïse* and *The Sentimental Journey*. A new standardisation of personal feeling succeeded the revelation of its individuality. Sterne's sentiment could be imitated, and was imitated in Russia by Radishchev and Karamzin, and the gloom of young Werther and the sensibility of Julie de Wolmar had their echoes in Russia as in the rest of Europe. But by breaking the form Pushkin was able to escape the new conventions that had risen out of imitation. The sentimental novel of love and death appears in a wholly different light when told in glittering octosyllabics, and the poet accentuates the discrepancy by himself standing back, and withdrawing his sensibility from the scene which it should have dominated. As a sentimental novel *Evgeny Onegin* is like nature without God, and

---

[1] This stanza and two earlier ones in the chapter (15, 16) were published in *Pushkin and his Lycée Comrades and Teachers* (1887). See Nabokov's *Evgeny Onegin*, vol. II, p. 21.

Pushkin, the *deus absconditus*, turns the subjective sensibility into an objective property, ornament, and plaything.

As we shall see, the formalist critic Shklovsky, in a brilliant critique of *Evgeny Onegin*, demonstrates the ways in which it parodies the novel, the novel of sentiment in particular, and we shall return to discuss his findings. The question and quality of parody is never far away in Pushkin, and his novel in verse is bewitched by it. But it never appears schematic – ivory box arranged inside ivory box. (Nabokov's commentary and translation give the impression that *Evgeny Onegin* is not unlike one of his own novels, and are all the more stimulating and absorbing for this reason, and at times all the more misleading.[1]) The depth of the thing, as usual with Pushkin, is in the contrasts and confrontations which its artificiality makes possible. Even the most ingenious parodist is apt to be oblivious of the plain reality which involuntarily enters his fiction – chairs, typewriters, dirty glasses, ashtrays – while he concentrates on its point. Pushkin appears to take note of and describe these things at the same moment that he imitates a fellow-poet, plays variations on a sentimental landscape theme, or creates his heroine's consciousness in terms of the heroes and heroines she has read about in books. His characters, no less than himself, are surrounded by the mundane and unchanging facts and relations of life, and these are in the novel, along with every sort of literary and stylistic attitude towards them.

The gap between fact and fiction can open without warning, as in the duel scene. The reflections on Lensky's death, his memorial and its imagined visitor (6. 41), are all literary commonplaces; and the poet, while treating them with rare and moving skill, emphasises none the less that he knows they are, and depends on the relation to them that his art wins for him. But the duel and the death itself have the almost hypnotic accuracy of things which nothing can or should alter. Onegin and Lensky, existing elsewhere in the chequered shade of books, suddenly enter the world of action and determined time. In the same way Tatyana, in behaviour and provenance a sentimental heroine, has a nightmare which has the terrifying realism of folk-tale (it should be compared with *The Bridegroom*) and in which she and Onegin appear as the leading figures. We remember how in *Rusalka* Pushkin combines in dramatic form a folk-tale theme with contemporary romanticism.

---

[1] His novel *Pale Fire*, appearing after his work on *Evgeny Onegin*, shows how much he himself was aware of this.

Onegin thus appears in sequence as a folk-tale murderer in Tatyana's dream, as a duellist in the unforgiving world of fact, and then – again in Tatyana's mind – as a presence in his abandoned country house, experienced by her through his books, his furniture, and the gossip of his old housekeeper. Pushkin – never more the pokerfaced outsider – arranges for his parody heroine to examine Onegin's library and the marks his thumbnail has made in the margins of the pages, and to wonder if the man she loves and suffers for is after all perhaps nothing but a parody:

> Слов модных полный лексикон?...
> Уж не пародия ли он?...
>
> Ужель загадку разрешила?
> Ужели *слово* найдено?

A whole dictionary of fashionable words?...Might he not be a parody? ...Can she have solved the riddle? Can the 'answer' have been found? (7. 24, 25.)

The confident complexity of the novel is able to pose, without irony, the simple rhetorical question. Its answer is in the part of the novel itself, and in the density of the sequence which begins with Tatyana's walk:

> Был вечер. Небо меркло. Воды
> Струились тихо. Жук жужжал.
> Уж расходились хороводы;
> Уж за рекой, дымясь, пылал
> Огонь рыбачий. В поле чистом,
> Луны при свете серебристом
> В свои мечты погружена,
> Татьяна долго шла одна.
> Шла, шла. И вдруг перед собою
> С холма господский видит дом,
> Селенье, рощу под холмом
> И сад над светлою рекою.

It was evening. The sky darkened. The waters flowed quietly. The beetle droned. The hound-dancers had dispersed, and already the fishermen's fires, smoking, burned across the river. In the open field, by the moon's silver light, sunk in her dreams, Tatyana walked on alone...walked and walked. And suddenly before her from the hill she sees a manor house, a village, a grove below the hill, and a garden above the luminous river. (7. 15.)

Lensky is dead; her sister Olga has married and gone away. Like Rousseau's Julie de Wolmar, Tatyana walks in solitude. All the usual properties are there, with the addition of the crepuscular beetle, taken from English literature via Zhukovsky, but these time-honoured devices are transformed by the characteristically Pushkinian tempo. Its terse tranquillity appears even in the beetle verb, which here works not by suggestion ('droning flight', 'drowsy hums') but by definition.

The old housekeeper shows her 'the empty house where recently our hero had been living', the real shell from which the elusive tenant has departed, as Lensky, at the moment of his death, is compared to an abandoned house. Onegin's presence – in the forgotten cue on the billiard-table and the riding crop on the untidy sofa – is as overpowering to Tatyana as was his supernatural presence in her dream. Here he slept, the housekeeper tells her, here he took his coffee, read his books in the morning, and listened to his steward's report. In her words Onegin sheds his romantic individuality and his self-made pose as a *chudak* (an eccentric) and becomes simply one of his class and kind. So his forebears lived, and so – if he has any – will his children. But there is more than this in the old woman's words: without drawing breath she goes on to speak of her former master, Onegin's uncle:

> Вот это барский кабинет;
> Здесь почивал он, кофей кушал,
> Приказчика доклады слушал
> И книжку поутру читал...
> И старый барин здесь живал:
> Со мной, бывало, в воскресенье,
> Здесь под окном, надев очки,
> Играть изволил в дурачки.
> Дай бог душе его спасенье,
> А косточкам его покой
> В могиле, в мать-земле сырой!

This was the master's study; he used to sleep here; take his coffee; listen to the steward's reports; and read his book of a morning...and the old master lived here too. There used to be a time, on a Sunday, when at this window here, putting his glasses on, he would allow himself to play 'fools' with me. May God save him and give peace to his bones in the grave, in damp mother earth. (7. 18.)

The old master dies before the reader – who at the opening of the novel found himself travelling down to the estate in Onegin's company – could meet him; and the housekeeper's words take this reader back to the beginning, with Onegin exclaiming in exasperation at the boredom of having to sit beside the old invalid and entertain him. Fate spares him that duty, a miniature analogue of other things in the common human lot which he will miss in the poem.

This network of unobtrusive cross-reference has the quality of a certain kind of much later novel, and so has the changing reality of persons in terms of their environment; places and houses have more continuous personality than the individual. There is the sense of place, which we associate with women novelists, from Jane Austen to Elizabeth Bowen. Heathcliff in *Wuthering Heights* takes successive and discontinuous personality from place and speaker as Onegin does: his literary being is set against a real background, and his almost mystical status as a projection of Emily Brontë's consciousness is objectified by his relation to the solid structure of the plot and the other narrators. Pushkin, too, uses what is known and familiar to him with an instinctive ease which has something feminine about it, very different from the masculine geography of Balzac and the nineteenth-century realistic novelists. We recall again the remarkable metaphor at the moment of Lensky's death, an abandoned house, silent and shuttered, the windows covered with chalk, the mistress absent – *khosyayki net*. In the next chapter Tatyana finds Onegin's house empty and re-animates it with her image of him.

Pushkin never disturbs the elegant balance of parody and sentiment – indeed he makes us realise, somewhat as T. S. Eliot was to do in *The Waste Land*, how such a use of parody can move by suggesting a whole tradition and community of feeling behind what might appear local and ludicrous, or even pathetically banal.

> She turns and looks a moment in the glass,
> Hardly aware of her departed lover;
> Her brain allows one half-formed thought to pass:
> 'Well now that's done: and I'm glad it's over'.
> When lovely woman stoops to folly and
> Paces about her room again, alone,
> She smoothes her hair with automatic hand,
> And puts a record on the gramophone.

Eliot's seduction scene is based on correspondences – the gramophone and a sentimental poem of Goldsmith, the typist of the twenties and her age-old feminine gesture before the mirror. And when this comes off, whether in Eliot or in Pushkin's far more sustained but not so dissimilar technique, the effect is more natural than nature; and a timeless stateliness is achieved by art's byplay on the fashions and fragments of time.

Thus Tatyana stands 'enchanted' in Onegin's exotic cell (7. 20), like Lyudmila in the house of Chernomor. 'A young pilgrimess' she goes home, having obtained permission to revisit the 'deserted castle', and when she does she finds 'a different world' awaiting her in Onegin's books. The 'grim shade' before whom she trembled in her own garden at home is revealed as if in the helplessness of sleep.[1] Pushkin may have remembered Byron's account of Haidée watching the sleeping Juan.

> All that it hath of life with us is living...
> There lies the thing we love with all its errors
> And all its charms, like death without its terrors.

'The singer of the Giaour and Juan' is the first author excepted by Onegin from his general ennui with literature, and it would be typical of Pushkin's methods to imply that Tatyana may have read of the love of Juan and Haidée as she sat in Onegin's study, a further image of love to add to those of 'Clarissa, Julia, Delphine', with whom she had identified her first *Schwärmerei* for Onegin. Her discovery of him in his books, a parody man, paradoxically gives her a new possessive and assured affection, and a new confidence which we shall see in its full significance in her next encounter with Onegin, an encounter as much of a revelation to him as the first apparition of him had been to her.

Ideologically minded critics, from Dostoevsky onwards, have set the 'naturalness' of Tatyana against Evgeny the hollow man, a perfectly feasible distinction to which our general impression of the novel does correspond, but which none the less passes over the real interest and complexity of Pushkin's method. He was clearly fascinated by the ways in which modern literature had imposed its stereotypes on the men and women of the period, a process particularly marked in Russia, where the upper class tended to identify itself with a current European model. But the imported sensibility did not flourish in a vacuum: it made a contrast, sometimes a grotesque one, with the solid ramifications of Russian life, a contrast exploited in every context by the art of *Evgeny Onegin*. And it is this contrast which is simplified by the ideologists into notions of 'rooted' Tatyana and 'rootless' Onegin. In fact both depend equally, from the poem's point of view, upon their back-

[1]   Vezde Onegina dusha
         Sebya nevolno vyrazhaet
Onegin's soul has everywhere unconsciously expressed itself... (7. 23).

grounds, both are held by their environment in a way that is not at all like the novel of sentiment from which their style derives.

One of the novels upon which Onegin was able to bestow his continued esteem was certainly *Adolphe*, as we know from an anonymous note by Pushkin in the *Literary Gazette* of 1830 referring to Vyazemsky's translation of Benjamin Constant's masterpiece, quoting the stanza from *Evgeny Onegin* which mentions the 'two or three novels in which the epoch is reflected, and modern man pretty correctly represented' (7. 22). Adolphe has no background: the Poland and even the France in which he has his being exist because the novel's brilliant analysis of egoism and possessive jealousy must take place somewhere. But in *Evgeny Onegin* the local background is as functional as the literary one, and the drama depends on the tragi-comic relation between them. Pushkin's first idea was to send Onegin off on his travels at the moment (7. 24) of Tatyana's rhetorical discovery that he may after all be only a parody. The moment was well chosen but the plan misfired. For Onegin proved as dependent on his upbringing as Tatyana on hers. Wanderings to such places as Odessa, where the author – as a local expert – proposed to meet his friend again, would remove not only the narrative *raison d'être* but the physical apprehension of Onegin which we receive in the course of the first chapter's account of his Petersburg days, and which Tatyana experiences in his deserted house. Pushkin not only abandoned Onegin's journey at this point but substituted for it Tatyana's transfer to Moscow by her family in search of a husband.

In the original plan Tatyana was to find Onegin's album, filled with his actual comments and descriptions of life and books, which would then have been retailed to us at first-hand. This also was a wise alteration, for Onegin's silence and his absence (except in Tatyana's mind) tell us much more about him than his words do – it is typical of his precariously balanced creation that his actions reveal him clearly while his speech or writing (even his homily and his letter to Tatyana, 4. 12, 8. 27) blur his image. Pushkin must always remain separate from Onegin, and the latter's album jottings bear an uncomfortable resemblance to Pushkin's own comments and interventions throughout the poem: changed into interrogative form, one of the album stanzas becomes Pushkin's own comment on his hero's conduct in the next book (8. 9). Nabokov regrets that though Tatyana, as a well brought-up young girl, could scarcely have been allowed to eavesdrop on the album,

Pushkin did not allow the reader 'to dip into it behind her back'. But it is vital that we should not hear Evgeny's voice at this point, and that the author should not preside over Tatyana's new impression of him.

Meanwhile her relations at home are discussing her and deploring her silent depression and her lack of interest in possible suitors. Can it be that she is in love? But with whom? They can think only of the neighbours whom we met at Tatyana's disastrous name-day party. Her preoccupation with Onegin, and her relatives' unconnected concern with her, make an admirable transition to the next stage in the novel. Taken to the marriage-market in Moscow, Tatyana is eclipsed while her family comes alive. As if their reality would not stand up to continuous exposure, Pushkin is careful not to remain with one of his characters for long; and thus he avoids as well the Rousseauesque unity of author with hero and heroine, or the more objective but equally unmistakable identification of Constant with Adolphe and Flaubert with Madame Bovary. The reunion in Moscow of Tatyana's mother with her cousin Aline puts in the background both Tatyana's troubles and the absent Onegin, and Tatyana will only be clicked back into focus when we see her (8. 14) as a calm and dignified apparition at the ball. Onegin himself is there, and we see her through his own startled eyes.

> «Ужели», думает Евгений:
> «Ужель она? Но точно...Нет...
> Как! из глуши степных селений...»
> И неотвязчивый лорнет
> Он обращает поминутно
> На ту, чей вид напомнил смутно
> Ему забытые черты.
> «Скажи мне, князь, не знаешь ты,
> Кто там в малиновом берете
> С послом испанским говорит?»
> Князь на Онегина глядит.
> – Ага! давно ж ты не был в свете.
> Постой, тебя представлю я. –
> «Да кто ж она?» – Жена моя. –

'Can it', thinks Evgeny, 'can it be she? But really...No...What! from that remote country village...' And he keeps an importunate lorgnette directed every minute at her who has dimly reminded him of forgotten features. 'Tell me, Prince, you don't know who that is over there in the *framboise* head-dress, talking to the Spanish ambassador?' The prince stares at Onegin. 'Aha, it's a long time since you were in the world; wait, I'll present you.' 'But who is she?' 'My wife.' (8. 17.)

The shock of transformation is like the moment at the end of
Proust's novel when the narrator at a party finds himself surrounded by old people and suddenly realises that he too is old. The
relations who met Tatyana in Moscow exclaim incessantly at the
way the years have flown, and what a short time it seems since they
carried her in their arms and gave her ginger-bread. Before we see
Tatyana married, changed, barely recognisable, we have felt
already in the Moscow scenes the full impact of time, which makes
nonsense of youth's problems and endows the old with a terrible
innocence in their suffering and enjoyment which the preoccupied
young do not begin to understand. Tatyana is projected from her
childhood home, her dear woods and fields, as stylised in Pushkin's
description as in her consciousness of them, into the world of time
in which there is no defence in dreams, books, and illusions. Exhausted by the joy of seeing them, her mother's invalid cousin
soon begins to shed tears.

> Ох, силы нет...устала грудь...
> Мне тяжела теперь и радость,
> Не только грусть...душа моя,
> Уж никуда не годна я...
> Под старость жизнь такая гадость...»
> И тут, совсем утомлена,
> В слезах раскашлялась она.

'Oh, I've no strength...my chest's worn out...now even joy is too
much for me, not only misery...my dear, I'm good for nothing now.
Life's terrible when you're old.' And here, quite exhausted, she started
coughing till the tears came. (7. 42.)

Age and infirmity have made this old cousin spontaneous as
Tatyana and Onegin cannot be. The old people's unconditional
acceptance of life animates the Moscow arrival and gives it a flavour
unlike anything else in the novel – here is life as it has to be lived,
and not as the young dream of living it, or of rejecting living it.
Compared to Tatyana's beloved groves and fields, Moscow has a
swarming and business-like vitality – Nadezhdin in the *European
Messenger* described the scene as 'truly Hogarthian' – though
Pushkin may in fact be remembering the stanza on London in the
tenth canto of *Don Juan*:

> Ну! не стой,
> Пошел! Уже столпы заставы
> Белеют; вот уж по Тверской
> Возок несется чрез ухабы.

Мелькают мимо будки, бабы,
Мальчишки, лавки, фонари,
Дворцы, сады, монастыри,
Бухарцы, сани, огороды,
Купцы, лачужки, мужики,
Бульвары, башни, казаки,
Аптеки, магазины моды,
Балконы, львы на воротах
И стаи галок на крестах.

Come! Don't stop, get on. The turnpike posts show white ahead. Along
Tverskaya Street the coach jolts over the potholes. Watchmen's huts
and peasant women flick past, urchins, shops and street lamps, great
houses, gardens, monasteries, Bokharans, sledges, kitchen gardens,
merchants, hovels, *muzhiks*, boulevards, towers, cossacks, chemist shops,
fashion stores, balconies, lions on the gates, and flocks of jackdaws on
the crosses. (7. 38.)

And all this has the function of preparing us for Tatyana's transformation in the final scene of the novel, as if she was emptied out
into time and life with this mass of other objects and other lives.
She shrinks back in a dazed unapprehension of it all, and the
nightmare continues with her sleepless night under the unfamiliar
silken bed canopy, the church bells in the morning, and the view
from the window of fence, stables and kitchen shed. In the midst
of balls and gaiety she 'mutely guards her heart's secret', but
the last touch of Chapter 7 shows her willy-nilly depersonalised
by the generations into whose pattern she will be merged. At
the ball her aunts nudge her and point out a general who has
been giving her his attention. 'Who? That fat general?' she
exclaims, a cry at once spontaneous and quite uncharacteristic of
the image in which she has been presented up to now – her mother
or Aunt Aline might have uttered it in their time and in that
context.[1]

In his review of it in *The Northern Bee*, Bulgarin called Chapter 7
a complete comedown – *chute complète* – and proceeded to parody

---

[1] In the first draft: 'Who? That old general?' Our impression of Tatyana's
future husband (or presumed husband, for we cannot be sure it is him she
marries) is certainly of someone elderly – Dostoevsky refers to him as a
venerable old gentleman. It is a typical instance of Pushkinian double-take,
for, as critics have pointed out, he is a friend of Onegin's and cannot be much
older: there is certainly no generation gap. The man she loves is considerably
older than she is and so is the man she marries, but Pushkin certainly implies
that Tatyana has sacrified herself to an old man, as well as one she does not
love: or perhaps he only seems old to her, as Onegin might have done if she
had not fallen in love with him.

its content in rhyme. They decide to marry off Tatyana; they take her to Moscow where she is bored and her mother makes a fuss, and that's it – end of chapter. (Bulgarin added that the beetle was a promising new character whom he expected to be better sustained than the existing ones.) In a note written at Boldino Pushkin took the beetle jest in good part, but went on to answer the main criticism in a preface projected, but not published, for the last two chapters of the poem, the concluding one and the appendix on Onegin's journey, originally planned as the penultimate chapter. 'The most insignificant subject', he says, 'may be selected by the author for his poem. Critics need not discuss *what* the author describes – they should describe how he discusses it.' Bulgarin's complaint, in fact, was that of a philistine who could not see what a novel set out to do, and how the author's method could reveal its progress and depth, irrespective of the apparent triviality of his subject-matter. Henry James would have emphatically agreed.

Though Chapter 7 has none of the great passages which the anthologist selects, it shows the nature of the novel; how it combines its diverse manners, tones and ingredients; and above all how it handles time and change at the moment when the pattern of inevitability is beginning to reveal itself. A detailed commentary on the whole being out of the question, I have tried in a discussion of Chapter 7 to suggest how the novel works, and how its method relates to other great fictions. It is also the vital bridge chapter (and gave Pushkin great trouble for that reason) between the climax of Lensky's death and the *dénouement* of Tatyana's marriage. It begins, in a verse of exquisitely delicate pastoral, with the coming of spring in the country and ends with the animation and bustle of the family arrival in Moscow. And its greatest technical triumph is the answer it makes to those critics, from Katenin onwards, who have objected to the hiatus or gap between the young girl in the country and the *dégagée* hostess of the last chapter, receiving in her Petersburg salon.[1] In its suggestions of time, age, the family, and the fragility of the young and isolated Tatyana, it accomplishes the transition with all the 'insignificance' which the art in depth of the novel can command.

By substituting Tatyana's journey to Moscow for an account of Onegin's wanderings, Pushkin gauged the psychological timing that would ensure the impression made by his climax. Tatyana's

---

[1] Referred to in 'Fragments from Onegin's Journey' (v, 199).

world has really changed. She has had to grow up: she has had to become someone else. Through Onegin Pushkin converts into social reality the gothic changelessness and timelessness of the heroes who manifest themselves at moments throughout the poem like the goblins of Tatyana's dream – Melmoth, Childe Harold, the mysterious Sbogar. 'What other mask will he now put on?' The irony in Pushkin's question and in the last line of 8. 8: 'You know him? – Yes and No' – is that Onegin is always the same. As F. D. Reeve aptly remarks in *The Russian Novel*, 'However superficial Onegin seems to us, we understand that he understands'. This 'understanding' is certainly vital to the atmosphere of the poem but it is also equivocal: the man who understands cannot learn. We might compare the 'understanders' in Tolstoy's *Boyhood and Youth* and in *War and Peace*: it is Pierre, who is not one, who can learn from life.

Compared to Onegin, both Tatyana and the 'always cheerful' Olga – Lensky too, had he lived – are persons capable of change. Like their mothers and fathers, they are open to the processes of life, are carried along with it while Onegin stands outside. Pushkin recognises the fact with humorous resignation (8. 10), neither being censorious about his hero nor praising the *prekrasny chelovek*, the admirable man who lets life lead him through its right and proper stages. Pushkin does not have to be, in the modern sense, 'on the side of life'. But the epigraph of Chapter 4, taken from Necker – *La Morale est dans la nature des choses* – is coming home to roost. Tatyana, and even Olga, demonstrate *la morale* because they submit to the nature of things. Onegin does not, and he is abandoned in the limbo of his own detachment. He carries out, in a realistic social context, the role of the contemporary gothic and romantic hero; and it is all the more effective, and damning, that he does not intend to do so. He has no desire to ruin Tatyana's future or destroy Lensky's life and happiness, but he does both as if he had schemed like a literary villain.

Dostoevsky felt that Onegin's actions spring from thwarted idealism, unconscious disgust at the life he has to lead and his inability to do anything about the society in which he leads it – an idea developed in his own *Crime and Punishment*. Adopting the diction of modern psychology, Edmund Wilson observes that it is the poet in Lensky whom Onegin has unconsciously hated. 'For all Lensky's obtuseness and immaturity Evgeny has been jealous of him because Lensky has been able to feel for Olga an all-absorbing emotion, whereas Evgeny, loved so passionately by Tatyana, has been unable to feel anything at all.' As with Shakespeare, these kinds of comments reveal the depth of a work of art, though they do not allow for the insulating effect of the poetic artifice which Shakespeare and Pushkin have at their disposition. If we follow up Edmund Wilson's line of argument there is nothing to stop us ending by seeing Onegin as a portrait of Alexander Raevsky (the 'demon') and Lensky as an ironical self-portrait of Pushkin himself. But here Pushkin has already forestalled us, with the artifice of a Shandean 'false admission':

> Несносно (согласитесь в том)
> Между людей благоразумных
> Прослыть притворным чудаком,
> Или печальным сумасбродом,
> Иль сатаническим уродом,
> Иль даже Демоном моим.

It's unbearable (we're agreed on that) to pass among the *bien pensants* for a pretence eccentric, a gloomy half-wit, or a satanic monster, or even for my Demon. (8. 12.)

By the artifice of such devices *Evgeny Onegin* is sealed off from the contingent touch of life, and it is by these means that Pushkin is able to speculate about his characters with such friendliness and composure, a kind of composure not possible to a novelist who has to invert or disguise in order to conceal. Pushkin's prose novels and stories are kept right outside his own life and circle, because prose for him called for a simplicity and objectivity which could only be maintained in a fiction that did not involve the author personally at any level. His presence in *Evgeny Onegin*, and his introduction of his friends – Kaverin dines with Onegin in the first chapter, and Vyazemsky is kind to Tatyana in the seventh – secures for Pushkin the kind of distance possible in his lyrics, but which in his prose could only be attained by formal anonymity. And of course Pushkin's simplest, commonest, and most final device of dissociation from his characters is to keep assuring us how much he 'loves' them.

Onegin lives by thinking he cannot be bothered with anything, good or bad. Detached, he can survey the follies of the world and comment on them with an impartial judgement and a biting tongue. Like most cynics he enjoys being censorious (he is categorised as a 'pedant' in the first chapter) and he enjoys preaching at Tatyana in their confrontation after her love-letter.[1] Yet in fact he is as much the sport of impulse and occasion as his victims are. He agrees on an impulse when Lensky asks him to come to the name-day party (4. 49), and then finds that instead of a small family affair it has swollen to a grotesque provincial entertainment, with a band, dancing, speeches and cardplaying. His resentment is petty but very human, and is increased by the sight of Tatyana's pale face (she has just had her nightmare about him). Insensibly he starts to act in the way her nightmare has led her to expect: she already influences him to a degree he would never admit. He flirts with Olga, who is temperamentally incapable of not responding to his attentions, and continues to do so until Lensky leaves in a rage, determined to send a challenge the next day. When it arrives Onegin has already regretted his behaviour, but the challenge is brought by a former duellist and malicious gossip, Zaretsky. Were he to seek a reconciliation now this man might spread rumours about his courage. He half perceives the totally undetached and 'non-Oneginlike' impasse to which his impulse has committed him, and the exasperation of it seems to make him behave like an inhuman automaton for the rest of the dire sequence. As committed to his impulse as Tatyana is to love, and Lensky to his own and Olga's honour, he makes no attempt to use his will or sense in the time that yet remains. He could have stood Lensky's fire (possibly not a very great hazard) and himself fired in the air. Instead he raises his pistol as the duellists approach each other, pulls the trigger at the psychologically correct moment, and kills his opponent instantly.

The account of the duel – the loading of the pistols, the directions and the positioning – expresses the determined world, the blank necessity which has suddenly taken over. The dinner of the two friends together at Onegin's house had been a corresponding climax of freedom and enjoyment. And this balance or 'spring' between freedom and necessity is a vital part of the novel's structure.[2] The freedom of the two friends is echoed by the happy movement of the novel into winter: the peasant travelling again in his sledge, the boy putting his dog in a toboggan, the red-footed goose

<hr />

[1] By means of contemporary quotation, Brodsky in his *Commentary* seeks to prove that 'Pedant' had in Pushkin's world the sense of a man of integrity and of principles, indeed of liberal principles. Nabokov ridicules the idea, citing Brodsky's other attempts to make political capital out of the poem, and indeed Pushkin's context suggests only the sense of one who derives pleasure from the precise dryness of his observations, and their emotional detachment.
[2] The term is used by Shklovsky in his analysis of the novel's structure: *Roman pruzhinit* (the novel is sprung).

sprawling on the ice of the pond. In this atmosphere even Onegin unbends a trifle, but Lensky is a part of it, as absurd as the goose and as gleeful as the peasant and boy. We see that the query of Pushkin's epitaph – would he have become a poet, or lapsed into the dressing gown of contented middle-age? – is not so much antithetical as movingly elegiac. Immersed in life as he is, the two destinies for Lensky would have been the same. We remember the epitaph above the grave of old Larin, who had planned his daughter's match with Lensky's father years before.

> Он был простой и добрый барин,
> И там, где прах его лежит,
> Надгробный памятник гласит:
> *Смиренный грешник, Дмитрий Ларин,*
> *Господний раб и бригадир,*
> *Под камнем сим вкушает мир.*

He was a kind and simple squire, and there, where his dust lies, his gravestone states: 'The humble sinner, Dmitri Larin, servant of the Lord and Brigadier, enjoyeth peace beneath this stone.' (2. 36.)

Lensky as a poet and a married man is neither more nor less absurd than the epitaph of the man who would have been his father-in-law (*gospodny rab i brigadir*). He is as helplessly incongruous as life itself, as he revealed when he poetically apostrophises the departed Brigadier as 'Poor Yorick' and in the next breath recalls how often as a child he played with his Ochakov medal. Tatyana herself is not dissimilar. Though she hated gossip she could not help listening with elation to the buzz of speculation on her behalf when Onegin first came to call.

In *War and Peace* Tolstoy drives home with his usual thoroughness the acceptance of incongruity which life dictates, and which is implicit in Pushkin. The mercurial Natasha, after waiting to be used by life, becomes the contented and blowzy housewife absorbed in her family. Tolstoy tacitly invokes Tatyana's situation – the love affair with Kuragin, which he regarded as the 'pivot' of the whole novel, parallels Tatyana's fatal entanglement with Onegin – but he brings Natasha through to the destiny she should have. *War and Peace* is an idyll in which freedom triumphs by becoming synonymous with destiny; in *Evgeny Onegin* the pair cannot join, but are held in a balanced and opposing tension.

In fact necessity in Pushkin's novel is deformed. It is the conditioned reflex of custom which compels the duellists to behave like automata, embodying the whole absurd mechanics of duelling without a word being said directly about it. Lensky falls asleep scribbling down in his last poem the word *ideal*, and the next morning he is to die at the climax of an implacable sequence of actual events, dictated by convention. Those measured paces at the duel have already been foreshadowed in the slow return of Onegin and Tatyana to the house after he has lectured her on her folly.

> Он подал руку ей. Печально
> (Как говорится, *машинально*)
> Татьяна молча оперлась,
> Головкой томною склонясь;
> Пошли домой вкруг огорода.

He offered her his arm. Sadly (as the phrase is, 'mechanically') Tatyana leaned on it in silence, bending her poor little head; home they went round the kitchen garden. (4. 17.)

Slonimsky points out how characteristic of the novel is that casual reference to the vegetable garden at the moment when Tatyana's heart is breaking. But Pushkin does not say, as Byron would: isn't this typical of life? He refers it without comment to a specific area of the psychological drama: Onegin's inability to accept the incongruity in which he, like all the others, is involved by life. He is absorbed in his own image as the truth-teller, the elder brother whose duty and pleasure it is to reveal her folly to the poor girl, and how he might have taken advantage of it.

Crushed Tatyana and complacent Evgeny, walking back arm in arm, are as far apart from each other as are Olga and Lensky at their meeting after the disastrous name-day party, but their mutual incomprehension is at the level of comedy and potential happy endings. Even the static, novelettish charms of Olga, ironically emphasised, become unpredictable in Pushkinian action. Naturally she flirts with Onegin at the dance, but when Lensky calls next day – tormented by jealousy and with the challenge to Onegin already sent off – she skips out blithely to meet him:

> Резва, беспечна, весела,
> Ну точно та же, как была.

Playful, carefree, gay – in fact just the same as she had always been. (6.13.)

Her very insensitiveness can bestow love and restore it:

> Она глядит ему в лицо.
> «Что с вами?» «Так.» И на крыльцо.

She looks into his face. 'What's the matter with you?' 'Nothing.' And he makes for the porch. (6. 19.)

Lensky goes happily off to his death. Pushkin's first idea was to return Olga, so to speak, to the commonplace love story from which he claims to have borrowed her. She was to visit Lensky's grave and shed tears over it, like Charlotte over Werther's in the engraving famous throughout Europe, before allowing herself to be led off by the broad-shouldered Uhlan who is her new admirer. Pushkin retains her as his own character, in the final text, by making her consistent – she does not visit the grave. As her incomprehension of his feelings made Lensky feel himself still beloved, so – after his death – it removes all thought of him from her head.

In the stylised pattern of the novel, Olga and Lensky are unaware of themselves and are seen from outside; while Tatyana and Onegin have all the elegance of self-consciousness that poetry and story need. But that awareness does not of course extend to realising how much their behaviour and expectations are formed from books. In Tatyana's talk with her nurse the word *vlyublena* (in love) occurs four times, and each time with a different intonation that marks her increasingly forlorn but defiant determination to apply this term from books to the state she finds herself in. Acoustically the exchange is one of the most marvellous in Pushkin, and like Tatyana's letter which follows it, and which is as masterly a recreation in an idiom of composition as the exchange is in that of dialogue, it has survived all the banality of anthologies and rote learning. Tatyana first uses her word with deceptive casualness, encouraging her nurse to talk about her own childhood and hoping that the word will seem normal to her:

> ...– «Расскажи мне, няня,
> Про ваши старые года:
> Была ты влюблена тогда?»

'Nurse, tell me about your old days. Were you in love then?' (3. 17.)

She is soon undeceived:

> – И, полно, Таня! В эти лета
> Мы не слыхали про любовь;
> А то бы согнала со света
> Меня покойница свекровь. –

'Oh come now Tanya! We never heard of love in those days. That sort of thing would have made my late mother-in-law chase me off the face of the earth.' (3. 18.)[1]

---

[1] Nabokov quotes a draft of notes by Pushkin for the 1833 edition: 'Somebody asked an old woman: Was it passion that brought you to the altar, Granny? 'Yes, my dear, passion', she answered. 'The steward and the bailiff were in such a passion they almost beat me to death.'

My ne slykhali pro lyubov is a rumble of amusement, the substantive seeming down-to-earth even in the old woman's derisive utterance of it. She ignores the faint high syllables of Tatyana's romantic participle as if they were too absurd for her, and she tells how the matchmaker arranged her marriage and how she cried when she went to a strange family. Too immersed in her own sensations to listen, Tatyana interrupts, striving desperately to convey the significance of her magic word while pleading for some reassurance about the state she is in. Uncomprehending, the old nurse can only tell her she is not well and offer to sprinkle her with holy water, and Tatyana in desperation repeats her word twice more as if to convince herself that it does describe what she is feeling:

> «Я влюблена», шептала снова
> Старушке с горестью она.
> – «Сердечный друг, ты нездорова».
> – «Оставь меня: я влюблена».

'I am in love', she murmured again sorrowfully to the old woman. 'Sweetheart, you aren't well.' 'Leave me: I am in love.' (3. 20.)

Something must be done, and by the light of the 'inspiring moon' (probably Delille's *lampe inspiratrice*) Tatyana sits down to write her letter.[1] The whole passage has remarkable affinities with one of a similar kind in another novel in verse – Chaucer's *Troilus and Criseyde* – in which Criseyde, distracted by Troilus's passion for her, and by what she should do and feel about it, walks out into the moonlit garden and hears 'a nyghtingale, upon a cedir grene'. Both Chaucer and Pushkin use the lyricism of their art not to describe the states of mind of their characters but to suggest them by their surroundings and Chaucer uses the mediaeval convention of courtly love, as Pushkin the contemporary literary conventions of romance, to reveal pyschology and actuality.

The responses of the Tatyana of Chapter 8 are as much dictated by literary precedent as those of the girl who sits down to write her letter to Onegin: it is another aspect of the continuity between them. In his sermon to her (4. 16) Onegin comments that a girl has new loves as a sapling puts out new leaves each spring: the world-weariness in the metaphor of repetition is very typical of him. As

---

[1] Nabokov's highly plausible conjecture. He points out that in one of Madame de Staël's books, *De la Littérature considérée dans ses rapports avec les institutions sociales* (a suggestive title in the context of *Evgeny Onegin* and very likely known to its author) she observes that '*Delille...s'est servi d'un mot nouveau, inspiratrice*'.

with so much else in the two passages, there is an echo when, after his winter spent shut up in Petersburg trying to forget her, he rushes out in the spring (8. 39) for his final confrontation with Tatyana. For him spring means something real at last, but ironically the genuineness of his impulse is misunderstood. She puts it aside as the calculated move of a professional seducer, alive to the reputation to be acquired from a liaison with a married woman of the *haut monde*. As she says, it is now her turn, and she deals with him as firmly, and with the same slightly priggish virtuousness that he once meted out to her. But like her letter her speech is from books:

> Я вышла замуж. Вы должны,
> Я вас прошу, меня оставить;
> Я знаю: в вашем сердце есть
> И гордость и прямая честь.
> Я вас люблю (к чему лукавить?),
> Но я другому отдана;
> Я буду век ему верна.

I married. You must, I must ask you, leave me. I know that in your heart is both pride and real honour. I love you (why deny it?) but I am given to another, and I shall remain faithful to him for ever. (8. 47.)

Compare the stylised composure of that *Ya vas lyublyu (k chemu lukavit?)* with the feverish whispered repetition *Ya vlyublena.* And we may compare, too, the scene with her nurse to Tatyana's touchingly formal evocation of her:

> Сейчас отдать я рада
> Всю эту ветошь маскарада,
> Весь этот блеск, и шум, и чад
> За полку книг, за дикий сад,
> За наше бедное жилище,
> За те места, где в первый раз,
> Онегин, видела я вас,
> Да за смиренное кладбище,
> Где нынче крест и тень ветвей
> Над бедной нянею моей...

At once I'd gladly give up all the rags of this masquerade, all this glitter and noise and vapour, for a shelf of books, a wild garden, our poor house; for the places where I saw you, Onegin, for the first time; and for the humble church-yard where now there is a cross and the branches' shade above my poor nurse... (8. 46.)

Pushkin makes use of the pathetic sentiment of Rousseau, but so deep and strong by now is the novel's impression of verisimilitude that Tatyana seems to be taking refuge in this image of herself, as she once explored, in ecstatic anguish, the image of being 'in love'. And as the bookish tone of Onegin's sermon to her seemed to conceal his satisfaction in being a 'pedant', so that of hers to him is an instinctive disguise for her real grief. Pushkin contrives (as Rousseau does not) to distinguish between his own literary flights – the description of Lensky's grave for example – and those of his hero and heroine, in whose speech literature plays both a formative and an immediately dramatic role. This impression of Tatyana's last speech is heightened by its contrast with her reported conversation at their first Petersburg encounter:

> С ней речь хотел он завести
> И – и не мог. Она спросила,
> Давно ль он здесь, откуда он
> И не из их ли уж сторон?
> Потом к супругу обратила
> Усталый взгляд; скользнула вон...
> И недвижим остался он.

He wished to begin a conversation with her and – could not. She asked how long he had been here, where he had come from, and whether he had been in their own part of the world? Then she turned a tired glance on her husband; slipped away...and he remained motionless. (8. 19.)

Self-possession then was achieved by recourse to conventional queries which the verse renders with rapid naturalism (and was she quite so self-possessed as Onegin thought? – as Nabokov observes there is 'the ghost of a stutter' in the flurried monosyllables of that reported line: *i ne iz ikh li uzh storon?*).

Hero and heroine have changed places. In order to deal with life she has had to acquire the same persona that it suited him to cultivate in order to remain outside it. As the novel ends we see that they have never understood each other and do not do so now. She was once eager to commit herself to him without understanding and 'make with him life's humble journey' – *svershit smirenny zhizni put* (8. 28).[1] With an equal straightfaced irony Pushkin says

---

[1] In an earlier MS version *vesely zhizni put* (life's happy journey). The change in the poetic cliché emphasises the difference between what Tatyana has become ('how changed Tatyana is!') and the simple life she hoped to have with the man she loved. See *Poeticheskaya frazeologiya Pushkina*, ed. V. D. Levin (Moscow 1969), p. 175. The earlier version would have chimed with Tatyana's cry to Onegin at their last interview: '*A schaste bylo tak vozmozhno, tak blizko!...*' ('But happiness was so possible, so near!...') (8. 47), but the revision does bring out the contrast between her nature and her destiny, as well as having more, perhaps, of the *alliteratio Pushkiniana*.

yes, there's no doubt of it, he's fallen in love with her now like a child (*kak ditya vlyublen*). In his lecture he had professed to see all too clearly what she was, and what would become of her if he were weak enough to be flattered by her passion for him, or unscrupulous enough to make use of it. Now she retaliates this false understanding upon him. He has fallen for her with the spontaneous clumsiness she once had, but she sees it as the manœuvre of a cynic, who feels he now owes it to his reputation to compromise hers. The remarkable thing about his letter is that every word of it is true. What he valued, he says, is freedom and quiet, and not the happiness of a 'dear habit', the habit of the marriage bond, and he now sees that freedom and quiet in her possession: *sidit pokoina i volna* – 'she sits calm and free' (8. 22). His own ideal for himself now appears infinitely attractive in her, and he is forced to contemplate, like a mirror-image, his own insulation in another person. But even now it does not occur to him to wonder what Tatyana feels about this 'calm and freedom' and what sort of satisfaction they are to her.

In spite of this final alienation there is nothing depressing about the end of *Evgeny Onegin* – it is not like *Adolphe*, a demonstration of hopelessness in which the author himself is deeply involved. Pushkin's novel in verse is too free and too various to end on a note of claustrophobic gloom. The very incomprehension of one character by another, the abyss of distance between them, is as much an earnest of possible happiness as of deprivation. When Tatyana says: 'yet happiness was so possible, so near...' (8. 47), her words have something more than the pathos of illusion. The happiness of 'life's humble journey' was near at hand for Olga and Lensky and was taken from him – but not from her – by 'blind fate', as it was taken from the other Evgeny in *The Bronze Horseman*. The perspective of 'life's humble journey' opens out from every point in *Evgeny Onegin* where artifice, irony, and the patterning of the novel of sentiment are most dazzlingly and triumphantly in control.

II

We have been talking about the novel in naturalistic terms because we first read it, I am sure, as if it was a real story about real people, as we read other masterpieces of the genre, from *Don Quixote* to *Pride and Prejudice*, all of which tell a story that grips the reader, and in which he becomes involved as if it were something in his own life. But the true subject of *Evgeny Onegin*, according to Shklovsky, is not the story of Tatyana and Onegin but 'a game with this fable' (*a igra s etoy fabuloy*).[1] By making use of *Beppo* and *Don Juan* Pushkin adapts the novel in verse to the prose model of his admired *Tristram Shandy*. Like Sterne's novel, Pushkin's is a parody not of the sentiments and manners of the age itself but of the conventions of the novels which reflect them.[2] Like *Tristram Shandy*, *Evgeny Onegin* seems to start and does not: after fifty-two stanzas Pushkin returns to the point at which he began. Once again we are travelling down from Petersburg to the estate of Onegin's uncle: 'and it is with this that I began my novel.' At the end of Chapter 7, with the story almost done, Pushkin invokes the epic muse: 'Here is an introduction, though a belated one.' He pays his respects to classicism, and thus emphasises the artificial symmetry of his tale, which is a logical extension of the initial false start. For Tatyana falls in love with Onegin but nothing comes of it; then Onegin falls in love with Tatyana and equally nothing comes of that. We are back where we began.

In his 'Theory of Prose' Shklovsky lays down the general principle that 'the perception of its form reveals the content of the work'. Since forms are by definition enclosures, the world of content and meaning cannot be open-ended; and Pushkin, says Shklovsky, not only parodies the traditional world of the novel of sentiment, but even parodies his future critics – 'from Dostoevsky to Gershenzon' – by proposing morals and meanings for his poem. How serious is he? Is he really crying over Tatyana or joking? Shklovsky dryly concludes that Russian literature, headed by Dostoevsky, 'is sure that Pushkin wept', and thus has removed a masterpiece of formalism into the debatable land of emotional and psychological speculation, the realm of contingency in which human beings have to operate but the creations of art do not.

But if it was removed it was worth removing. This is the short

[1] V. Shklovsky, *Teoriya Prozy* and *Pushkin i Sterne, Volya Rossii*, no. 6 (Prague 1922). One of the most brilliant of the early formalist critics, Shklovsky anticipates most of the premises of the 'new novel' and the 'anti-novel' today. The anti-novel is of course as old as the novel itself, for as soon as the form acquired sophistication and self-consciousness it began to examine the story it told and its claim to be able to tell it. Novel and 'anti-novel' can thus be said to alternate and develop in parallel since the middle of the eighteenth century and even earlier.

[2] In a later essay *Zametki o proze Pushkina* (1937), Shklovsky emphasises that it is only in *Evgeny Onegin*, and not in Pushkin's prose, that the influence of Sterne is important.

answer to all formalist strictures, which, though they clear the ground, seldom make the all-important value-distinction between the work whose content is indeed determined by the perception of its form, and the work whose content – for whatever reason or reasons – transcends them. Most 'new novels' of today, those of the French school of Butor, Simon, and Robbe-Grillet, certainly give the impression that they cannot be taken over by their public and their critics because they remain inside the enclosure the novelists' artistic consciousness has made for them. Even the deliberate permissiveness of Robbe-Grillet, with his advice to the reader to recreate the work in his own image and according to his own wishes, stirs the most languid response by reason of this very invitation. 'A masterpiece of formalism' – if it means anything – must mean a work whose artifice has liberated meaning and created a wide field of human speculation, and this is what happens to the formalism of Shakespeare, Pushkin, Jane Austen, Sterne, Henry James.

There is also an important difference between our attitude to forms in *Evgeny Onegin* and in *Tristram Shandy*. However we may respond to Sterne's novel we cannot read it as a straight story, oblivious of its peculiarities: its peculiarities are its story, to paraphrase Shklovsky. In Pushkin, story and parody are interrelated but independent. Every 'strange-making' device of Pushkin may pass us by, and we may be aware only of a tale of four persons and their fates. Hence the interpretations begin and – as Shklovsky would be quick to point out – they begin from an imperfect awareness of the structure designed; an awareness, however, licensed by the dual nature of the form as a whole. The tale is necessarily more free than the telling, which may explain why Dostoevsky genuinely thought that Tatyana married an old man, and Mérimée that Onegin travelled abroad, neither having any warrant from the text.

These errors reveal not so much an inattention to the poem as an engrossment of its story. It is significant that the idea of Onegin abroad, and the idea of Tatyana's husband, are *outside* the enchanted bounds which Pushkin creates. They are real because possible: they are not determined aesthetically; they are not a part of '*my* Tatyana' and '*my* Onegin'. Arguably indeed, none of the marginal characters in the poem is determined in this way. Onegin's uncle, Tatyana's nurse, mother, and aunt, live in the story but not in the parody. Dostoevsky's error is illuminating. He could not have made it if he had been talking about *Tristram Shandy*, because no one tries to take over the story of *Tristram Shandy*. Its form covers it completely: no one in it has the extra-Shandean existence that the older persons have in Pushkin's novel. No one, for the same reason, tries to take over *Adolphe*, or *La Jalousie* or *L'Emploi du Temps*.

We may agree with Shklovsky that Pushkin's frequent assertions of love and pity for Tatyana, of friendship and regard for Onegin, are in fact a proclamation of their non-reality: he loves them because they don't exist, because they are creatures of his imagination: 'The products of my fancies and of harmonious devices' (4. 35). But as another Russian critic no less truly observes, Tatyana's words to Onegin at the end – 'happiness was once so possible, so near' – echo throughout the novel.[1] The reason is, surely, that these words remain outside art; they cannot refer to what is in the novel but only to what might be outside it. Expressed formalistically, Pushkin has parodied as part of his art-form the 'happy ever after' marriage that is lived through after the conventional novel has ended; he has made the happiness towards which such a novel leads up an integral – but negative – part of his plot. None the less it shows where the sovereignty of the poem breaks off and the world outside becomes imminent and unavoidable – hence its real and wholly 'unaesthetic' pathos. The 'spring' which Tatyana's words hold tense is between the poem and the world outside, and makes us suddenly and finally aware that though she is the product of Pushkin's fancy she was created for that world and not for the poem. Onegin, its eponymous embodiment and justification, has held her inside it like a prisoner; and she releases herself and causes him to vanish by the 'password', which invokes the possibility for which she was made and he was not. Dramatically, the contrast between what the poem circumscribes and what is outside it is now revealed as the contrast between Onegin as Art and Tatyana as Life; and though such a formula sounds depressingly theoretical it does show why the atmosphere of *Evgeny Onegin* is that of the open world, not that of the enclosed aesthetic one.

Onegin is the embodiment of every aesthetic device in the poem, the focal point at which they all meet and assume a human form which exactly contains and expresses them. His fate is indeed to be a method. Shklovsky remarks that the famous 'sentiment' of

[1] Slonimsky, *Masterstvo Pushkina*.

Tristram Shandy is merely the form it assumes; but he omits to mention that when the success of Sterne's novel turned sentimentality into a cult it ceased to belong to Sterne and became merely a vulgar possession of his readers; and the same thing happens when Onegin is removed by critics and readers from the novel which embodies *Oneginshchina* as *Tristram Shandy* defines Shandyism. The more an eponymous character owes his success to the exclusiveness with which he embodies the work of art, the more he is used as a generalising image. Onegin is made for Pushkin's verse novel as Hamlet is made for the revenge drama, with its discovery, its prolongation, and its *dénouement*; and yet his fate, like that of Hamlet, is to exemplify persons whose situation in no way corresponds to that for which he was created. The more formally adequate the hero, the more disintegrated and widespread is his human appeal.

Shklovsky is so far justified, however, in that Pushkin's method does lay ironic and stylised emphasis on his hero's fatal adequacy for the poem in whose image he is made: rather as Henry James, in his story *The Beast in the Jungle*, caricatured the heroes of his own and other novels in the man whose fate was that nothing could ever happen to him. Hamlet might have been a scholar and a soldier, and had he become king might 'have proved most royally'. The novel revealed to Pushkin that Onegin could not become a Decembrist or even a traveller, only a man who *has* travelled – outside the formal boundaries of the novel. In the stress of his disappointment over Tatyana's refusal to notice him he began to resemble a madman, or even a poet. But:

> Дни мчались; в воздухе нагретом
> Уж разрешалася зима;
> И он не сделался поэтом,
> Не умер, не сошел с ума.

Days went by – winter was already resolving itself in mild airs. And he did not become a poet, he did not die, he did not go mad. (8. 39.)

The most severe judgement on Onegin is itself a variation of Pushkin's formulaic love for his characters. At the end of Chapter 6, after Lensky's death, we are told that though Pushkin loves his hero 'with all his heart', he is not just at that moment in the mood for him. This withdrawal of existence, coupled with the re-assertion of love, reminds us that the duel which seemed so hypnotically real never in fact took place, that Onegin is not a real person. But it also suggests an aesthetic judgement on him of the most severe and mortifying kind – a parallel to the moral judgement that might be passed on such an event in life. For his part in the duel Onegin is to suffer a temporary but total aesthetic eclipse: the eye of his creator will be withdrawn from him.

This temporary withdrawal of favour is all the more convincing because Pushkin is himself, like Onegin, a character in his own novel. In four stanzas of Chapter 1 (45–8) we see the pair together, Pushkin at first disconcerted by Onegin's cynicism, but coming to enjoy his wit and caustic turn of phrase. Drawn together by their youthful disenchantment with life, they lounge on summer nights by the parapet of the Neva. But the character Onegin is bored by the country (1. 54) whereas the character Pushkin finds it of all places the most congenial to him. Their mutual attraction is tacitly contrasted with that between Onegin and Lensky (2. 13–16), who become inseparable through being as different from one another as 'verse and prose, ice and flame', and from having nothing else to do in the country. The poet Lensky is fortunate in being able to read his verses to his beloved (even though she may not be listening); the poet Pushkin has only his old nurse as audience for 'the products of my fancies' (the real Pushkin almost certainly never read any of *Evgeny Onegin* to the old lady, or indeed any of his other poems).

One reason for all this artifice is undoubtedly Pushkin's deliberate policy of dissociating himself from the romantic attitudes, as opposed to what he considered the romantic 'free forms'. He deplored modern excess, and the determination to feel strongly about life, society, and love ('The French poet of today has systematically said: let us be religious, let us be political, and even, let us be extravagant') and he admired Constant's dry detachment for the same reason that he thought Hugo's *Les Derniers Jours d'un Condamné* a repellent work in spite of the talent it displayed.[1] But detachment also can be too determined a goal, which is why Pushkin's natural ease and forthcomingness are allowed to appear in such guises as a stylised affection for his characters.

A more specific reason is the dissociation from Byron, often implied, and stated openly (1. 56) when Pushkin observes that 'he is always glad to note the difference between Onegin and myself' in case some reader or publisher claims that he has produced a self-

[1] From a review of Delorme's *Poésies et Pensées* and Sainte-Beuve's *Les Consolations* which appeared in the *Literary Gazette* in 1831 (vii, 235).

portrait like Byron, 'the poet of pride'. The claim to detachment implies a total artifice where Byron had insisted that Don Juan was real life, the 'real thing'. But there are drawbacks in Pushkin's dissociative emphasis. Byron's egoism does at least unify digression and narrative; 'rattling on exactly as I'd talk' produces a complete homogeneity in which we do not distinguish between the poet telling us his story and telling us about himself. The link-passages in *Evgeny Onegin* can be arch, self-conscious, and artificial in the bad sense. The reader soon comes to prefer the poet who is the virtuoso of his characters (including himself) and his story, to the poet who treats us *in vacuo* to an elegant commonplace or a *causerie autour de soi*; and it is significant that the greatest number of Pushkin's own cancellations in revision are of such commonplaces about life, woman or society. In order to evade *Don Juan*, Pushkin must dissociate himself from its club-room atmosphere as well as from its dominating personality. The least successful digressions – like that on friends (4. 18–20): 'God preserve us from them' – are those in which a conversational man-to-man approach is used instead of a switch in style. At such moments the complex charms of *Evgeny Onegin* are momentarily eclipsed by the possessive gusto of *Don Juan*. The note is struck at the opening of Chapter 4:

Чем меньше женщину мы любим,
Тем легче нравимся мы ей...

The less we love a woman the easier it is to be liked by her... (4. 1.)

The first stanza, numbered 1–7, records the demise of six stanzas of worldly wisdom, as if the Byronic egoist had been left to hold forth on his own in the deserted smoking-room. His profound comments on the Sex have been quietly dropped, though the first four of them were published separately in 1827 in the *Moscow Herald* under the title *Women: A Fragment from 'Evgeny Onegin'*. And at the opening of stanza 9 Pushkin discloses who it is who has been thinking along these lines. *Tak tochno dumal moy Evgeny* ('exactly thus my Evgeny was thinking') – a line that echoes the opening of the second stanza of Chapter 1: *Tak dumal molodoy povesa* ('thus a youthful rake was thinking') – when the young Evgeny is reflecting on the boring prospect of sitting with his invalid uncle. A generalisation turns out to have been part of an isolated consciousness in the poem, not that of its author.

Digressions and generalisations in the last two chapters have a different tone from those in the early part of the poem, and with the knowledge of hindsight we can connect these with the changes that had taken place in Pushkin over the years of its composition. Blest is the man, he writes (8. 10), who was youthful in his youth and who then grew up at the right time; the admirable fellow who did not shun society and go in for strange dreams; who married at thirty and at fifty discharged his debts. When Pushkin completed Chapter 8 in the Boldino autumn of 1830 his marriage, after several postponements, was about to take place. A few days before the wedding he wrote to his friend Krivtsov: 'My youth has passed tumultuously and fruitlessly. Up to now I have lived in a different way from most people. There has been no happiness for me. *Il n'est de bonheur que dans les voies communes* [The last sentence of Chateaubriand's *René*.] I am past thirty. At thirty people usually get married – I am acting as people usually do and I shall probably not regret it...Trials and tribulations will not surprise me: they are included in my family budget. Any joy will be something I did not expect.'

In his letter to Tatyana Onegin wrote:

> Я думал: вольность и покой
> Замена счастью. Боже мой!
> Как я ошибся, как наказан.

I thought: freedom and quiet are a substitute for happiness. God! What a mistake I made, and how I am punished! (8. Onegin's letter.)

Four years later Pushkin was to echo the phrase in one of his finest short poems:

> Пора, мой друг, пора! покоя сердце просит –
> Летят за днями дни, и каждый час уносит
> Частичку бытия, а мы с тобой вдвоём
> Предполагаем жить...И глядь – как раз – умрём.
> На свете счастья нет, но есть покой и воля.
> Давно завидная мечтается мне доля –
> Давно, усталый раб, замыслил я побег
> В обитель дальнюю трудов и чистых нег.

It's time, my dear, it's time! The heart begs for peace – the days fly past and every hour carries off a little bit of life, and we make plans together to live...and all of a sudden we (shall) die. There is no happiness in the world, but there is peace and freedom. I have long been dreaming of an enviable lot – a weary slave, I have long been planning a flight to a distant sanctuary of work and pure pleasures. (III, 278.)

There is an intimate link between the immediacy of the lyric and the artifice of the long poem, for in both the personal identity and environment of the poet himself is absent, irrelevant, not required. The lyric despair of Shelley in the *Stanzas written in dejection near Naples* (the penultimate verse of which offers some kind of equivalent of the quality of Pushkin's lines); the haunted melancholy of Tennyson and Baudelaire – these create a static world, enclosing the poet and his own destiny. Pushkin's, by contrast, express perfectly the emotion of a moment, making out of its very intimacy something universal and anonymous – the effort to anticipate and impose order upon the passing moment (*predpolagaem zhit*) is swept away with each word of the poem. In the lyric, as in the ironic portrait in *Evgeny Onegin* of the family man Pushkin saw himself as on the threshold of becoming, there is only the barest flicker of connection between art and the situation of the artist, and the connection is all the more moving for that reason.

Compared with the romantic styles of the period, the style and diction of *Evgeny Onegin* are the instruments of distance and of variations exactly anticipated and controlled. We have discussed earlier the typical romantic weakness of inadvertent *incongruity* in styles, and their tendency – especially in narrative and ballad – to show each other up. Wordsworth's finest poetry, for example, puts on loftiness or a penetrating simplicity under the impulse of the poet's desire to communicate, so that incongruity seems almost like a needful aspect of the very urgency of communication. Compare the declamation of the 'Immortality Ode' with the sudden drop into a vocabulary of the most searching and haunting accuracy:

> Not for these I raise
> The song of thanks and praise;
> But for those obstinate questionings
> Of sense and outward things,
> Fallings from us, vanishings;
> Blank misgivings of a creature
> Moving about in worlds not realised...

Wordsworth seems to blow his blasts as if absent-mindedly: his argument is too intensely scrutinised to justify a change of diction which in a more formal poet would signify the discarding of a sufficiently handled commonplace and the taking up of another. When, in *The Excursion*, he settles into a uniformity of style it is a sign that the pressure of examination has dropped – exposition has taken the place of excited and groping utterance. Keats's finest poems depend equally on a seemingly uncontrolled mixture of the sublime and the banal; and when, in *Hyperion*, he seeks to confine his utterance to an artificially sublime diction, it rises like that of *The Excursion* into an inflexible monotony.

By reason of its very uncertainty, its absorption in the feel of its experience rather than in any attention to appropriateness of diction, romantic poetry can generalise and philosophise in a way that is not available to Pushkin. When Keats speaks of 'the feel of not to feel it', or Wordsworth of 'blank misgivings of a creature moving about in worlds not realised', they make a break-through in the verbal exploration of human experience. Such things can be implied by Pushkin in the drama of narrative – Keats's phrase might describe the impression Tatyana gives in her Petersburg salon – but Pushkin's styles have no power to give the thing in itself. His generalisations are the weakest things in *Evgeny Onegin* and redeem their weakness only by not taking themselves too seriously: their elegance seems good-humouredly to patronise an emptiness for which it is itself largely responsible.

The ability of the English romantic poets to be clumsy with point and power is inherited from Shakespeare and Elizabethan poetry, and from an instinctive sympathy with a much earlier poetic idiom. In terms of a literary tradition Pushkin has only the eighteenth century behind him. Though he knew of *The Excursion* – the first lines of which he attempted to translate in 1834 with the aid of a French/English dictionary – he was as ignorant of the best features and examples of English romantic poetry as were his con-temporaries on the continent. Nor is there any likelihood that he would have responded to them. *Vulgar* was an English word he was fond of (he uses it to imply everything that Tatyana in her Petersburg persona was not) and he would certainly have found much of Keats and the *Lyrical Ballads* as vulgar as did the *Edin-burgh* and *Quarterly* reviewers – reviewers whose attitudes were the model of his own *Sovremennik*. He was equally conservative about the French romantics, agreeing with Nodier's view that their diction was a corruption rather than a revival of the styles of the French renaissance. Deploring Hugo, he reserved his admiration for the diction of Chénier, 'a real Greek' who had distilled a pure style with nothing romantic in it from the diction of his eighteenth-century predecessors.

In *Evgeny Onegin*, then, the style is not the man but a complex instrument manipulated by him. Curiously enough, Goethe's pronouncement: 'I have no style, only styles' is also true of

Pushkin's verse novel, and places it in the classic and European tradition of controlled rhetoric and the use of the 'High' and the 'Low'. In English verse the parallel here is Chaucer's use of the formal principles of poetic decorum to achieve a rich and delicate acoustic background for each personality – the Knight, the Franklin, the Miller – allotting the pilgrims in the *Canterbury Tales* a poetic appropriateness in keeping with their social status and profession. The complexity of Pushkin's technique is of course much greater, but something of the same formal artifice is involved, an artifice that can probably only be achieved in a poetic language at an early stage of its development, when freedom and formality are allies who can bring out the best in one another. Pushkin's fiction in poetry anticipates many of the later stylistic devices of the novel in prose – particularly those of James Joyce – as it has already adapted into verse technique the prose innovations of *Tristram Shandy*.

Lensky is encompassed with the spiritual aura of his poetic dreams, 'parting and sadness, and a kind of *something*, and the *cloudy distance*, and romantic roses' (2. 10). Gabriel, in Joyce's story *The Dead*, is a poet in much the same sense that Lensky is, and his reflections at the end of the story reveal a discovered emotion whose depth is registered through an appropriately eloquent indulgence continuous with the total effect of the story but not identified with it.[1] In the same way, Lensky's romantic attachment to love and death are not the same as the novel's own imagination of them. In his own account of the poet's death Pushkin alternates between the empathy of a similar style to Lensky's own ('the storm blew, the beauteous flower has withered at sunrise, the flame is extinguished on the altar!...' (6. 31)) and a sudden and moving withdrawal into an older and more impersonal commonplace, of the kind that is accessible only to the greatest of poets.

> Мой бедный Ленский! за могилой
> В пределах вечности глухой
> Смутился ли, певец унылый,
> Измены вестью роковой,
> Или над Летой усыпленный
> Поэт, бесчувствием блаженный,

---

[1] Better pass boldly into that other world, in the full glory of some passion, than fade and wither dismally with age. He thought of how she who lay beside him had locked in her heart for so many years that image of her lover's eyes when he had told her that he did not wish to live.

Generous tears filled Gabriel's eyes... (James Joyce, *The Dead*.)

Уж не смущается ничем,
И мир ему закрыт и нем?...
Так! равнодушное забвенье
За гробом ожидает нас.

My poor Lensky! Beyond the grave, in the borders of voiceless eternity,
was the sad singer disturbed by the fateful news of his betrayal? Or
lulled to sleep by Lethe, blest with insensibility, was the poet no longer
disturbed by anything, the world for him cut off and silent? So it is!
Indifferent oblivion awaits us beyond the grave. (7. 11.)

The rhetorical alternative echoes the one already asked: would
Lensky have become an immortal poet or a comfortable landowner
in a dressing-gown – and both are alternatives of style rather than
of fact. The modulation into the conclusion – *Tak! ravnodushnoe
zabvene*... – has the perfect ease and simplicity of a Shakespearen
sonnet, and the same power to withdraw from story into generalisation in such a way that the personal slips out of both, leaving a
relaxed and colloquial perfection that is the ghost of the artist's
presence.

It is strange that Pushkin's stylistic achievement in *Evgeny
Onegin* should summon up the ghost of two Irish writers, and
should often in fact be closer to the tenderness of Joyce than the
sentiment of Sterne. He shares with both an easy eighteenth-
century relationship with poetic facility and cliché. What Wordsworth and the romantic poets forgot in their strictures on the
poetic diction of their predecessors was that the best poets who
used it never took it very seriously, just as a great rhetorician does
not take the rhetoric he makes use of very seriously. The sparkling
conventionality which attends the opening of the champagne at
Onegin's restaurant dinner (1. 16), and at his country festivity with
Lensky (4. 45), give such moments the memorable character of the
musical supper in *The Dead*, and Bloom's breakfast kidney in
Ulysses. Language is perfectly at home with these simple quotidian
festivals even while it confers on them the aura of heroic celebration. Compare Tennyson's attempt in *In Memoriam* to treat such
an occasion with linguistic decorum:

> Let all my genial spirits advance
> To meet and greet a whiter sun;
> My drooping memory will not shun
> The foaming grape of eastern France.

We cannot but smile, because the graceful and indeed exceptionally accurate poeticism for champagne offers itself to us with an

unwinking gravity which is suited neither to the beverage itself nor
to the occasions on which it is imbibed. The calm grave diction
suited to the overall tone of the poem trips itself up at such a
moment; we do not have the sense of participation which Pushkin
achieves by the kind of artifice which in Tennyson draws too much
attention to itself. The clichés of Pushkin's champagne are aware
of their own obviousness and emphasise it with gusto.

> Вдовы Клико или Моэта
> Благословенное вино
> В бутылке мерзлой для поэта
> На стол тотчас принесено.
> Оно сверкает Ипокреной;
> Оно своей игрой и пеной
> (Подобием того-сего)
> Меня пленяло: за него
> Последний бедный лепт, бывало,
> Давал я. Помните ль, друзья?
> Его волшебная струя
> Рождала глупостей не мало,
> А сколько шуток и стихов,
> И споров, и веселых снов!

The blessed wine of Veuve Clicquot or Moet is brought on the instant to
table for the poet in its frosted bottle. It sparkles like Hippocrene, and
with its play of bubbles (a comparison for all sorts of things) it used to
captivate me: for it I was wont to part with my last poor lepton. You
remember, my friends? Its enchanted stream gave rise to no little
foolishness, but how many jokes and verses too, arguments and happy
dreams! (4. 45.)[1]

Friendship is the theme, a gift as 'blessed' as the wine, and
Pushkin glances at all the convivial comparisons beloved by poets –
from Voltaire and Byron to his own friends Baratynsky and
Vyazemsky – the former in his poem *The Feasts* called it 'a simile
of youthful life'. (He also spoke of the 'freedom and pride' of the
wine that cannot 'bear captivity', phrases which the watchful
censor seized on as too anthropomorphic by half, and required to be
altered. Nabokov conjectures that Pushkin's friends would perceive a sly reference to this episode.) At Tatyana's name-day party
in the next chapter Pushkin produces to suit the different context
a different exercise in the art of the disembottling cliché. In keeping

---

[1] To be sure in point of language, descriptive density, metrical virtuosity, there
is a distinct affinity between *Evgeny Onegin* and *In Memoriam*. The variation
of rhythm in the first line of the quotation from the latter is typical of Pushkin's continual play on the possible variations of the four-stress iambic line.

with the pretensions of a rural gathering a sparkling Don wine –
Tsimlyansky – is brought forth in a bottle sealed with pitch, and
the amateur poet Triquet stands up to read Tatyana a special poem.

> Освободясь от пробки влажной,
> Бутылка хлопнула; вино
> Шипит; и вот с осанкой важной,
> Куплетом мучимый давно,
> Трике встает.

Freeing itself from the moist cork the bottle pops; the wine foams; and
now with portentous mien, long tormented by his couplets, Triquet
arises. (5. 33.)

The laborious syllables and the pause before the last stress of the
second line make even the wine seem to flow in slow motion and
exquisitely convey the solemn moment as the poet rises to his feet –
an antithesis in onomatopoeia of the scene at Talon's restaurant in
Chapter 1:

> Вошел: и пробка в потолок,
> Вина кометы брызнул ток.

He came – and the cork flew to the ceiling, the Comet wine spurting
forth. (1. 16.)

In his *The Art of Sinking in Poetry* Pope had produced a model
formula for the bottle-opening poet:

> Apply thine engine to the spungie door,
> Set Bacchus from his glassy prison free,

and he would doubtless have enjoyed an art as referential as his
own and a diction that availed itself as brilliantly of the stock
phraseology of other poets. Pushkin can emphasise the process
with a display of mock modesty, as when he breaks off his superb
description of the coming of winter (itself carrying more than an
echo of the French version of Thomson's *Seasons*) to point out that
two other poets, named by him in a note as Vyazemsky and
Baratynsky, have already done it much better.

Pushkin is as much a master in *Evgeny Onegin* of the new
romantic clichés as of the classic diction of the eighteenth century,
and the Gallicisms that go with it. And both are emphasised by the
art of the novel in verse for its purposes of characterisation and
depth of colour. He exaggerates the provenance of a diction that
in his shorter poems becomes invisible: the language that is
deliberately and promiscuously *local* in the novel can seem trans-
parently simple and pure in the context of his finest lyrics. This

phenomenon was not unnaturally disconcerting to his friends and contemporaries, who were puzzled by the ebullient linguistic antics of *Onegin*; Baratynsky disliked it particularly, though most likely because he suspected a dig or two at his own work (Lensky and Olga do have a certain resemblance to Vladimir and Eda in his poem *The Finnish Maid*). Küchelbecker, the 'severe critic' referred to (4. 32) in connection with Lensky's tendency to write elegies and love-poems instead of dignified odes, had mentioned Pushkin amongst others in his essay in *Mnemosyne* in 1824, 'On the tendency of our poetry, especially lyrical, in the last decade'. Küchelbecker was as ardent a Schillerian as Lensky himself, but he retained a preference for the clumsy if vigorous diction of the eighteenth-century Russian composers of odes, Derzhavin and Lomonosov. Reversing Wordsworth's strictures on poetic diction (itself an illuminating sidelight on the simultaneous and rapid development of Russian poetic style in its great age) he attacked what seemed to him the mechanical use of a new *romantic* poetic diction, borrowing in the process ideas already expressed by a French critic in the *Journal des Débats* on the new cult of the 'vague' in poetic vocabulary.[1] He lists such stock terms as *pokoy* (peace), *pechal* (sadness), *mechta* (reverie), words which were indeed as popular with Pushkin as with his contemporaries. In his reference to Küchelbecker *à propos* Lensky's poetic efforts, Pushkin says he will keep quiet because he does not want 'to make two ages quarrel' (*no ya molchu: | Dva veka ssorit ne khochu*) and shrugged his shoulders at being thus 'placed' in the new romantic camp. The whole point, of course, of his linguistic practice in *Onegin*, with its elements of 'burlesque' disapproved of by contemporaries, was to make the fullest use of all kinds of poetic diction, and in so doing he reveals the ways in which diction mirrors the conditioning of a changing society.

When Lensky uses words like *pokoy* and *mechta* they are a trademark of 'poetry'; when Pushkin uses them they disappear into the purity of his art.[2] It is a very obvious paradox, which Pushkin

[1] See Nabokov, *Evgeny Onegin*, vol. II, p. 447.
[2] An oblique comment on this is made in Pushkin's comment on Lensky's last poem on the night before the duel: 'Thus he wrote, *darkly* and *languidly* (what we call romanticism, though I do not see any romanticism at all here, but what is that to us?)' (6. 23). Pushkin, in fact, adopted the conventional view that Shakespeare is 'romantic', and hence held that the romanticism of his own age was a kind of fashionable and fallacious imitation of an ideal, in much the same way that the minor French neo-classic writers were travesties of the classic ideal.

implies in *Evgeny Onegin* and demonstrates in his shorter poems. Its most moving manifestations in the novel, as we have noted, are things like the simplicity of poetic comment on one who was 'poetically' in love with the romantic properties of death, love and the ideal. *Tak! Ravnodushnoe zabvene | Za grobom ozhidaet nas...* But the transparent use of the most poetically 'placed' diction was also the genius of Racine:

> Et tout dort, et l'armée, et les vents, et Neptune...
>
> *(Iphigénie en Aulide*, i, i, 9)

and of Pope too, as his own favourite couplet shows:

> Lo! where Maeotis sleeps, and hardly flows
> The freezing Tanais through a waste of snows.
>
> *(The Dunciad*, Book 3, 87)

We might compare the use that Pushkin makes of romanticism, via Lensky, with the much more soundless comment on it (more delicate, less placing) that Tatyana invites:

> Она любила на балконе
> Предупреждать зари всход,
> Когда на бледном небосклоне
> Звезд исчезает хоровод,
> И тихо край земли светлеет...

She loved to anticipate the coming of dawn upon her balcony, when the choral dance of stars disappears in the pale sky and the horizon softly lightens... (2. 28.)

Metre and melody here give her own sense of herself; but when she sits down to write to Onegin the lines echo, in their purposeful flatness, her own now firm and unselfconscious determination:

> «Поди, оставь меня одну.
> Дай, няня, мне перо, бумагу,
> Да стол подвинь; я скоро лягу;
> Прости».

'Go now, leave me alone. Give me a pen and paper, nanny, and move up the table. I'll soon go to bed – goodnight.' (3. 21.)

As hero, and as vacancy, with a being that embodies the whole novel but is nowhere determined in it, Onegin himself is outside the use of diction as a medium that decorates, criticises and makes visible. His non-involvement in the visible charms of poetry is in

some sense a comment on his non-involvement in the positive
necessities of life. Though we are closer to his physical being than
to that of the other characters – we are familiar with his clothes,
his meals, the furnishings of his rooms, how he gets through his
time – we have no sense of his *style*, the style that in the art of
Evgeny Onegin is the equivalent of a living individuality. Lensky,
Olga, Tatyana, involuntarily possess such a style but Onegin does
not. His blankness as a being is in a sense comparable to the nullity
of Byron's Don Juan; but whereas that of Byron's hero is merely
an aspect of the Byronic uniformity of style and diction, Pushkin's
reveals and contrasts with individuality and diversification: the
import of Onegin to a later generation outside the poem is dramatised within its own world of language.

That language also dramatises the world of nature in the poem,
intermingling it with the consciousness of the actors. Nature is
their reaction to it, and the style in which that reaction expresses
itself. Tatyana watches the sunrise, roams the woods, and pines in
Petersburg for the wild garden of her childhood home, and these
responses are juxtaposed with her deep, involuntary acceptance of
her surroundings: the currant bushes where the girls are picking
berries as she has her fateful meeting with Onegin; the river landscape through which she wanders unseeing to his manor house with
its romantic associations. Nature and our response to it are always
two separate things for Pushkin, and this is mutely emphasised in
the contrast between what she sees and what is noted about her by
the poem. The snowy wood through which the bear follows her in
her dream, the branches that tear off her ear-rings and the snow
that engulfs her drenched slipper, are as hallucinatorily vivid as the
scene of the duel between Onegin and Lensky, and in both cases the
protagonists are too absorbed in action to be aware of their surroundings.

The shifting subtlety of the relation is most marked at the
opening of Chapter 5:

В тот год осенняя погода
Стояла долго на дворе,
Зимы ждала, ждала природа.
Снег выпал только в январе
На третье в ночь.

That year autumn weather went on for a long time. Nature waited and
waited for winter. Snow fell only in January, on the night of the second.
(5. 1.)

Tatyana sees the new world with all the surprise of simplicity,

> В окно увидела Татьяна
> Поутру побелевший двор,
> Куртины, кровли и забор,
> На стеклах легкие узоры,
> Деревья в зимнем серебре...

In the morning Tatyana saw from the window the yard, the flowerbeds, roofs and fence grown white; the airy patterns on the window-panes, the trees in winter silver... (5. 1.)

and in the second stanza Pushkin himself steps in with a rhetorical flourish – 'Winter!' – and proceeds to describe its animation in literary and pictorial terms, borrowing from French versions of Thomson and from a poem of his friend Vyazemsky.[1] But the opening: 'That year autumn weather long continued', is fiction at its purest and most sober. Like the beginning of many great nineteenth-century novels it turns contingent accuracy into the universality of a story and then modulates into the poetry of the picturesque while remaining separate from it. To achieve these transitions between poetic pictures and the solid natural background of the novel, Pushkin needs not only the story but the locale which insensibly imposed itself more and more as the novel developed – the triangle of the Larins' estate, Moscow, St Petersburg. When, in the stanzas of Onegin's journey, he goes outside the triangle, nature can only be represented one-dimensionally, as views of the Caucasus and Odessa witnessed by Onegin and recalled by Pushkin (Onegin follows Pushkin, as it were, to the Fountain of Bakhchisarai and remembers him there), or views 'of the Flemish school' which have now become Pushkin's ideal.

> Иные нужны мне картины:
> Люблю песчаный косогор,
> Перед избушкой две рябины,
> Калитку, сломанный забор,
> На небе серенькие тучи,
> Перед гумном соломы кучи
> Да пруд под сенью ив густых,
> Раздолье уток молодых...

Other pictures are needful to me: I like a sandy slope, two rowans in front of a little cottage, a wicket gate, a broken-down fence, little grey

---

[1] Probably the French translation of 1802, *Les Saisons*. *Pervy Sneg* (*The First Snow*) was written by Vyazemsky in 1819. Pushkin also admired his *Zimnie Karikatury* (*Winter Caricatures*), printed in 1831.

clouds in the sky, heaps of straw by the threshing-floor, and a pond in the shelter of dense willows, the domain of ducklings... (Fragments of *Onegin's Journey*, stanza 17.)

Pushkin gives a 'picture' here of what has already been embodied in the background of the novel. Nowhere inside the novel itself could such a pictorial convention have been employed, for there the presence of what is here described is indirect, oblique and cumulative. 'Nature' in the novel is pictorial and poetic except when it is apprehended through action and character; and Pushkin now, with a certain irony, himself takes over and stylises the kind of setting the novel suggested and established by other means. (Tolstoy's novels also build up an immense and spacious impression of homely landscape without direct description, but in the chinks of action and in the oblique apprehension of the characters.) Stylising from the distant and impersonal viewpoint of Onegin's journey, Pushkin comments on the transformation in his own tastes – from the romantic to the realistic – which has taken place during the long composition of the novel and whose real significance is buried within it. 'The variegated litter' (*pestry sor*) of the Flemish school is an apt description of Pushkin's rural scene, with its key image of disordered *density*; but in fact its impact as a picture is more like that of a Constable or an Impressionist, although Pushkin typically suggests a homely luxuriance of disorder with a few spare and telling phrases.[1]

Three years after he had discontinued work on the stanzas of Onegin's Journey Pushkin wrote a meditative nature poem *Vnov ya posetil* (*I visited again*), quite possibly an exploration of the Wordsworthian manner which he had encountered the year before when improving his English with *The Excursion*.[2] It is his only poem of meditative communion with nature, and as such it is curiously bad. The verse is flat, as if Pushkin were deliberately subduing himself to a Wordsworthian context, though it is significant that the poem turns out to be the meditation not of a nature-lover but of a landowner. Unlike Coleridge's larch 'which pushes out in tassels green its bundled leafits', the young pines of Mikhailovskoye did not lead Pushkin to reflections about himself, but about his heirs. Pushkin did not subscribe to Coleridge's view that 'our most interesting poems are those in which the author

---

[1] It is almost like a slight sketch anticipating the luxuriant thicket of Gogol's prose poem in *Dead Souls*, describing Plyushkin's garden.
[2] III, 345.

develops his own feelings', and in its completed form (though the poem was not published in his life-time) he omitted passages of meditation on the feelings the country scene aroused in him which for Coleridge would have constituted the poem's proper egocentric and sympathetic charm. The revised ending – the poet's grandson riding past the same pines and thinking perhaps of his forebear – is a *topos* which Horace might have used, and is incongruous with the loose meander of the form. The earlier ending is conscientiously in keeping with it, but shows how unapt Pushkin is for joining nature to himself in an anthropomorphic meditation. The poem is a singular instance of how a form and diction explored by Pushkin can impose a mode of feeling which is not suited to him and which does not allow free play either to his own individuality or to his objective sense of things.

III

It is arguable that something rather similar occurs in *The Little House at Kolomna*, written in the Boldino autumn of 1830, although here the inhibiting influence is not Wordsworth but Byron, and the problem of being taken over by a model is confronted on a larger scale and in a far more interesting way. The model here is *Beppo*, which bears a far closer relation to *The Little House* than does any other poem of Byron to a poem of Pushkin's. *Beppo* is a pilot poem and an artistic polemic, an exploration of the stanza and method used in *Don Juan*: *The Little House* is also polemical, but instead of being a preliminary poem it is a deliberate breakaway from the completed *Onegin*.

In the spring of 1830 Bulgarin had attacked Pushkin as a 'French versifier', who copied Byron without understanding him. Other attacks followed, both from Bulgarin in the *Northern Bee* and Polevoy in the *Moscow Telegraph*, deriding Pushkin's pride in his aristocratic origins and suggesting that as a writer he had become a back number, turning out increasingly inferior chapters of a poem already *passé*. Pushkin's immediate reply was an epigram (*Ne to beda, chto ty polyak...*); his real response was the extraordinary burst of creation that autumn at Boldino. All he wrote there was a new departure, and the opening stanza of *The Little House* makes – as a kind of symbol of the real and remarkable innovations of the *Little Tragedies* and the *Tales of Belkin* – a humorously defiant gesture of novelty:

Четырехстопный ямб мне надоел:
Им пишет всякий. Мальчикам в забаву
Пора б его оставить. Я хотел
Давным-давно приняться за октаву.
А в самом деле: я бы совладел
С тройным созвучием. Пущусь на славу!
Ведь рифмы запросто со мной живут;
Две придут сами, третью приведут.

The four-stress iambic line bores me: everyone writes it. It's time to leave it as an amusement for the little fellows. I have long wished to take up the octave. And in fact together with it I would make myself master of the three-rhyme ending. Off we go towards fame! Rhyme and I live together on simple terms; two come of themselves and they bring along the third. (IV, 323.)

In invoking the metre, Pushkin by implication summons Byron to his side, both as an ally against the attacks of grovelling professionals – 'in foolscap uniforms turned up with ink' – and as a fellow aristocrat who wrote with negligent ease. Byron too had brushed aside the vulgar notion that trivial events were not suited to poetic narrative; he too disliked the talk of men of letters ('One hates an author that's *all author*') preferring

Men of the world who know the world like men...
Who think of something else beside the pen.

The Byron whom Pushkin had been careful to place in *Evgeny Onegin*, with amused neutrality, as an egoist and the reason for so much studied egoism in others, is now a fellow sufferer (and fellow aristocrat) with whom Pushkin is glad to carry on the fight against 'the would-be wits and can't-be gentlemen', toadies, journalists, bourgeois fashion and bourgeois hypocrisy.

But Byron can prove an embarrassing ally. Once his tone and manner have been adopted (and Byron's sniping at mere men of letters is far more vindictive than Pushkin's instinct against protesting too much could have found comfortable) it is difficult to get outside him and use him as a point of departure. Pushkin surrenders to his idiom in *The Little House* as he does on a smaller scale to that of Wordsworth in *Vnov ya posetil*, but the boisterous dexterity of Byron is more easily accommodated than is Wordsworth's insidious quiet. In both poems Pushkin contrives none the less to set a distance between himself and his overpowering model: in *Vnov ya posetil* by changing the 'I' persona from rural wanderer to reflective landowner; and in *The Little House* by adopting a subtly different poetic stance from that of his fellow nobleman while remaining, so to speak, fraternally arm in arm with him.

The first version of *The Little House* contained several stanzas of direct polemic against Bulgarin and the offending periodicals, and this Pushkin may have intended to publish separately and anonymously in Delvig's *Literary Gazette*, an unsuccessful periodical which Pushkin had helped to launch as a rival to the *Northern Bee*. But at the end of 1830 the *Literary Gazette* was suppressed for printing a poem celebrating the change of regime in France, and when *The Little House* was published under Pushkin's name three years later in the almanac *Novoselye* the stanzas were removed, and in the absence of this localised polemic the general intention shows up clearly; a new stanza, a new kind of poem, a humorous *conte* which gentlemen – if not critics and journalists – should enjoy.

Suburban Kolomna was a long way from fashionable Venice – here is one big initial difference from *Beppo* – and yet Pushkin's poem gives no impression of deliberately selecting a scene from humble life. Tales with such a scene have by tradition a very obvious point and moral, either a lachrymose one (Karamzin's *Poor Liza*) or a bawdy. Remove such a point and moral, and the result appeared to contemporary critics nothing but a frivolous exercise in the new art of the Russian octave, though it earned the admiration of Gogol and later of Belinsky, who referred to the creation of a 'special class of poem' by Pushkin as the first hint of the new Russian school of naturalism. M. L. Gofman, who did much to establish the poem's text and who emphasised its polemical origin in the journalistic skirmish, expressed a measure of judicious agreement in his view that Pushkin was seeking a new kind of realistic style by using the octave less flamboyantly than Byron, with no grotesquerie of enjambement and dialogue. An anonymous critic in the magazine *Galatea* (1839) robustly maintained that the sole function of the piece was to naturalise the Italian octave, while at the other end of the scale there are (as always with Pushkin) no lack of speculations about its possible profound and hidden meaning. Gershenzon in *Mudrost Pushkina* finds in it a concealed revelation of the passionate love of Pushkin's youth when he lodged in Kolomna; and the poet Khodasevich thought it revealed his superstitious sense of the intervention of diabolical powers in human life (the devil, presumably, can vanish away at will, but has to shave while living among the humankind he seduces). The sensible Bryusov concentrates on the verbal parallels with *Beppo* and with another of its successors – Musset's *Namouna*. Pushkin, we remember, excepted Musset from his condemnation of modern French poetry 'because he is the first French poet who has been able to grasp the tone of Byron's facetious works, which are in reality no joking matter'.

Is *The Little House* then no joking matter? The interpretative Pushkinians certainly do not think so, but it is possible to feel that Pushkin, and Musset too, may have taken Byron too much *au pied de la lettre*. Like his scorn of the scribbling tribe, his insistence on the laughter that 'leaves us so doubly serious shortly after', is a pose that goes with the technique rather than a considered reference to the nature of the tale he tells. Yet Pushkin, who was himself contemplating the same step, must have been struck by Byron's two references to prose, for which he would keep more serious matters ('I'll keep them for my life (to come) in prose') and by the 'Beppoid' convention that here is a form as down-to-earth as prose but which can avoid its logic and disclaim its need to complete a proposition it has begun. The Beppoid poet makes a virtue of being at the mercy of his medium, as Tolstoy's Anna Scherer 'smiles at her own impetuosity' and exploits her 'charming defect' of never finishing a sentence, and it is here that Pushkin, with quiet emphasis and perhaps deliberately, dissociates himself from his model.

> This story slips forever through my fingers,
> Because, just as the stanza likes to make it,
> It needs must be, and so it rather lingers...

Pushkin's will not linger. When he has explained his premises he is going to get down to business – unlike Byron and Musset – and show that the poet need not adopt a comically helpless stance before the exigencies of the octave. The tail need not wag the dog, nor the dog point out how well the motion becomes him. Instead, like Napoleon or Tamerlane, Pushkin will marshal his rhymes like an army and put them through their exercise: to vary the metaphor, he will keep the pert muse of the genre in order.

> Усядься, муза: ручки в рукава,
> Под лавку ножки! не вертись, резвушка!
> Теперь начнем. – Жила-была вдова,
> Тому лет восемь, бедная старушка,
> С одною дочерью. У Покрова
> Стояла их смиренная лачужка
> За самой будкой. Вижу как теперь
> Светелку, три окна, крыльцо и дверь.

Sit, muse; little hands in sleeves, little feet under the bench! Don't twirl about, giddy creature! Now, let's begin. – There was once a widow, about eight years ago, a poor old lady with one daughter. Their humble dwelling was by the church of the Intercession, just behind its gatehouse. I see, as if it were today, an attic, three windows, the porch and the door.[1]

From now on there will be no digressions except ones that are in keeping with the dramatic *atmosphere* of the poem, in which Pushkin himself will become not a commentator but an actor, wandering round Kolomna and surveying the three-storied house (conceivably a parallel to the triple rhymes of the octave) which has replaced the *domik* in which his characters used to live. Are they still alive? His own youth has vanished as they have done.

> Мне стало грустно: на высокий дом
> Глядел я косо. Если в эту пору
> Пожар его бы охватил кругом,
> То моему б озлобленному взору
> Приятно было пламя. Странным сном
> Бывает сердце полно; много вздору
> Приходит нам на ум, когда бредем
> Одни или с товарищем вдвоем.

> Тогда блажен, кто крепко словом правит
> И держит мысль на привязи свою,
> Кто в сердце усыпляет или давит
> Мгновенно прошипевшую змию;
> Но кто болтлив, того молва прославит
> Вмиг извергом... Я воды Леты пью,
> Мне доктором запрещена унылость:
> Оставим это, – сделайте мне милость!

I became sad: I looked askance at the tall building. If a fire had enveloped it utterly at that moment the flame would have been agreeable to my embittered eye. The heart is full of strange fantasies; so much

---

[1] This stanza might be contrasted with the end of the first part of *Namouna*, in which the poet compares himself to Aeneas, the poem to Anchises, whom he bears on his shoulders, and his muse to the wife of Aeneas, Creusa, who is continually dropping behind, or stopping to fasten her garter. Musset exaggerates with *élan* everything he admired in Byron. His poem is brilliant, but over-emphatic, and over-long: Pushkin is concerned to take the steam out of Byron, rather than increase the pressure. With a certain air of *de haut en bas* Musset observes of his poem (which is in *sixains*, lacking the final couplet of *ottava rima*):

> Byron, me direz-vous, m'a servi de modèle.
> Vous ne savez donc pas qu'il imitait Pulci?

and the epigraph from Chamfort with which he heads his second canto –
Qu'est ce que l'amour? L'échange de deux fantaisies et le contact de deux épidermes
– is a perfect example of the kind of Gallic wit which Pushkin had avoided both in the mottoes and the text of *Evgeny Onegin*.

nonsense goes through one's head when one strolls alone or together with a friend.

He is in bliss then indeed who is absolute master of his words and holds his thoughts well in control, who can put to sleep or stifle the serpent who hisses by moments in his heart. But he who babbles all is at once marked down as a cad...I drink Lethe's waters...the doctor has forbidden me sadness: let's leave this – do me the favour.

We can see here how the Beppo poet's artlessly random utterance is ingeniously converted by Pushkin into a fictional narrative method – the narrator's inability to control his thoughts about the past, and the memories that assail him when he wanders through familiar streets like Baudelaire or Dostoevsky's underground man. Between such a narrator and the story he tells there will clearly be some undisclosed and sensitive connection. The authorial 'I' of Evgeny Onegin is by its convention a free man: his tastes, griefs, adventures may be referred to openly and neutrally. The author of *The Little House* is in terms of its convention a haunted man. Instead of being separated from the frothy tale and appearing in exclamations about former days and the seriousness that follows laughter, the idea of 'no joking matter' is now integrated into the tale's narrative perspective, its wry uncertainty. The author is both involved and detached; he has his wounding memories, and yet the characters of his story were seen by him only through a window or when he attended church. The tale's inconsequence faithfully reflects the lack of any continuous relation with them.

They have the vividness of a picture studied from well back, and the author tells us that he has seen a hundred times figures like his old widow in the portraits of Rembrandt. He is seeing them from a very different perspective from that which Evgeny in *The Bronze Horseman* desperately imagined two very similar people (the daughter's name Parasha is common to both poems) but he too is seeing them from a distance and in a kind of dream. The author's dream likes to play round the picture of Parasha and her mother leading their quiet life in Kolomna. All depends on the angle of vision, and here again we have a clue to Pushkin's comment on such a poem as 'no joking matter'.

> Зимою ставни закрывались рано,
> Но летом до́ ночи растворено
> Всё было в доме. Бледная Диана
> Глядела долго девушке в окно.
> (Без этого ни одного романа
> Не обойдется; так заведено!)

Бывало, мать давным-давно храпела,
А дочка – на луну еще смотрела

И слушала мяуканье котов
По чердакам, свиданий знак нескромный,
Да стражи дальный крик, да бой часов –
И только. Ночь над мирною Коломной
Тиха отменно. Редко из домов
Мелькнут две тени. Сердце девы томной
Ей слышать было можно, как оно
В упругое толкалось полотно.

In winter the shutters were closed early, but in summer all the house was open to the night. Pale Diana gazed long on the young girl in the window. (No novel could do without this; so it is decreed.) And so it chanced that when the mother had long been snoring the daughter still gazed at the moon and heard the mewing of tom-cats on the tiles, the indication of some shameless encounter, the distant cry of the watch, the striking of the hours – and that was all. The night is wonderfully calm in peaceful Kolomna. Occasionally two shadowy forms glimmered forth from houses. In her lassitude the girl could hear her heart nudge the yielding cloth of her bodice.[1]

The run on between the stanzas is admirable, as are the stops in mid-line which suggest in depth the monotony of the scene as in a novel of Balzac. The moon watches the girl as the poet watches her in memory: the parenthesis shows the widening gap between the author as a brooding Jamesian *conscience* and as the facetious poetic commentator on a non-tale, a parody of an event. This commentator tells the 'Beppoid' tale which acts as a stalking horse for the real preoccupation of his colleague, which delares itself at the beginning of stanza 21, introduced by the visits of mother and daughter to church.

Туда, я помню, ездила всегда
Графиня...(звали как, не помню, право)
Она была богата, молода;

There, I recall, a countess always came in her carriage...(what her name was I really don't know). She was rich, young;

[1] There is no doubt that Pushkin is 'parodying' here the concluding lines of his own sequence of Tatyana and her nurse in the moonlight in *Evgeny Onegin*. A cancelled variant of those lines – 'and everything slept in the stillness beneath the inspiring moon' – reads: 'and all was silent; under the moon only a cat mewed by the window'. The same kinds of zestful and delicate manipulation of the tones of art can be found by an English reader everywhere in Chaucer – compare the Miller's 'low' parody, in his tale, of lines in the *Knight's Tale* which are themselves stylishly and sympathetically parodic. Chaucer and Pushkin share to a remarkable extent the same pleasure in compounding and adjusting stock effects.

The 'I' who remembers here, sensed an intriguing melancholy behind the proud bearing of the countess to whom he never spoke; and the interest with which he studied her must only have produced, as he now realises, her mechanical reaction to yet another obvious admirer. The persona of this countess could be related to the married Tatyana, and to Donna Anna of *The Stone Guest*, while Gershenzon was no doubt right that Pushkin summons up here the memory of an actual *grande dame* whom he used to see when he lived in Kolomna. It is more important, though, that Pushkin has taken a hint from *Beppo* and used it in a very unBeppo-like fashion.

> I've seen some balls and revels in my time,
> And stayed them over for some silly reason,
> And then I looked (I hope it was no crime)
> To see what lady best stood out the season...
> I never saw but one (the stars withdrawn)
> Whose bloom could after dancing dare the dawn.
>
> The name of this Aurora I'll not mention,
> Although I might, for she was naught to me
> More than that patent work of God's invention,
> A charming woman whom we like to see;
> But writing names would merit reprehension...

The woman who was naught to Byron is a good deal to the Jamesian speculator, brooding over and shaping his memories. The idea of a Beppo tale with a lighthearted surface and a wry, unappeased undercurrent of emotion, with two distinct narrative tones instead of digressions, begins to take on a functional possibility. But unfortunately there is no more to be done with the countess. The Jamesian recollector disappears, and the Beppo commentator can only use her for a series of sententious comparisons with Parasha, comparisons where Pushkin may have intended to impress the journalists with his preference for simple, unfashionable topics and people, but which only strike the reader as a new version of an old cliché.

> Блаженнее стократ ее была,
> Читатель, новая знакомка ваша,
> Простая, добрая моя Параша.

Our new acquaintance, the simple and good Parasha, was a hundred times more fortunate than her, reader.

We hear no more of the countess, and the rest of the tale is a brilliant exercise in *ottava rima* narration, brisk, witty, and economical. The old cook dies; Parasha sets out to engage a new one, and returns with a tall awkward girl who seems to know nothing of household matters but is modest, quiet, and cheap. At church next Sunday the widow is assailed by a sudden fear that the new servant may have stayed at home to steal: she runs home and finds her shaving in Parasha's mirror. The servant vanishes – did Parasha blush? 'I know nothing more.' 'You mean that's all? What about a moral?' 'There is none – or rather yes there is. Wait a moment.' The moral of course is that shaving is not suited to female servants who, besides, should not be engaged for nothing.

Though the adventure of the new cook is as spirited as the *Beppo* recognition scene, *The Little House* cannot be called a masterpiece by Pushkinian standards. The word is no doubt as beside the point as the complaints of the imaginary reader (and the actual critics) about the story's pointlessness, but Pushkin is the kind of artist who cannot but invoke even in a *jeu d'esprit* the logic and the shapeliness of great art. *Count Nulin*, written five years earlier, has these on its small scale as much as *Evgeny Onegin* on its wider one, and so have the *Skazki*. But *The Little House* is filled with suggestions and loose ends which it does not help to explain away as an aspect of its genre, for the fact is that neither stanza nor genre really suited Pushkin. The swinging knockabout satire that Byron commands is not his forte, and the alliance he tacitly invokes – between two gentlemen and men of the world against the scribbling tribe – proved unworkable. Haunted memories, farce, polemic chat, make uneasy bedfellows in the poem, and cannot be synergised like the equally heterogeneous elements in *Evgeny Onegin*. In modifying the *Beppo* technique Pushkin has not really transformed it, and *The Little House* is his only poem in which modification and paraphrase of a source does not yield a commensurate gain.

In *Count Nulin*, on the other hand, a notion from Pushkin's reading of Shakespeare had been worked up into a triumphant success. Annenkov first recorded a note of Pushkin's in which the idea of doing a parody of *The Rape of Lucrece* is mentioned. He had been working on the fourth chapter of *Evgeny Onegin*, and *Count Nulin* is virtually a comic transposition of the Lucrece situation into the world of the Larins: we can imagine the heroine and her husband attending Tatyana's name-day feast. Pushkin had found Shakespeare's poem 'pretty feeble' – its conceits are certainly tedious in French prose – but the idea of a different outcome to Tarquin's advances appealed to him. If Lucrece had resisted

Tarquin's advances would the course of history have been changed? It is clear from Pushkin's note that he does not take the idea very seriously; indeed the idea itself is included in the parody by being embodied in the comical and comfortable disorder of a *pomeshchik*'s household. Tarquin is a Frenchified Russian nobleman from Paris; Lucrece a plump, amiable and animated wife, whose husband is just setting off for the hunting-field as the poem opens on a late autumn morning.

> Выходит барин на крыльцо,
> Всё, подбочась, обозревает;
> Его довольное лицо
> Приятной важностью сияет.

The master comes to the porch and surveys the scene, hand on hip; his satisfied face gleams with engaging self-importance. (iv, 237.)

Nothing even in *Evgeny Onegin* is so electrically charged with life as the beginning of *Count Nulin*. The expectant huntsmen, their master, his appurtenances: all are swept before us on the invigorating gale of Pushkin's octosyllabics. Then they are away, and for the rest of the poem we are completely absorbed into the static world of the mistress of the house. Her boredom is not like that of Onegin, playing billiards all day and waiting for the moment of dinner. It is an endlessly diverted and distracted boredom, in which one incident leads to another like a visual equivalent of the conversation of Jane Austen's Miss Bates.

> Наталья Павловна сначала
> Его внимательно читала,
> Но скоро как-то развлеклась
> Перед окном возникшей дракой
> Козла с дворовою собакой
> И ею тихо занялась.
> Кругом мальчишки хохотали.
> Меж тем печально, под окном,
> Индейки с криком выступали
> Вослед за мокрым петухом;
> Три утки полоскались в луже;
> Шла баба через грязный двор
> Белье повесить на забор;
> Погода становилась хуже:
> Казалось, снег идти хотел...
> Вдруг колокольчик зазвенел.

Natalia Pavlovna began to read it [a sentimental novel] attentively, but was soon distracted by the battle below her windows of a billy-goat with a watch-dog, and watched it with silent absorption. Urchins were laughing around them; and meanwhile under the window turkey-hens uttering their mournful cries were running round after the bedraggled cock. Three ducks were dabbling themselves in the pond; an old woman crossed the muddy yard to hang washing on the fence; the weather didn't look so good – it might even be going to snow...Suddenly a carriage bell could be heard jingling.

A bell! A carriage! Count Nulin, his conveyance in need of repair, presents himself. Natalia Pavlovna bubbles over with excitement at this unexpected treat, the thrill of supping with the Count and discussing the fashions and theatres of Paris, and her vivacity is misinterpreted by the Count, who is not innocently self-satisfied like Natalia's husband, but merely conceited. In bed that night, and supplied by his valet with an uncut novel, a glass in a silver holder, a cigar, a bronze candle-stick and snuffer, and an alarm clock (properties that directly correspond with the heroic appurtenances that decked the *Barin* as he set out for the hunt) he asks himself whether he could be in love; in an early draft Onegin had asked himself the same question about Tatyana over his bedside Walter Scott.

But Onegin is the hero of a novel of sentiment. He is incapable of action, comic action least of all, and it was perhaps as a relief from the atmosphere of one kind of parody that Pushkin took a brief holiday with another and abandoned Sterne for the world of Fielding and Lesage. The Count snuffs out his candle and falls to reflecting on the charms of his hostess. The recollection of them excites him so much that he puts on his silk dressing-gown, and accidentally knocking over a chair in the dark, fumbles his way with very unTarquinian strides to his hostess's bedroom door. Waking with a start to find him at the foot of her bed she gives a shriek, boxes his ear, and sends him fleeing back to his room. The atmosphere next morning is at first constrained, but soon she is chattering gaily, and the outraged Count thaws, responds, and is on the verge of becoming amorous all over again when the husband returns from the hunting field. The worthy squire is as delighted as his wife to find company, but Nulin declines his warm invitation to stay.

> Когда коляска ускакала,
> Жена всё мужу рассказала
> И подвиг графа моего
> Всему соседству описала.

Но кто же более всего
С Натальей Павловной смеялся?
Не угадать вам. Почему ж?
Муж? – Как не так. Совсем не муж.
Он очень этим оскорблялся,
Он говорил, что граф дурак,
Молокосос; что если так,
То графа он визжать заставит,
Что псами он его затравит.
Смеялся Лидин, их сосед,
Помещик двадцати трех дет.

Теперь мы можем справедливо
Сказать, что в наши времена
Супругу верная жена,
Друзья мои, совсем не диво.

When the carriage had departed the wife told her husband everything
and described the Count's action for the benefit of all the neighbours.
And who had the biggest chuckle over it with Natalia Pavlovna? Can
you guess – why then? The husband? Oh no. By no means the husband.
He was considerably put out, and said that the Count was a clown and a
milksop, and that if he had been there he would have set the dogs on
him and made him squeal. The man who laughed most was Lidin, their
neighbour, a twenty-three year old landowner.

Now we must say, in all fairness, that in our age, my friends, a wife
faithful to her husband is not altogether a prodigy.

Nadezhdin deprecated the 'low and immoral' tone of *Count
Nulin* in the review he wrote at the time, while admitting its
excellence as a piece of 'Flemish genre painting'. Belinsky praised
it, in the same terms as *The Little House at Kolomna*, as a pioneering
work of Russian realism. With the growth of Pushkinolatry the
usual deeper meanings were discovered in it, and several critics
have linked its composition with that of *Boris Godunov*. Gukovsky
stresses the interest in historical causation which the study of the
source material for his play had awoken in Pushkin, and sees *Count
Nulin* as a diversion on this theme in terms of place and custom.
Pushkin's Lucrece is fully of her time and place: her conditioning
and class determine her actions – both the rebuff she gives to the
Count and her implied affair with a young squire of the neighbourhood.[1] Female virtue is an aspect of social relation and context, as

---

[1] In a commentary in Vengerov's edition of Pushkin's works P. Morozov first
stressed the significance of the Shakespeare parallel, and Eykhenbaum
pointed out the further link with a fantasy of Küchelbecker's on Shakespearean themes. 'O zamysle "Grafa Nulina"', *Vremmenik Pushkinskoy
Komissii*, III (1937).

Pushkin's conclusion equivocally emphasises, and not something to be measured in absolute terms. There is a good deal in this, though like most extrapolations of Pushkinian 'meaning' it ignores the actual and peculiar art of the poem. The hint of a relation between Natalia Pavlovna and young Lidin is not a blanket generalisation about the habits of her class, but refers to her alone, as a specific and individual character. The sudden perspective of unexplored possibility that Pushkin opens up at the end of the poem is typical of his method, and might be compared with the role of the countess in *The Little House* and – still more – with the buried idyll of Parasha and her disguised admirer, to which Pushkin only refers by remarking that the new cook got everything wrong in spite of all Parasha's efforts to help and instruct her. In the mutual entertainment of Natalia Pavlovna and Lidin, as in the unspecified manœuvres of the widow's daughter, we glimpse a private and intimate world that seems – because of the privacy in which art has left it – as innocent as the world of Ferdinand and Miranda in *The Tempest*. Pushkin has deliberately hidden it from our open scrutiny, and hence from our judgement and our generalisation. Neither poem has any of the grossness of farce.

The glimpse left to the imagination in both is a link between them, but though both have the air of a light-hearted *fabliau* they are really very different from each other. A metre for Pushkin was not only a form to be explored but a different mode of being, and the joyous tone of *Count Nulin*, its supple and merry octosyllabics, is far removed from that of the octaves of *The Little House*, which are at once self-regarding and – for Pushkin – curiously diffident. He never quite came to terms with the pure octave, but three years after *The Little House* he triumphantly modified its metre to produce one of his finest poems, the 'fragment' *Autumn (Osen)*, in which the last traces of the Byronic manner have been totally subdued to Pushkin's own personality. Among other things it is Pushkin's only poem about writing poetry, a sudden and marvellous disclosure of the feel of the Boldino autumn, upon which he had come to depend for the delivery of what he called his *dryan*, the 'load of rubbish' which under these conditions he could produce with such extraordinary rapidity.

The tone of *Osen* combines unbuttoned ease with something of the more formal and musical intimacy of Leopardi's *Sempre caro mi fu quest'ermo colle...*

PUSHKIN

Унылая пора! очей очарованье,
Приятна мне твоя прощальная краса –

Melancholy season! Enchanting to the eye, your valedictory beauty
delights me – (III, 262.)

It has the always faintly wistful delicacy of an exquisite miniature,
and yet the spacious and comfortable interior of a long conversational poem. Yeats and Valéry are also masters of this peculiar
kind of formal/informal genre, joining the note of conversation to
a fine eloquence and elegance of phrase and metaphor, but neither
quite fuses the two into one with the ease Pushkin seems to. Leopardi is much the closest parallel, even though his meticulous
despair is the antithesis of Pushkin's passionate enjoyment of the
season which brings him inspiration and resource.

The metre brings together the octave's jaunty rhyming continuity and the lyric and elegiac possibilities of the alexandrine.
Feminine and masculine endings alternate, each stanza consisting
of three lines rhyming on each, and a couplet which may be either.
Pushkin thus exploits to the full the Russian resources in feminine
rhymes, achieving both the harmony of eleven and twelve syllable
lines, and a formal variation, like a Mozart harmony, between
stanza patterns of 11–12–11 or 12–11–12, using the former mostly
for description and metaphor and the latter for explanation and
confidences. The opening stanza is full of the movement and also
the stillness of autumn:

Октябрь уж наступил – уж роща отряхает
Последние листы с нагих своих ветвей;
Дохнул осенний хлад, дорога промерзает.
Журча еще бежит за мельницу ручей,
Но пруд уже застыл; сосед мой поспешает
В отъезжие поля с охотою своей,
И страждут озими от бешеной забавы,
И будит лай собак уснувшие дубравы.

October is here already – the grove is already casting the last leaves
from its bare branches. The autumn cold has breathed, the road begins
to freeze; the stream still runs murmuring beyond the mill, but ice has
formed already on the mill-pond; my neighbour with his pack hastens
to the hunting fields; the winter crops suffer from the furious sport, and
the hounds' baying arouses the sleeping woods.

The caesura is used in the fifth line to arrest the movement, as the
ice grips the pond, and then it breaks out again in the wild anima-

tion of the hunt. In the eighth stanza we have the alternative pattern:

> И с каждой осенью я расцветаю вновь;
> Здоровью моему полезен русский холод;
> К привычкам бытия вновь чувствую любовь:
> Чредой слетает сон, чредой находит голод;
> Легко и радостно играет в сердце кровь,
> Желания кипят – я снова счастлив, молод,
> Я снова жизни полн – таков мой организм
> (Извольте мне простить ненужный прозаизм).

And every autumn I blossom anew; the Russian cold suits my constitution; once more I enjoy the habits of ordinary life: in due time and order comes sleep, comes hunger; lightly and joyfully the blood sports in my heart, desires seethe – I am once again happy, young; I am full of life once more – such is my organism (if you will be good enough to excuse me this needlessly prosaic term).

There is a remarkable contrast between the Byronic traces in this octave and those in *The Little House*. Instead of the straightforward borrowing of the Byronic idiom we have a parody of it, a lyric enthusiasm that carries the poet away and then recalls him and the reader – in a conspiracy of amusement – to the mock apology of the concluding line. So the poem moves up to its climax, the moment when the physical sense of heightened life, and of unity with the expectant fertility of the season, will disappear into literature, into the creation of a poem.

> И забываю мир – и в сладкой тишине
> Я сладко усыплен моим воображеньем,
> И пробуждается поэзия во мне:
> Душа стесняется лирическим волненьем,
> Трепещет и звучит, и ищет, как во сне,
> Излиться наконец свободным проявленьем –
> И тут ко мне идет незримый рой гостей,
> Знакомцы давние, плоды мечты моей.
>
> И мысли в голове волнуются в отваге,
> И рифмы легкие навстречу им бегут,
> И пальцы просятся к перу, перо к бумаге,
> Минута – и стихи свободно потекут.
> Так дремлет недвижим корабль в недвижной влаге,
> Но чу – матросы вдруг кидаются, ползут
> Вверх, вниз – и паруса надулись, ветра полны;
> Громада двинулась и рассекает волны.
>
> Плывет. Куда ж нам плыть?...
>   . . . .

And I forget the world – and in the dulcet silence I am sweetly lulled by my imagination, and poetry awakens within me: my soul is seized by lyric excitement, it stirs and murmurs, and seeks, as in a dream, to release itself at last in free expression – and now towards me comes an invisible throng of guests, old acquaintances, the products of my fancy.

And thoughts swirl with audacity in my head, and airy rhymes run to meet them, and fingers beg a pen, the pen paper, a minute – and verses flow freely forth. Thus sleeps a ship motionless on still waters, but look – the sailors suddenly jump to it, race up and down the rigging, and the sails swell, filled by the wind – the great bulk moves and cleaves the waves.

It sails. Where then shall we sail?...

The image of the becalmed ship, breaking out into a bustle of movement as she sets sail, parallels in metaphor the first stanza's picture of the freezing pond, and the wild zest of dogs and huntsmen.

Osen is Pushkin's most remarkable example of the calculated fragment, shaped to underline the completion and harmony of its theme by its air of breaking off where a theme is about to begin. This both echoes *Tristram Shandy* and carries to a logical conclusion the comic structure of the *Beppo* poem, advertised by Byron as a story which never gets started and is no story at all; but it transcends the limitations of that genre by merging its genial, unpoetical intercourse between poet and reader into the isolation of lyric and elegy, in which the poet is alone and indifferent to his audience. *Beppo* poems play with the topics of poetry, and it is essential to the effect of hushed and expectant isolation at the end of *Osen* that these topics should be present only by implication. Originally Pushkin had a stanza between the last two complete ones, describing with a whimsical orgy of detail 'the old acquaintances and products of my fancy': knights in armour, Spaniards in cloaks, captive princesses and evil giants, and mistresses with smooth foreheads and yearning eyes. He even continued the final stanza in rough draft, specifying some of the romantic countries he might 'sail' to:

> Ура!...куда же плыть?...какие берега
> Теперь мы посетим: Кавказ ли колоссальный,
> Иль опаленные Молдавии луга,
> Иль скалы дикие Шотландии печальной...

Hurrah!...where to sail then?...what shores shall we now visit: the towering Caucasus, or the parched steppes of Moldavia, or the wild cliffs of gloomy Scotland...

These stanzas show us how close the poem in its first inspiration was to the mere exuberance of a minor occasional poem. Only when Pushkin had written it, most likely, did its real pattern emerge for him, as the pattern of *Evgeny Onegin* revealed itself on its greater scale.[1] And as Onegin's journey turned out to be only an excrescence, outside the bounds of the true novel, so the possible fields of poetic inspiration (referred to in any case with Pushkin's customary lack of seriousness) were outside the world of the poem that had come into being, the world of autumnal expectancy, when nature falls asleep and the poet wakes.

The poem dies, its span completed: its beauty is that of a matrix from which other poems will be born. The last half-line tempers the expectation and excitement of the preceding stanzas with a touch of wry melancholy, the breath of mortality in the moment of creation. *Dokhnul osenny khlad* – the autumn chill breathes in the unfinished line as at the opening, giving the poem as a 'fragment' the symmetry it would have lacked if Pushkin had retained the omitted stanzas. The weighty satisfaction in *plyv*yot, completing the onomatopoeia of *ploy*, turns into the plangent resonance of the infinitive form *Kuda zh nam plyt?* ... – a remarkable contrast to the cheerful bustle of departure in the first draft. Though the melancholy is stylised, and has more of eighteenth-century elegance than romantic longing, Pushkin's query has something of the same measured balance as the line of consummation in the last stanza of Keats's *Ode to Autumn*: 'or sinking as the light wind lives or dies', and Keats's alteration of the line, by the substitution of 'or' for 'and', was in its way as decisive as Pushkin's breaking-off in achieving the implied balance between life and death, fulfilment and extinction.

When it modulates from the confiding innocence and exuberance of converse to the solitary voice of Lyric (a feat, incidentally, which seems so natural to Pushkin that we may forget no other poet of the time can do it with a comparable ease and grace[2]), the span of *Osen*

---

[1] 'Not to read life's novel to the end but all at once to part with it' is a pattern for Pushkinian endings, and a part of the logic of not 'spelling it out'. It would hardly be too much to say that he inaugurates a tradition of Russian fictional endings (compare those of *War and Peace* and *Resurrection*) which imply a kind of suspension before further impending and implied development – Eykhenbaum in his formalist criticism is continually preoccupied with the notion of such 'endings'.

[2] Keats perhaps comes closest in *Sleep and Poetry* and the *Epistle to Reynolds*, but Keats's tone is more artlessly confiding, as if the lyric passages were a demonstration of the poetic immaturity he feels.

recalls the finest of Pushkin's love poems, written three years before, *Dla beregov otchizny dalnoy* (*For the shores of your distant country*). The poem is in memory of Amalia Riznich, who had died of consumption in Italy, and it gives a great intensity of feeling to an utterance that is soberly impartial and retrospective. Its words seem to wonder at the strength of the emotion they display: they exhibit a wondering curiosity as far removed from the commonplace note of bitter-sweet recollection as from the immediacy of the remarkable lyric of physical passion written in the same year *Net, ya ne dorozhu myatezhnim naslazhdenem* (*No, I do not treasure that frenzied enjoyment*):

> Для берегов отчизны дальной
> Ты покидала край чужой;
> В час незабвенный, в час печальный
> Я долго плакал пред тобой.
> Мои хладеющие руки
> Тебя старались удержать;
> Томленья страшного разлуки
> Мой стон молил не прерывать.
>
> Но ты от горького лобзанья
> Свои уста оторвала;
> Из края мрачного изгнанья
> Ты в край иной меня звала.
> Ты говорила: «В день свиданья
> Под небом вечно голубым,
> В тени олив, любви лобзанья
> Мы вновь, мой друг, соединим».
>
> Но там, увы, где неба своды
> Сияют в блеске голубом,
> Где тень олив легла на воды,
> Заснула ты последним сном.
> Твоя краса, твои страданья
> Исчезли в урне гробовой —
> А с ними поцелуй свиданья...
> Но жду его; он за тобой...

For the shores of your distant country you were leaving a foreign land. In an hour unforgotten, in an hour of sadness, I wept long before you. My stiffening hands tried to keep you; my cry besought you not to break off the terrible anguish of parting.

But you plucked your lips away from our bitter embrace; from a land of dismal exile you called me to another land. You said: 'In the day of our meeting again, in the shade of the olive beneath a sky always blue, we shall once more, my darling, join in a kiss of love.'

But there, alas, where the arch of the sky shines radiantly blue, where the shadow of the olive trees lies on the waters, you are sleeping the last sleep. Your beauty and your sufferings have vanished in the tomb – and with them the kiss of our meeting...But I still wait for it; it is due from you... (III, 204.)

The poem begins by reproducing the anguished clumsiness of an actual parting, with a kind of attentive detachment. In the second stanza it is the imagination which supplies what is said, and which relieves with the expedients of literature the raw confusion of a real moment, but it does not hide the true and pitiful subterfuges of leave-taking: that we shall meet again and everything will be wonderful. The simple vocabulary of blue skies is as moving as a popular song, and for that reason begins to generalise a unique experience into that of all lovers. The Mediterranean as the place where lovers meet is – as in Mignon's song from Goethe's *Wilhelm Meister, Kennst du das Land wo die Zitronen blühn?* – a part of the romanticism of the age, but in Pushkin the single image of the olive tree's shadow on the water is enough to suggest the whole southern landscape. The fourth line in each stanza is like a bell, tolling in the first and third with its impartial memorial of fact, pealing with illusory hope in the second. His expedient in the last line echoes hers in the second verse: she tried to soften the parting with the hope of meeting again, and his voice in the fifth and seventh lines of the last stanza echoes her high hapless syllables to answer them in the deep tones of the sixth and eighth. (Because of a mistake in the MS of Pushkin's amendment to them, some editions print the draft version of the last two lines:

> Но сладкий поцелуй свиданья...
> Его я жду; он за тобой...

But the sweet kiss of our meeting...I wait for it: it is due from you...

– but the movement of the last line, as a contrast to its predecessor, is surely perfected by Pushkin's correction.)

The more we read Pushkin's finest lyrics in his later period, the more we feel in them the same kinds of organisation that the longer poems possess. In the shorter poems this involves a hidden separation between lyric statement of subjective and emotional intensity, and the other level of implied and oblique objective comment – the poet both feels and watches himself feeling. In one of his last great short poems, the magnificent paraphrase of Horace's *Exegi*

monumentum written in 1836, the process seems to become almost
sardonically explicit. Pushkin is following Derzhavin's version,
itself based on Lomonosov's original Russian translation, and the
two poems make a contrast so revealing that it is worth quoting
them in full. Here is Derzhavin's:

Я памятник себе воздвиг чудесный, вечный,
Металлов тверже он и выше пирамид;
Ни вихрь его, ни гром не сломит быстротечный,
И времени полет его не сокрушит.

Так! – весь я не умру, но часть меня большая,
От тлена убежав, по смерти станет жить,
И слава возрастет моя, не увядая,
Доколь славянов род вселенна будет чтить.

Слух пройдет обо мне от Белых вод до Черных,
Где Волга, Дон, Нева, с Рифея льет Урал;
Всяк будет помнить то в народах неисчетных,
Как из безвестности я тем известен стал,

Что первый я дерзнул в забавном русском слоге
О добродетелях Фелицы возгласить,
В сердечной простоте беседовать о Боге
И истину царям с улыбкой говорить.

О муза! возгордись заслугой справедливой,
И презрит кто тебя, сама тех презирай;
Непринужденною рукой неторопливой
Чело твое зарей бессмертия венчай.

I have raised up for myself a monument, wondrous, everlasting; it is
stronger than metal and higher than the pyramids; neither whirlwind
nor sudden thunderbolt shall shatter it, nor the flight of time cast it
down.

And so! – not all of me shall die, but a great part of me, escaping
corruption, shall live after death, and my glory – unfading – grow as
long as the Slavic race is held by all in honour.

My fame shall travel from the White Sea to the Black, where the
Volga, Don, Neva flow, and the Ural from the Riphean mountains.
Throughout unnumbered peoples it shall be remembered how I rose
from obscurity into fame,

How I presumed, the first, to proclaim Felitsa's virtues in the style of
Russian comedy, to speak of God in heartfelt simplicity, and to tell truth
to kings with a smile.

O Muse! Glory in your righteous desert, and you yourself scorn anyone who may scorn you; with unconstrained, deliberate hand, garland
your brow with the dawn of immortality.

And Pushkin's:

Я памятник себе воздвиг нерукотворный,
К нему не зарастет народная тропа,
Вознесся выше он главою непокорной
Александрийского столпа.

Нет, весь я не умру – душа в заветной лире
Мой прах переживет и тленья убежит –
И славен буду я, доколь в подлунном мире
Жив будет хоть один пиит.

Слух обо мне пройдет по всей Руси великой,
И назовет меня всяк сущий в ней язык,
И гордый внук славян, и финн, и ныне дикий
Тунгус, и друг степей калмык.

И долго буду тем любезен я народу,
Что чувства добрые я лирой пробуждал,
Что в мой жестокий век восславил я свободу
И милость к падшим призывал.

Веленью божию, о муза, будь послушна,
Обиды не страшась, не требуя венца;
Хвалу и клевету приемли равнодушно,
И не оспоривай глупца.

I have raised up to myself a monument not built with hands, and to it the path trodden by the people will not be overgrown; it has raised its unsubmissive head higher than Alexander's column.

No, I shall not wholly die – the spirit in my sacred lyre shall outlive my dust and escape corruption – and I shall be famous as long as one single poet lives still in the sublunary world.

Tidings about me shall pass throughout all great Russia, and all peoples living in her shall name my name: both the proud descendant of Slavs, the Finn, and the now wild Tungus, and the Kalmuk, the friend of the steppes.

For long shall I be dear to the people, because noble feelings I awoke with my lyre, because in my cruel age I glorified freedom and called for mercy on the fallen.

To the commandment of God, O Muse, lend an obedient ear; fearing no insult, demanding no crown, receive indifferently both praise and slander, and do not quarrel with a fool. (III, 373.)[1]

Both superb poems celebrate their authors' pride in doing what Horace had done. Derzhavin joins his fame with that of his

[1] The end of the first stanza could also read 'the Alexandrian column', i.e. the Pharos of ancient Alexandria. Pushkin probably intended the equivocation, but there is no doubt that he had in mind the monument to Alexander I in St Petersburg.

imperial mistress. His monumental lines express and embody the pride of the new empire as unmistakably as Catherine's statue of Peter the Great, her palaces and art collection and the pantheon to her generals in Tsarskoe Selo. The peoples of the empire will remember the poet as they celebrate the emergence of the power with which he is identified – *kak iz bezvestnosti* – the resounding line heralding the gesture of the Muse, garlanding her brow like a national statue.

In his first stanza Pushkin dissociates himself from the stone and marble of the imperial achievement; but he slyly sees and raises the nationalistic claim – he will be known so long as any poet remains in the world. Derzhavin evokes the geography of power and space: Pushkin the peoples who fill it – various, uncouth, steppe-loving not empire-worshipping. He will be loved by the people, for his liberal thought, for his pleas for the defeated Decembrists. The fourth stanza is, significantly, the weakest in the poem: the sudden localisation of its claim after the magnificent deliberation of the previous line (the most Horatian of the poem) does not quite come off, but it is in a sense a stand-in for the original version of the stanza, which made an explicit though oblique reference to Derzhavin's praise of Catherine.

И долго буду тем любезен я народу,
Что звуки новые для песен я обрел,
Что вслед Радищеву восславил я свободу
И милосердие воспел.

And for long I shall be dear to the people, because I found out new harmonies for my songs; because, following the example of Radishchev, I glorified freedom, and celebrated in song the merciful in heart.

Radishchev, the eccentric author of the outspoken *Journey from Petersburg to Moscow*, and himself a poet of no mean talent, was one of the martyrs of Catherine's reign, in which he had been exiled to Siberia, being only fully rehabilitated by Alexander I. To this point the Ode, which was not published in Pushkin's lifetime, fully justifies the encomiums of latter-day critics on his *narodnost* and his measured hostility to the imperial regime. But in the last stanza the claims of the poet, though not deflated, are quietly set aside. It is not for the Muse to accept the crown of the people's poet, to engage in polemic or to argue with fools – even, perhaps, with fools who assert their immortality whether in stone or bronze or poetry – and Pushkin characteristically avails himself in his final line of a precept that had appealed to him in some rendering of the Koran.

Burtsev and Nabokov have suggested that the first four stanzas should be in inverted commas, but this would replace the deadpan gravity of Pushkinian equivocation with the open irony of – for example – Horace's famous second Epode, *Beatus ille*. It seems to me possible that Pushkin may have taken a hint from this poem, in which the money-lender Appius is discovered in the coda to have uttered its fine panegyric on rural happiness. Even there the sincerity of Horace's usurer is no more in question than the sincerity of Pushkin's poet, for Derzhavin in his sonorous ode is Derzhavin himself, while Pushkin, as so often, is not so much Pushkin but Pushkin as poet. And in this he resembles Shakespeare, whose paraphrase of Horace in the Sonnets is stylised and impersonalised by being set in the convention of another's interest. For Shakespeare it is the loved one ('O none, unless this miracle have might / That in black ink my love may still shine bright'), for Pushkin the immortal powers, who are as indifferent to the poet's fame as he himself should be to the fools who award or withhold it.

Such a miracle, as Pushkin reminds us, comes within the province of the Almighty, to whom poets are as subject as emperors. It is fitting that in one of his last poems the great national poet should seem to dissociate himself from the more idolatrous manifestations of his own impending national status.

7

PROSE

The spurt of creation in the Boldino autumn of 1830 produced both
the *Little Tragedies* and the *Tales of Belkin*, Pushkin's first considered and completed venture into prose, which were published
anonymously in the following year. Perfection of expression in the
Little Tragedies, as in Shakespeare's mature style, seems merely the
perfection of human speech, poetry which is like 'a gum which
oozes from whence 'tis nourished', as the poet says in *Timon of
Athens*. We are not specially conscious of their being written in
poetry, but it is very clear from the first sentence that the *Tales of
Belkin* are written in prose. Every sentence is carefully deprived of
cadence, made flat, transparent, and effective.[1] 'Voltaire may be
regarded as an excellent example of prose style', Pushkin had
written eight years earlier. 'Precision and tidiness are the prime
merits of prose...poetry is another business. Whose prose is the
best in our literature? Karamzin's. This is no great praise.'[2]

But it was Karamzin and the French authors from whom he had
learnt so much who were Pushkin's models in the *Tales of Belkin*.
He intended them as pilot pieces in the Russian art of the prose
story, and they are exemplary and experimental as *Boris Godunov*
had been and as the *Little Tragedies* were not. Plays and stories
were written together in the same few days, but there is hardly a
link between them; they belong to different worlds. 'No writer of
both prose and verse, in Russia or even in the west', observed
Shevyrev, 'has made such a severe and firm boundary between the
two kinds of utterance.' And this was certainly intentional. The
avant-garde was demanding a new school of Russian prose.
Pushkin's contemporary Bestuzhev made the famous comment:
'A child is attracted by a rattle before he is attracted by a compass
...one has ceased to listen to poetry since everyone became able to

---

[1] Critics (e.g. Lezhnev in *Proza Pushkina*) have established that the phrases of
a sentence bear a marked relation to the length of an octosyllabic line – the
line in which Pushkin must habitually have 'thought' – but none to its
rhythm.

[2] *On Prose*, an unfinished piece. (VII, 14.)

write it...there is a general outcry: "Give us prose – water, plain water!"'

The writer of romance is echoing, strangely enough, the attitude of Bacon and other writers of the later European Renaissance. Remember poetry is the work of a liar, Rapin had said. Separate it, give it its own world of make-believe, cordon it off from the world of fact and from the advancement of true learning. After the great Russian poetic renaissance some such reaction was perhaps inevitable, and in both cases it is hard to say whether the natural authority and confidence of poetry had begun to diminish before the change of attitude, or whether its decline was hastened by compartmentalisation. The Jacobeans who spoke poetry are succeeded by the Augustans who spoke prose; and in Russia the change took place with the foreshortening typical of that astonishingly rapid literary cycle.

Yet Bestuzhev's prose style is very far from being 'plain water': it has all the ebullient expansiveness of the nineteenth century, of the Waverley Novels. These move and operate by sweep and volume, not by any discrimination of sentence or phrase; and Balzac, Dickens, Stendhal and Gogol all in their different ways use the medium of prose abundantly and unselfconsciously. They can be rhapsodical and they can be startling, but all build up their fictions by sheer bulk and flow – they run on. Even Lermontov in *A Hero of Our Time* uses the kind of easy imperfections and clichés that are common to Scott as to Stendhal, and that Pushkin is careful to exclude. His prose sounds prosaic, but never banal.

His prose, too, followed more old-fashioned models than Scott, and already sounded old-fashioned in its time. This was remarked on by his contemporaries, and the *Tales of Belkin* acquired no general popularity even when it was known that Pushkin was their author. It was Mérimée who first took to them and made them known in France by his translations – significantly, for Mérimée was by temperament an antiquarian, a recreator and even a forger of styles and idioms. And he liked economy – the understatement of the ballad, the precision of the anecdote – which in his treatment become distinctly *choses préservées*. Even so, Pushkin's prose was too unexciting for him, and in *Le Coup de Pistolet* (*Vystrel*) and *La Dame de Pique* (*Pikovaya Dama*) he makes attempts to bring out his author. The alteration of tone is revealing, for it shows that in spite of the model and the self-consciousness Pushkin's tone is not really so French after all. Where Mérimée (in his own tales as well as in these translations) is pointed and sprightly, Pushkin is plain and unobtrusive. At the end of *Vystrel* the hero, Silvio, having had his revenge by sparing the young count for the second time in their duel encounter, lets fly at the hole in a picture made by the count's miss. 'He shot at it, almost without seeming to take aim, and disappeared.' Mérimée cannot resist translating: *il doubla ma balle.* We know that Silvio never misses, and the narrator has already noticed the nearly coincident holes in the picture – Mérimée's phrase is sensational for its own sake. In Pushkin the sensationalism is in the tale itself. But Pushkin is equally careful not to exaggerate understatement, as Mérimée clearly piques himself on doing at the end of *Matteo Falcone. Vystrel* ends simply with a report of Silvio's death in action: 'They say that. . . ' (*Skazivayut*), thus adding a fourth, impersonal narrator to the other three through whom the story is told.

The device of multiple narrators, taken up by Lermontov in *A Hero of Our Time*, is the main technical feature of the *Tales of Belkin*. The author is anonymous; he has merely undertaken to arrange the publication of the stories of 'the late Ivan Petrovich Belkin'. He writes to Belkin's heir and next of kin, who turns out never to have met him and refers the editor to a friend, whose letter is then quoted. The portrait of Belkin thus comes to us from the pen of a 'candid and simple' neighbour, who was attached to Ivan Petrovich 'although we did not resemble one another in habits or manner of thinking or character'.

Beside the tales you are pleased to mention in your letter, Ivan Petrovich left several manuscripts, some of which are in my care, the remainder having been used by his housekeeper for a number of domestic purposes. For example all the windows in her quarters were stuck over last winter with the first part of a novel which he did not complete. The tales already mentioned it seems were his first effort, and, as Ivan Petrovich said, it seems they are for the most part true stories which he had heard from various persons. But the proper names in them he mostly made up himself, while the names of big and little villages were taken from our own neighbourhood, for which reason too my own village is mentioned somewhere.[1]

[1] To save lengthy and on the whole unnecessary reduplication, prose quotations will be given in translation. It is true that the flavour of complete stories – in particular *The Queen of Spades* and *The Captain's Daughter* – is almost as impossible to convey in an English translation as that of *Evgeny Onegin*, but extracts in English will usually serve to illustrate critical argument.

A footnote refers to the putative sources of the tales:

In Mr Belkin's MS there is an inscription, in the author's hand, before each story: 'Heard by me from so-and-so' (there follows the rank and title and the initials). We quote for the curious student: 'The Postmaster' was narrated to him by Titular Counsellor A.G.N.; 'The Shot' by Lieutenant I.L.P.; 'The Undertaker' by B.V., shop assistant; 'The Snow-Storm' and 'Mistress into Maid' by Miss K.I.T.

Devices for referring authorship further and further back do not end there, for *The Shot* has three internal narrators, and *The Station-Master* two.

Pushkin's purpose here may have been to secure a sterile field for his prose experiment, without the single narrative tone of most types of anecdote and nouvelle. He may have realised that the narrative mode of *The Negro of Peter the Great* had operated against him, for in that fragment the style takes a colour from whatever circumstances are being described – either the traditional tale of gallantry and intrigue (French) or the local colour of the historical novel (English). The elaborate security measures which hedge about the *Tales of Belkin* defend the work from the intrusion of such recognisable tones: if we hear the echo of one we cannot tell from what direction it comes. Anecdote becomes unpredictable; the stories escape into a dramatic limbo in which elements of parody appear and vanish without the apparent consent or intention of the compiler. The tales thus renew and liberate the form of the pointed anecdote, as the *Little Tragedies* renewed that of the dramatic fragment.

The unnaturalness of prose to Pushkin, which he emphasises like an acquired virtue, makes the process a highly theoretical one; but it can none the less act on later writers, for whom prose has become as native a medium as poetry was to Pushkin, as a salutary reminder of the basis of their craft. Writing to Golokhvastov in 1873 Tolstoy urges a re-reading of the tales: he cannot exaggerate the debt of his own prose technique to their 'beneficent influence'. Yet it was only when Pushkinolatry was well under way that they came to be treated with the same reverence as the rest of his work. Polevoy called the collection 'a farce, tightened into a corset of simplicity without any kind of compassion', and Vyazemsky thought the tales too trivial and too 'quiet', with 'too much suspicion of poetical expression'.

It is true that Pushkin in his poetry uses all the devices of prose narrative naturally and expansively. The 'I's are there, both confirming the impersonal and removing the impression that great trouble has been taken to secure it: the narrative artifice is both unobtrusive and unconstrained. Eykhenbaum, for whom Pushkin as artist was not 'an innovator but a completer' (*ne zachinatel a zavershitel*), feels that his prose remains that of a poet, a synthesis of the same story-telling elements.[1] And yet the difference is surely fundamental, for whatever 'I' is present in Pushkin's poetry – or if none is – he never makes us feel that he is withholding himself: he is too natural a poet to do so. In prose he deliberately seeks the goal of impersonality, and the apparatus of Belkin seems to be constructed so that he can, as it were, get the worst over at once. The devices of multiple narrative, to hedge anonymity about, can be discarded after they have served their purpose. *The Queen of Spades* and *The Captain's Daughter* do not require the artificial aids of Belkin. Yet the development is a secret one. As Lezhnev points out in *Proza Pushkina*, the poetic development is proud and open, dramatically obvious; and Lezhnev comments that the parallel development of two other writers of prose and poetry – Heine and Lermontov – is 'more natural and more typical' than that of Pushkin.

The anonymous external control exercised in Belkin – Polevoy's 'corset' – shuts out the possibility of natural growth, the growth that reveals itself at the conclusion of *Evgeny Onegin*. But this does not mean that Belkin lacks of the warmth of a human presence, though this is by convention that of Titular Counsellor A.G.N., Miss K.I.T., etc. Polevoy was right about the corset but wrong about the absence of 'compassion'. Compassion is there, wherever it comes from. *The Station-Master*, the best of these anecdotes, is full of solicitude for the unfortunate official and – more important – of a kind of surprise, conveyed with admirable drollery, that human nature should turn out so unexpectedly well. The hussar who abducts Dunya, the station-master's daughter, does not desert her but makes her happy; Dunya herself, though unforgiven by her

---

[1] He comments (and it is indeed more of a paradox than he makes it sound) that Pushkin creates his prose on the basis of his verse, but that it is never 'poetic prose', like that of Bestuzhev and Gogol. *Count Nulin, The Little House in Kolomna*, and *Evgeny Onegin* itself, are on the road to prose as regards subject-matter, and the four-stress iambic line (so unlike the 'musical' verse of the Romantics) provides the foundation for a sober and 'classic' prose rhythm. Eykhenbaum analyses very interestingly the phrase structure of the opening of *Vystrel* and of the fragment *Tsesar puteshestvoval* (*Caesar was on a journey*). B. M. Eykhenbaum, 'Problemy poetiki Pushkina', in *Pushkin–Dostoevsky*, ed. A. L. Volynsky (Petrograd 1921).

father, does not forget him but comes to kneel by his grave. Polevoy presumably wanted the 'compassion' that had made Moscow weep buckets over Karamzin's tale of *Poor Liza*: Pushkin's tale not only implies an ironic comment on its predecessor but supplies solicitude of a more discriminating kind.

It also contains a more elaborate element of parody. As earlier readers must have spotted, and Gershenzon convincingly demonstrated, it reverses the Parable of The Prodigal Son, texts and pictures from which adorn the walls of the station-master's little house. And when Dunya goes off with the hussar her father persists in interpreting the event in the light of the parable. He will search for his 'lost lamb', forgive her and bring her home. When he traces the hussar to Petersburg the trail of the unexpected begins. He begs his daughter to be restored, even though her honour is lost, but the ashamed and yet exasperated young man assures him that Dunya is very well off: 'Why do you want her? She loves me; she has become unaccustomed to her former style of life. And neither you nor she will forget what has happened.' The last sentence goes to the heart of the psychological situation which the Parable necessarily passed over. The young man pushes some notes into the station-master's sleeve which he indignantly throws on the pavement as he walks away. 'After having gone a few steps, he stopped, reflected, and returned...but the notes were no longer there.' A young dandy has picked them up and made off in a cab. As he tells the tale to the Titular Counsellor the old man wipes away his tears, 'tears partly induced by the punch, of which he had drunk five glasses in the course of his narrative, but for all that they moved me deeply'. The final irony is that it is the old man and not his child who goes to the bad. He dies of drink, grieving over the fall of his prodigal daughter, who is bringing up a family in happiness and security.

It is not uninteresting that one of Pushkin's first prose tales should parody the scriptures, as did his early narrative poem the *Gavriliiad*, though far more unobtrusively. Like all Pushkin's parodies it does not deride or belittle the source, but gives it a further dimension of humanity. Satire with Pushkin, as with Fielding, is always a humanising process, but Pushkin never openly makes fun of his target as Fielding made fun of *Pamela*. In *The Snowstorm* the concealed target is the contemporary vogue for tales of romantic elopements and demon bridegrooms, and the narrator – Miss K.I.T. – not only enthusiastically shares the romantic feelings of her hero and heroine, rejoicing in the co-incidence that brings Burmin to the feet of the girl on whom he had played his joke, but also herself seems unconscious of the parallels with Bürger's *Lenore* that are hinted at in the nightmare of the heroine Masha. In Miss K.I.T.'s other story, *Mistress into Maid*, a sentimental pleasure is taken in the fact that the young hero should think of marrying a peasant girl for love; like Darcy and Bingham he is seen from the woman's viewpoint. The shop assistant who is the anecdotalist of *The Undertaker* takes for granted the pride of trade, of securing customers, cheating them, and even feeling a kind of touchy dignity on their behalf after they have been buried.

Yet in none of the *Tales* is there an acoustic presence. The same supple impersonal tone prevails throughout, justified by the con-vention that narratives come to us at two, three or more removes, on both sides of the shadowy raconteurs whose tales were compiled by the comic lay-figure of Ivan Petrovich. We can see traces, it is true, of the Pushkinian dramatic principle that was being em-bodied in the same few weeks in the *Little Tragedies*, the principle he had expressed theoretically in his contrast of the misers of Shakespeare and of Molière. His undertaker, for example, is not all undertaker: he has just bought 'for a considerable sum' a new cottage which he has long desired, but when he enters it 'he was astonished to find his heart did not rejoice'; he pines for his old and squalid and comfortable home; he has the same human instincts as his 'customers', who he has come to assume must want to die and be buried, because it is his business to bury them. And affronted by his friends' lack of respect for the mysteries of his craft he decides to invite to his house-warming party not his prospective live customers but his 'orthodox' dead ones (quite likely a parodic glance at the invitation that Don Juan issues in *The Stone Guest*).

Nothing in the *Little Tragedies* takes place outside the deter-mining structure of the characters' speech and consciousness; and in the *Tales of Belkin* nothing takes place inside them. It is as if Pushkin felt that prose should not commit itself, as dramatic poetry does, to the separate worlds of individuals. The narrators do not impose themselves on their material; the objective reality of things remains alike outside the stories and the individuals in them, as if the resistance of the prose medium was revealed in the resistance of things as they are to the individual's attempt to see them other-wise. The old station-master cannot grasp that events in real life do not follow the traditional pattern of the moral law and the

scriptures. Silvio's determination to impose his will on the indifferent world of fact, represented by the insouciant young count
who insults him and does not take the ensuing duel with a proper
seriousness, is magnificent but futile. Silvio is a mystery man, a
melodramatist cut off from the prosaic world, and sober prose
reveals him as a figure isolated by eccentricity of will from the
reality which it represents.

In Pushkin's prose the world seems alienated from the medium
that describes it by the very operation of that medium. As Lezhnev
puts it, poetry and truth cannot co-exist in this atmosphere; there
is in it 'either mood without nature or nature without mood'. But
because this is not a psychological stance of Pushkin's but a property of the prose virtues he is investigating, we feel none of the
chill that penetrates the meticulous sentences of Flaubert. Silvio
and the station-master are not seen dispassionately, but with
sympathy and understanding as well as humour. The *Tales of Belkin*
are not *contes* like Flaubert's or like Joyce's *Dubliners*, in which the
medium is manipulated with the greatest nicety to produce the required result. Exemplary as they are, there is an element of diffidence
and even evasiveness about them; Pushkin gives the impression of
honouring prose by remaining outside it and not slipping into it
with familiar ease as he slips into the garment of poetry. (Gogol,
who much admired the *Tales*, may be said to have developed this
evasiveness as a professional and personal manner.)

Pushkin only created the figure of Belkin after the tales were
written, as a part of their mechanism of anonymity; but so
promising a figure was he that Pushkin at once went on to write the
History of the Village of Goryukhino, in which Ivan Petrovich
appears in the first person. This brilliant and engaging piece relaxes
all the constriction of the previous tales. We learn how Ivan
Petrovich, after a brief and uneventful army career, enters into his
paternal inheritance and out of boredom (not a Russian Faust's
but rather an Oblomov's) determines to become a writer.

All the kinds of poetry – for I still did not think of humble prose – were
considered and appraised, and I at last opted for an epic poem, drawn
from the history of the fatherland. A hero was not far to seek. I chose
Rurik, and got to work.

The epic hangs fire and is turned into a tragedy, finally into a
ballad, and then discontinued. Ivan Petrovich decides instead on a
series of aphorisms.

Ideas, unfortunately, did not come easily to me, and in two days I produced only the following observation: *The man who does not follow the law of reason but is accustomed to follow the prompting of the passions, often goes astray and condemns himself to remorse at a later date.* This thought is of course a just one, but is hardly new. So abandoning thoughts I turned to tales, but having no experience in creating the events of fiction I chose memorable anecdotes which I had heard at various times from various persons, and I tried to adorn the truth with liveliness of narration and sometimes even with flowers of my own fancy. Little by little I formed my style and learned to express myself correctly, pleasantly and fluently. But soon my supply of tales gave out, and I began to seek another subject for my literary activity.

The subject is history, and Ivan Petrovich is gratified to find that material is available in plenty in his own manor-house, principally in the diary of his great-grandfather.

This [writes Ivan Petrovich] is distinguished by clarity and brevity of style, e.g.:

May 4   Snow. Trishka flogged for insolence.
6   The dun cow fell. Senka flogged for drunkenness.
8   Clear weather.
9   Rain and snow. Trishka flogged because of the weather.
11   Clear weather. Powder snow. Hunted down three hares.

– and so forth, without reflections.

Ivan Petrovich's experiences are a burlesque on Pushkin's own literary progress – both a commentary on the advance towards prose realism and a sly comment on an aspect of that realism. But 'after six whole months of preliminary study' the history is completed, and 'like another historian whose name escapes me' Ivan Petrovich lays down his pen: 'with a kind of sadness I went into my garden to reflect on what I had accomplished'.

Although he cannot remember Gibbon's name, Ivan Petrovich mentions with awe the great Niebuhr and the new school of Russian scientific historians; but the effectiveness of the 'History' does not depend on the fact that Pushkin is parodying the crude imitations of Niebuhr by Polevoy and others. No historical survey evades the scope of Pushkin's deadpan humour, because this is how all historians have to see their subject. They can only render things and events by convention and notation, reconstructing human actions, whether isolated or repetitive, from back to front. 'To be the judge, observer, and prophet of centuries and of peoples seemed to me the highest station obtainable by a writer.' Pushkin

anticipates not only the levity of *1066 and All That* but the narrative
philosophy systematised in such different writers as Proust and
Sartre. One of the implied functions of prose is to reveal the
relative, and the nature of the gap between words and things.

We see the inimitable Ivan Petrovich behaving towards the
reality of the world as Silvio and the station-master had behaved
in his tales. Oppressed by the weight of things as they are, he seeks
relief in writing them down as they are not, as Silvio sought relief
by isolating himself in his fantasy of revenge and the station-
master in his fantasy of the Prodigal Son. But as usual Pushkin
avoids consistency. Ivan Petrovich does not know he is 'writing'
when he describes his homecoming, the birches that had grown
taller, the familiar and unfamiliar faces, the reaction of the
servants. 'To the women I said without ceremony – "How old
you've got" – and they answered me with feeling – "And you,
master, how ugly you've got!"' His introduction stands in mute
contrast to the 'History' itself, where spontaneity gives place to
method, and he begins to write both history and prose. Here too
Pushkin's point shows at moments, as when Ivan Petrovich
comments magisterially on the tendency of the denizens of Goryukhino to look back on a mythological 'happy time':

The idea of a golden age occurs among all peoples, and only demonstrates
that people are never satisfied with the present, and having learnt from
experience to place little hope in the future they adorn the irrevocable
past with all the flowers of the imagination.

The 'History' ends with the tyranny of the Goryukhino steward,
and the disappearance of history into the bleak facts of the
present.

'Either mood without nature or nature without mood' – there is
certainly no correspondence between the two in Pushkin's prose.
In *Poltava*, as we noted, the 'still Ukrainian night' was a part of
the guilty conscience of Mazepa and the last hours of Kochubey.
Petersburg in *The Bronze Horseman* reflects the mood of the happy
'insider' of the Prologue and the tormented Evgeny of the tale.
The waves of the rebellious Neva enter the houses of the capital
like hooligans and robbers, and in Evgeny's mind the statue of
Peter the Great turns into a pursuing demon. At the end of *The
Station-Master* a cold wind is blowing and leaves are falling from
the trees; autumn has arrived, but as an objective fact: it has no
connection with the dead man and the daughter who comes to

visit his grave. The snow-storm of the title is a wild irruption of nature which destroys the fantasy of the projected elopement; and the snow-storm in *The Captain's Daughter* is equally unconnected with human mood and action.

Out of it looms Pugachev the rebel, but not as a portent and symbol of the wild force that is to be unloosed on Russia. He is lost in it as the hero and his servant are, and like them he can do nothing about it. It accompanies him but it does not symbolise him (as some critics have maintained) for Pugachev himself was not the embodiment of *Pugachevschina* but the rider of the whirl-wind and in the end its victim. (The point becomes explicit later in the novel when he hints to the hero how little control he has over his generals and the course of the revolt.) He appears out of the storm not as an apparition but as a crafty and humorous peasant who saves the travellers by his practical skill – the smoke he smells in the darkness tells him in what direction the village lies. Pushkin distinguishes the reality of the storm and of the peasant from the dream of the tired hero as the carriage lurches through the snow-drifts. In the dream the young man returns home and is told his father is dying. The bed-curtains are opened and there lies a bearded peasant, winking at him. The peasant jumps up, waving an axe, and the room is filled with dead bodies. Here we have the symbol of revolt and dispossession – the peasant with his axe was a traditional figure of the threat of class war in Russia – but it is unconnected with the real snow-storm and the real peasant guide outside.

Pushkin's narrative genius had always lain in his capacity to balance and to separate, to present a tale whose unity is complete but whose elements and actors are held in unobtrusive but rigorous isolation from one another. Prose brings out a new side of this gift, and *The Queen of Spades*, written three years after the *Tales of Belkin*, displays it in its starkest yet most melodramatic form. Its success is in the tension which holds the protagonists so far apart, and in particular Hermann, the Napoleonic hero, the man of will, obsession and dream, and the old Countess with her magic secret for success in gambling which might put power and wealth within his grasp. The background of the story, as of many tales which Pushkin left unfinished, is high society, the world of the old Countess and her grandson Tomsky, and this world is completely established in the opening sentence: 'They were playing cards with Narumov, of the Horse Guards.'

'They' are the 'we' of *The Bronze Horseman* – the best people, who have too much confidence to think of themselves as such, or to look down on others. The old Countess accepts this world, and herself, with the *dégagé* apathy of those who in their position have always retained, under all circumstances, every advantage. She holds that position now simply by being alive – 'the hideous but indispensable ornament of the ball-room' – whom it is necessary for everyone to greet at all functions 'in accordance with established custom'. They pay no further attention to her, or she to them, but it would no more occur to her to give up going to every party than to give up receiving society, which she does with rigorous etiquette and without recognising anyone. She mentions a contemporary of hers who has been dead seven years, and her young ward, Lizaveta Ivanovna, makes a meaning face to restrain her grandson from pointing this out, but the old Countess hears the news of the death with complete equanimity. By surviving, she has continued to keep every advantage. Pushkin understands her through and through, as Tolstoy was to do with his society characters, and he clearly feels the same affection for her as her grandson Tomsky feels in the story. For the imagination of the tale she has all the assurance of absolute fact.

And it is this settled fact that Pushkin confronts with the visionary stratagems of Hermann, the young man on the make. Tomsky and his friend Narumov are in the Guards, Hermann in the Engineers; and in a piece of by-play as brilliant as that which reveals the old Countess's moment of satisfaction at having survived her old friend and contemporary, Tomsky makes gentle fun of Liza Ivanovna for thinking Narumov might be in the Engineers! The reader does not grasp the significance of the exchange until it becomes clear why Lizaveta Ivanovna – in her betwixt-and-between position – has created the misunderstanding. A young man in Engineer's uniform has been standing in the street and gazing at her window, and the significance of this portent is only revealed after the social scene has been set. The spring of the story oscillates between the Countess's house, with all its stuffy and overpowering detail, and the shadowy figure of Hermann, glimpsed outside it and in the casual references of Tomsky.

Shklovsky has observed that *The Shot* unfolds itself in the narrative pattern 2–1–3: first the retirement from the world of Silvio, then his narration of the duel that gave rise to it, and finally the *dénouement* told to the original narrator by the other participant in that duel. The six short chapters of *Pikovaya Dama* move with a denser and less schematic irregularity. After Hermann has confronted the old Countess with his unloaded pistol and she has died of shock, the scene shifts back, via Lizaveta Ivanovna waiting for him in her room, to the ball that she and the Countess had attended, and the shrewd comments that Tomsky had made there about Hermann. When Hermann comes he tells her what has taken place, and though she is full of horror, and remorse at being his dupe and involuntary accomplice, the scene is one of curious intimacy. Hermann confides in her because like him she is young and homeless. They sit in silence together till the dawn, and as he leaves he presses her hand and kisses her bowed head. The future has killed the past.

At first reading *Pikovaya Dama* seems both flat and confusing. It 'impresses less at first to impress more later', when every aspect and detail acquires the muted resonance of a scene cut from a longer novel. It may be this characteristic that made Yazykov object on its first appearance that 'Pushkin has put his tale together very badly'. Its parts are indeed centripetal, not only preserving the difference between the different worlds of super- natural magic, ambition, and society, but forcing them still further apart. The conclusion, compressed to the verge of parody, is that of a novel: Hermann in the lunatic asylum; Lizaveta Ivanovna happily married; Tomsky promoted and engaged to the Princess Pauline, whom we have never even met but whose presence has been a part of the social echoes. When Hermann enters the house of the Countess in Part Three all he sees in the lighted vestibule – the footman asleep in a soiled armchair, the ornaments and the portraits by Madame Lebrun – engulfs him in a clutter of dispro- portionate detail which seems to have nothing to do with his quest. Like a lover he witnesses in secret the repellent ritual of the Countess's toilet, and as he leaves by the winding stair he thinks of the lovers of sixty years back, 'hair dressed *à l'oiseau royal* and pressing a three-cornered hat to a fast-beating heart'. The vast interior of the house stretches the distance between past and present to immense length and then brings them together in Hermann's reflection; for though all the details of the story seem to recede from one another there is a constant play of reference between them. Hermann is both the last lover and the destroyer – his Napoleonic will destined to succeed the ancient assurance of class and property.

As the old Countess lives in another world from Hermann's, so she is herself totally detached from her 'secret', the mysterious trick of winning at the game of 'shtos' which she learnt – according to her grandson's account – in her youth in Paris. We hear of the secret before we meet her, and Pushkin exploits without comment the contrast between the Countess as she is and the aura of power and mystery with which Tomsky's tale has invested her in the eyes of the young gamblers. In his treatment of the secret Pushkin implies an irony which is muted by his creator's affection for her *byt*, the way of life and the period of history she represents. Her reality is used in the interest of parody, parody of the 'diabolical' tales of Hoffmann and Balzac, which depend on the straightforward fantasy of the supernatural, which gives power to the possessor but in the end corrupts and destroys him. Anyone less suited to this role than the old Countess it would be hard to imagine. She was not corrupted by the magic formula because she was incorruptible: she had no need of money, she thought nothing of it. Once her temporary embarrassment in Paris was disposed of and her debt of honour paid (as Pushkin reminds us, she would not have been concerned to discharge a debt to a tradesman) she was never tempted to use her secret again, except once to help out a young *protégé*, and she never passed it on to her four sons. The moral is obvious: class has no need of magic. Adhering to a way of life with all the tenacity of unconscious conviction, it can neither be corrupted nor reformed. The old Countess is exactly as she would have been if the extraordinary secret had never been revealed to her.

And indeed was any secret revealed to her? We have only Tomsky's account of the family tradition – and the confrontation between the old Countess and Hermann, an encounter without communication, the personified will meeting the conditioned reflex. The Countess never reveals if she has a secret or not: faced with this brutal intrusion of the future her only resource is to die. But Hermann thinks she has one. Like most men of will he is the victim of superstition, which replaces in him the religious habit and the observances of tradition. At her funeral the Countess is as distant from him as ever. She is surrounded by the members of her household: 'the servants in black caftans, with armorial ribbons on their shoulders, and candles in their hands; the relatives – children, grandchildren, and great-grandchildren – in deep mourning. Nobody wept; tears would have been *une affectation*.' In her death the ugly exasperating old creature begins to attain in reality something of the macabre grandeur with which Hermann's imagination has invested her.

The relatives go up to bid farewell to the corpse; only the ancient lady's maid sheds tears. Hermann too goes up, and falls in a faint, convinced the old Countess has opened one eye and winked at him. The final touch to the macabre worldliness of the ceremony is the old court dignitary's whispered comment to the English bystander that the young officer was the Countess's natural son. The idea is grotesque, but the old fellow cannot resist the temptation to gossip, and it echoes other references in the story: we remember the Countess asking Tomsky for novels, but not the kind in which the hero strangles his mother or father...The *monde*'s automatic desire for scandal becomes here symbolic truth, for the Hermanns and all they stand for are indeed the natural sons of the old regime. There is irony in the fictional happy ending – Hermann removed, Lizaveta married, Tomsky and the Princess Pauline betrothed – for the deeper implications of the tale are not so reassuring.

And this is because Pushkin uses the supernatural not as an instrument of moral allegory but of social suggestion. The future is haunted by the past it has sought to exploit and profit by. Dead, the old Countess enters into a sinister intimacy with Hermann unthinkable while she was alive. The wink from the coffin is grotesquely at variance with her living self and with the funereal decorum around her. But as Pushkin does not manipulate the supernatural for a Faustian allegory,[1] so he does not revel in the grotesque for its own sake, like Gogol. Though much about the tale baffles our expectation of an intensifying and sinister tension, Hermann's gambling is none the less exciting in its own right. Pushkin himself was pleased with the success of the story in his Petersburg circle, noting that 'young gamblers now punt on the three, seven, and ace'.

In the *dénouement* our familiarity with the niceties of *shtos*, or Faro, is certainly taken for granted. Without it we can only have a general and not an exact impression of what happened in Hermann's duel with Chekalinsky on three successive nights, and his climactic blunder in drawing a queen from the pack and punting on it instead of on the ace. The procedure would have been as follows. Punter (Hermann) and banker (Chekalinsky) each had a fresh pack of cards. Hermann selected his card – the three on his first night –

---

[1] Writing to Turgenev in 1856 Herzen's friend N. Ogarev compared the story with Goethe's poem.

and put it face down on the table with his stake. The banker began
to deal from his pack, facing a card alternately left and right. If a
card of the same points as the punter had selected came up on his
right the banker won, and if on his left he lost. Hermann therefore
wins on his first deal two nights running. The game could be far
more complex than this and there were many possible permutations
in punting. The most audacious was the *quinze et le va* of *Evgeny
Onegin* (2. 17, a cancelled stanza), in which the punter risked his
stake and all his previous winnings (as Hermann does on the third
night) by bending down three corners of his card. Both in *The Shot*
and *The Queen of Spades* reference is made to the banker straighten-
ing out the corners of cards which were improperly staked, i.e.
with no winnings to back them. The precision of prose here has
become exclusive: Pushkin assumes the reader belongs to his set,
and we can understand the disapproval of the social critics of the
forties and fifties. Belinsky observed that the tale was not a *povest*
but a *masterskoy rasskaz*, not a story with universal application but
a specialised study of the grotesque; and Chernyshevsky dismissed
it as an unimportant piece, well-written.

In a sense nothing that Pushkin wrote more clearly reveals his
eighteenth-century side than *Pikovaya Dama*. He takes it for
granted, as Pope does, that his sort of reader will understand his
references: almost as much as the *Moral Essays*, or the *Dunciad*,
Pikovaya Dama is written for those in the know.[1] Byron, for all his
parade of eighteenth-century virtues, never writes like this. Like a
good actor – 'getting up rapture and enthusiasm with an eye to the
public', as Thackeray says – he takes care to make clear exactly
what he means, while Balzac, like Kipling at a later date, would have
explained the whole gambling operation in great detail, and with
the typical enthusiasm of the nineteenth-century writer demonstrating his familiarity with the inner ring and the ways of the world.

Both *Pikovaya Dama* and *The Bronze Horseman* were completed
within the same few weeks in 1833, the second great Boldino
autumn. *The Bronze Horseman* is also a tale, a *rasskaz*, but it is a

[1] Pushkin himself was an enthusiastic gambler who preferred keeping the bank
to punting. It is of some interest that he cancelled the gambling stanzas in
Evgeny Onegin, with their specialised terminology, and employs them in the
anecdotal *Pikovaya Dama*, together with a reference to the practice of saying
atandé if one wished to punt, in the epigraph to Part Six. Detail in Onegin is
always self-explanatory, as in the beautifully fashioned account of the
preparations for the duel and the loading of the pistols.

There is an excellent account of these gambling practices in Nabokov,
Evgeny Onegin, vol. II, p. 259.

tale in poetry, and addresses itself naturally to a wider audience. Its Prologue, as we have seen, contrasts with its story; the first is intimate, the second externalised, and the two tones, so distinct in the unpublished poem, invisibly combine in the prose of *Pikovaya Dama*. Moreover Hermann and Evgeny have a good deal in common. Both are outsiders; both hope to win their way in the world by prudence and hard work. Hermann's plea to the Countess echoes Evgeny's reverie about his future. The former may be the plea of a demon, who uses a demon's rhetoric (foreshadowing Lermontov's passionate octosyllables in his poem *The Demon*) but it is not a question of the devil quoting scripture for his purpose. Hermann implores the Countess to remember the love she has felt as a wife and mother, and vows that his own children and grandchildren will bless her name if she tells him her secret. But the Countess is unmoved: the distance between Hermann and her is as great as that between Evgeny and the statue. 'Love' as the Countess has understood it is worlds away from the passion which Hermann feels, and which is so tellingly equivocated between romantic yearning and cold ambition – the emotions with which Stendhal had endowed his hero in *Le Rouge et le Noir* (there is even an odd hint of the same relation to the mother figure as Julien Sorel's to Madame de Rênal).

As we should expect of the Pushkin of *Angelo* and the *Little Tragedies*, he does not make Hermann appear to the reader as the 'Napoleonic profile with the soul of a Mephistopheles' that he appears to Tomsky and Lizaveta Ivanovna. Hermann is as much victim as villain, and a comic figure into the bargain, a thrifty young German (all Germans are apt to be ridiculous in Russian fiction) who is so careful not 'to risk the necessary in the hope of gaining the superfluous'. His comicality is inherited from an abandoned novel in letters which forms one source of *Pikovaya Dama*. Pushkin had planned it in 1829 as a kind of exercise in modern love, with reference to *Clarissa Harlowe* and *Adolphe*. The exchange of letters between Hermann and Lizaveta parodies both *Clarissa* and Pushkin's own abortive novel in letters, for Hermann's object is not the seduction of Lizaveta but the secret of her employer (whom he even thinks of making love to in order to obtain it). So passionate is his wish that he soon abandons the German love-letter models he begins by using: he is 'sincere' because his real target is not the girl herself, and Lizaveta is as pleased by the tenderly respectful tone he has copied from books as she is thrilled by the language of real passion he then begins to use. When he sees 'the fresh little face and black eyes' at the window of the house he desires so much to enter in order to possess its owner's secret, 'that moment decided his fate'. Pushkin transposes the language of the novel of sentiment into the story of ambition and intrigue.

No text of the story exists in Pushkin's autograph, but two MS fragments obviously represent early versions: one describes the climactic game of cards, and the other a variant of the Lizaveta–Hermann situation. Hermann and the daughter of a worthy German in whose house he is living 'love each other as only Germans in our time can'. Though satirically observed, this Hermann has clearly much in common with the Evgeny of *The Bronze Horseman*. He is virtuous and resolute, and it is this resolution which survives to become the keynote of the hero of *Pikovaya Dama* – a faint aura of the earlier bourgeois idyll still surrounds our Hermann as it surrounds the figure of Evgeny. Bartenev, an indefatigable collector of Pushkiniana, records a note of Pushkin's to his friend Nashchokin in which he says that the model for the old Countess was Natalia Petrovna Golitsyn, whose grandson had told Pushkin a story of her life in Paris very similar to the one used in *Pikovaya Dama*.[1] Thus the story grew up from abandoned story-projects and the characters in them, was grafted on to an anecdote from real life, and given a colouring of fashionable literary *diablerie*.

But it is the weight of a novel which is most in evidence. Pushkin was on the verge of a form which he might have called 'Little Novels', in succession to the *Little Tragedies*. Like the latter they might have depended on a contrast and a confrontation – Hermann and the Countess parallel the contrasting figures of Mozart and Salieri, Juan and Carlos, Inez and Donna Anna. But while the *Little Tragedies* take place in a setting historical or picturesque, the novels would have depended on the contemporary social setting and Pushkin's interpretation of it. In the fragment that begins 'On the corner of a little square'...we have the Adolphian theme of a mature woman about to be abandoned by her lover; and in the related piece 'The guests had assembled at the *dacha*'...(which Tolstoy said had given him the impulse to begin *Anna Karenina*) the concept of a woman, both *exaltée* and unsophisticated, whose passions are too strong to fit the society in which she has to live.

[1] P. I. Bartenev, *Rasskazy o Pushkine* (Stories about Pushkin).

The link between this fragment and *Egyptian Nights* suggests that Pushkin may have had it in mind to combine and contrast the kind of exotic background he used in the *Little Tragedies* with a contemporary Petersburg setting. In *A Russian Pelham* he had evidently intended to transpose the theme of Bulwer Lytton's *Pelham: Or the Adventures of a Gentleman*. In all these fictional fragments – none of which is longer than a few pages – we see Pushkin experimenting with forms immediately related to his life in the capital and the social world in which he moved. Whether he would successfully have developed any into a full-scale novel it is impossible to say, but it seems more likely that he might have hit on the form of the 'novel as story', concentrated, pointed, and carrying the fullest suggestion of a complex social background established in the dialogue or description of the opening lines. *Pikovaya Dama* can be seen as the only completed example of this genre, in which a deep interest in society and its tensions is concealed by the lightness of a weird anecdote.

As Tolstoy expanded on his massive scale a hint in 'The guests had assembled at the *dacha*'..., so Dostoevsky – a great admirer of *Pikovaya Dama* and himself at one stage of his life an obsessive gambler – made use in *Crime and Punishment* of the confrontation between Hermann and the old Countess. What in Pushkin is a social situation – in the fullest sense – becomes in *Crime and Punishment* a metaphysical problem. Raskolnikov and his victim, the old money-lender, exist in the abstract, in a metaphysical void. The old woman is worthless, evil; killing her, in order to get the money to realise his potentialities, can be seen by Raskolnikov as a kind of duty. Hermann does not ask the question, because Pushkin does not put such questions in abstract form. The 'value' of the old Countess cannot be measured, because she is embedded in a whole social system, a system which Hermann is endeavouring to enter. Had Pushkin lived to write more novels we can be sure that they would be novels of society, not fantasies – however humorous and realistic – for purposes of metaphysical drama and moral regeneration. Dostoevsky's novels are of course swarming with real people: drunks, prostitutes, the destitute and the casualties of life, but like Dickens's heroes, Raskolnikov remains outside this world in a way that Hermann is not outside his. That is why he is closer to the French models – Julien Sorel and Lucien de Rubempré of Balzac's *Les Illusions Perdues* – whose relation with society is both obsessive and self-destructive, and who reveal its nature to us by the in-

tensity of that relation. Society breaks them because they have to
work through it.

It is interesting that there is no comparable prototype in the
literature of the time for the heroine whom Pushkin has sketched
in the two or three beginnings which he never continued. Ellénore
in *Adolphe* has something in common with his Zinaida Volskaya,
but Constant's heroine lives in a vacuum determined by the egoism
of Adolphe himself and his attitude towards her as narrator, while
Pushkin seems to have envisaged his as trapped in society and
seeking to abandon its values and conventions even while she needs
them and lives by them. In conception Volskaya is as original a
figure as Tatyana Larin turned out to be. Separated from her
husband and living alone in Kolomna ('On the corner of a little
square'...) she has tried to give up the *monde* and feed wholly on
her lover Valerian. He was pleased to court her as a conquest but is
now irked and unnerved by her possessiveness and is planning to
leave her. She tries to reproduce *à deux* the things he enjoys in
society – champagne suppers and so forth – but he misses the
monde and is irritated to discover that because of her he no longer
holds the same accepted place in it: the dull balls which he would
not have bothered to attend he is now not even asked to.

A pen sketch by Pushkin on the MS of 'On the corner of a little
square'...shows a face at once passionate and pathetic, innocent
and dissatisfied, a face that could light up like Anna Karenina's
'with the terrible glow of a conflagration on a dark night'. Anna,
we might note, is not drawn from the life in the way that Kitty
and Natasha are. She belongs to a definite literary tradition, and
may stand in the same relation to Volskaya as Volskaya to the
Constant and Stendhal heroine, and they to Clarissa and Julie de
Wolmar. What is fully developed and explored in Anna is the condition of unnaturalness to which a natural self has come, and the
pressure of custom and society which both inhibit her nature and
channel it into the protest of possessive and unlawful passion.
Referring (and not altogether ingenuously) to his 'discovery' that
Anna commits suicide, Tolstoy quotes Pushkin's comment: 'My
Tatyana has gone and got married, I should not have thought it of
her.' What is certainly true in the implied comparison is that
Pushkin is as much at home in his verse novel as Tolstoy in his
massive sphere of prose fiction. Only in verse, not in prose, does
Pushkin demonstrate the instinct and flexibility of a novelist whose
characters reveal their own destinies in such a way. His prose plans

are for fictional investigations, like the dramatic investigations of the *Little Tragedies*: the synopses are calculated; the beginnings already have an air of finality. It is possible that Pushkin would never have produced a novel of contemporary society while he held to his view of prose as a severe and impersonal instrument, in contrast to the unbuttoned ease and fluency of verse. Indeed it is possible that he would never have produced such a novel at all. His fragments and plans remain mines for others to quarry, and Tolstoy was undoubtedly the chief beneficiary.

Pushkin seems to have abandoned the idea of treating Volskaya as a wholly contemporary social character when he tries her out for the role of a modern Cleopatra who would make her lover's destruction the condition of the privilege of her love. Her potential for danger – that 'glow of a conflagration by night' – is suggested in the fragment 'We spent the evening at the *dacha* of Princess D . . . ', in which it is related not to social realism but to a legendary and mythological background. We have the impression that Pushkin is falling back on a more conventional contemporary mode. True, he had made Hermann live as a social being through the fashionable romantic atmosphere of the supernatural *conte*, but Volskaya is a different proposition. Her potential as a character is in her woman's lack of social and intellectual *independence* – her will cannot operate in isolation like that of the male heroes Hermann or Julien Sorel – and to realise this potential Pushkin would have had to entangle her completely in a tale of modern society and emotional intrigue. Instead he seems to have intended a parallel between ancient Alexandria and modern St Petersburg. The conversation turns on ideal women, and Alexei Ivanich quotes from an account of Cleopatra by Aurelius Victor, which he admires (as no doubt Pushkin himself had) for its Tacitean concision. He translates it for the benefit of the company.

'It signifies that Cleopatra traded in her charms, and that many bought a night with her at the price of their lives.'
'How dreadful!' exclaimed the ladies. . .

At the end of the fragment, which has several variants, Alexei Ivanich asks Volskaya what she thinks of Cleopatra's legendary condition. She replies that there are women in Petersburg who might exact a similar kind of bargain. He is incredulous, and she repeats the point, gazing at him meaningfully with her fiery eyes.

This is more like Theda Bara than Anna Karenina. Though the

atmosphere of the *monde* is promising, any *dénouement* must have been more melodramatic than psychological. Perhaps Pushkin himself felt this, for he recasts the Cleopatra motif into the frankly hybrid form of *Egyptian Nights*, in which interest is concentrated on two types of 'poet'. One is the aristocratic young Petersburger Charsky (a sardonically drawn self-portrait and based on the sketch of 'my friend' an author, from a story projected four years previously) and the other a down-at-heel Italian *improvvisatore*, intent on making money by performances in fashionable society. After Pushkin's death *Egyptian Nights* appeared in the *Sovremennik*, and it is most unlikely that he would have published it in its present form, but like *Rusalka* and *Osen* it has something of the air of a fragment that breaks off at the right moment. It is not, like the prose pieces, put aside undeveloped as well as unfinished.

The *improvvisatore* comes to visit Charsky, who to test his powers suggests as a theme for demonstrating them that 'the poet himself choses the subject of his songs, and the crowd has not the right to command his inspiration'. At once a superb piece of rhetoric is produced. How is it done? The improviser himself cannot explain why 'the idea issues from the poet's head already equipped with four rhymes measured in ordered and regular feet'. The second part of the improvisation is borrowed by Pushkin from the last stanzas of *Ezersky*, which made the same point as *Poetu* (*To the Poet*): the poet is his own master, a Tsar, who may ignore at his pleasure the elevated topics which the public thinks he should compose upon – 'as the eagle flies past mountains and towers to perch upon a rotted stump'. In *Ezersky* and *Poetu* the point is made explicitly: here it is presented in an ambiguous and even farcical context, as if to display the doctrine in a realistic setting rather than to state it.[1] Whom is the laugh on? Charsky (and Pushkin) believe passionately in the poet's independence, and now the improviser takes this very theme and brilliantly illustrates it at his patron's behest.

It is the paradox at the heart of great art; the independence of genius is in fact an aspect of its subtle versatility. The claim that the poet in his own kingdom is priest and Tsar, and that his integrity must be religiously respected, can become a piece of solemn romantic dogma unless it is tempered by the realisation

---

[1] It is not certain, from the MS, that Pushkin did indeed intend the insertion of the verses at this point, but there is a very strong supposition of it, on which his editors have acted.

that the same divine gift also makes the poet both mountebank and chameleon. He needs freedom but not the hush of idolatrous respect. The great poets of the Renaissance would have been amused by the notion that they were forfeiting their independence by producing the kind of works which their patrons expected of them. Their genius was in its nature both independent and compliant, and in the confrontation of Charsky and the improviser Pushkin brings together two complementary conceptions of a poet, as later in *Egyptian Nights* the lovers of ancient Alexandria with the *beau monde* of Petersburg.

German aesthetic theorists, particularly Schelling,[1] were fashionable among Pushkin's younger acquaintance, and one of these, Prince Odoevsky, had produced in 1833 a story called *The Improviser* which debates the question of poetic inspiration, but Odoevsky's Hoffmannesque fantasy is most unPushkinian. It is of interest that both Russian stories (Odoevsky's, the first in time, was later published in *Russian Nights*) take a down to earth view of the phenomenon, though Odoevsky's is a satire in the form of a fantasy. As passive as an X-ray, his Improviser can see everything, but can feel and appreciate nothing: his gift has deprived him of every human response. Pushkin is equally sceptical but less inquiring; he is not interested in the metaphysical questions raised by such a performance but in its dramatic paradox – the poet whose inspiration enables him to compose on any subject must none the less retain his own judgement, taste and independence.[2]

Romantic theories of poetic inspiration emphasised the god-like nature of the poet's gift, and improvisers – almost a class of professional performers in Italy – became fashionable and revered throughout Europe. Pushkin had become fascinated in Moscow by the art of poetic improvisation, and had admired Mickiewicz's skill at it as much as he admired his poems. But he did not care for the arrogance and flamboyance of the Polish poet, and it is conceivable that the theatrical figure of the *improvvisatore* expresses a hint of this. Charsky is repelled by the theatrical costume he puts on for his public performance, but he has to admit that there is nothing

---

[1] Schelling's theories concerning the 'unexpressible' certainly influenced Tyutchev, some of whose poems appeared in the first issue of *Sovremennik*, and form the vague aesthetic background to his famous and succinct line *Mysl izrechennaya est lozh* (A thought spoken is a lie).

[2] The whole subject is admirably examined in Viktor Weintraub's essay 'The Problem of Improvisation in Romantic Literature', *Comparative Literature*, XVI (1964).

ridiculous about the Italian when he appears before the audience with his pale face illuminated by the stage lighting. As the theme given him takes hold, the improviser can be seen to 'feel the approach of the god' and his eyes 'sparkle with a strange fire'. The theatrical and the dramatic, the banal and the impressive, are mixed inextricably together. Poets are both absurd and inspired.

Pushkin certainly caricatures himself in Charsky, who would rather talk to the shallowest man of the world than to literary people, who hates being asked what he is writing, yet who only knows true happiness when the *dryan* (Pushkin's term for his own bouts of composition) demands expulsion and he shuts himself up and scribbles for twenty hours a day. Pushkin distances Charsky by a touch or two outside himself (his own study was emphatically not 'furnished like a lady's boudoir') but the main effect is one of good-humoured self-mockery, creamed over with a complacent acquiescence in the fact that 'the calling of poet does not exist' among Russian gentry. Amusement extends both to Pushkin's cherished idea of the poet's dignity and his ability to strike a good bargain – Russian gentleman and needy *improvvisatore* pass instantly from aesthetic discussion to the price of tickets for the public performance, an account of which forms the second subject of the tale.

Charsky dryly assures his new friend that the fashionable world will come, even if they don't understand Italian, in order to display their culture to their acquaintance and not to miss a new sensation. After some comic by-play, a statuesque 'goddess of the Neva' draws from the urn a paper with the subject *Cleopatra e i suoi amanti*, and the recitation begins, a magnificent passage of octo-syllabics in Pushkin's best bravura style.[1] At a feast in her palace Cleopatra makes her scornful offer of a night of love to any who will pay the price of death the next morning. Three candidates are eager: a grizzled soldier, an Epicurean philosopher and poet, and an unnamed boy on whom the queen bestows a brief glance of emotion. She makes her vow to Aphrodite and the poem breaks off, and the story with it.

Bryusov supposed that Pushkin intended a contrast between the meretricious world of modern Petersburg and ancient Alexandria with its cult of the flesh and its acceptance that 'the goddess of love

[1] In 1825 Pushkin had written a poem, partly in five-stress iambics, on the same Cleopatra theme, and this he now modified and cannibalised for the benefit of his improviser.

and the goddess of death' are one and the same.[1] And Bryusov himself continued the poem along these lines,[2] making it a *fin de siècle* work suited to the taste of the nineties, and embellished with 'emblematic accessories' – in Zhirmunsky's phrase – which contrast with Pushkin's own severely simple use of local colour. He is also careful to save the third and youngest suitor, as did Théophile Gautier in his version based on the anecdote of Aurelius Victor. Weighted as they are with the arcane solemnity of their era, both the interpretation and the 'continuation' of Bryusov ignore the dazzle of levity and caricature with which Pushkin has surrounded the work. The paradox of poethood in the first part is echoed by the paradox of historical recreation in the second. The denizens of the Petersburg salon, the *improvvisatore* in his flashy costume, and his chagrin at the hilarity which greets his timid request for a little more information on the theme of 'Cleopatra and her lovers' – 'because the great queen had many' – all suggests a submerged but pointed satire on the whole pretentious fashion of historical fiction and the aping of picturesque legend by modern taste. And yet, despite the ludicrousness of the setting, 'the god approaches', the poem takes fire, and momentarily bridges the gulf between the reality of the past and its attempted recreation in the romanticism of the present. That the process can be only momentary is perhaps shown by Pushkin's breaking off before the inevitable banality of any outcome to the situation so graphically sketched out by the improviser's declamation. Because of the enigmatic element of humour and caricature in the story, Pushkin's brief conjuration of Cleopatra gives her something of the earthy and comic vigour and passion she has in Shakespeare's play, and *Egyptian Nights* belongs to the world of Shakespeare and Gogol rather than to the meticulous and hieratic recreations of Flaubert or of Bryusov himself (he wrote a lengthy historical novel about fourth-century Rome entitled *The Altar of Victory*).

[1] V. Bryusov, *Moy Pushkin*, pp. 107–18. For Dostoevsky the contrast was rather different. 'Here is the ancient world!...here are the earthly gods who seated themselves on the people's backs...segregated Gods, despising the genius of the people...who grew mad in their isolation, who in their weariness foresaw death, and who in their agony sought diversion...' Dostoevsky, 'The Pushkin Address'.

[2] Several later Russian poets attempted the completion of Pushkin fragments. In 1850 Pushkin's brother Lev recited from memory a few octosyllabics which seem to have been the beginning of a verse tale taken from the story of the Doge and Dogaressa in Hoffmann's *The Serapion Brothers*, and Maikov completed the poem on the lines of Hoffmann's tale. See N. O. Lerner, *Rasskazy o Pushkine*.

Pushkin may well have realised the impossibility of recreating the ancient world in the detailed perspective of a historical novel. About the time he wrote *Egyptian Nights* he planned a story of Roman life in the days of Nero, and produced the fragment which begins: 'Caesar was on a journey and with Titus Petronius I followed him at a distance.' Its sonorous, nervous prose suggests a deliberate recreation of Latin authors – Pushkin had been reading Tacitus and Petronius's *Satyricon* in a French translation. But he must soon have realised that the experiment could not be continued to the length of a novel or even a *nouvelle*. Antiquity could not be summoned up on a conventional shape of the present, but only suggested through the oblique and offhand medium of the *Egyptian Nights*, whose burlesque and magpie form recalls the spirit of Petronius more effectively than a historical novel about him could do. Annenkov first suggested that Pushkin was absorbed at this period of his creative life in the contrast between antiquity and modernity, and later commentators have emphasised his increasing interest in ancient history and his notes on Polevoy's historical work which stress the significance of the unbridgeable gap between the pagan and the Christian consciousness.

Though he admired 'the Scottish enchanter', Pushkin was well aware of the shortcomings of his imitators and the weakness of the genre as a whole. 'Like Agrippa's apprentice they have evoked the demon of antiquity but do not know how to handle him, and have become the victims of their own rashness...These pale productions, however, are read all over Europe...Is it because the portrayal of bygone times, even if feeble and inaccurate, has an inexplicable charm for the imagination sunk in the humdrum monotony of the present?'[1] Only the most recent history, Pushkin may well have reflected, could be used by art for the art of the novel; and his most sustained achievements in the form, *The Captain's Daughter* and the unfinished *Dubrovsky*, are both set in the reign of Catherine, virtually 'Sixty Years Since', like Scott's

[1] From a review of Zagoskin's novel *Yury Miloslavsky or the Russians in 1612*, which Pushkin published in the *Literary Gazette* in 1830 (VII, 102). Pushkin thought Zagoskin 'carries us really back to 1612', and excepted him from his general condemnation of ill-informed costume novels, among which – in the first draft of the article – he had numbered Vigny's *Cinq-Mars*. In the same draft he significantly excepted the names of Fenimore Cooper and Manzoni from his condemnation of those 'who were so far from the Scottish enchanter', possibly because both wrote novels which were not costume pieces from remote history.

Waverley. Pushkin's prose style is admirably suited to the tale of adventure in the recoverable past – better suited, it may well be, than to the society novels which he projected but never wrote. Yet like much of Scott's best work, *Dubrovsky* and *The Captain's Daughter* could be said to be social novels by other means.[1] The archetypes of Russian society and character which they bring into existence are more important in both than story or history. Pushkin evokes the gentry of the period, the heirs of the Petrine system, from the great Troyekurov, whose fortunes had been made by his relation to Princess Dashkov, the favourite of Catherine, to the more modest ex-officer landowners like the elder Dubrovsky and the elder Grinev, whose estates and family life are very similar to those of the Larins in *Evgeny Onegin.*

Pushkin's are the first of the great nineteenth-century portraits of Russian landowners, and the only ones which make us feel at each re-reading: this is what such men were really like. Unlike Tolstoy and every other celebrant of the landowning class, Pushkin has no apparent axe to grind.[2] He is retrospective without being in the least nostalgic: he both celebrates and loves, but his criticisms are as unanswerable as they are unobtrusive. The core of both novels, as we shall see, is a revolt against the Petrine system, that rigid and artificial hierarchy of power which has so much in common with the party apparatus in Russia today. Yet none of Pushkin's squires – Dubrovsky, Troyekurov, or Grinev – is deliberately typical or exemplary, just as Captain Mironov and his lieutenant are not offered to us as characteristic of the courage and the simple virtues of the Russian army. The supreme advantage of Pushkin's

---

[1] The combination becomes explicit in Lermontov's novel *Vadim*, whose back-ground is the Pugachev rebellion, and whose hero, like Pushkin's Dubrovsky becomes a rebel leader from the motive of personal revenge.

[2] In his book on Tolstoy *O romanakh L. N. Tolstogo*, which repeatedly stresses not only the threat of 'superfluous detail' to *War and Peace* but also the 'impurity' of placing contemporary characters in a historical setting, Leontiev concludes that in *War and Peace* we get 'not so much the spirit of the age as the individual genius of the author', and that in Pushkin's historical novels we are aware of both. Tolstoy himself noted in his diary in 1853 'I read *The Captain's Daughter*, and alas it must be said that Pushkin's prose is already old-fashioned, not in its style but in its manner of exposition'. Tolstoy's attitude to Pushkin was always equivocal – on one occasion in conversation with V. Lazinsky he maintained that his strength lay in his prose and that his verse was 'rubbish' – but it is notable how many times he re-read things (*The Stone Guest*, *The Gipsies*, *The Tales of Belkin*) and experienced a feeling of sudden illumination, recorded in such phrases as 'I only now understand Pushkin'. (See B. M. Eykhenbaum, 'Pushkin i Tolstoy'.)

carefully developed and controlled prose is that it is incapable of the portentousness which goes with moral generalisation and the suggestion of moral archetypes. Tolstoy's Captain Tushin, in *War and Peace*, does strike us as such an archetype, particularly in his relation to his superiors; though made as unlike Mironov as possible he clearly descends from him, but what is resonantly typical in Tolstoy is in Pushkin no more and no less than a memorable portrait, even though Soviet critics have made Pushkin's Captain a forerunner of those pattern types whose function it is to illustrate the 'human' qualities which are the prop and stay of the Russian people and fully recognised and rewarded only under socialist enlightenment. But even the salt of the earth loses its savour if it is held under our noses too often.

A good example of Pushkin's method is the beginning of Chapter 3 of *The Captain's Daughter*, when the narrator Grinev arrives as a young ensign at the fortress in the steppes commanded by Captain Mironov.

'Is it far to the fortress?' I asked the driver. 'No, not far' he replied. 'That's it over there.' I looked on all sides, expecting to see frowning bastions, towers and a moat, but saw nothing except a small village surrounded by a wooden palisade. On one side of it stood three or four haystacks half-buried under the snow; on the other a derelict windmill with sails of bast hanging idly; 'But where's the fortress?' I asked in surprise. 'There', answered the driver, pointing to the village, and as he spoke we drove into it.

The arrival deflates his romantic expectation of what a fortress in the middle of nowhere would be like, and he is then cast into the depth of depression by the thought of his probable associates in such a place. But the second assumption is as misleading as the first. He finds himself in a family, as unassuming as the one he has left at home, though far humbler. But he does not patronise it and nor does Pushkin. The only person who does is the villain, Shvabrin, who comes from the same background as the hero-narrator, and treats the fortress family with all the disdain of one who is – like the hero – a former guards officer. Shvabrin's subsequent villainy is dictated by the plot, but his real odiousness is indicated by Pushkin in his contrast of the attitudes and behaviour of the two young men. They are bound to quarrel, because Grinev's growing pleasure in the fortress family arouses Shvabrin's self-protective disdain. Grinev cannot help laughing when Shvabrin mimics the family, or hints at an improper relation between the

Captain's wife and the elderly lieutenant, but this mephistophelean denial leads eventually to the only way in which Grinev can express his rejection of Shvabrin, even though it ironically confirms their similar backgrounds – a duel. The family regard such a thing as both absurd in itself and contrary to regulations; the old lieutenant does not even understand the function of a second, and the duel is reduced to the status of a farce by their impenetrable good sense. But the malignity of Shvabrin detaches Grinev from the family which he would otherwise enter so naturally. Shvabrin writes (as it appears) to Grinev's father, who forbids any engagement between the hero and the Captain's daughter.

As Shvabrin's fictional villainy is convincingly established by his malignant dissociation,[1] in terms of daily life, from the fortress family, so the true nature of Masha is revealed through her being a part of it. She is, as the Captain's daughter, a heroine at one with her surroundings and the life she leads. She has none of the artificial detachment of a Scott heroine, though her journey at the end of the novel to intercede for the hero at the court of the Empress is clearly modelled on the action of Jeanie Deans in *The Heart of Midlothian*. Scott's heroine is an admirable figure, and the nature and quality of her conscience is wholly convincing, but it remains at one side of her environment rather than a logical and necessary part of it. Masha's action in going to the Empress is at one with the devoted tenacity that her family have already displayed – her father by his defence of the fortress and her mother in staying with him to the end. It is this instinctive steadfastness which has already endeared her to Grinev's family, who have come to accept her – without any suggestion of patronage – as 'one of us', just as their son had found himself doing with the family in the fortress.

The development of romance and plot in terms of social units and their interaction is one of the triumphs of *The Captain's Daughter*. Its moral background is democratic, 'human', without the slightest display of the fact. As a part of this social pattern it is even convincing that Shvabrin should go over to Pugachev. Rejecting the virtues of a unit which he regards as beneath him, he joins the rebels among whom he can be a leader (as Pugachev claims to be Tsar) without feeling he is lowering himself. His

---

[1] It is perhaps not too fanciful to see in Shvabrin – especially in the 'malign smile' which he gives the hero when he denounces him at the end to the court of inquiry – a hint of Dostoevsky's malignant solitaries and his 'underground man'. Certainly there is nothing of the stage villain in Pushkin's economical sketch of Shvabrin's nature.

treachery is in keeping with his would-be aristocratic detachment, whereas the garrison officers he despises have a true sense of class solidarity which only appears *in extremis* but which makes them die rather than swear allegiance to an impostor and ex-convict. Old Grinev shows the same instinct and background when it does not occur to him to doubt the finding of an official verdict, even though he is overwhelmed by the charge that his son has conspired with the rebels. He is proud that his own father should have been executed for being on the wrong side in a court rebellion, but broken-hearted that his son should seem to have joined a revolt whose object was to 'exterminate the gentry' in a class war.

But the pattern is nowhere forced on our attention. The massive demarcation in *War and Peace* between the Moscow and the Petersburg nobility – Rostovs and Kuragins – and between the Russian 'family' and the French 'system', have their parallels in the bare narrative of Pushkin, but they give no hint of the purpose and design in Tolstoy's giant project to remake the past. *War and Peace* is an idyll in Schiller's definition of the term, in that it creates on the widest and most complex scale things 'not as they are but as they ought to be'. But this is not the impression that we retain from Pushkin's two historical narratives.

We might contrast the great landowner Troyekurov, in *Dubrovsky*, with Aksakov's portrait in his family history of grandfather Bagrov. Both are men of strong passions, natural tyrants, who can exercise their total authority without let or hindrance. Bagrov is on the whole a benevolent patriarch, despite his fits of rage, and though we accept this we do not forget that the old man is seen through the grandson's eyes, and that much was hidden from him which is necessarily omitted from the narrative. Pushkin's Troyekurov is not necessarily typical, but he embodies, with a totality at once grotesque, majestic and terrifying, the logic of his position. He is not a bad man – he even wants others to be happy – but the habit of domination is so compulsive that the ordinary virtues, as Slonimsky observes, cannot breathe in the atmosphere around him. He is not corrupt – he has usually no need to be – but he assumes that a corruption advisory service will be at his beck and call when he wants it, like his dogs or his serfs. He cheats the elder Dubrovsky out of his modest estate for a whim, in much the same spirit in which he introduces tutors and visitors into a small room with a chained-up bear. Far from being discomfited when the beast is pistolled by the new French tutor (young Dubrovsky in disguise) he recounts the episode with the greatest satisfaction 'for he had the happy faculty of priding himself on all that in any way belonged to him'. He is pleased with the rich prince who wants to marry his daughter, not so much from snobbery as from gratification that the prince has been at such expense, '*tous les frais*', to please him. And yet he is never pleased. He 'gave little thought to winning the case he had set in motion', and when victorious he even sets out to visit his victim with the intention of making it up. The madness and death of his victim, which might have gratified an ogre, are for him a genuine source of disappointment and embarrassment: unforeseen consequences upon which it is no longer possible for him to exercise the impulses of his power. Troyekurov is not in fact capable of glimpsing what Vronsky is compelled to discover in *Anna Karenina* – 'the eternal error that men make in supposing that happiness consists in the gratification of their wishes' – but he is an infinitely more meaningful as well as a more majestic figure than the ogreish and self-tormenting landowners of Saltykov – 'Iudushka' Golovlyov and the squires of *Old Days in Poshekhonie*.

Pushkin quotes *in toto* in *Dubrovsky* the transcript of a lawsuit which took place in the province of Tambov between 1826 and 1832 and resulted in the unjust expulsion of a poor landowner by a rich one. Such reliance on recorded fact was to be very much in the spirit of his more tendentious successors in Russian realism, but in *Dubrovsky* the *résumé* – quoted without comment – admirably sets off the colourful account of Troyekurov himself. Even the censorship helped, enabling Pushkin to record the event with dispassion as something that took place in the past. There is no need for further comment, and the contrast between the joviality of Troyekurov and the cold black and white of his legal swindle is all the more telling.

But as the nineteenth century progressed the novelist was compelled into one camp or the other; Tolstoy in *War and Peace* embarks on a monumental historical defence of the landowning class, although in sheer size it transcended the factional barriers of the time. Pisemsky, Goncharov and Leskov were all labelled as reactionaries for doing something rather similar on a smaller scale, while even Turgenev's *Sportsman's Sketches* was claimed for the radical and reformist side. However much their work was made use of by later polemicists, both Pushkin and Gogol have the transparency and independence of vision that is only possible in nineteenth-century Russia before the ideological frontiers are drawn and the armies entrenched.

Like the *Tales of Belkin*, *The Captain's Daughter* is booby-
trapped by the device of an editor, publishing memoirs which have
come into his hands. Grinev is no Ivan Petrovich, but he can be
used by Pushkin on occasion in a somewhat similar way, as Voltaire
made use of the reactions of Candide. Captain Mironov orders a
Bashkir to be flogged to extract information from him, and then
finds the man's tongue has been cut out as a barbarous punishment
for some previous rebellion. There follows a paragraph of commentary by Pushkin's hero.

When I think that this happened in my lifetime, and that I have now
lived to see the gentle reign of the Emperor Alexander, I can only
marvel at the rapid progress of civilisation and the spread of humane
principles. Young man! If these notes of mine ever fall into your hands,
remember that the best and most lasting changes are those which
proceed from an improvement in moral custom, without any violent
upheaval.

The worth of the sentiment conceals the irony of its context. We
know how Pushkin felt about Alexander and about the tyranny of
Arakcheev that had darkened the last years of his reign. 'Arakcheev may be dead', he had himself remarked, 'but *Arakcheev-
schina* continues.' Though the worst features of the military
settlements had been abolished by Nicholas, barbarous punish-
ments were still commonplace. And yet neither Swift nor the author
of *Candide* would have thought of making the men who took for
granted such barbarities and carried them out, comical, even
lovable and good-hearted. The tripwire pegged by Pushkin into
Grinev's sentiments does not entangle his humanity as a narrator.
It engages with the narrative as naturally as the remark of the
Captain's wife that she does not much care for torture herself and
will take good care to keep Masha out of earshot; or her realisation
that something serious is afoot when, 'returning from morning
service', she sees the lieutenant pulling out of the cannon 'bits of
rag, small stones, wood shavings, knuckle-bones, and rubbish of
every sort that the children had stuffed into it'. Satire is, as it were,
so fully humanised by Pushkin's method that it never shows up in
a meaningful isolation but is dissolved into the whole weight of the
incongruous that presses down on any sequence of events.

Such incongruity becomes in *The Captain's Daughter* the principle of epic narrative. In the last minute of their lives, when they
have refused to swear allegiance to Pugachev, the Captain and his
old lieutenant instinctively address him in the same idiom which

we are accustomed to hearing them use in the fortress family: '*Ty mne ne gosudar*' – *govorit Ivan Kuzmich* – '*ty vor i samosvanets, slysh ty!*' ('You aren't my Sovereign', said Ivan Kuzmich, 'you're a thief and impostor, do you hear!'). *Slysh ty!* is the Captain's invariable and unavailing exhortation to his wife, while his lieutenant addresses Pugachev as *Dyadyushka* (uncle), his habitual term of familiarity. At the moment of 'heroic decision' he is still the same man who held her wool for the Captain's wife, and threaded mushrooms under her eye to dry for the winter.

The assault on the fortress is an anti-climax, all over in five minutes, but before it Grinev's feelings are wholly romantic as he grips the hilt of his sword and 'imagined myself the chevalier' of his beloved Masha. The contrast of romantic expectations with the actual baldness of objective events may remind us of Fabrice's experiences at the battle of Waterloo at the opening of Stendhal's *La Chartreuse de Parme*, and also of Nikolai Rostov's 'rescue' of the Princess Mary in *War and Peace*, in which there is a similar contrast between his own romantic idea of what he is doing and what actually occurs.[1] In *War and Peace* such incongruity is of course employed on a huge scale and developed in modes of narration which alternate and intertwine with each other like the branches of a forest. What Shklovsky, as we have noted *à propos Evgeny Onegin*, calls 'making it strange', the device used with exaggerated emphasis in *War and Peace* (for example in the account of a ballet), is never found in Pushkin's prose, for it is subsumed under the whole premise of his prose writing – 'simply, shortly, clearly'. In *The Captain's Daughter*, as in any series of episodes from life, the events are not clear, the time is not short, the characters are not simple. It is Pushkin's artistic achievement to make them appear so, and hence it is the words on the page which themselves 'make strange' what they call into being.

This uniform unexpressiveness which none the less expresses everything is nowhere more remarkable than in the scene in *Dubrovsky* in which the law officers, who have come to take possession for Troyekurov, are burnt alive in the manor house. When they arrive the peasants wish to attack them and are dissuaded by their dispossessed owner, young Dubrovsky. Coming downstairs later,

---

[1] Yu. N. Tynyanov, *Pushkin i ego Sovremenniki* (Moscow 1969) points out Tolstoy's probable debt to Pushkin's account of a skirmish with the Turks in his short factual description of his experiences in the Caucasus in 1829, *A Journey to Arzrum*; and Tolstoy himself expressed his debt to Stendhal's description of Waterloo.

he finds the blacksmith Arkhip hanging round with an axe, and
asks him what he is doing.

'I thought...I came...sort of to find out, if they were all here' –
mumbled Arkhip in a low voice.
  'And why the axe with you?'
  'Why the axe then? Can't go round without an axe these days. These
court fellows are up to anything – got to watch out...'
  'You're drunk. Leave the axe and go and lie down.'
  'Me drunk? Vladimir Andreevich sir, God's my witness I haven't
touched a drop...would I go getting my head all muddled up now, with
this going on? – office fellows laying a plan to get possession of us,
chasing our masters out of the big house...'[1]

Arkhip clearly intends to take revenge on his master's behalf for
this scandalous and unheard-of situation, and it is not explained
whether Dubrovsky gets the idea from him or has already been
meditating on it himself. Unlike Grinev as narrator, Dubrovsky is
seen from a distance and is interpreted by the reader through his
actions, which are always impulsive and abrupt. He now checks
that the house is empty except for the drunken officers, and sets it
alight.

'Wait' – he said to Arkhip – 'I think I must have shut the doors into
the hall – go and open them, quick.' 'Arkhip ran into the hall – the doors
were open. He locked them, muttering to himself: 'Open them! Not
likely' – and returned to Dubrovsky.

Did he send back the smith deliberately, knowing what he would
do? Or did he order the doors to be opened, both to increase the
draught and give the officers a chance to escape? From his later
confession to Troyekurov's daughter we know he intended to burn
the landowner in his bedroom, when he had taken service in his
house disguised as a tutor. At any rate Dubrovsky drives off and
the clerks are burnt to death, the smith looking on with sardonic
satisfaction, and later rescuing a cat from the roof of the burning
barn.

The poor creature mewed piteously for help. The boys roared with
laughter, watching its predicament. 'Why are you laughing, you little

[1] Arkhip's sheepish, self-righteous, and inconsequential replies are difficult to
render without losing their flavour. As Russian critics have noted, Pushkin
does not convey peasant speech through any elaboration of dialect or
phraseology, as Leskov and Ertel were later to do, but he gets a tone exactly.
He individualises too: Arkhip the smith and Anton the coachman have quite
a different speech idiom.

devils?' demanded the indignant smith. 'Don't you fear God? – one of his creatures perishing and you fools think it's funny' – and putting a ladder against the burning roof he climbed up to the cat. It understood his purpose and clutched gratefully on to his sleeve. Half-scorched, the smith climbed down with his prize.

The villagers thoroughly enjoy the fire, which spreads to their own homes, and the chapter ends with them wandering disconsolately in the darkness round the piles of red-hot embers.

Herzen in his memoirs records how often fire – 'the red cock' – was used as a weapon against unpopular landlords. Here it seems quite natural that Dubrovsky's serfs should watch with satisfaction the destruction of the property, as natural as the burning of Moscow when the French are in occupation. Pushkin is as matter-of-fact about the hatred of Dubrovsky's serfs for the interloper as he is about the satisfaction and pride which Troyekurov's serfs take in their master's tyrannical personality, of which they regard themselves as an extension – the quarrel between the two neighbours originally arose because one of Troyekurov's servants insulted the elder Dubrovsky. Like master, like man. Freedom, in such circumstances, comes from complete identification with the master, and when the dispossessed young Dubrovsky sets up as a kind of guerrilla and brigand his people automatically become brigands too. It is impossible that Pugachev should be a liberator, in any other sense of the word, because his followers regard him as they regard the Tsar or their estate owner. As we know from the *History of the Village of Goryukhino*, demoralisation sets in when there is no master but only some impersonal agency, and the peasants look back nostalgically to the days of identity with the true owner.

As the hero of a romance Dubrovsky remains mysterious, though his relation with Arkhip and the serfs is as revealing as that of Grinev with his servant Savelich on its more detailed scale – the master and servant relation is vital to the characterisation of both novels. Troyekurov and his entourage belong to a different world, and we enjoy them as static portraits while we follow Dubrovsky's actions and disguise for the unfolding of plot suspense. The increasing discontinuity between the background of *Dubrovsky* and the nature of its hero none the less presents Pushkin with a technical problem, which may have contributed to his suspending work on the novel. Dubrovsky is an intruder on the old world of country gentry and their pursuits, and a figure from the future, for where Pushkin adopts a relaxed and retrospective ease in describing Troyekurov and his family he gives Dubrovsky the temperament of a romantic hero of the eighteen-twenties. Pugachev is a rebel from the past: Dubrovsky, even though he has no idealistic political motivation, has the unpredictability of what may be to come.

The novel could no doubt have been completed on the level of melodrama and suspense. Masha Troyekurov, like Tatyana before her, refuses to elope with Dubrovsky because her father has already married her to the Prince, but whereas Tatyana's dismissal of Onegin terminates the pattern of sentiment in the verse novel, Masha's refusal is that of the good heroine in melodrama whose problems will have to be solved by the turn of events, not by the logic of her own nature. In Pushkin's plan Dubrovsky was to return to Russia, disguised as an Englishman, after Masha has become a widow. The pair will meet perhaps in Moscow. Another synopsis is given in a few words: *Moscow, the Surgeon, Solitude, the Tavern, Denunciation, Suspicion, the Chief of Police.*[1] Clearly Dubrovsky was to have been recognised, perhaps by a scar, and either have escaped again with his beloved or perhaps been exiled with her to Siberia.

Such a novel, as Pushkin must have known, would have had little chance of getting past the censor, who did in fact raise objections when the novel was published as a fragment after the author's death. The censor probably had the Decembrists in mind, but that is hardly the point. Dubrovsky is not an idealist, wishing to replace one political system by another, but a kind of nihilist in spite of himself, a man astounded by the flagrant injustice possible in a society to which he had previously belonged as a privileged member. He is not a Robin Hood figure, or even a Karl Moor, but more like Kleist's Michael Kohlhaas, whose acceptance of the social order is transformed into violent rejection when his eyes are opened by personal experience. The qualms of the censor were not misplaced: such a portent is all the more telling when placed in the lavish and homely opulence of rural Russia, a rogue landowner operating against his own neighbours, for whom hoary iniquity is so much a part of the established order of things that they are unable even to understand the nature of the injury that has been done to him. Though the young ladies, 'gorged with the mysterious

[1] See P. Kaletsky, 'Ot "Dubrovskogo" k "Kapitanskoy Dochke"', *Literaturny Sovremennik*, I (Leningrad 1937).

horrors of Mrs Radcliffe', see Dubrovsky as a romantic figure, their elders, including Troyekurov, are too comfortably accustomed to corruption to suppose that its victims would suffer it with anything other than fatalistic acceptance: for them he is unnatural, a creature turned against its own kind.

Romance itself in *Dubrovsky*, as in *Evgeny Onegin*, is used not in good faith as a literary fashion but to reveal the psychology of those for whom it is a part of consciousness. Masha, though a good warm-hearted girl, is uncertain how to act when she decides to keep a clandestine appointment with her tutor (the disguised Dubrovsky) who she suspects has fallen for her. 'Should his declaration be received with aristocratic indignation, with friendly advice, good-humoured banter, or silent sympathy?' The lines might come straight from *Sense and Sensibility*. But brought up as she is, Masha is conditioned to feel that 'servants and peasants are not men' and that a tutor is only a kind of servant. And such conditioning can be heroic as well as inhuman; married against her will to an elderly Prince, she will not leave him when she is spectacularly 'rescued' by Dubrovsky; and this decision is not just that of a romantic novelette, it is proved by the whole weight of the novel. Nor is heroism confined to one class. When Dubrovsky's serf-boy is caught by Troyekurov a manuscript variant records that he is whipped to make him reveal his master's hiding-place, and that 'he said nothing under the punishment, suffering like a little Spartan'. In the definitive text the same point makes itself indirectly and laconically (it was not, after all, the Spartans who told the story of the Spartan boy). Masha's half-brother, a bastard of Troyekurov's by her former French governess, is in the secret and is threatened with a beating if he does not reveal it. He does so instantly, whereas the serf-boy remains silent.[1]

Dubrovsky is another example of Pushkin's curious philosophy of endings. His reluctance to 'spell it out' seems to inhibit him from continuing the kind of tale in which the *dénouement* is predictable in terms of the overall convention. Masha is married and Dubrovsky's dramatic rescue-bid miscarries. She will not now leave with him, and in the struggle he is wounded by the Prince, whom he does not harm. He disbands his guerrillas and leaves the country.

---

[1] Slonimsky, *Masterstvo Pushkina*, notes the point as characteristic of Pushkin's social sense: the spoilt child of the manor has not the native courage of the peasant boy. But the change is really for technical reasons. Instead of emphasising the boy's fortitude, Pushkin merely implies it by contrast with the other's instant collapse under threat of punishment.

Like the play *Rusalka*, the novel has to all intents and purposes gone far enough. 'Blest is he...who never read life's novel to the end and all at once could part with it...' *Evgeny Onegin* is Pushkin's only sustained work of fiction in which the end declares itself naturally and incontrovertibly. It is not a contrived finale: we do not see it coming, but when it arrives, it shows – to the author as to ourselves – the whole shape of the work. We cannot know whether Pushkin would ever have developed a less 'instinctive' attitude towards prose fiction; whether he would ever have come to terms with the 'instalment' novel in which the ending occurs after a prescribed number of chapters. It seems unlikely. As Tolstoy was to observe dryly: 'We Russians do not understand how to write novels in the sense in which this genre is understood in Europe.' All the great Russian classics, from *Dead Souls* to *War and Peace* and *The Brothers Karamazov*, share a kind of breaking-off, a promise of continuation which is an aspect of their life as art although it does not belong to the artifice of the form, and in this – as in so many other things – Pushkin may be said to set a precedent.

The anecdote was a different matter. Here Pushkin stipulated an appropriate dramatic conclusion, as we can see from the *Tales of Belkin* and from the brief anecdotes related in *Table Talk*. In *The Captain's Daughter* he goes through to the end, and the device of the memoir helps him (as does the borrowing from Scott) but it is none the less a trifle mechanically. A chapter in the manuscript, omitted in the published version, shows him casting about for an appropriate climax. The villain Shvabrin and his band attack the Grinev estate, and the family are rescued in the nick of time. It is shamelessly melodramatic, and Pushkin probably dropped it for this reason, but as a 'false climax' it shows a high degree of narrative ingenuity of the 'make 'em laugh, make 'em cry, make 'em wait' kind. When all seems happily settled we still have the drama of the false charge against young Grinev and the intercession of the Captain's daughter. Moreover her pursuit by Shvabrin reaches an appropriate climax. Grinev only gradually comes to realise (a little like Nikolai Rostov with Dolokhov in *War and Peace*) that Shvabrin's malign cynicism may be the result of jealousy and wounded pride. Masha reveals that he had asked for her hand:

'I don't like him. I loathe him, but in a strange way, I wouldn't at all like to think that he disliked me. That would bother me a great deal.'

Masha's honesty is touching; Shvabrin repels her, yet she wants him to admire her. The melodrama of his pursuit is made acceptable in the outcome from the realism of its origins. Defeated at last and badly wounded, 'his face expressed nothing but physical pain'. Yet he survives to lay a final slander against the hero.

Pugachev himself, however, is the real centre of the novel, and when he disappears from the foreground the epic breadth begins to be squeezed into the stricture of a conventional plot. By casting *The Captain's Daughter* as a family memoir Pushkin can present a subjective view of the rebel which reveals him more fully than the factual account in his *History* of the Pugachev Rebellion. 'Memoir' and *History* are totally different, not so much in style as in approach, and yet they have one thing significantly in common: the sense of a past that is not done with yet. Here is the last paragraph of the *History*:

So ended a rebellion, begun by a handful of insubordinate cossacks, which the inexcusable neglegence of those in authority had caused to grow in strength until it shook the government from Siberia to Moscow, and from the Kuban to the forests of Murom. It was long before peace was finally restored. Panin and Suvorov remained a whole year in the pacified provinces, reasserting enfeebled authority, rebuilding towns and fortresses, and extinguishing the last traces of the defeated revolt. At the end of 1775 a general amnesty was proclaimed, and it was decreed that the whole business be consigned to eternal oblivion. Wishing to extirpate all memory of that dreadful time, Catherine abolished the old name of the river whose banks had first witnessed the revolt. The Yaik cossacks were renamed 'Ural cossacks' and their town Uralsk. But the name of the terrible mutineer still echoes in the lands where he spread desolation. The people preserve a vivid memory of the bloody epoch which – so expressively – they have called the *Pugachevshchina*.

Names have been changed; authority has done all in its power to blot out the past. But the quiet ending, so lacking in any Gibbonian finality, suggests that insurrection is not dead but sleeping. Neither the revolt, nor its suppression, has been forgotten. At the close of Chapter 13 of *The Captain's Daughter* Grinev describes the desolation and horror of the final pacification, and adds fervently: 'May God not bring to be seen such another Russian rebellion, senseless and merciless.'

Soviet critics have found comment needful here. Gukovsky observes that Pushkin is the first writer, apart from Radishchev, to understand the nature of a peasants' revolt, which must indeed be 'hopeless, and therefore meaningless', before the historical process has produced the enlightened few who can both inspire and control it. Meilakh points out that the sentence actually echoes some of Radishchev's comments in *A Journey from Petersburg to Moscow*, and adds that Pushkin is not of course objecting to revolt as such.[1] But in fact the sentiment is Grinev's, not Pushkin's – its very openness and fervour proclaim the narrator in the open and not the author in hiding – and it refers back logically to Grinev's own experiences of Pugachev and his doings. After the intercession of his old servant Savelich had saved him from hanging, Grinev had been summoned to Pugachev's presence by a Cossack who naively extolled the leader as bearing all the signs of royalty: 'they say in the bath-house he showed them the marks of Imperial dignity on his breasts: the two-headed eagle on one, the size of a penny, and on the other his own likeness'. 'I did not consider it necessary to dispute the Cossack's opinion' the narrator dryly informs us, but during his interview with Pugachev the name of Dimitri is mentioned, the pretender of *Boris Godunov*, and Pugachev claims that even if he suffers the same fate his attempt will have been worthwhile. In such contexts the word 'meaningless' begins to assume a very particular meaning. Pugachev seeks to replace Catherine's imperium with his own, and his followers are as blindly self-interested as her nobility.[2] Pushkin can express through the art of his novel, as he could not in his history, his profound sense of the *perpetuum mobile* of the Russian power structure.

He had been given special permission to study in the archives – itself a remarkable favour, for autocracy does not favour a public post-mortem on its embarrassments – and Nicholas himself had insisted that his study must be called 'the History of Pugachev's Revolt' and not the 'History of Pugachev', for 'a rebel could have no history'. In 1836, when both History and novel were completed, Pushkin tried unsuccessfully for permission to publish a projected essay on Radishchev. In *The Captain's Daughter* he had at least been

---

[1] B. S. Meilakh, *Pushkin i ego epokha* (Moscow 1958).

[2] Pushkin observes in the *History* that three of Pugachev's followers called themselves Counts Panin, Orlov, and Vorontsov – three of Catherine's noblemen – but adds in a note that he doubts whether the rebels took this 'parody' very seriously. He also quotes Voltaire's reassuring letter to Catherine, pointing out that the phantom of a Pretender might have been a thing to cause tragic trouble in the days of Demetrius, but was a farce in the eighteenth century. It was not a farce to Catherine's generals, however, who knew Russia better than Voltaire did. At his execution on the Red Square Pugachev was commanded to identify himself to the crowd as a Cossack, which he duly did, earning himself an easier death in consequence.

able to echo some of Radishchev's sentiments without risking his fate. No reader would suspect Grinev of disloyal thoughts, but Pushkin himself was another matter.

As Pugachev is trapped by history and by his essentially 'meaningless' role in it, so is Catherine the Empress. Her nature found nothing unattractive in hypocrisy, and the logic of her position exacted it. Proud of her liberalism and her friendship with the *philosophes*, this highly intelligent and far from inhuman ruler had no wish to meddle with the entrenched interests bequeathed by Peter on which her rule depended. Her enlightenment won her the friendship of Voltaire but it did nothing for the Russian peasant, as Pushkin observed in some notes on eighteenth-century Russia that he made in 1822 at Kishinev.[1] When she died, serfdom was more widely established than at the beginning of her reign; and though her code of legal instructions – based on Montesquieu – was so advanced in theory it could not be published in pre-revolutionary France, it was well understood to be only for show, and undertaken from the same motives of vanity and self-advertisement which may also have moved her victim Radishchev to compose his polemical *Journey*.

The censorship would expect from Pushkin a benign portrait of Catherine, but what is remarkable is that in giving one he contrives to do the same for her rival. Their portraits in *The Captain's Daughter* have a significant amount in common. As Grinev meets and talks to Pugachev for the first time without realising who he is, so his betrothed tells her story to an unknown lady in the palace grounds who turns out to be the Empress. Both have a magnetic physical presence expressed in the animation of the eye. Both are terrifying if contradicted – the incognito Empress turns red with rage when Masha cries out that the charge against Grinev is not true. Both can be appalling and yet amiable, and Pushkin suggests the combination with mesmeric immediacy. We are as aware in *The Captain's Daughter* as in *The Bronze Horseman* of the relation between humanity and power, their coincidence and yet their fearful separateness. As the charm of the Petersburg prologue gives place to the nightmare of the poem's story, so the physical being of the two autocrats contrasts with the realities of *Pugachevshchina* and its repression.

Grinev is saved by them both. As in Shakespeare's last plays, and some Greek tragedies, the novel celebrates for individuals the

<hr>

[1] VIII, 125.

possibility of an almost supernatural good fortune, which measures up to its epic stature in asserting not just a perfunctory requirement of romance but a Shakespearean tribute to 'the clearest gods who make them honours of men's impossibilities'; and it is here most profoundly the progenitor of the spirit of *War and Peace.* Grinev is not a pilgrim like Pierre; but though he is cleared of the charge of desertion he has indeed in some sense gone over to Pugachev in the spirit.

... Released from imprisonment towards the end of the year 1774 at the order of the Empress... he was present at the execution of Pugachev, who recognised him in the crowd and nodded the head to him which a moment later was shown lifeless and bleeding to the people. Shortly afterwards Piotr Andreich and Maria Ivanovna were married. Their descendants still flourish in the province of Simbirsk.

Grinev's memoir endorses the impact of that recognition and fulfils its tacit plea. When the revolt was over he could think joyfully of going home and getting married, 'but notwithstanding, a strange feeling poisoned my joy'. That Pugachev had spared his life and saved his betrothed affects him less than a disturbing sense of sympathy with a man now awaiting the revenge of power:

But a strange feeling poisoned my joy: the thought of the terrible creature, steeped in the blood of so many innocent victims, and the execution awaiting him, disturbed me in spite of myself. 'Emelya, Emelya!' – I thought wretchedly – 'why didn't you get stuck with a bayonet or knocked over by a grape-shot. That would have been the best thing to have happened to you.'

'*Emelya, Emelya!*' – *dumal ya s dosadoyu* is a cry from the heart. Pushkin conveys through it a degree of strong feeling, submerged and confused in the narrator's mind, and only gradually infiltrating our own. The process begins with our realisation that the christian name of the rebel who, like an impersonal force, has created such havoc, has not been mentioned before.[1]

We can see how unobtrusive the process is, and yet how ultimately effective, if we compare the relation of Grinev and Pugachev

---

[1] And only occurs once again, when Savelich, who has refused throughout to recognise the rebel as anyone special, uses its familiar form – Emelka Pugachev – in admitting that his master has been his guest. Both uses are unobtrusively and perfectly timed and expressed, but both are omitted in the translations, presumably because of the confusion of a new name that Grinev's exclamation might cause.

with the one Tolstoy endeavours to establish in *War and Peace* between the prisoner Pierre and the French Marshal Davout.

Davout looked up and gazed intently at him. For some seconds they looked at one another, and that look saved Pierre. Apart from conditions of war and law, that look established human relations between the two men. At that moment a very great number of things went fleetingly through both their minds, and they realised that they were both children of humanity and were brothers.

Tolstoy's eloquence moves us not at all. It is quite clear, it is virtually admitted – a characteristic example of Tolstoyan double-take – that what influences Davout is the recognition that Pierre is a gentleman like himself, who knows how to address a man of rank. The pair establish a human relation by finding they belong to the same class, and this truth is at once true to life and typical of Tolstoy's power of shutting for an instant when it suits him an eye that can see all too well.

The relation between Pugachev and Grinev is by contrast both simple and enigmatic.[1] Pugachev remembers the old servant who intercedes for the young officer, and through him the episode in the snow-storm when Grinev gave him a hareskin coat which he had outgrown and which was a great deal too small for the recipient. There is no parade of gratitude or of one good deed deserving another. The human impulse is largely a whim, arising from a coincidence. The two have nothing in common and their subsequent talk does not bring them together. (It is significant, too, that Grinev's later distress, and his '*Emelya, Emelya!*', contain an element of vexation, expressed in the word *dosada*, that Pugachev could not have relieved Grinev's conscience by simply getting himself killed.) The relation is as matter-of-fact as that of Grinev to his old servant, who pleaded for his 'child's' life, asking to be hanged in his place. Before the book is over Grinev has come to perceive his servant's attachment instead of taking it for granted, as he is impelled to take a final leave of Pugachev on the Red Square. In the course of the book, without an indication being given on the subject, he has learnt to live, and to become – like the hero of Pindar – what he is.

There are many resemblances between *The Captain's Daughter* and the *Waverley* novels, and one fundamental difference. The

---

[1] This is briefly brought out at Grinev's examination, when the prosecutor observes: 'How did such a strange friendship spring up, and what could it be founded on?...'

brevity of Pushkin's novel is an index of its contemporaneousness: the leisure of Scott's reveals their happy domicile in the past. But the similarity between the plot patterns of *The Captain's Daughter* and *Waverley* itself can hardly be accidental. Like Grinev, Waverley is a landowner's son who goes to take up a military appointment in rebel territory. He too becomes involved with the rebels through his attachment to MacIvor, one of their chiefs, and is accused of treason to his sovereign. Pushkin, as we have seen, combines this situation with the *dénouement* of *The Heart of Midlothian*. The two heroines of *Waverley* show why the novel is a prototype, and had such influence on its successors and on romantic attitudes to the past. The past is the era of romance, and by journeying to the Highlands young Waverley penetrates its very shrine, falling romantically in love with Florence MacIvor. But romance, like the past, is for visiting and not for living. Waverley is restored to his English estate and the sensible heroine, Rosa Bradwardine. Of course the fascination of the formula does not lie in any explicit contrast between England and Scotland, the establishment and the rebels, romance and prosaic fact. Scott makes romance itself comfortable and knowable, investing a Highland hunt and feast with all his genius for combining the actual and the antiquarian. Waverley is received at the Baron Bradwardine's into a family as unfamiliar yet as congenial as the one which welcomes Grinev in the Belogorsky fortress – indeed it is possible that Pushkin caught the characteristic charm and detail of Scott here even through a French translation.

But when it comes to the rebellion itself Scott's genius turns against him. It is not that he evades the grim side of it, but as a good North Briton he is concerned to present the '45 as the very stuff of antiquity, more irrevocably in the past even than the covenanting times of *Old Mortality* or the Highland and Lowland confrontation of *The Fair Maid of Perth*. Waverley's love for Flora MacIvor and admiration for the Young Pretender are generous and misguided daydreams which he will recall with the nostalgia of maturity remembering the follies of youth. Grinev's experiences and acquaintance with Pugachev are by contrast premonitory, deeply educative, haunting not in their recall of the past but by revealing the scope and shadow of the future.

Scott's art puts history behind us. Pushkin, in *The Captain's Daughter* no less than in *The Bronze Horseman* and *Poltava*, brings it into the present and leaves it to imply what is to come. Yet he takes Scott as a model for plot and situation and not, as Balzac did, as an inspiration for the exhaustive survey of 'man as whole in the whole of society'.[1] And there were plenty of conventional Russian historical novelists – Zagoskin is one – who followed Scott faithfully in equating the past with Romance, even though – as Pushkin notes of Zagoskin's novel – they may both know the past and feel for it. So Tolstoy, as a part of his huge and complex work, celebrates the old life of the Russian country gentry. But Tolstoy's first idea had been to go to the roots of the Decembrist conspiracy, and *War and Peace* indicates these almost as an accidental by-product of its lavish resources. Tolstoy's ideal gentry were those who might have made a last stand against the service *apparatchiki* created by Peter and perpetuated by his successors. At the end of *War and Peace* history is standing at the door, and the question is: should our duty be to resist public tyranny or to support and protect our family life, and ensure its survival? Of course there is no natural lodgement for such a query at the end of *The Captain's Daughter*, and no swarming *dramatis personae* to sustain it, but in his concluding note the 'editor' of Grinev's memoirs remarks that 'they were given to us by one of his grandchildren who had heard that we were engaged on a work dealing with the period described by his grandfather'. By a narrative device the projected history of Pugachev is thus made to engender a 'memoir' of him, and the viewpoints of the two silently complement each other. In the history he is an impersonal force which shed rivers of blood, in the memoir an individual whose memory is preserved out of gratitude, and who himself displayed that rare virtue, in however incongruous a form.

Pushkin must be the only great writer to have written a history and a novel on the same subject. And he keeps the two separate. History is one thing and the novel another: each has its own laws and its own truth. 'It is not our purpose to intrude on the province of history' says Scott towards the end of *Waverley*, but in fact he

[1] G. Lukacs, *Studies in European Realism*. His references to *The Captain's Daughter* in *The Historical Novel* do not, it seems to me, sufficiently distinguish its outlook and method from that of Scott and his successors. It is of some importance that Scott did not belong to a nation or society in which history counted, and the past haunted and shaped the present. Rightly or wrongly he saw the present as happily detached from the past, and in consequence all the more amenable to the art of the novelist. For Pushkin, as for all Russian writers, past and present were not detachable, but this is not necessarily a premise of the good historical novel. If it were, the best of such novels should logically have been written by Jews, Poles and Irishmen.

does, intermingling imaginary and historical events in his own relaxed manner. Comfortable as the process is, history is none the less used by it, and misused. The true desperation of the revolt and the inhuman repression that followed are alike glossed over; MacIvor's parting with Waverley and execution offstage have a Virgilian decorum; the Highlanders are presented as a lovable but misguided people whom progress can afford to patronise, as Addison patronised Sir Roger de Coverley; the enduring legacy of hatred and extinction by impoverishment is ignored, though this is compensated, one must add, by the trial scene in which MacIvor's clansman makes his memorable speech. Scott can rise to an epic dignity without effort or display. And it is significant that though neither Scott nor Pushkin lingers on the suffering and atrocities which modern taste would consider obligatory to establish the 'reality' of their violent subjects, both suggest such reality obliquely by the prominence they give to what might be called the servile aspect of historical revolt. Being the absolute possession of their hereditary chieftains, Scott's clansmen had no choice but to follow them to the war, and this is shown as clearly by Scott as their unquestioning loyalty and devotion. Savelich is as unquestioningly the possession of the Grinev family, and he never thinks of regarding himself as being 'liberated' by Pugachev, who for his part demonstrates in the most natural way possible his unconscious acceptance of Grinev's status as a gentleman and a superior being. The '45 rebellion, as Scott implies in the words he gives to the judge at MacIvor's trial, was only made possible by an obedience of the rank and file unthinkable in the more progressive society against which it was directed. There are many hints that Pugachev's revolt is doomed to failure from the fact that the rebels continue to *believe* in the gentry even as they destroy them – Savelich and Pugachev have the mutually scornful but inescapable kinship of a devotee and an inconoclast. Lermontov was to observe that one of the 'hidden reasons' for Pugachev's revolt was that the nobility, which had lost its former power and independence, 'did not know how to change its pattern of behaviour'. Perhaps it was this that saved it.

At the other extreme Flaubert uses history in *Salammbô*, and with evident and mordant relish, to attack the present day for possessing the vileness of the past without its style. The Carthaginians are different from the bourgeoisie of the Second Empire because their rapacious and dedicated commercialism can be presented, after the passage of eleven centuries, almost as an aesthetic virtue. The ancient world – just because it is the ancient world – cannot be vulgar; its materialism has nothing *Biedermeier* about it. This inverted romanticism may have tempted Pushkin in the treatment of *Egyptian Nights*; if so he was wise enough to forgo it, for nothing more completely falsifies the past than the suggestion that it reveals the nature of the present by being so different from it, yet so similar.

As historian and historical novelist Pushkin's great merit is that he does not begin with the assumption of different 'worlds' – the past and the present, romantic and prosaic, heroic and mundane – but with the intention of treating a given subject in a given form. In much nineteenth-century fiction which descends from and develops the historical fashion and genre, backgrounds, scene-painting, and minor picturesque characters assume a disproportionate importance and often become the real *raison d'être* of the work.[1] History and geography replace the proper human hierarchy of interest. In *The Captain's Daughter* hero and heroine are the most interesting as well as the most important characters, and all the others in descending order of importance – down to the hussar Zurin who takes a hundred roubles at cards off the young Grinev who meets him again playing cards at the crisis of the campaign – fill their parts in exactly the right proportion and perspective. In the *History*, on the other hand, the human actors shrink into insignificance by comparison with the narrative of events and campaigns.

Since his characters are in the forefront of Pushkin's fiction their fates too must appear in a perspective which the decorum of the form exacts. The story of *The Captain's Daughter* may have been suggested to Pushkin by an episode which he had come across in his research, and which he describes in the *History*. A certain Major Kharlov was in command of a fortress near Orenburg which was taken by Pugachev. Already severely wounded, he was hanged in the sight of his young wife, who was then raped by Pugachev and became his mistress until she too died at the hands of his followers, who feared her possible influence over him. This blank atrocity, typical of so many in the period of *Pugachevshchina*, is transposed by Pushkin into the key of historical romance, and yet we can put one beside the other without thinking: this is true and this is false;

---

[1] See Mario Praz, *The Hero in Eclipse in Victorian Fiction*, an admirable study which reveals much indirectly about the legacy of the historical novel.

this is what must have occurred in life and this is dressed up for the make-believe of fiction. The inviolability of the Captain's daughter and the singleminded devotion of Grinev are the stuff of romance, but by his mastery of the form, and by the care with which he excludes the rival form of factual exposition, Pushkin makes romance like the ancient artifice of saga and epic, in which the nature of fact cannot be separated from the craft of its objective presentation.

It is the destiny of the Captain's daughter (and the phrase itself suggests a ballad heroine) to save another and to be saved herself; her fate makes her the character she is and becomes, and so with the fate of her mother and father. Captain Mironov dies not as Major Kharlov did, though the facts are the same, but as the character whom Pushkin had not taken from history but created for his fiction. (Interesting, in this connection, that Pushkin had jotted down in his own notes for the history that Kharlov was drunk when his fortress was under attack, but also observes he will not mention this out of respect for the death of a brave man – a good instance of Pushkinian decorum being identified with the sense of proportion. We know that Captain Mironov had his daily decanter of vodka, but this has no proportional significance in the characteristics of his end.) Husband and wife in the *History* have the blank anonymity of atrocity victims, sealed off from the life they once had, the life which art would first have had to establish in its own terms in order to make their fate a part of it, but it is the one detail of the *History* which Pushkin refers to, using the convention of the memoir form which would make it intelligible to those who had shared the experiences of *Pugachevshchina*. In her letter to Grinev the Mary Ivanovna of fiction refers to the Lizaveta Kharlovna of history, and prays that she may not suffer the same fate.

It was Pushkin's final requirement of prose fiction that it should not create a world belonging wholly to the author, as the verse world of *Evgeny Onegin* belonged to him. The art of a Constant, a Flaubert or a Turgenev, creates a world whose reality is both contained in and circumscribed by the author's style, in the fullest meaning of that term. And in this sense Pushkin's prose has no style. It is a medium purely and simply, in which events and people appear to go their own way and exist in their own independent manner. This may strike us particularly in contrast with one of the most conscientious and self-conscious of Russian prose-stylists and naturally a great admirer of Pushkin – Isaac Babel.

The horrors of *Pugachevshchina* were repeated a hundredfold in the Civil War and the Polish campaign which Babel describes in *Konarmiya* (*Red Cavalry*). But the numerous atrocities in these stories all have the appearance of existing in order that Babel can respond to them and realise himself in relation to them, realise himself in the laconic intensity and care with which he makes into a part of himself what he has seen. For Pushkin these were facts like others, which prose and its writer could not absorb but must apportion in the proper perspective which the forms of history or of fiction required. Babel's famous and meticulous terseness is as subjective as Pushkin's is objective.

The objectivity comes in part from a kind of masterful perfunctoriness in *The Captain's Daughter* and still more in *Dubrovsky*; they do not take themselves very seriously or press themselves into the subjective world of creation with the earnestness of dedicated prose style. Gogol may have understood this quality in Pushkin and transformed it to find his own manner of airy sly evasiveness; Gogol and Pushkin are the first and the last Russian prose writers who are not – or in Gogol's case do not seem to be – intent on the *sérieux*, on the engrossed matching of words with experience; and Gogol certainly realised that the simple freshness of Pushkin could never be recalled. As he wrote in *Selected Passages of Correspondence with Friends*: 'We can no longer serve art for art's sake...without having first comprehended its highest purpose and without determining what it is given to us for. We cannot repeat Pushkin.'

Pushkin could serve art for art's sake because he was not serving art for the sake of the artist. Fiction in prose during the nineteenth century – in Russia as in the rest of Europe – became increasingly the medium for self-expression that poetry had already been in the earlier romantic period. In the *nouvelle* style tends to become the man, in the absolute sense in which the style of a modern film is that of its director. The technical seriousness of Babel, the personal obsession of Kafka and Genêt, the yet more claustrophobic self-obsession of Hemingway – all display prose as a means to find the writer's self, and all possess the concomitant inability to allow the reader to manœuvre on his own. He must either identify with the author or get out. But prose fiction for Pushkin is a liberating because a genuinely impersonal instrument, taking for granted the neutral existence of everything to which it gives artifice, proportion, and accord: it can never create its own exclusive world of style.

SELECT BIBLIOGRAPHY

IN ENGLISH

INTRODUCTION

By far the best selection of Pushkin's poetry in English is in the Penguin Poets Series (ed. J. Fennell) giving plain prose translations, and there is also a good selection of his prose in the Penguin Classics Series (ed. Rosemary Edmonds). A wider selection of prose and verse, including *Evgeny Onegin* and *Boris Godunov*, is edited by Avrahm Yarmolinsky (Nonesuch Press, 1939) but the quality of the translations is uneven. Much of Pushkin's verse and prose remains still untranslated. V. Nabokov's monumental edition of *Evgeny Onegin*, with translation and commentary (Routledge, 1964 (4 vols.)) is excellent value, and there is a slighter but still valuable edition and commentary by D. Chizhevsky (Harvard University Press, 1953). All Pushkin's letters have been translated and well annotated by J. Thomas Shaw (Oxford, 1963). *A Pushkin Verse Reader*, edited with notes and a vocabulary by I. P. Foote (Allen and Unwin, 1962), makes a very good introduction for the student learning Russian in order to read Pushkin.

The earliest appreciation of Pushkin in English is in Maurice Baring's *Landmarks in Russian Literature* (Home University Library, 1910), and in his preface to the *Oxford Book of Russian Verse* (1924, 2nd ed. 1948). A forthright and civilised general introduction to Pushkin by D. S. Mirsky in the Republic of Letters Series (Routledge, 1926) is unfortunately no longer in print, and neither is Janko Lavrin's useful *Introduction to Pushkin and Russian Literature* (Teach Yourself Library, 1947), but there is a section on Pushkin in Mirsky's *History of Russian Literature* (Routledge, 1949), and a more comprehensive one in *A History of Russian Literature*, ed. Fennell (Faber's, to be published in 1971). *Pushkin on Literature*, selected and edited by Tatiana Wolff (Methuen, 1970) is a useful anthology of Pushkin's critical writings, from essays and letters, with a biographical commentary.

Biographies include that of Ernest J. Simmons (Cambridge, Mass., 1937), Henry Troyat (Paris, 1947, 2 vols., and an abridged translation, London, 1951), and David Magarshack (Chapman and Hall, 1967). W. N. Vickery's *Pushkin: Death of a Poet* (Indiana University Press, Bloomington and London, 1968) gives a detailed account of Pushkin's duel and death, based on up-to-date Russian sources.

BIBLIOGRAPHY

STUDIES OF VARIOUS ASPECTS OF PUSHKIN'S WORK

J. C. Fiske, 'The Soviet Controversy over Pushkin and Washington Irving', *Comparative Literature*, VII, 1954.

G. Gibian, 'Love by the Book: Pushkin, Stendhal, Flaubert', *Comparative Literature*, VIII, 1956.

'*Measure for Measure* and Pushkin's *Angelo*', *P.M.L.A.* LXVI, 1952.

H. Gifford, 'Pushkin's *Feast in Time of Plague* and its Original', *American Slavic and East European Review*, VIII, 1949.

R. A. Gregg, 'Pushkin and Shenstone: The Case Re-opened', *Comparative Literature*, XVII, 1965.

B. F. Kirtley, 'National Character and Folklore in Pushkin's Skazki', *West Virginia University Philological Papers*, XI, 1958.

W. Lednicki, 'Pushkin's *Bronze Horseman*: The Story of a Masterpiece', *Slavic Studies, University of California Publications*, I, 1954.

R. A. Maguire, 'A. S. Pushkin: Notes on French Literature', *American Slavic and East European Review*, XVII, 1958.

R. E. Matlaw, 'Poetry and Poet in Romantic Society as reflected in Pushkin's *Egyptian Nights*', *Slavonic and East European Review*, XXXIII, 1954.

'The Dream in *Evgeny Onegin*, with a note on *Gore ot Uma*', *Slavonic and East European Review*, XXXVII, 1959.

V. Nabokov, 'Pushkin and Gannibal', *Encounter*, XIX, 1962.

J. J. Pauls, 'Two Treatments of Mazeppa: Ryleev's and Pushkin's', *Études Slaves et Est Européennes*, VIII, 1963.

F. Seeley, 'The Problem of *Kamenny Gost*', *Slavonic and East European Review*, XLI, 1963.

J. T. Shaw, 'The Conclusion of Pushkin's *Queen of Spades*', *Studies in Russian and Polish Literature in honour of Wacław Lednicki*, The Hague, 1962.

G. Struve, 'Mickiewicz in Russia', *Slavonic and East European Review*, XXVI, 1948.

W. N. Vickery, '*Medny Vsadnik* and the Nineteenth-Century Heroic Ode', *Indiana Slavic Studies*, 1964.

E. Wilson, 'In Honour of Pushkin', *The Triple Thinkers*, John Lehmann, 1952.

T. A. Wolff, 'Shakespeare's Influence on Pushkin's Dramatic Work', *Shakespeare Survey*, 5, 1952.

IN RUSSIAN

INTRODUCTION

The alphabetically arranged lists that follow are not intended as a comprehensive bibliography, but as an indication of the main biographical and critical studies of Pushkin in Russian, including those which I have worked on or mentioned in the text. The exhaustive recent

BIBLIOGRAPHY

Russian bibliographical survey *Pushkin, Itogi i problemy izucheniya*, is an indispensable aid for the serious student, as is the Pushkin thesaurus *Slovar Yazyka Pushkina*, and its supplement, *Poeticheskaya frazeologiya Pushkina*.

After Pushkin's death, an edition of his works appeared in 1838, reprinted – often carelessly – from the publications done under his own supervision in his lifetime. This was followed in 1841 by three volumes of his posthumous works, edited by Zhukovsky, who made a number of changes, some to meet the requirements of the censorship, some as a result of his own preferences. Between 1855 and 1857 there came out in seven volumes the first comprehensive edition, edited by P. V. Annenkov, *Sochineniya Pushkina. S prilozheniem materialov dlya ego biografiii, portreta, snimkov s ego pocherka i s ego risunkov i proch* (St Petersburg). The first volume contained the 'materials for the biography of Pushkin' which give the work its special value; but Annenkov's editorial methods were free and easy, and though most of Zhukovsky's changes in the interests of the censorship were put right,[1] his other alterations remained.

Pushkin's copyrights expired in 1887, and there began a new series of comprehensive *Collected Works*, aiming at including all that Pushkin had written, but set down in arbitrary chronological order, and restoring passages that Pushkin had himself omitted in the latest versions of his MSS. The best example is Morozov's edition of 1905 in twelve volumes. Between 1907 and 1916 appeared the immense and unwieldy edition in six huge quarto volumes edited by S. A. Vengerov, of which the text and method are totally unreliable but the mass of commentary of considerable interest: the best of it has been quarried and quoted by later Pushkinists.

In 1899 the 'Academy' edition was taken in hand, with the idea of producing at last an authoritative edition, based on the final fair copies of Pushkin's manuscripts, but progress was slow, and by 1929 only the first six volumes had appeared. In 1921 M. L. Gofman published a short work on the principles of Pushkin editing (see bibliography of Russian criticism) and in the following year B. V. Tomashevsky, perhaps the most able of all Pushkin's modern editors, brought out a model edition, with commentary, of the *Gavriliiad*. The seventeen-volume 'Academy' edition, Akademiya Nauk SSSR (Moscow–Leningrad, 1937–59), is the most thorough and reliable in textual matters, but unlike later 'Academy' editions has no commentary, except for vol. VII *Dramaticheskie Proizvedeniya*, which was also published separately with notes and articles (including that by G. O. Vinokur cited on page 179) in 1935. Several scholarly editions followed, some more complete than others. A full commentary is given in 'Academy' 1959–62, 10 vols., ed. Blagoy, Bondi,

---

[1] For example Zhukovsky had printed in the fourth line of Pushkin's ode after Horace, *Ya pamyatnik sebe*, the more harmless *Napoleonova* instead of *Aleksandriiskogo stolpa*, for which Gogol took him to task in a letter. See D. Yakubovich, 'Chernovoy Avtograf *Pamyatnika*', *Vremennik Pushkinskoy Komissii*, III, 1937.

BIBLIOGRAPHY

Vinogradov and Oksman which also includes in their context the drawings that Pushkin made in the margins of his manuscripts. 'Academy' 1962–6, 10 vols., general ed. Tomashevsky, is rather more compact, with notes and variants better arranged and the emphasis on textual rather than biographical details. Also useful are the separate editions of Pushkin's letters, criticism, and occasional writing, listed below.

PUSHKIN'S LETTERS, CRITICISM AND OTHER PIECES

Pushkin Dnevnik, 1833–5, ed. (with commentary) B. L. Modzalevsky, Moscow–Petrograd 1923.

Pushkin Kritik, ed. N. V. Bogoslovsky (revised ed.), Moscow 1950.

Pushkin Pisma, ed. B. L. and L. B. Modzalevsky, Moscow–Leningrad 1926–35 (letters 1815–33, with a full biographical commentary).

Pisma poslednikh let 1834–7, ed. N. V. Ismailev, 1969 (a completion of the foregoing edition).

Sochineniya Pushkina: Perepiska, 3 vols., ed. V. I. Saitov, St Petersburg 1911 (letters to and from Pushkin).

Rukopisi A. S. Pushkina, ed. V. E. Yakushkin, Russkaya Starina, 1884, XLI–XLIV.

Rukoyu Pushkina, Nesobrannye i neopublikovannye teksty, ed. M. A. Tsyavlovsky, L. B. Modzalevsky, T. G. Zemger, Moscow–Leningrad 1935.

The last two concern Pushkin's MSS and unpublished fragments in his own hand from the Rumyantsev Museum and the Pushkin House.

COLLECTIONS AND PERIODICALS

Pushkin i ego Sovremenniki, I–XXXIX, St Petersburg–Leningrad 1903–30.

Literaturnoe Nasledstvo, XVI–XVIII, Moscow 1934.

Pushkin, Vremennik Pushkinskoi Komissii, I–VI, Akademiya Nauk SSSR, Moscow–Leningrad 1936–41.

Pushkin, Issledovaniya i materialy, I–IV, Akademiya Nauk SSSR, Moscow–Leningrad 1956–62.

The third collection listed, particularly vol. III, contains essays and material of considerable interest. Earlier numbers of the second collection contain some essays of peripheral interest, e.g. V. Zhirmunsky on the influence of Goethe on Russian poetry 'Gete v russkoy poezii', nos. 4–6.

RUSSIAN CRITICISM

Akhmatova, A. A., 'Poslednyaya skazka Pushkina', *Zvezda*, no. I, 1933, pp. 161–76.

'*Kamenny gost* Pushkina', *Pushkin, Issledovaniya i materialy*, vol. II, ed. M. P. Alekseev, Moscow–Leningrad 1958.

Azadovsky, M. K., *Literatura i Folklor*, Leningrad 1938.

BIBLIOGRAPHY

Belinsky, V. G., 'Literaturnye Mechtaniya', *Polnoe Sobranie Sochineny*, vol. I, Moscow 1953–6.

'Sochineniya Aleksandra Pushkina', *Polnoe Sobranie Sochineny*, vol. VII, Moscow 1953–6.

Blagoy, D. D. *Sotsiologiya Tvorchestva Pushkina. Etyudy*, Moscow 1929 (2nd ed., Moscow 1931).

Masterstvo Pushkina, Moscow 1955. -

Tvorcheskii put Pushkina, Moscow–Leningrad 1950.

Boris Godunov A. S. Pushkina, Sbornik statey, ed. K. N. Derzhavin, Leningrad 1936 (a collection of important articles).

Brodsky, N. L., 'Commentary: A. S. Pushkin, *Evgeny Onegin*', Moscow 1932 (4th ed., Moscow 1957).

Bryusov, V., *Moy Pushkin*, ed. N. K. Piksanov, Moscow–Leningrad 1929.

Chernyshevsky, N. G., 'Sochineniya A. S. Pushkina', *Polnoe Sobranie Sochineny*, Moscow 1947–9, pp. 424–516.

'A. S. Pushkin, ego zhizn i sochineniya', *Polnoe Sobranie Sochineny*, Moscow 1947–9, pp. 310–39.

Eykhenbaum, B. M., 'Problemy poetiki Pushkina', *Pushkin–Dostoevsky*, ed. A. L. Volynsky, Petrograd 1921, pp. 76–96. Reprinted in the essay collection *Skvoz Literatury, Voprosy Poetiki*, Leningrad 1924, and in '*Slavistic Printings and Reprintings*', The Hague 1962.

'Put Pushkina k proze', *Pushkinist*, ed. N. V. Yakovlev, vyp. IV, Moscow–Petrograd 1922, pp. 59–74.

'Pushkin i Tolstoy', *Literaturny Sovremennik*, I, Leningrad 1937, pp. 137–47.

Feinberg, I. L., *Nezavershennye raboty Pushkina*. Moscow, 1955 (2nd ed., Moscow 1958; 3rd ed., Moscow 1964).

Gershenzon, M. O., *Mudrost Pushkina*, Petrograd 1918.

Gofman, M. L., *Pushkin, Pervaya glava nauki o Pushkine*, Petrograd 1922 (2nd ed.).

Pushkin, Psikhologiya tvorchestva, Paris, 1928.

Gorodetsky, B. P., *Dramaturgiya Pushkina*, Moscow–Leningrad 1953.

Lirika Pushkina, Moscow–Leningrad 1962.

Gukovsky, V. P., *Ocherki po istorii russkogo realizma, Pt. 1: Pushkin i russkie romantiki*, Saratov 1946. *Pushkin i russkie romantiki* (2nd ed.), Moscow 1965.

Pushkin i problemy realisticheskogo stilya, Moscow 1957.

Istoriya Russkoy Literatury, Akademiya Nauk SSSR, vol. VI, 1953, pp. 159–328.

Izmailov, N. V., 'Is istorii zamysla i izdaniya *Mednogo Vsadnika*', *Pushkin i ego Sovremenniki*, vyp. XXXVIII–XXXIX, 1930, pp. 169–90.

Kireevsky, I. V., 'Nechto o kharaktere poezii Pushkina', *Polnoe Sobranie Sochineny*, vol. I, Moscow 1911.

Levin, V. D. (ed.), *Poeticheskaya frazeologiya Pushkina*, Moscow 1969 (supplementary to *Slovar Yazyka Pushkina*).

Lezhnev, A. Z., *Proza Pushkina, Opyt stilevogo issledovaniya*, Moscow 1937 (new ed., Moscow 1966).

BIBLIOGRAPHY

Lunacharsky, A. V., 'A. S. Pushkin' (introduction), *Polnoe Sobranie Sochineny*, 6 vols., Moscow–Leningrad 1930–1. (Vol. I), *Prilozhenie k Krasnoy Nive*, pp. 7–37.

Maikov, L. N., *Pushkin*, St Petersburg 1899.

Meilakh, B. S., *Pushkin i russky romantizm*, Moscow–Leningrad 1937.

Pushkin i ego epokha, Moscow 1958.

Khudozhestvennoe myshlenie Pushkina kak tvorchesky protsess, Moscow–Leningrad 1962.

Merezhkovsky, D. S., *Vechnye Sputniki*, St Petersburg 1897.

Nusinov, I. M., *Pushkin i mirovaya literatura*, Moscow 1941.

Oksman, Yu. G., 'Pushkin v rabote nad romanom *Kapitanskaya dochka*', *Kapitanskaya dochka*, ed. Yu. G. Oksman, Moscow 1964, pp. 149–208.

Shevyrev, S. P., 'Sochineniya Aleksandra Pushkina', *Moskvityanin*, 1841, pt. 5, no. 9.

Shklovsky, V. B., *Zametki o proze Pushkina*, Moscow 1937.

Slonimsky, A. L., *Masterstvo Pushkina*, Moscow 1959 (2nd ed., Moscow 1963).

Stepanov, N. L., 'Literaturnaya Gazeta', *Ocherki po istorii russkoy zhurnalistiki i kritiki*, Leningrad University 1950, vol. I, pp. 383–401.

'Sovremennik', *Ocherki po istorii russkoy zhurnalistiki i kritiki*, Leningrad University 1950, vol. I, pp. 402–14.

Lirika Pushkina, Moscow 1959.

Proza Pushkina, Moscow 1962.

Tomashevsky, B. V., 'Poeticheskoe Nasledie Pushkina', *Pushkin-rodonachalnik novoy russkoy literatury*, Akademiya Nauk SSSR, Moscow–Leningrad 1941, pp. 263–334.

Pushkin, Bk. I (1813–24), Moscow–Leningrad 1956.

Pushkin, Bk. II (Materialy k monografii (1824–37)), Moscow–Leningrad 1961.

Pushkin i Frantsiya, Leningrad 1960.

Tynyanov, Yu. N., 'Arkhaisty i Pushkin', *Arkhaisty i Novatory*, Leningrad 1929. Also included in following title:

Pushkin i ego Sovremenniki, Moscow 1969.

Veresaev, V., *V dvukh planakh*, Moscow 1929.

Vinogradov, V. V., *Yazyk Pushkina: Pushkin i istoriya russkogo literaturnogo yazyka*, Moscow–Leningrad 1935.

Stil Pushkina, Moscow 1941.

Problema avtorstva i teoriya stilei, Moscow 1961, pt. 3.

(ed.) *Slovar Yazyka Pushkina*, 4 vols., Moscow 1956–61.

Vinokur, G. O., 'Slovo i stikh v *Evgenii Onegin*', *Pushkin. Sbornik Statei*, Moscow 1941, pp. 155–213.

Zelinsky, V. A., *Russkaya kriticheskaya literatura o proizvedeniyakh A. S. Pushkina*, 7 parts, Moscow 1887–99.

Zhirmunsky, V. M., *Byron i Pushkin, Iz istorii romanticheskoy poemy*, Leningrad 1924.

BIBLIOGRAPHY

RUSSIAN BIOGRAPHIES

Annenkov, P. V., 'Materialy dlya biografii Pushkina', *Sochineniya Pushkina*, I, St Petersburg 1855.

Bartenev, P. I., *Pushkin v Yuzhnoy Rossii*, Moscow 1914 (first published in *Russkii Arkhiv*, 1866, nos. 8 and 9).

Brodsky, N. L., *Pushkin. Biografiya*, Moscow 1937.

Grossman, L. P., *Pushkin*, Moscow 1939 (2nd ed., Moscow 1958, 3rd ed., Moscow 1960).

Grot, Ya. K., *Pushkin, ego litseiskie tovarishchi i nastavniki*, St Petersburg 1887.

Izmailov, N. V., *Pushkin. Ocherk zhizni i tvorchestva*, Moscow–Leningrad 1924.

Lemke, M. K., *Nikolaevskie zhandarmy i literatura 1826–55 gg. Po podlinnym delam Tretego Otdeleniya Sobstvennoy E. I. V. Kantselyarii*, St Petersburg 1908.

Lerner, N. O., *Trudy i dni Pushkina*, Moscow 1903 (2nd ed., Moscow 1910).

Rasskazy o Pushkine, Leningrad 1929.

Modzalevsky, B. L., *Pushkin pod tainym nadzorom*, Petrograd 1922 (first published in Byloe 1918, new ed., Leningrad 1925).

Pushkin na yuge, Trudy Pushkinskikh Konferentsii Kishineva i Odessy, ed. A. T. Borshch, Kishinev 1958 (2nd ed., Kishinev 1961).

'Pushkin v neizdannoy perepiski sovremennikov', *Literaturnoe Nasledstvo*, vol. LVIII, 1952, pp. 3–154.

Pushkin v vospominaniyakh sovremennikov, ed. A. L. Dymshits and D. I. Zolotnitsky, Leningrad 1950.

Shchegolev, P. E., *Duel i smert Pushkina, Issledovaniya i materialy*, revised 3rd ed., Moscow–Leningrad 1928.

Tomashevsky, B. V., 'Pushkin': *A. S. Pushkin, Sochineniya*, Leningrad 1935, pp. 25–42.

Tsyavlovsky, M. A. *Rasskazy o Pushkine, zapisannye so slov ego druzey P. I. Bartenevym v 1851–60 godakh*, Moscow–Leningrad 1925.

Letopis zhizni i tvorchestva A. S. Pushkina, vol. I (1799–1826), Moscow 1951.

Tynyanov, Yu. N., *Pushkin, Roman*, pts. 1–2, Moscow 1937 (part 3 in *Znamya*, 1943, nos. 7–8, pp. 13–91).

Veresaev, V., *Pushkin v zhizni*, 2 vols., revised 6th ed., Moscow 1936.

BIBLIOGRAPHICAL WORKS IN RUSSIAN

Bibliografiya proizvedeny A. S. Pushkina i literatury o nem, Akademiya Nauk SSSR. Separate volumes by various authors cover 1886–99, 1913–36 (partly), 1937–48, 1950, 1951, 1952–3, 1954–7, Moscow–Leningrad 1949–63.

Fomin, A. G., *Pushkiniana 1900–10*, Leningrad 1929.

Pushkiniana 1911–17, Leningrad 1937.

BIBLIOGRAPHY

Meilakh, B. S. and Gornitskaya, N. S., *A. S. Pushkin, Seminarii*, Leningrad 1959 (a series of special bibliographies for different aspects of Pushkin's life and work).

Mezhov, V. I., *Pushkiniana*, Moscow 1886.

Muratova, K. D., *Istoriya russkoy literatury XIX veka. Bibliografichesky ukazatel*, Moscow–Leningrad 1962.

Pushkin, Itogi i problemy izucheniya, ed. B. P. Gorodetsky, N. V. Izmailov, B. S. Meilakh, Moscow–Leningrad 1966 (a 650-page critical survey of all that has been written about Pushkin in Russia, from the poet's own lifetime to the present).

INDEX

INDEX

INDEX

365

INDEX

INDEX